ISBN 978-0-484-87839-5
PIBN 10768580

THE REED GENEALOGY

(Signature at the age of 95.)

THE

REED GENEALOGY

DESCENDANTS OF

WILLIAM READE

OF

WEYMOUTH, MASSACHUSETTS

From 1635 to 1902

Which following the descendants of his four sons, for convenience are divided into four branches, namely:

A. Branch Descendants of his eldest son William, who settled in Abington, Massachusetts.

W. Branch Descendants of his second son, Thomas, who settled in Weymouth, Massachusetts.

T. Branch Descendants of his third son John, who settled in Taunton, Massachusetts.

M. Branch Descendants of his youngest son James, who settled in Middleborough, Massachusetts.

Volume 1

BY

CONTENTS

ILLUSTRATIONS

PREFACE

William Reade, our emigrant ancestor, who was born in England in 1605, sailed from London, on July 26, 1635, on the ship "Assurance." He landed at Boston shortly afterwards, and proceeded at once to Wassegusset (now Weymouth), where he located permanently. In a very short time he became prominently identified with the affairs of the new colony.

He was made a freeman on September 2, 1635, and it is a noteworthy coincident that on this very day the General Court, sitting at Boston, passed an order changing the name of the settlement theretofore known as Wassegusset and establishing it as a plantation under the name of Weymouth. On the following day, September 3, the Court ordered the inhabitants of Weymouth to send a deputy to represent them at the General Court. The selection of this deputy does not seem to have been made until the following year. At this early day in the history of the community there seem to have been three distinct opposing factions or elements in the colony, each supported by a strong following, and each desiring to be represented in the Court, and probably as a compromise they determined to send three deputies instead of one, leaving it to the Court to decide which one should be admitted. William Reade, John Bursley and John Upham were the three persons elected. It is supposed that John Bursley represented those who remained of the Gorges Company and friends who followed them; William Reade representing those who came in from other towns in the colony, with an interest centering in the capital, and John Upham those who came with Rev. Joseph Hull and his sympathizers.

At a session of the General Court, held in Boston on Sep-

tember 8, 1636, these three deputies presented themselves to the Court, and under that date we find among the records of the Court the following order:

"Whereas the town of Waimoth hath sent 3 deputies to this Courte being a very small towne, at the request of the said deputies two of them were dismissed by Court viz: Mr. Bursley and John Upham."

It may be inferred from the foregoing that William Reade was permitted to take his seat in that body at once, and while his name does not appear among the list of those in attendance at that session, this may be accounted for by the fact that he was admitted after the opening of the Court. He is recorded as being present at the next assembling of the General Court, on December 8, 1636.

From the foregoing it will be noticed that William Reade was Weymouth's first representative or deputy in the General Court.

An interesting and important event which occurred during the session of the Court at which William Reade was admitted to membership was the voting by the Court, on October 28, 1636 (O. S.), or November 7, 1636 (N. S.), of an appropriation for a school or college, which proved to be the establishment of Harvard College, the first institution of learning in the colony, and indeed on the continent. The record of this appropriation reads as follows:

"The Court agreed to give 400£ towards a schoale or colledge whereof 200 to bee paid the next yeare & 200 when the work is finished & the next Court to appoint wheare & wt. building."

This action of the Court was a noteworthy one, as it shows the interest of the early settlers in the cause of education. The sum appropriated was a large one in that day, and was double the amount of the entire receipts in any one previous year from taxes, levied by the General Court.

Within the last few years many persons have been interested in looking up the record of their ancestors, to ascertain if they rendered such service or held office, which entitled

their descendants to membership in the various patriotic societies of the country.

In this connection it will be seen that all the descendants of William Reade of Weymouth are eligible to membership in the Society of Colonial Wars and kindred societies, having similar requirements for membership, by reason of his service as a member of the General Court of Massachusetts Colony in 1636 and 1638. And as additional title to such membership, the descendants of each of the several branches can claim this right by reason of the several ancestors having been soldiers in the King Philip's war, namely:

William Reed, A 4, was a private in Lieut. Edward Oaks' Company, April 26, 1676.

Thomas Reed, W 7, was a private in Lieut. Gillam's Company, Maj. Savage's command, February to May, 1675-76.

John Reed, T 9, was a private in Capt. Johnson's Company, later Capt. John Jacobs, in 1675.

James Reed, M 10, was a private in Capt. Johnson's Company in 1675, and later, on April 8, 1682, was a member of a military company in Taunton.

Besides these, many other titles to membership can be established by reason of services rendered by ancestors on the maternal side.

Following page 385 the author has inserted a table showing his own ancestry, both paternal and maternal, in which he designates twenty-four ancestors under whom he claims title to membership in the Colonial Wars Society.

Many of our ancestors did service in the French and English Wars, as will be seen by a search of the genealogy, but I have not deemed it necessary to compile a list of them.

Membership in the "Mayflower" Society is highly prized by those who can establish their title to it. It will be seen that about one-half of the descendants of William Reade of Weymouth may claim title to membership in this society, through their maternal ancestor, Esther Thompson, the wife of William Reed, A 4, whose father, John Thompson, married Mary Cook, daughter of Francis Cook, one of the "May-

flower" Company. Thus all of the A branch (descendants of William Reed 4) are entitled to such membership. This is the largest branch of the four, and indeed about equals the other three combined. In addition to these it will be seen that a considerable number of the descendants of the M branch (descendants of James Reed 10) can claim title through Sarah Warren, wife of William Reed, M 121. She was a lineal descendant of Richard Warren, one of the signers of the compact in the cabin of the "Mayflower," as is shown by a sketch of her on page 82.

On page 407 will be seen a note which reads as follows: "The descendants of David and Jane (Reed) Stockbridge are also 'Mayflower' descendants through Elder William Brewster, the leading figure in the Pilgrim Church." The line of descent is through Margaret Turner, who was the wife of John Stockbridge, who were the parents of David Stockbridge. Margaret was the daughter of Joseph and Bathsheba Hobart (Leavitt) Turner, Joseph Turner being the son of John Turner, Sr., and Mary (Brewster) Turner. Mary was the daughter of Jonathan and Lucretia (Oldham) Brewster. Jonathan was the son of Elder William Brewster. There are a number of scattered cases of intermarriage of "Mayflower" descendants, note on page 546. Susan Clark Reed, A 789, who married Emory Alden, a direct lineal descendant of John and Priscilla Alden. And doubtless there are a great many others if they were traced out.

The descendants of fifteen at least of the Reeds can claim title to membership in the societies of the Sons of the Revolution and the Sons of American Revolution and similar societies, by virtue of the service of the following ancestors, in the Revolutionary War, viz.:

T 91, page 70, John Reed.
T 109, " 80, John Reed.
A 156, " 89, Capt. William Reed.
A 178, " 99, Abel Reed.
A 182, " 100, Rev. John Reed.
A 205, " 110, Samuel Reed.

A 209, " 113, Benjamin Reed.
W 238, " 126, Thomas Reed.
W 244, " 128, John Reed.
T 282, " 134, Job Reed.
M 324, " 140, Benjamin Reed.
W 558, " 185, Thomas Reed (Capt.).
W 560, " 185, Samuel Reed (Lieut.).
W 562, " 185, Isaac Reed (Ensign).
W 594, " 195, Ezra Reed.

The descendants of the following Reeds can claim title to membership in the Society of the War of 1812, namely:

A 381, page 146, Joshua Reed.
A 472, " 166, Joseph Reed.
A 497, " 172, Noah Reed.
A 511, " 173, Rev. David Reed.
W 585, " 193, Henry Ludovicus Reed.
T 678, " 210, Charles Leonard Reed.
M 714, " 217, Simeon Reed.
A 725, " 220, Abel Richmond Reed.
A 748, " 223, Jonathan L. Reed.
W 1107, " 268, Goddard Reed.
W 1119, " 272, Abiah Reed.

I have not mentioned those who can claim membership in the above-named societies by descent through their maternal ancestry, except in the case of the "Mayflower" descendants, for the reason that the latter must necessarily have been maternal ancestry, as there were none of the Reeds on the "Mayflower," William Reade having come over some fifteen years later on the "Assurance" of London.

Many inquiries have been made as to the change in the manner of spelling our family name, and as to when the spelling was changed from Reade or Read to Reed. I can only state that when I took up this work, I found the almost universal custom was to spell it Reed, but later I found some few of the connection, principally in the Taunton branch, and among those of families who had removed to

Maine and New Hampshire, spelt it Read. There was, however, no uniform rule even among these, as in many cases where the father would spell it Read, the sons would spell it Reed, and it was so difficult to follow it in the families who preferred Read, that I concluded to adopt the uniform spelling of Reed. As to when the change took place, I should say in the second generation, as it will be seen by the will of William Reed, A 4, on pages 10 to 13, that he spells his children's names in three different ways, viz.: Reade, Read and Reed, and on page 10 it will be noticed that to an agreement, which he entered into, he signed his own name William Reed, and from that time on documents signed by the Reeds are mostly signed Reed, and the town records refer to them in most instances as Reed.

In the history of the Reeds, published in 1861, by J. Whittemore Reed, he gives an interesting account of the "Origin of the name and history of the clans," in which he mentioned seventeen different ways in which the name is spelled, namely: "Reed, Read, Reid, Rede, Red, Rad, Rheade, Rheadus, Wrede, Whrede, Reda, Rada, Radha, Wada, Wrade, Raad, Ried, are all derived from Rhea, which had its origin in Phoenicia."

JOHN LUDOVICUS REED.

11 S. Gay Street,
Baltimore, Md., Jan. 2, 1902.

INDEX

(See also General Index, page 711.)

Embracing Christian names of descendants of William Reade of Weymouth, male and female. The figures before the names denote the year of birth; those after, the number given to the individual in the record.

The letter (A) denotes the Abington branch, being the descendants of William, the eldest son; (W) denotes the Weymouth branch, the descendants of Thomas, the second son; (T) denotes the Taunton branch, the descendants of John, the third son; and (M) denotes the Middleborough branch, the descendants of James, the fourth son.

1790 Hannah ....(A) 498
1786 Hannah ....(A) 519
1759 Hannah ....(W) 557
1764 Hannah ....(W) 559
1782 Hannah ....(W) 568
1788 Hannah ....(T) 655
1798 Hannah ....(T) 672
1795 Hannah ....(A) 856
1795 Hannah ....(W) 1120
1816 Hannah ....(W) 1876
1848 Hannah ....(W) 1930
1823 Hannah E. ......(T) 621
1838 Hannah Flint ...(A) 834
1839 Hannah G. ......(A) 1076
1803 Hannah Howard (A) 903
1823 Hannah Jane ...(A) 940
1851 Hannah Jane ...(W) 2468
1844 Hannah Maria ..(A) 1640
1827 Hannah Perkins (W) 1918
1787 Hannah Willard .(A) 423
1878 Harlan ....(W) 2602
1886 Harold C. ....(W) 2725
1889 Harold Whitman (A) 2305
1883 Harold Williams (A) 2712
Harriet ....(M) 1422
1802 Harriet A. ......(T) 659
1843 Harriet A. ......(A) 1006
1849 Harriet Emily ..(M) 2268
1862 Harriet J. ....(T) 2130
1860 Harriet Loud ...(W) 2020
1833 Harriet M. ......(A) 1667
1821 Harriet Newell ..(A) 928
1838 Harriet Pauline (W) 1216
1856 Harriet Swain ..(A) 2338
Harriet W. ......(A) 907
1819 Harriet Witherell(T) 2049
1861 Harris Corner ...(A) 1810
1865 Harris Herman Jackson ....(T) 2218
1892 Harris Spilsted ..(A) 2306
Harry ....(A) 1756
1854 Harry Duncan ..(W) 2527
1869 Harry Lathrop ..(A) 1519
1860 Harry Irving ....(A) 2287
1869 Harry S. ....(A) 2356
1870 Harry W. ....(T) 2631
1791 Harvey ....(W) 595
1876 Harvey Dennett (W) 2041
1819 Harvey H. ......(W) 1205
1820 Harvey H. ......(W) 1206
1822 Harvey H. ......(W) 1208
1817 Harvey, Jr. .....(W) 1204
1836 Harvey L. ....(A) 1003
1831 Harvey Williams (A) 1466
1886 Harvey Wilson .(W) 2594
1852 Hattie ....(W) 2498
1857 Hattie Frances ..(A) 1819
1871 Hattie H. ....(A) 2406
1847 Hattie Jane .....(A) 1726
1888 Hazel M. ....(A) 2429
Helen ....(A) 820
Helen ....(A) 844
1837 Helen ....(A) 1648
Helen ....(A) 1828
1873 Helen ....(W) 2030
1885 Helen Ainsworth(W) 2755
1885 Helen Adeline ...(T) 2626
1844 Helen Ann Titterton, (W) 1222
1842 Helen Augusta .(W) 1932
1883 Helen Erfuth ...(A) 2719
Helen Frances ..(T) 1320
1891 Helen Frances ..(A) 2714
1840 Helen M. ....(A) 1005
Helen M. ....(A) 1766
1879 Helen M. ....(A) 2420
1833 Helen Maria ....(A) 1488
1857 Helen Marion ...(M) 2262
1853 Helen May ......(A) 1697
1891 Helen Laurana .(W) 2555
1891 Helen Margaret (M) 2706
1894 Helen Sampson .(A) 2452
1835 Helen Sophia ....(A) 1789
1840 Henrietta Bryant(W) 2534
1878 Henrietta Lillian (A) 2448
1841 Henrietta Maria (A) 1759
1846 Henrietta Manly (W) 2536
1815 Henrietta Morse (A) 993
1799 Henry ....(A) 757
1833 Henry ....(W) 1219
Henry ....(M) 2664
1842 Henry ....(A) 1490
1864 Henry ....(W) 2473
1876 Henry Alonzo ...(A) 2705
1846 Henry Arthur ..(T) 2071
1832 Henry Augustus (A) 833
1853 Henry Beecher .(W) 2574
1869 Henry Bicknell .(A) 2302
1850 Henry C. ....(T) 2124
1874 Henry Clarence .(M) 2670
1827 Henry Clark ....(W) 1188
1873 Henry Curtiss ..(W) 2732
1842 Henry Dyer .....(A) 1638
1842 Henry E. ....(T) 1316
1854 Henry Elliot ....(A) 1768
1857 Henry Francis ..(T) 2074
1810 Henry Gooding .(T) 1250
1840 Henry Harrison (W) 2521
1853 Henry Horatio .(W) 2032
1858 Henry J. ....(T) 2620

9
R
V

G
9
R
v

Redesdale.

FIRST GENERATION

1

William Reade. Son of William and Rebecca Reade

b. 1605. Boston Transcript 4-9-1913

m. Avis Deacon. " " 7-15-1912

m. Avis Chipman " " Jan. 1914

William Reade was born in 1605, and sailed from Gravesend in the County of Kent, England, in the "Assurance" of London (Isaac Bromwell and George Percy, Masters). There were on board this vessel, at the time of sailing, two hundred and twenty-one persons, the most of whom were very youthful. Of the whole number, but one of them was sixty years of age. The average age was from twenty-three to twenty-five years. The date of the sailing of this expedition cannot be accurately ascertained, but from information procured from ancient records, it may be fairly assumed that the correct date was about the 24th July, 1635. This party landed in Boston and William Reade proceeded to and settled in Weymouth, Massachusetts.

It is supposed he came from ~~Maidstone near~~ Somersetshire London. On March 9, 1636-7, he purchased from the estate of Zachery Bicknell, his house and farm, which was located on the western side of Middle street, the old house stood on the knoll opposite the junction of Middle and Charles streets. The premises are at this time owned by James Clapp. Some members of the family occupied this farm until 1769, when John Reed who married Mary Bates, purchased the old farm of about forty acres, situated on both sides of Front street, near and adjoining the old Reed Cemetery (so called).

William Reade was among the earlier settlers of Weymouth, it having been made a plantation May 8, 1635. On September 2, 1635, he was made freeman, and was very soon

9
F
V

called upon to take part in public affairs. Was representative at the General Court, December 7, 1636, and also September 6, 1638. In the spring of 1635, Rev. Joseph Hull and his company came to Weymouth, having sailed from England on March 20, 1635. Prior to this time, a very undesirable element had located at Weymouth, but upon the arrival of Hull's company, the township or plantation took on a new growth, and a different and more desirable class of people than those who had previously located there, took up their abode in Weymouth.

On July 13, 1635, the ship "Alice" (Richard Orchard, Master) sailed from Gravesend. She had thirty-two passengers on board, among whom was Avis Deacon, then but nineteen years of age. The oldest of this party was but thirty-five years, and the youngest but nine months. The average age of the entire company was but twenty-two years. It is a fact, worthy of note, that in those early days, nearly all of the emigrants who came to this country were very young, and few men or women, of mature age, could endure the hardships and privations of the new world, or cared to leave the place of their birth, to make their homes in a new country, about which so little was known at the time.

There was a Thomas Deacon, nineteen years of age, on board the "Assurance" with William Reade, supposed to be a twin brother of Avis Deacon.

Avis Deacon must have married William Reade soon after her arrival in this country.

Appended is the official record of the services of William Reade in the General Court, and also of his purchase of the house and land mentioned above.

1636 7, Dec. "Certificate of the Secretary of the Commonwealth of Massachusetts. A General Court houlden at Boston, the 7th day of the 10th month, 1636. Pr'sent.

Deputies, * * * *

* * * * * * Goo-Will-Reade."

1636/7. "William Reade, having bought the house and twenty acres of land at Weymouth, unfenced, for £7, 13s, 4d, wch was Zachary Bicknels (after Bicknels death), of Richard Rocket and his wife, is to have the same sale confirmed by the child when he cometh to age, or else the child to alow all such costs as the Court shall think meet."

1638. 6, Sept. "At a General Court, held at Boston, the 6th Day of the 7th Month, a 1638. Pr'sent.

Deputies, * * * *
* * * * * * * Will-Reade."

Vol. 1, Records of Colony Mass., pp. 184, 189, 235.

1638. 6, Sept. "There is a rate of 400. granted, but the warrants not to be sent out until the other accounts be cleared, and that to be done, within eight weeks, and these afternamed are to meet the first Tuesday in November, and to take the Treasurer's account, and then to appoint the warrants to be sent out. The committee are, * *
* * * * * * * William Reade."
* * * *

Vol. 1, Records Colony Mass., p. 242.

Commonwealth of Massachusetts,
Office of the Secretary,
Boston, March 12, 1894.

I certify the foregoing citations to be true abstracts from the printed Records of Massachusetts, Vol. 1, 1628-1641.

Witness the Seal of the Commonwealth.

(Seal) WM. M. OLIN, Secretary.

The name of William Reade is the eleventh on the list of names in the first division of land in Weymouth, and eighteen acres were allotted to him.

The following abstracts are taken from the Town Records of Weymouth, Massachusetts:

"Sould by Edward Smith unto William Reade the 25th of the 3d month (May) 1644" "Ten acres & half of land

in the Westerneck Eight acres & half of it was first given to him the said William Reade two acres first given to Rich Addams bounded on the east with the land of said William Reade on the west with the land of Richard Addams, North & South with the Commons."

"At a meeting of the Town the 26th of the 9th, month (November) 1651, There were chosen Townsmen. John Rogers, Nicholas Byram, David Hunt, John Burge, Thomas Dyer, William Reade & William Dyer, & are to be invested with power for the carring on the Towns affayers for the ensuing year."

We have no record of the exact date of death of William Reade. From the foregoing records it will be noticed that William Reade was chosen Townsman on the 26th day of November, 1651. This is the last mention we have of him in public life. That he died sometime between the years 1651 and 1658, is evident from the following abstracts, taken from the above-mentioned record and which relate to his widow, Avis Reade.

On the 6th of April, 1658, the Townsmen,

"Ordered that the Widow Read shall have liberty to take in a garden plott in the swamp before her House, provided she lay up that garden plott to common, formerly granted, Neere Macnith Pratts barne & that she take no more, than the aforesaid plott contaynes."

The 6th day of the 12th Month (Feb.), 1659.

"At a meeting of the Townsmen (or Selectmen) it was further granted that Widow Avis Read, should have a swamp lott by virtue that her Husband was then an Inhabitant, when the sayd swamp lotts were granted."

"At a general Town Meeting held March 7-1659./60. Voted that Elder Bate, John Bicknell, Richard Porter, & Others, should have lotts in the Pine Swamps, and that Widow Read should have one lott in the same Pine Swamp and that Sergt Whitmarsh should Measure all the lotts."

In the first division of lands in 1663, Widow Reed received Lot No. 13, of 10 acres, beginning at the Braintree line, and Lot. No. 4, of 30 acres, in second division.

v

CHILDREN

2. Margaret, b. 1636; d. July 6, 1659; m. May 11, 1651, John Vining. Hedded 1657
3. Hannah, b. 1637; m. April 2, 1658, Nicholas Whitmarsh.
4. William, b. Oct. 15, 1639; m. 1675, Esther Thompson.
5. Esther, b. May 8, 1641. m. Jones Austin of Taunton.
6. Ruth, b. 1642; d. in 1663; m. Dec. 19, 1662, John Whitman.
7. Thomas, b. 1645; d. Nov. 14, 1719; m. in 1670, Sarah Bicknell.
8. Mary, b. 1647; d. 1655; unmarried.
9. John, b. 1649; d. Jan. 13, 1720; m. Bethiah Frye.
10. James, b. ———; d. July 21, 1726; m. April 18, 1683, Susanna Richmond.

SECOND GENERATION

A 4

William Reed, son of William and Avis (Deacon) Reade.
b. Oct. 15, 1639; d. in 1706.
m. 1675, Esther Thompson, daughter of John Thompson, who came over in Wesson's company when six years of age, and Mary Cook, daughter of Francis Cook, who was of the Mayflower company. She died in 1706.

William was constable in Weymouth in 1675, which was in those times the principal office of the town. He was selectman in 1681, and an extensive dealer in land. His will, dated Oct. 26, 1705, a copy of which is hereto appended, was proved Sept. 12, 1706, and may be found in the probate office (lib. 16, fol. 73), he and his wife dying between the time of making and the time it was probated. He lived on Pleasant street on the southwesterly side, a part of the old house still standing at this date (1888) having been remodeled and occupied by Palmer Loud. The old dam which he built across the river is near the house, and was probably built between 1680 and 1690. He owned all the land both sides of the street from Hingham line to Ragged Plain (so called) and from the river to a point westerly of the house owned by William

V

Dyer and later built a double house on the site that had been occupied by William Dyer's house, also one between that and his residence, a portion of the old house had the diamond glass as late as 1850.

It may be interesting to some of their descendants to know the parentage of Esther. It appears by a genealogy published by Ignatius Thompson in 1841, that Lieut. John Thompson, father of Esther, was born in Wales, and was six years old when he landed in Wesson's company in May, 1622, and when he came of proper age, Dec. 6, 1645, married Mary Cook, daughter of Francis Cook, who was one of the Mayflower's company (she was born in Plymouth in 1626; died March 21, 1715). He settled and built a log house thirteen miles west of Plymouth, on the confines of what was then called Plymouth, now Halifax and Middleborough. He lived there until his house was burned by the Indians. While living there either he or his wife would walk to meeting every Sunday. The only place where they had an elder to speak to them was Plymouth, a distance of more than thirteen miles. "We have," says Thompson, "orally received information that during one year of his residence there, his wife on two of the Sabbaths in June, after breakfast took a child six months old in her arms and walked to Plymouth to attend meeting, and returned on the same day." We have in this a picture of real life as it existed in those times, as well as a striking illustration of the indomitable energy and perseverance of the Puritan ancestors. The descendants of William Reed and Esther may thus distinctly trace their ancestry through her to the Pilgrim company of the Mayflower who landed on Plymouth Rock. John Thompson died June 16, 1696. He and his wife are buried at Middleborough. After the death of her husband the widow removed from Weymouth to Abington. He was a private in Lieut. Edward Oak's company, April 26, 1676. (See Soldiers of King Philip's War, by W. S. Bodges, p. 43.)

The site of his house was pointed out to the compiler on

a visit to Weymouth July, 1900. Another house had been built on the spot where the old house stood, some of the timbers from the old, were found to be good and sound, and were worked into the new house, they were of oak, and apparently as sound as the day they were put in originally. The land was purchased of John Raue, whose house was burned by the Indians, at the time of King Philip's War (about 1675).

A Bridgewater newspaper of April 25, 1900, notes the sale of the John Thompson farm on Thompson street, Halifax, to John Ljinberg the past week which is remarkable from the fact that the farm now passes out of the Thompson family for the first time since the settlement of Halifax. The site of the first house built in the town is on this farm. And it is a matter of record that with this sturdy family the thirteen miles walk to Plymouth church was the regular order of things Sundays.

The following abstracts, taken from the town records of Weymouth, Massachusetts, refer to William Reed:

"In 1662, William Reed was fined twenty shillings for cutting thatch on the Town fflatts."

"At a General Town Meeting 2d of March 1663/4 Voted on Motion of William Reed, that the said William Reed shall have forty Pole of Land, so that he could straighten his Wall & c Next to Reeds Marsh (so called)."

"March 1669/70 William Reed was appointed fence viewer."

"1676/7 William Reed appointed fence viewer."

"At a General Town Meeting 28th of Nov. 1681, William Reed was chosen one of the Selectmen."

"At a Meeting of the Selectmen, the 4th of April, 1682, they appointed to run the perambulation lines on both sides of the Town of Weymouth Corp^ll^ French & William Reed for Hingham line and Lt. White and Corp^ll^ Kingman for Braintree line."

"William Reed, was chosen Selectman at a General Town Meeting of the inhabitants of Weymouth, Nov. 27 1686. He was again chosen Selectman in 1686/7."

"At a General Town Meeting Convened the 2d day of March Anno, 1695/6 Maj Hunt, Chosen Moderator.

"The Selectmen Chosen, Edward Bate 33, Joseph Dyer 13, Maj Hunt 12 Lt. White 14 William Reed 12."

"At a General Town Meeting, the first day of March 1696/7 by vote of the town were chosen for Selectmen, Capt. White, Lt. White, William Reed, Abiah Whitman & Edward Bate."

"At a General Town Meeting November 27-1682, Capt Holbrook is chosen Moderator.

"After severall agitations concerning the old Meeting house the insufficiency of it, and the inconveniency of it, both for want of Room & for want of light &c., The town passed a vote that the should be a Committee appointed, 2dly, That Lieut White, & Corpl French doe warne the sd committee appointed to meet & at what place, & the time when, which said Committee or the Major part of them have full power to act in all respects for the accomodating the towns with a Meeting house either for the repayring the old, or building of a New Meeting house to doe as they see cause upon the Towns Charge, The Men Nominated & Appointed by the town for the Committee are,

Capt Torrey,
Lieut Holbrook,
Lieut White,
Deacon Humphrey,
Ensigne Hunt,
Quartermaster Nash,
Sergt Whitmarsh,
Corpl French,
Corpl Kingman,
Sergt Vining,
John Pratt,
Richard Phillips,
James Smith,
Phillip King,
Joseph Pitty,
James Lovell,
John Shaw Senr,
Joseph Pratt,
William Reed,
John Richards,
William Holbrook,
Thomas Reed,
Joseph Dyer,
John Porter,
Joseph Poole,
Ebenezer White,
John Rogers."

V

"The 13 day of March 1688, Wee, whose Names are underwritten have agreed with Thomas Randal, to Ring the Bell and Sweep the Meeting house for the year ensueing the date hereof for fortie Shillings in Money In behalf of the Town

Samuel White,	Abiah Whitman,
William Reed,	Joseph Dyer." —
James White,	

William Reed was chosen Waywarden in 1692/3.

"At a Meeting of the freeholders of the Town legally Convened the 24th day of April, 1693, Its to be understood that the waye over the great playne is to be between the two divisions of the great lotts when it Comes to the divisions, and if any be agrived they May Come to the Committee for Satisfaction Thomas Reed, Abiah Whitman, Nathl. Humphrey, Joseph Green, John Holbrook, John Whitmarsh, James Lovell, William Torrey, John Rogers, William Reed, Joseph Pratt, Ebenezer White, Joseph Dyer

(Committee)"

"At a Generell Town Meeting Legally Convened the 4th day of March 1695/6. The town past a vote that there shall be a Committee added to the present Selectmen with reference to the agreement for the settlement and procureing a School Master, The Committee by the town is Lt. Nash, John Rogers, Lt. Whitmarsh, William Reed, James Lovell, Senr. Corpl. Hunt, John Pratt Sr. Sergt. Reed, Deacon Torrey, Joseph Green, James Richards and Sergt. Holbrook."

"At a Meeting of the Selectmen the third day of March 1695/6 An agreement Made for the Macking a Substantial New Pound in the manner & form of the old pound Now Standing, William Reed hath engaged with the Selectmen to erect, Make, finish, and set up where the said Selectmen Shall appoint a pound with all sorts of timber of the same dementions both posts railes & Gate with Substantial lock and Key as is Expressed in page (78) And alsoe the said

William Reed doth alsoe engage to put a good Slab or Slabs all rounf with the pound to be ffastned to the Posts and all to be done suffisint & work man like, betwixt the day of the date hereof and the first day of May next insueing the date here of in consideration whereof the said William Reed is to be truly paid out of the next town rate the Sum of eight pounds in or as Money, In Witness whereof the said William Reed hath hereunto Sett his hand the day & year above written.

William Reed."

"At a General Town Meeting the 6th day of March Anno Domi. 1698/9 The following votes were passed by the Town of Weymouth, Chosen for fence viewers Sergt. Reed & others Chosen for a Committee to New Seat the Meeting house & to erect Seat or Seats as they Shall See Meet, Mr. Torrey, Corpl. Hunt, John Pratt Senr. Lt. Nash, Cornet White, Dea. Torrey, Mr. French & John Rogers, William Reed, Joseph Diar, Sergt. Reed, Joseph Poole Sergt. Whitman, William Torrey, Sergt. Porter, Edward Bate."

WILL

"I William Read, Being through the Great Decay of Nature and Weakness of Body, aprehensive of my Mortality, and being of perfect memory and a disposing mind, Doe make this my last will and Testament as followeth:

"I doe humbly and hopefully Give up my self unto God my heavenly father, through Jesus Christ his son, my only Savior, in Whom through Grace I believe for Eternal Life, and salvation, and upon whom I wait Instantly, for an entrance into his Everlasting Heavenly Kingdom, adoring that Infinite Grace, through which notwithstanding my Exceeding Great unworthiness, I have obtained this hope of Salvation, I Doe also Commit and Commend my Dear wife and Children unto the saving Grace of god in Christ Jesus according to his Everlasting Covenant

"Concerning my Woorly Estate my Will is that my funeral

Expenses being Discharged and all my Lawful Debts being Duely paid my beloved. Wife Hester Read Shall Have the Sole use and Improvement of my Dwelling House and some land and Meddor adjoining bound westerly by the High way and Southerly by the fenc of my Rye lot as the fence standeth at the date of these presents and Easterly by the Damm made to flow Sd Meddor and Northerly from the Northwest Corner of sd Meddo to the high way and my barne and orchard on the west Side of the way being about four acres as it is now fenced in and also the sole use and Improvement of all my Movables that I shall be possest of att my Decease and I Doe Injoyne my sons William Reade and John Reade to manage and improve the sd lands meddow for their mother according to her direction and appointment without any other Recompense then they shall have by what I shall give and bequeath unto them by this my will and Testament and this During her natural life:

"Item. I Doe give and bequeath unto my Eldest son William Read the new Dubble house and land adjoining that I built for him and all my land on the west side of the way bounded Easterly by the high way, Southerly by land belonging to John Shaw Dec his heirs Westerly by the Towns Common lane, Northerly by the land of John Richards Children with all the orchard upland and meddow land Contained in sd bounds and limitts and all my Meddo lying by the pen River provided always that the barn and orchard about four acres contained in the sd bounds or limmits shal be to the use of my wife as before during her natural life.

"Item. I Doe Give unto my son John Reed my Dwelling house wherein I live on the East side of the high way and all that my land adjoining and Meddo land bounded Westerly by the High way, Northerly by land belonging to the heirs of John Richards Dec. Easterly by hingham line and Southerly by land of Joseph pool provided always that that part of the land and Meddow and also my house shall bee for the use and Improvement of my wife During her natural life as before Expressed.

V

"Item. I Doe give unto my son Jacob Reed my lot of land in Ragged plaine bounden Easterly by the high way Southerly by land of Cont. Whitmarsh Westerly by the Town Common land, Northerly partly by Ebenezer Whitman and partly by land belonging to the heirs of John Shaw Dec. and a part of a lott of land in the thicket; the Westerly End of that lot and also a lot of land in the great plain and half a lot in the pine swamp and all my Meddo att Reads Marsh so caled near John Blanchards land:

"Item. I Doe give unto my Daughter Bashna porter twenty pounds in Money or current pay all money price.

"Item. I Doe give unto my Daughter Mercy Whitmarsh twenty pounds in Money or current pay all money price.

"Item. I Doe give unto my Daughter Mary Reed twenty pounds in Money or Current pay all Money price.

"Item. I Doe give unto my Daughter Hester Reade twenty pounds in Money or Current pay all money price.

"Item. I Doe give unto my Daughter Sarah Reade twenty pounds in Money or Current pay all money price.

"Item. I Doe give unto my sons John Reed and Jacob Read aforementioned my lot running throw the birch swamp and my swamp lot in Bicknells Swamp so called.

"Item. I Doe give unto my aforementioned three sons William Read and John Read and Jacob Read my part of the wharf and my Common lot by the great pond and all my land in the Township of Bridgewater and my part of the sawmill in sd Bridgewater to bee Equally Divided amonght them both for quantity and qulity and further I Doe oblige my son William Read and John Reed to pay my four daughters first Mentioned above to Each of them twenty pounds in Money or Current pay all Money price within two years after my decease and to Doe what work their Mother shall need or Require in Improving her land yearly During her natural life and I Doe hereby oblige my son Jacob to pay twenty pounds in Money or current pay all Money price to my youngest Daughter Sarah Read within two years after My Decease if shee Require it so soon

v

"Item I Doe give unto my five Daughters before mentioned in this my will all my movables which shall Remain after my wifes Decease to be Equally divided amonght them And finally I Doe appoint my beloved wife Hester Read to be Executrix and my sons William Read and John Reed and to be Executors together with her of this my last will and Testament. Also it is my Desire and I Doe request my loving friends Edward Bate sen and James Humphrey both of Weymouth to be overseers to see this my will performed acording to the true intent and meaning thereof and I Doe hereby Revoke all other former wills Declaring this to be my last will and Testament In witness Whereof I have hereunto set my hand and seale this twenty sixth Day of October annoque Domini one thousand seven hundred and five

The Mark W of William Read Seal

Signed sealed and published in the presence of

Edward Bates Sen
John Bate Jun } Witnesses
Samuel Bate Jun

"This will presented by William Read and John Read Executors herein named for probate the Executrix being dead

"Boston Sept. 12th 1706
Suffolk S'S

"Edward Bate Sen and John Bate Junr made oath that they saw the above named William Read Senr sign and Seale and heard him publish this Instrument and for his last will and Testament and that he was then of sound Disposing Mind to them best Discerning: and that they the Depon^s and Samuel Bate Jun set to their hands as witnesses thereof in the Testators presence

H. Addington J Probate"

CHILDREN

11. John, b. Oct. 21, 1680; d. young.
12. William, b. May 24, 1682; d. June 3, 1753; m. 1703, Alice Nash.
13. John, b. July 10, 1687; m. 1st. Sarah Hersey; m. 2d. Mary Whitmarsh.

v

14. Jacob, b. Nov. 6, 1691; d. 1766; m. 1st. Sarah Hersey; m. 2d. Hannah Noyes (widow).
15. Bashna, b. ———; m. Nicholas Porter.
16. Mercy, b. ———; m. ——— Whitmarsh.
17. Mary, b. ———.
18. Hester, b. ———; m. in 1707, Joseph Allen.
19. Sarah, b. March 21, 1694; m. Hezekiah King.

W 7

Thomas Reed, son of William and Avis (Deacon) Reade.

b. 1645; d. Nov. 14, 1719.

m. in 1670, Sarah Bicknell, daughter of John and Mary Shaw Bicknell, b. about 1651, who d. at Weymouth, Aug. 21, 1719.

The following is a statement by Quincey L. Reed, of South Weymouth, Massachusetts, as to who "Sarah," the wife of Thomas Reed, was:

"In the Genealogical History of the Porter family, by the Hon. J. W. Porter, of Bangor, Maine, published 1878, on page fourteen, a very imperfect account is given of John Bicknell, and his first wife Mary, and their children. Of course it is all that can be found on the records, but does not tell who this Mary was, nor whether the three children given, were all of that branch; neither does it give dates of birth of all of them. Then on page fifteen, it reads, that James Richards (2d), son of William Richards (1st), married Ruth Bicknell, oldest child of John and Mary (Porter) Bicknell. John Bicknell's first wife was Mary Shaw, William Richards' wife was Grace Shaw, both daughters of Abraham Shaw. The children of these two families were cousins, but James Richards was in no way related to the children of John and Mary (Porter) Bicknell, and married their oldest daughter Ruth. This James Richards was a business man at that period, before 1700, and his books are in existence at this time. In his books he speaks, in 1693, of 'Brother John Dyer of Boston'—1694, 'Brother John Richards' and 'Cousin Thomas Porter'—1695, 'Brother

Joseph Richards'—1696, 'Sister Hannah Bicknell'—1698, 'Uncle Shaw'—1701, 'Uncle Vinson'—1702, 'Brother Thomas Reed'—1705, 'Sister Reede'—1706, 'Brother Reed'—1707, 'Enoch Lovell on his father Reeds account'—1709, 'Brother Maurice Trufant.' In addition to all this, I have many more of the different citizens of that period, referred to in this same manner, and in every instance, where they are known, they bear the same relationship as is expressed in his language. It was customary to some extent, at that period, upwards of two centuries ago, to refer to the relationship of the parties, in making entries in their account books. The first reference is 'Brother John Dyer of Boston.' Dea. Thomas Dyer, in his will 1676, gives his house in Boston to his son John, who married Mary Bicknell, probably oldest child of John and Mary (Shaw) Bicknell. The next is 'Brother John Richards'—he was an older brother of James; then 'Cousin Thomas Porter,' he was a son of Thomas Porter, brother of Mary (Porter) Bicknell, and cousin to Ruth Bicknell, wife of James Richards; then 'Brother Joseph Richards,' another older brother to James; then 'Sister Hannah Bicknell,' she was sister to Ruth Bicknell, the wife of James Richards; the next is 'Uncle Shaw,' this was John Shaw, who married Alice Philips, brother to Grace, the mother of James Richards. The next is 'Uncle Vinson,' who was he? Who could he have been and uncle to James Richards and his wife? I can find no one but Thomas Vinson, who married Martha Shaw, sister to Grace. The name of Martha has been in the Vinson family to the present time. Then comes 'Brother Thomas Reed' and 'Sister Reed.' How were they brother and sister to James Richards and his wife? According to the ages of John Dyer and Thomas Reed, the wife Sarah, of Thomas Reed, was probably the second child of John and Mary (Shaw) Bicknell. John Bicknell was thirty-four years of age when his first wife, Mary Shaw, died in 1658, and was probably married sometime between 1645 and 1650. He had a son John, born 1654, a daughter Naomi, born 1657,

a daughter Mary, date of birth unknown, but probably the oldest child bearing her mother's name, who married John Dyer, and between the birth of his daughter Mary and his son John, his daughter Sarah was probably born, who married Thomas Reed. (John Dyer was born 1643.) Thomas Reed was born 1645. Then comes 'Brother Maurice Trufant'; he married Mary Bicknell, own sister to Ruth, the wife of James Richards. Then compare the names of the daughters of the two families, those of John Bicknell were Mary, Sarah, Ruth, Hannah, Elizabeth, Joanna, Experience; those of Thomas Reed were Mary, Sarah, Ruth, Hannah, Elizabeth. These are not given according to their ages, but the names are all there. To a person of the present generation this may appear of little account, but to one acquainted with the customs of that period, two and one-half centuries ago, it has far more significance than appears on the face of it. It is now nearly fifty years since I first began investigations to ascertain who this Sarah was who married Thomas Reed, my own ancestor, about 1670. I have exhausted all the records of Weymouth, and other records, but could never find any indication who she could be, and had given it up as an impossibility, until these records of James Richards were found. In the land grants of Weymouth, 1663, every family was represented. After following through all of these families, and disposing of all the Sarahs but one, 'Sarah Rogers,' it would be supposed she must be the person, but I have never been able to find the first point to sustain that, with the exception that her name was Sarah, while there are circumstances, facts and records, much that I do not write, in connection with Thomas Reed, and the Bicknell family, the Vinsons and the Shaws, that are unaccountable, only for this solution, which verify these records of James Richards, beyond a doubt."

Thomas Reed was chosen fence viewer, March 22, 1668-9, March 1673-4, March 1675-6, Feb. 23, 1679, in 1680, 6 March, 1698/9 and 7 March, 1708-9; constable, November 27, 1676; way warden, 1681-2 and 1690.

"At a Generall Town Meeting the 2d day of March 1690/1 Capt. Holbrook Chosen Moderator, There is chosen for Constable to serve for the year Ensueing William Torrey Senr and Edward Bate, There is Chosen for Selectman for the year Ensueing Sergt Reed, Capt. White, Ebenezer White Abiah Whitman, Capt Hunt James Smith Senr and John Rogers."

"A vote past with reference to a Motion Made or Caused to be made by Matthew Pratt Senr Concerning some towns Common land behind his house by way of exchange with the town to save fencing, The Town voted that James Lovell Senr and John Hunt should lay out and view the land so as may be to accomodate and Not to deprive if it May be Thomas Reed of his Wartering place Viz, Not to prevent Thomas Reed of his wartering place at any time in the year, and to make return of it to the Clerk."

On the first Monday in March, 1692-3, Thomas Reed (Sergt.) was again chosen selectman, at a general town meeting.

"At a Generall Town Meeting Legally Convened the 4th of March 1694/5 There was chosen for Surveyors for the year ensueing Lt. Nash, John Pratt senr, Thomas Randal, Nathl Ford and Joseph Green, of Highways, There was Chosen tithingmen, John Rogers, John Hunt, James Humphrey, Nicholas Shaw, Sergt Reed, John Shaw Jr, and Peregrine White."

He was also, on November 27, 1682, at a general town meeting appointed one of a committee "for the repayring of the old or building of a new Meeting house . . ." [See abstract under William Reed (4).]

At a meeting of the freeholders of the town of Weymouth held on the 24th day of April, 1693, the "waye over the great playne" was determined, and a committee, to whom any one who might "be agrived they May Com" for satisfaction, was appointed. Thomas Reed was a member of this committee. [See William Reed (4).]

1694/5. March 4. "The town past a vote that there shall be a Committee added to the present Selectmen with reference to the agreement for the settlement and procuring a School Master." Sergt. Reed was a member of this committee. [See William Reed (4).]

"At a General Town Meeting Convened the 2d day of March Anno 1695/6 Maj. Hunt, Chosen Moderator.

. . . .

"Surveyors, Natl Humphrey, Sergt Thomas Reed, Joseph Pratt, John Rogers, Lt. Whitmarsh, Haywards, Joseph Drake and Richard Davenport.

"Fence Viewers, John Pratt Senr. Stephen French Jr. for to view all the fences above Thomas Porters and Thomas Reeds & so to Jonathan Whitmarshes Easterly, Thomas Richards James Humphrey, from Thomas Reeds down to Zachery Bicknells, and so all the lower plantation."

At a general town meeting, held on the 6th of March, 1698-9, Sergt. Reed, his brother William (4) and a number of others were chosen "for a committee to New Seat the Meeting house & to erect Seat or Seats as they Shall See Meet." [See abstract under William Reed (4).]

"At a generall Town Meeting the 4th of March 1705/6 Samuel Porter & Thomas Reed, Jr. (20), Chosen Constables, Col Hunt, Capt French, Elder Rogers, William Torrey, & Sergent Reed Chosen a Committee to Make or draw up some town orders or by laws for the benefit of the town, to present to the town for their aprobation and see to present the quarter Sessions to be aproved of and confirmed as the law directs."

He was a private in Lieut. Gillam's company, King Philip's War. Was under the command of Major Savage, Feb. to May, 1675-6.

Of Weymouth.

CHILDREN

20. **Thomas**, b. Sept. 12' 1671; d. Oct. 2, 1719; m. Jan. 4, 1701, Hannah Randall.

21. **Mary**, b. 1672; m. Nov. 24, 1697, Capt. Enoch Lovell.

22. Sarah, b. ———; m. July 28, 1697, Thomas Stockbridge.
23. John, b. Dec. 30, 1679; d. Dec., 1757; m. pub. Nov. 11, 1715, Sarah Whitmarsh.
24. Samuel, b. April 12, 1681; d. June 25, 1739; m. Jan. 7, 1704, Abigail White.
25. Ruth, b. Feb. 20, 1685; m. Benjamin White.
26. William, b. Feb. 4, 1688; m. Dec. 13, 1716, Jane Torrey.
27. Hannah, b. Sept. 25, 1689; m. Nov. 6, 1714, John Hunt.
28. Elizabeth, b. Nov. 9, 1694; m. Dec. 19, 1717, Thomas Hunt.

T 9

John Reed, son of William and Avis (Deacon) Reade.

b. 1649; d. in Dighton Jan. 13, 1721, aged 72.

m. Bethia Frye, daughter of Geo. Frye; d. Oct. 20, 1730, aged 77.

He was a house carpenter, and appears to have been a man of considerable property, and an extensive dealer in land.

" At a Meeting of the Selectmen the 6th day of September 1680 Whereas there is information given against John Reed, John Vinson, & James Reed, for Cutting timber upon the Towns Commons contrary to the Towns order the Selectmen on the hearing of the Case & the evidence produced do order that the said John Reed John Vinson, & James Reed do forthwith pay each of them twenty Shillings the one half to the informer & the other half to Joseph Dyer Constable for the use of the Towne, and in case of refusall to be levied by a Warrant from the Selectmen to the Constable."

We learn from tradition this action, on the part of the selectmen, so offended John Reed and James Reed, that they determined to change their residence, and subsequent records show that they immediately removed from Weymouth to Taunton (South Purchase) about 1680, and John remained there until he was set off in the new town of Dighton, May 30, 1712, and died there. James afterwards removed with his family, about 1705, to Middleborough. In 1682 they were both enrolled on the military roll of Taunton.

The records describe about a dozen pieces of land bought

by him in Taunton, and several pieces sold by him. Annexed is appended a deed of his home place purchased of John Woodward in 1680.

He was quite a business man in Taunton, but removed from there to Dighton. He and his wife were buried in Dighton, on Burying Hill, between upper and lower Four Corners. Their grave-stones are in good condition, and their inscriptions read thus: "Here lieth ye body of Battieah, wife of John Read: died October ye 20, 1730, aged 77 years." "Here lieth ye body of John Reed, aged 72 years: and died January ye 13th 1720-1."

His estate was valued at a hundred and sixty-two pounds at his decease. He was the ancestor of the Taunton Reeds. He, with his brother James, were privates in Capt. Johnson's company, later Capt. John Jacob's, in the "King Philip's War" (see Bodge's, pages 113 and 114). About 1675, before he removed to Taunton, he leased the farm belonging to Wm. Tynge, of Braintree, later the farm of Josiah Quincy.

DEED

"To all Christian People before whom these presents shall come, John Woodward of Taunton in the Collony of Plimouth in New England Sendeth Greeting Know Yee y[t] y[e] s[d] John Woodward for & in Consideration of nine pounds sterling to him in hand payd by John Reed of Taunton abovesd Carpenter the Receipt whereof he doth hereby acknowledge & thereof & of every part & parcell thereof, Doeth fully, Clearly & absolutely exonorate, Acquitt, & Discharge the said John Reed his heirs & Assignes forever by these Presents Hath given granted Bargained sold Aliened enfeoffed & confirmed and by these presents doeth give grant Bargaine sell alien enfeoffe and Confirme Unto the said Reed a Certain percell of land Lyeing scittuate & being with in the Township of Taunton afores[d]. westerly from the Meeting House of the said Town Bounded by the lands of Thomas Lincon Sen[e]. on the south side, and the

three mile River on the West End and the lands of Samuel Hoskins on the North side, & the Commons on the East End Containing by Estimation Twelve Acrees be it more or less, with all the priviledges profitts therin thereupon & therefrom ariseing with the appurtenences thereunto belonging.

"To Have To Hold the said Twelve acrees of land with all the Rights priviledges and appur[ces] thereof as before Bounded with the true copie of any such Original Deed or other writings as concern the s[d]. Barganed Premisses, with any other lands, if he the said John Woodward have any such Deed or Writing To him the s[d]. John Reed his heires executors Adm[es] and Assignes; to the only p[e]per use and behoofe of him the said John Reed his heirs executors & Assignes forever And the said John Woodward for himself his heirs executors and Assignes Doth Covenant & grant, to and with the said John Reed his heirs executors & Assignes by these presents that the said John Woodward the day of the date hereof is and standeth Lawfully Seized to his owne use of and in the said Bargained Premises and every part thereof in a good perfect & absolute Estate of Inheritance in fee Simple and hath in himself full power good Right & lawfull authority to Grant Bargain sell Convey and assure the same in manner & form aboves[d]. And that the said John Reed his heires executors & Assignes & every of them shall & may forever hereafter Peaceably and Quietly have hold & enjoy the aforesaid Bargained Premisses with benefitts and appurtenances thereof free & cleare & Clearely Acquitted & Discharged of & from all other Bargains sales gifts grants Joyntures Dowers titles of Dower Estates Mortgages forfeitures Judgements Executions and all Acts of Incumbrance whatsoever to be Holden as of o[e] Sovereigne Lord the Kind as of his Mann[e] of East Greenwicth in the County of Kent within the Realme of England in free & Common Soccage and not in Capite nor by Kn[ts] Service, to his only proper use & behoofe of him the said John Reed his beires and Assignes forever with Warrantees against all People by these presents: From by or under

the said John Woodward his heires Executors & Admes and every of them, Claimeing any Right title or Interest of or into the said pemises.

"And further the said John Woodward and Sarah his wife Do for themselves their executors & Admes Covenant promise & grant, to and with the said John Reed his heires & Assignes that they the said John Woodward & Sarah his said wife upon Reasonable and Lawfull Demand shall & will perform & do or cause to be performed and done all such further Act & Acts, whether by way of acknowledgment of this present Deed or Release of Dower with respect of the said premises, or in any other kind that shall or may be for the full Compleating, Conefirmcing and sure makeing the afore bargained premises Unto the said John Reed his heirs Executors and Assignes according to the true Intent hereof the laws of the Collony above. In witness whereof the Persons viz: John Woodward abovesd. & Sarah his said wife have hereunto putt their hands and seals this second Day of Decembe in the year one thousand six hundred & Eighty.

John Woodward (seale)
Sarah Woodward (seale)

Signed sealed & Delivered in
the presence of us
Shadrach Wilbore
John Crossman

"John Woodward above written pesonaly appeareing owned and Acknowledged this instrument to be his voluntary and Free Act & Deed Before Daniel Smith this 6th of July 1685.

"Thus Entered & Recorded Janey 14th 1698/9 By John Cary Recorde."

A true copy from Book 2 of Bristol Co. No. Dist. Land Records, pages 313 and 314.

Attest: J. E. Wilbar, Register.

CHILDREN

29. John, b. June 5, 1674; d. 1739; m. June 15, 1697, Bethiah Cobb.
30. William, b. ———; d. 1734; m. June 8, 1721, Mary Richmond.

31. Thomas, b. about 1677-78; d. Feb. 19, 1741; m. Sarah Tisdale.
32. George, b. ———; d. 1765; m. 1st. Sarah Whitmarsh; m. 2d. Jan. 1. 1730, Abigail Woodward.
33. Mary, b. 1681; d. April 23, 1748; m. Joseph Atwood, of Dighton.
34. Ruth, b. 1686; d. Aug., 1748; m. March 13, 1706, Joseph Tisdale, of Taunton, Mass.
35. Hannah, b. 1691; d. June 4, 1731; m. Sept. 2, 1713, Josiah Talbot.

10

James Reed, son of William and Avis (Deacon) Reade.

b. at Weymouth ———; d. July 21, 1726.

m. Apr. 18, 1683, Susanna Richmond, daughter of John Richmond, she was born Nov. 1661, at Bridgewater; d. Aug. 18, 1725.

On September 6, 1680, James Reed, together with his brother John and John Vinson, was fined twenty shillings by the selectmen of Weymouth, "for cutting timber upon the Towns Commons, contrary to the Towns order," and being offended at this action of the selectmen, removed to Taunton, where he resided for about twenty-five years, and afterwards, in 1705, he removed to Middleborough, and made it his permanent home. [See record of John Reed (9).]

While residing in Weymouth, in 1675, he served in Capt. Johnson's company in "King Philip's War." Later, on April 8, 1682, while residing in Taunton, he was a member of a military company. [See Bodge's, pages 113 and 114.]

CHILDREN

36. James, b. ———; d. Feb. 1, 1735.
37. William, b. May 1, 1685; m. Elizabeth ———; resided at Middleborough.
38. John, b. ———; m. 1st. Feb. 8, 1709, Susanna Rounds; m. 2d. Elizabeth ———.
39. Thomas, b. about 1684-89; m. 1st. March 1, 1707, Mary Fifield in Boston; m. 2d. Sept. 14, 1709, Sarah Niles.
40. Mary, b. 1697; d. July 17, 1724.
41. Martha, b. ———.
42. Ann, b. ———.
43. Susanna, b. ———.
44. Benjamin, b. 1699; m. Dec. 1, 1720, Hannah Chase

THIRD GENERATION

A 12

William Reed, son of William and Esther (Thompson) Reed.
b. May 24, 1682; d. June 3, 1753.

m. 1703, Alice Nash. She died Dec. 5, 1751. She was a daughter of Lieut. Jacob Nash, son of James Nash who settled in Weymouth in 1628. William Reed moved to Abington in 1708. At the first town meeting held in Abington, March 2, 1712, he was chosen selectman and town clerk.

At a general town meeting the 3d day of March, 1706/7, William Reed was chosen fence viewer.

"At a general town meeting held in Weymouth, May the 8th, 1727, Chosen for a representative for the year ensuing Joseph White, Esq., Chosen for Moderator for said Meeting, Joseph White, Esq., Chosen for a committee to lay out the wood lot which was voted to the South precinct in Weymouth, for the Minister in said precinct John Vining Jr, John Vinson & William Reed."

"At a general Town Meeting held in Weymouth on March 9th 1729/30 Voted that John Vinson, John Vining Jr, & William Reed be a Committee for running of lines & laying out land, & shall have three pounds & five shillings out of the town Treasury for their time and expence in said affair."

Aaron Hobart in his sketch of Abington, a book compiled by him in 1839, says:

"In 1665, Two Hundred acres of land were granted to the four younger Sons of Lieut James Torrey (of Scituate) lying above Weymouth near unto the line of the Massachusetts, to be at the disposal of Capt. William Torrey, for the good of said children, bounded &c—

"In 1714 William Reed, Samuel Porter, Nicholas Porter, John Reed and Jacob Reed, of Abington, and Thomas Reed, of Hingham owned this land, and divided the same into

lots, each owner agreeing to maintain his share of fence around the Meadow."

Hobart further states that "William lived where Ephraim S. Jenkins lives."

Rev. Mr. Dodge in his journal, 3rd of June, 1753, says: "Attended the funeral of the Aged Capt. Reed, the largest I have ever seen in town. Ten at least of his descendants in the Male line, have been liberally educated. Of these two have been Members of Congress, Viz, his grandson, the late Rev. Dr. John Reed, of West Bridgewater and his Son, the Hon. John Reed of Yarmouth, now a Member. After the Expiration of his present term, he will have been in Congress twenty-two years—Eighteen in succession."

Of Abington.

Children

45. Alice, b. in Boston, Oct. 19, 1703; d. Oct. 24, 1703.
46. William, b. Dec. 15, 1704; d. Nov. 21, 1724.
47. Obadiah, b. March 14, 1707; d. Nov. 4, 1753; m. Oct. 19, 1731, Mary Nash.
48. Ebenezer, b. July 13, 1709; m. Feb. 21, 1732, Hannah Thompson.
49. Alice, b. April 4, 1711; d. Sept. 29, 1724.
50. Daniel, b. Dec. 6, 1713; d. April 5, 1781; m. 1st. Sept. 15, 1739, Ruth White; m. 2d. Feb. 7, 1776, Sarah Hamlyn.
51. James, b. March 3, 1716; d. aged 37; m. May 10, 1739, Abigail Nash.
52. Solomon, b. Oct. 22, 1719; d. 1785; m. 1st. in 1748, Abigail Stoughton, of Conn.; m. 2d. Sarah Reed, widow of Elijah.
53. Jacob, b. ———.
54. Moses, b. Jan. 15, 1723; m. Phoebe ———.
55. Alice, b. April 19, 1725; m. Dec. 1, 1748, Jacob Reed.

A 13

John Reed, son of William and Esther (Thompson) Reed.

b. July 10, 1687, in Weymouth; moved to Abington in 1708.

m. 1st. Sarah Hersey.

m. 2nd. Mary Whitmarsh.

Was executor with his brother William of his father's will. He settled in what is now known as South Abington in 1708

and lived opposite the burying ground in the south part of the town.

Aaron Hobart, in his sketch of Abington, a book compiled by him in 1839, says:

"In 1665, Two Hundred acres of land were granted to the four younger Sons of Lieut James Torrey (of Scituate) lying about Weymouth near unto the line of the Massachusetts, to be at the disposal of Capt. William Torrey, for the good of said children, bounded &c.,

"In 1714 William Reed, Samuel Porter, Nicholas Porter, John Reed and Jacob Reed, of Abington, and Thomas Beal, of Hingham owned this land, and divided the same into lots, each owner agreeing to maintain his share of fence around the Meadow."

Of Abington.

DISTRIBUTION OF ESTATE

"Province of the Massachusetts Bay
Plymouth S. S.

"John Cushing Esqr. Judge of the Prob. of Wills
(Seal) &c. within the county of Plymouth To all whom these presents shall come Greeting.—

"Whereas it has been represented & made appear to me that the real estate of John Reed late of Abington in ye County of Plymouth, yeoman, decd. intestate, can't admit of division among all his children without great prejudice to, or spoiling of ye whole, and ye sd. real estate having been apprised at 190£. & his personal estate at 12-5-0 and 4£ afterwards given in by ye admr. sd. apprisal being made by sufficient freeholders according to law and John Reed, eldest son of ye sd. decd. having assigned and transferred his part in ye sd. decd. estate real & personal to James Reed second son of sd. decd. who has moved yt. sd. real estate may be settled on him, he paying to his brot[rs] & sisters & their legal representatives their ratable parts of ye apprised value thereof.

"Pursuant therefor to an act or law of this Province en-

titled an Act for the Settlement & Distribution of ye estates of intestates & ye direction power & authority to me therein given, I doe by these presents order & assign all the sd. real estate unto ye sd. James Reed to have, hold, possess & enjoy ye same with ye appurtenances to him sd. James Reed his heirs & Assigns forever (the widow of ye sd. decd. having quited her right of dower therein) and he having already given security to his eldest brother John Reed for his two ninths parts of ye apprised value thereof, and to his brother Joseph Reed his ninth part being 3-16-10, to his sister Mary Reed 3-16-10 being her ninth part & to Ezekiel Reed his brother 3-16-10 being his ninth part & to his brother Peter Reed 3-16-10 being his ninth part thereof, and to his brother Squire Reed 3-16-10 being his ninth part & to his brother Saml. Reed 3-16-10 being his ninth part of ye sd. estate, ye debts & allowances as pr. ye administrators acct. being first deducted.

"In testimony whereof I have hereto set my hand & ye seal of ye Court of Prob at Scituate, ye 12, Day of July A. D. 1740.

Jno. Cushing."

Child of John and Sarah

56. John, b. Aug. 10, 1713; m. June 20, 1734, Mary Torrey, and removed to Weymouth.

Children of John and Mary

57. James, b. Oct. 12, 1716; m. Ruth Ford Pool.
58. Joseph, b. Feb. 13, 1718.
59. Mary, b. Dec. 21, 1719; m. April 17, 1739, John Dyer.
60. Ezekiel, b. Nov. 14, 1721; m. in 1742, Hannah Beal.
61. Peter, b. March 29, 1723; d. Feb. 18, 1780; m. March 25, 1748, Lucy Hugens.
62. Squire, b. May 25, 1725.
63. Silence, b. Aug. 10, 1728.
64. Betty, b. April 8, 1730; d. young.
65. Samuel, b. July 13, 1732; d. young.

A **14**

Jacob Reed, son of William and Esther (Thompson) Reed.
b. Nov. 6, 1691; d. 1766.
m. 1st. Sarah Hersey, b. Sept. 26, 1692, daughter of

William and Sarah May (Langlee) Hersey. Her father was a soldier in Capt. Johnson's company Dec. 1675, was a representative in the Gen. Court 1698 and 1699, after 1704 he removed with his family to Abington. [See His. of Hingham.]

m. 2nd. Dec. 21, 1733, Hannah Noyes (widow).

He settled in Abington, the part now called South Abington, in 1708. He appears to have been a man of influence, from the fact that he was elected to the office of town clerk of Abington for nineteen years. He was one of the selectmen for eight years. His place is where John W. Jenkins afterward lived, formerly Lieut. Ephraim Whitmarsh's place.

Aaron Hobart, in his sketch of Abington, a book compiled by him in 1839, says:

"In 1665, Two Hundred acres of land were granted to the four younger Sons of Lieut James Torrey (of Scituate) lying about Weymouth near unto the line of the Massachusetts, to be at the disposal of Capt. William Torrey, for the good of said children, bounded &c.,

"In 1714 William Reed, Samuel Porter, Nicholas Porter, John Reed and Jacob Reed, of Abington, and Thomas Beal, of Hingham owned this land, and divided the same into lots, each owner agreeing to maintain his share of fence around the Meadow."

Children of Jacob and Sarah Hersey

66. Sarah, b. May 2, 1718; m. in 1748, Rev. Solomon Reed.
67. Jacob, b. July 7, 1720; d. Oct. 11, 1806; m. 1st. Nov. 26, 1741, Mary Ford; m. 2d. Dec. 1, 1748, Alice Reed, daughter of William.
68. Hannah, b. Feb. 26, 1722; m. Dec. 26, 1754, Joshua Howe.
69. William, b. Sept. 20, 1725; d. Dec. 4, 1807; m. in 1750, Silence Nash.
70. Elijah, b. Feb. 14, 1727; m. July 10, 1755, Sarah Reed, daughter of Obadiah.
71. Betty, b. March 1, 1731; d. young.

Child of Jacob and Hannah Noyes

72. Betty, b. 1734.

W 20

Thomas Reed, son of Thomas and Sarah (Bicknell) Reed.
b. Sept. 12, 1671; d. Oct. 2, 1719.
m. Jan. 14, 1701, Hannah Randall, a daughter of John Randall, who died Sept. 4, 1730. She died April 16, 1767.

They were married by Ephraim Hunt, a justice of the peace.

At a general town meeting of Weymouth the 4th day of March, 1705-6, Thomas Reed was chosen constable, and on Feb. 4, 1707-8, he was chosen Haywards or field driver.

Of Abington.

CHILDREN

73. Thomas, b. Oct. 18, 1701; d. Feb. 27, 1768: unmarried.
74. Daniel, b. Sept. 10, 1704; m. Feb. 22, 1728, Ruth Torrey.
75. Hannah, b. March 14, 1706; m. Jan. 8, 1730, James Pettee.
76. John, b. ———.
77. William, b. ———.
78. Sarah, b. Aug. 1, 1715; m. May 3, 1739, Abiah Whitman (3d) his second wife.

W 23

John Reed, son of Thomas and Sarah (Bicknell) Reed.
b. Dec. 30, 1679; d. Dec., 1757.
m. pub. Nov. 11, 1715, Sarah Whitmarsh.

"At a general town meeting held in Weymouth the 13th day of March, 1726-7, chosen for sealer of leather John Reed."

He was again chosen sealer of leather on March 4, 1727-8, and again on March 5, 1732-3.

Of Weymouth.

WILL

"In the name of God Amen, I John Reed of Weymouth, County of Suffolk, after the payment of my funeral expenses, which I order my executor to pay out of what I have given him, I do will and bequeath to my beloved wife

Sarah, the improvement of one half of the Housing and Barn, and of that part of my real estate which I do not give unto my son John, the one moiety of my outdoor movables and the improvement of all my indoor movables, together with such grain & wood yearly as she shall want for her own consumption, during her widowhood, except my gun and sword.

"Item. I do give unto my son John, to him and his heirs and assigns forever, all my housings and lands, my barn, my Homestead land, Upland and Meadow ground, fresh, English, and salt meadow and flats lying and being in Weymouth, the one Moiety at my decease, the other moiety at the marriage or decease of my wife; except that part of my fresh meadow I bought of Thomas Blanchard, and except my house and Barn and land I bought lately of John Burrell; I do give unto my son John all my outdoor movables the one moiety at my decease, the other moiety at the expiration of his mothers widowhood. I do give unto my son John my gun, my sword, and military accoutrements, my wearing apparall, my Monies, Bonds, Notes of hand, Book debts, except as herein excepted. I do give unto my daughter Sarah, to her and her heirs and assigns forever, about seven or eight acres of land more or less being in Abington, and being part of that estate which descended to me from my brother Samuel deceased. I do also give her a bond of one hundred pounds, be it more or less which I have against her husband provided, and is my will that if my son-in-law Adam Cushing at any time or times after my decease, by himself, or by any, by or under him shall make any demands upon my estate, for any sum or sums of money, as due to him from me on ye account of any Bills, Bonds, Notes of hand, Book debts, or by any pretence whatsoever, then I do give my daughter Sarah but 5 shillings, and what I have given her as above, I give to my son John. I do give my daughter Ruth, to her and her heirs and assigns forever, my home and land I lately bought of John Burrell, it being late the Estate of Elisha Lincoln, together with my

fresh meadow I bought of John Blanchard, called Puddle Meadow; and also I do give unto my daughter Sarah five pounds, six shillings, and eight pence, and to my daughter Ruth five pounds, six shillings, and eight pence to be paid within one year after my decease. I give unto my son John and to my daughter Ruth all my indoor movables not yet disposed of at the expiration of my wife or her widowhood. I order my son John to pay my legacies, whom I hereby appoint sole executor of this my last will and Testament, and all the residue of my estate not yet disposed of I do give unto him, May 31st, 1757.

John Reed (Seal)

Ezra Whitmarsh
William Beal } Witnesses.
Abner Pratt

Proved Dec. 23rd, 1757."

CHILDREN

79. Sarah, b. July 7, 1721; d. Oct. 25, 1751; m. June 9. 1743, Adam Cushing.
80. Ruth, b. Oct. 28, 1724; m. Feb. 18, 1747, Elisha Turner.
81. John, b. June 22, 1728; m. Dec. 26, 1745, Mary Bates.

W 24

Samuel Reed, son of Thomas and Sarah (Bicknell) Reed.
b. Apr. 12, 1681; d. June 25, 1739.
m. Jan. 7, 1704, Abigail White.

His wife was born in Weymouth March 3, 1683, and died in Mendon; they lived in West Abington just over the Weymouth line, on the site owned formerly by Isaac Jackson, now by his son. His (Samuel Reed's) farm consisted of about 600 acres. It will be seen by his schedule annexed that he left a considerable estate, leaving no direct heirs. His brother John was executor and inherited the principal part of his estate. He was selectman for two years in Abington.

see issue Mendon. V. R. p. 148

"A TRUE INVENTORY OF THE ESTATE BOTH REAL AND PERSONAL, WHICH SAMUEL REED, LATE OF ABINGTON, IN THE COUNTY OF PLYMOUTH, GENTLEMAN, DECEASED, DIED SEIZED OF AND APPRAISED AT ABINGTON, AFORESAID ON THE THIRTEENTH DAY OF OCTOBER, ANNO DOMINI 1739, BY US THE SUBSCRIBERS AS FOLLOWETH:

Imprimis.	His purse and Apparel	26– 4–3
Item.	To Arms and Ammunition	
Item.	" Books	
	" a Bed and Furniture	16– 0–0
	" a Comlet & Knife	0– 3–0
	" a Frying Pan	0– 8–0
	" a Basin & a Spoon	0– 6–0
	" a Mug & Pepper Box	0– 2–0
	" a Tramel	0–14–0
	" a Skillet & an Iron Pot	0–17–0
	" 7 Chains	1–10–0
	" a Cive	0– 2–6
	" 2 Earthen Jugs	0– 2–0
	" 2 Earthen Pots & a Pudding Pan	0– 1–6
	" a Milk Pan & a Tray	0– 3–0
	" 2 Pails & a Corn Basket	0– 4–6
	" Grindstone & Carpenter Tools	2– 5–0
	" Chains Yokes & Irons belonging	6– 2–0
	" a Cask Cops Pin & a Bolt	0– 5–0
	" Hames & Traces	1– 5–6
	" Cow Bell an Iron Dog & Shovel	1– 3–6
	" a Cart Rope Rye & Wheat	1– 8–0
	" a Razor	0– 8–0
	" Sheeps Wool	7–10–0
	" a Cain & Nails	1– 3–0
	" Glass Bottles	0– 2–0
	" a Cart 2 Pr. Wheels & old Iron	7– 0–0
	" Meat & Meat Tub	3–12–0
	" Barrels	0– 8–0
	" a Meal Bag a Runlet & a Jar	0– 6–0
	" two three year old Heifers	14– 0–0

	"	the largest pair of Oxen	26– 0–0
	"	another pair of Oxen	24– 0–0
	"	a three year old Steer	5–10–0
			£155–11–9
Item.	"	Boards & Planks	23– 1–0
Item.	"	a pair of Two year old Steers	8– 0–0
Item.	"	a year old Steer	3–10–0
Item.	"	4 Swine	12– 0–0
	"	6 Pigs	3–18–0
	"	32 Sheep & Lambs	17– 0–0
	"	a Mare Bridle & Saddle	20– 0–0
	"	3 Calves	3–15–0
Item.	"	about 75 acres of land purchased of	390– 0–0
Item.	"	about 20 acres of land purchased of Nicholas Whitmarsh	110– 0–0
Item.	"	about 150 acres of land purchased of Moses Cushing	964– 0–0
Item.	"	about 50 acres of land purchased of Thomas Wildes	250– 0–0
Item.	"	about 30 acres of land purchased of Stephen French	150– 0–0
Item.	"	about 13 acres of land purchased of David French	100– 0–0
Item.	"	Cedar Swamp lying in old Swamp	3– 0–0
Item.	"	about 5 acres of Fresh Marsh land purchased of Hezekiah Ford	40– 0–0
Item.	"	one eighth part of a saw mill with appurtenances belonging to it	2–10–0
Item.	"	about ten acres of land lying in Weymouth purchased of Joseph Lewis	280– 0–0
Item.	"	about 1 acre of salt Marsh, and about 1/2 acre of flats lying in S° Weymouth	40– 0–0
Item.	"	the homestead being about 116 acres of land with the dwellings & other appurtenances thereunto belonging	561– 0–0

Item. " land lying in S° Weymouth near Nashes .
Cedar Swamp 3- 0-0
Item. " the 1/16 part of the Iron work of an
old saw mill 1- 0-0

Sum total..................£3141- 5-9

William Reed.
Jacob Thompson.
Caleb Torrey."

"Plymouth, Nov. 13th, 1739, I John Reed, Administrator of the estate of Samuel Reed of Abington, deceased, made oath that the afore written Inventory contains all the deceased estate so far as he knows of, and when he shall know of more he will give it in before me.

John Cushing, Judge of Probate.

" * * (this line, in the original, could not be disciphered) that they should make the estate of Samuel Reed, Deceased, should be just & true according to the best of their judgment and understanding before me.

Samuel Pool, Justice of the Peace."

"A True Copy Examined by John Winslow, Register."

W **26**

William Reed, son of Thomas and Sarah (Bicknell) Reed.

b. Feb. 4, 1688, at Weymouth; d. Sept. 22, 1729.

m. Dec. 13, 1716, Jane Torrey of Weymouth; d. Jan. 24, 1730.

They were both of Weymouth and were married by Rev. Peter Thatcher. He was known as Sargt. William Reed.

Of Weymouth.

CHILDREN

82. William, b. Sept. 15, 1717; d. Oct. 18, 1717.
83. Deborah, b. March 24, 1719; d. before 1750; m. April 16, 1741, John Torrey, son of Haviland; no children.
84. Jane, b. Sept. 9, 1726; m. April 21, 1748, David Stockbridge.

T 29

John Reed, son of John and Bethia (Frye) Reed.

b. June 5, 1674; d. 1739.

m. June 15, 1697, Bethiah Cobb, daughter of Augustus Cobb of Taunton, Mass. and Barrington, R. I.

He removed to Swansey, and bought a tract of land known as Pompomunset, or Phebe's Neck. The tract of land bought by him is supposed to be located in what is now Barrington.

Of Swansey.

CHILDREN

85. John, b. Aug., 1701.
86. George, b. May, 1704; m. Jan. 1, 1730, Abigail Woodward.
87. William, b. Feb. 28, 1713; m. ———, Elizabeth ———.
88. Bethiah, b. Feb. 28, 1713; m. 1732, Matthew Watson.
89. Mary, b. ———; m. ———, Tiffany.
90. Marcy, b. ———.

T 30

William Reed, son of John and Bethia (Frye) Reed.

b. ———; d. 1734.

m. June 8, 1721, Mary Richmond; she d. March 4, 1770, aged about 85 years.

He lived at Taunton, Mass., the homestead was owned and occupied by one of his descendants as late as 1861.

His widow after his death married Stephen Andrews, Nov. 6, 1738, who was a man of learning and piety, and was known by his neighbors as St. Stephen. He lived to the age of one hundred years.

CHILDREN

91. John, b. 1722; d. Dec., 1788; m. 1st. Dec. 30, 1746, Dorothy Pinneo; m. 2d. Jan. 9, 1771, Mrs. Hannah Austin.
92. William, b. ———; d. 1780; m. March 27, 1755, Mary Perce.
93. Mary, b. ———.
94. Abigail, b. ———; m. July 29, 1750, John Haskell, of Rochester, Mass.

T 31

Thomas Reed, son of John and Bethia (Frye) Reed.

b. about 1677-8; d. Feb. 19, 1741.

m. ———, Sarah Tisdale, daughter of Joseph Tisdale of Taunton.

CHILDREN

95. Seth, b. Feb. 6, 1717; d. young.
96. Thomas, b. Aug. 20, 1718; m. in 1746, Rebecca Talbot.
97. Joseph, b. Nov., 1725; m. Oct. 31, 1747, Elizabeth Elliot.
98. Seth, b. Nov. 6, 1726; m. ———, Peddy Pool.
99. Sarah, b. Nov. 26, 1727; m. in 1746, Geo. Gooding.
100. Phebe, b. Aug. 20, 1729.
101. Elkanah, b. Oct. 8, 1730; d. March 4, 1777.
102. Job, b. March 13, 1731; m. Feb. 17, 1750, Jemima Talbot.
103. Simeon, b. April 17, 1733; d. July 10, 1804; m. ———, Deborah Codding.
104. Ruth, b. ———; m. Jan. 6, 1743, Joseph Talbot.
105. Mercy, b. ———; m. Dec., 1780, Elijah Bacon, of Providence.

(T) 32

George Reed (of Dighton), son of John and Bethia (Frye) Reed.

b. ———; d. in 1765 (or as J. W. Reed's book has it, "He died in Rehoboth Feb. 8, 1756").

m. 1st. Sarah Whitmarsh, daughter of Samuel Whitmarsh.

m. 2nd. Jan. 1, 1730, Abigail Woodward.

Of Dighton and Rehoboth.

CHILDREN OF GEORGE AND SARAH WHITMARSH

106. George, b. Aug. 21, 1718; d. May, 1727.
107. Avis, b. Sept. 5, 1720; d. July 7, 1755; m. Jan. 27, 1736, John Palmer.
108. Hannah, b. May 21, 1722; m. 1743, Reuben Clemens.
109. John, b. March 30, 1724; m. 1st. May 11, 1749, Miriam Talbot; m. 2d. March 27, 1752, Mary Perry.
110. Samuel, b. Nov. 29, 1725; m. in 1748, Rachel Williams.
111. Ruth, b. Nov. 3, 1727; m. 1st. Joshua Williams; m. 2d. Jan. Macomber; m. 3d. Ebenezer Myrick.
112. Rebecca, b. July 16, 1729; m. 1st. in 1752, John Coleman; m. 2d. Sylvester French.

CHILDREN OF GEORGE AND ABIGAIL WOODWARD

113. Isaiah, b. Oct. 14, 1730 (in Rehoboth).
114. George, b. Dec. 29, 1731; d. in 1758; m. Dec. 25, 1756, Mercy Phillips.
115. Sarah, b. Dec. 6, 1734 (in Dighton); d. young.
116. Sarah, b. Jan. 22, 1739; m. John Gilmore.
117. Loved, b. Feb. 26, 1741; m. 1st. Sept. 22, 1763, Charity Phillips; m. 2d. Oct. 15, 1786, Mary French.
118. Mary, b. Feb. 3, 1744; d. May 18, 1745.
119. Jonathan, b. Oct. 13, 1745; m. Miss Sheppard.
120. Bethiah, b. ———; m. 1754, John Jacob.

(M) 37

William Reed, son of James and Susanna (Richmond) Reed.
b. May 1, 1685.
m. ———, Elizabeth ———. Resided at Middleborough.
Of Middleborough.

CHILDREN

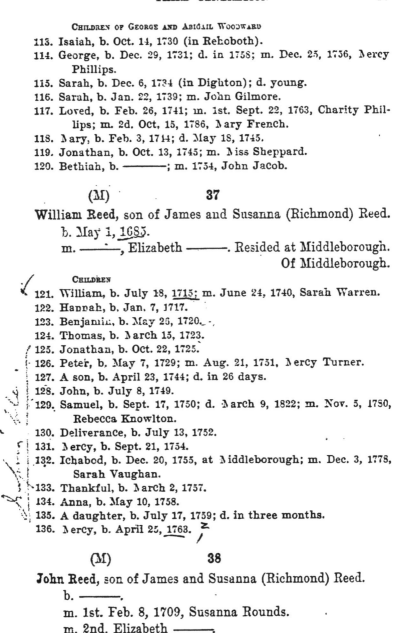

121. William, b. July 18, 1715; m. June 24, 1740, Sarah Warren.
122. Hannah, b. Jan. 7, 1717.
123. Benjamin, b. May 25, 1720.
124. Thomas, b. March 15, 1723.
125. Jonathan, b. Oct. 22, 1725.
126. Peter, b. May 7, 1729; m. Aug. 21, 1751, Mercy Turner.
127. A son, b. April 23, 1744; d. in 26 days.
128. John, b. July 8, 1749.
129. Samuel, b. Sept. 17, 1750; d. March 9, 1822; m. Nov. 5, 1780, Rebecca Knowlton.
130. Deliverance, b. July 13, 1752.
131. Mercy, b. Sept. 21, 1754.
132. Ichabod, b. Dec. 20, 1755, at Middleborough; m. Dec. 3, 1778, Sarah Vaughan.
133. Thankful, b. March 2, 1757.
134. Anna, b. May 10, 1758.
135. A daughter, b. July 17, 1759; d. in three months.
136. Mercy, b. April 25, 1763.

(M) 38

John Reed, son of James and Susanna (Richmond) Reed.
b. ———.
m. 1st. Feb. 8, 1709, Susanna Rounds.
m. 2nd. Elizabeth ———.
Of Middleborough.

CHILDREN OF JOHN AND SUSANNA

137. Elizabeth, b. Nov. 22, 1711.
138. Oliver, b. June 18, 1715.

CHILD OF JOHN AND ELIZABETH

139. Mary, b. May 13, 1726.

M 39

Thomas Reed, son of James and Susanna (Richmond) Reed.
b. in 1684 to 1689.
m. 1st. Mar. 1, 1707, Mary Fifield in Boston.
m. 2nd. Sept. 14, 1709, Sarah Niles.

CHILD OF THOMAS AND MARY

140. James, b. Sept. 16, 1707.

CHILDREN OF THOMAS AND SARAH

141. Sarah, b. May 12, 1711.
142. Mary, b. May 2, 1714.
143. Lydia, b. June 28, 1720, in Braintree; m. Dec. 6, 1739, George Smith, of Taunton, Mass., who was b. about 1715; d. about 1790.

M 44

Benjamin Reed, son of James and Susanna (Richmond) Reed.
b. 1699.
m. Dec. 1, 1720, Hannah Chase.
Lived at Middleborough.

CHILDREN

144. Benjamin, b. May 21, 1721; d. Feb. 12, ——; m. Elizabeth.
145. Hannah, b. Jan. 29, 1727.
146. Samuel, b. April 7, 1729.
147. Stephen, b. Nov. 7, 1732.

FOURTH GENERATION

A 47

Obadiah Reed, son of William and Alice (Nash) Reed.
b. Mar. 14, 1707; d. Nov. 4, 1753.
m. Oct. 19, 1731, Mary Nash, daughter of Ensign James

Nash; granddaughter of James Nash, of Weymouth (see History of Abington).

He is mentioned in Hobart's History of Abington, as Capt. Obadiah Reed, p. 415. He was selectman for eight years.

At a church meeting held in Abington in 1749, Capt. Obadiah Reed was "chose" clerk.

The first meeting house in Abington was a small Quaker-like building, unpainted, without steeple, tower, bell, pews or stoves. At the date of the organization of the society, they had eight male members. They were Samuel Brown, William Hersey, Andrew Ford, William Tirrell, Ebenezer Whitmarsh, Joseph Josselyn, William Reed (probably 12), and Joseph Lincoln. Benches were used in the meeting house to take the place of pews.

Jan. 14, 1751, the town voted to build a new meeting house with a steeple 70 ft. long, 50 ft. wide and 26-ft. posts, and appointed Lieut. Ephraim Spooner, Christopher Dyer, Jacob Porter, Capt. Obadiah Reed, Joseph Richards and Dea. Joshua Shaw, as building committee.

ORDER OF COURT DIVIDING THE ESTATE OF CAPT. OBADIAH REED

"Pursuant to a warrant from the Hon. John Cushing, Esqr. Judge of the Probate of Wills &c for the County of Plymouth in the Province of the Massachusetts Bay in New England, directed to us the subscribers for the appraisement & division of the estate of Capt. Obadiah Reed late of Abington deceased, which we have done in manner following, Viz:—

"First:—To Obadiah Reed the eldest son of sd. deceased the first share which is the dwelling house and land on the south easterly side of the road the barn and two acres and a half of land on the west side of the road beginning at the corner of Jacob Porter's land running south eighteen & an half, east twenty-one rod and four feet to a stake & stones from thence west eleven degrees, south thirty six rod

and an half to sd. Porter's land, thence near northeast by sd. Porter's land to the bounds first mentioned.

"The second share beginning at the corner by sd. first share, then running near south, by the way, thirty rod to a stake and stones standing by the road, then running west eighteen degrees south till it comes to the fourth share, then running north to a stake and stones standing in the four mile line, running east one degree, north till it comes to Jacob Porter's land, then running by Jacob Porter's land to the bounds of the first share, from thence eleven degrees north to the bounds first mentioned, about seventeen and an half to Obadiah Reed being his two seventh parts of the sd. estate.

"Thirdly:—The third share being one seventh part, we assign to Matthew Reed beginning at the north west corner of the third lot in the fourth share, running east one degree, north on the line of the sd. third lot one hundred and four rod to a stake and stones, then south thirty rod to a stake and stones, then running west one degree, south one hundred & four rod till it comes to Jacob Porter's land, then north by said Porter's land to the bounds first mentioned, about nineteen acres and a half, also a tenth part of the second lot in the fourth share, also six rods in width of a cedar swamp (called by the name of Streams Swamp) which is bounded easterly on the Young Men's shares, southerly on Lieutenant James Nash's land, westerly as far as the cedars grow, and northerly on Daniel Reed's, Benjamin Nash's & others land.

"Fourthly:—The fourth share being one seventh part, we assign to Silas Reed lying partly in the fourth share, beginning at the northeast corner of the third share, then running east one degree, north forty six rod, to the line of the fourth share, thence south one degree, west on said line about thirty four rod to Jacob Reed's land, thence west eighteen degrees, south twenty four rods to a stake and stones, thence north twelve degrees, west twelve rods, then west one degree, south thirty nine rods to a stake and stones

of the southeast corner of the third share, thence north by the said third share to the bounds first mentioned, about fourteen acres, also another piece in Bridgewater lying on the Old Mens shares, containing about twenty five acres, beginning at Beaver Brook by the Reed's land & running West about three hundred and twelve rod, then running north about thirteen rod, then east to the brook first mentioned, then south by the said Brook, thirteen rods to the sd. Reed's land, and also seven rod in width on the northerly side of a cedar swamp called Streams Swamp:

"Fifthly:—The fifth share being one seventh part we assign to Mary (the wife of Joseph Hearsey) containing about twenty two acres, beginning at the road on the northeast corner of Jacob Reed's land, thence running west eighteen degrees, south one hundred and forty rod to the line set off to Silas Reed in the fourth share, near north twenty five rod to a stake and stones thence east eighteen degrees, north one hundred & thirty seven rod to a stake & stones standing by the road, thence south fifteen degrees east to the bounds first mentioned—Also one quarter part of a piece of meadow land lying in Abington in the old Mill Pond on the easterly side of the river bounded northerly on Torrey's lot easterly on the young Men's Shares & south to Jacob Reed's & west on the river & a piece of Cedar swamp at Beaver Brook, six rods wide & twenty six rod long likewise one half of the pew in the Meeting House.

"Sixthly:—The sixth share being one seventh share, to Sarah, the wife of Elijah Reed, beginning at the road at the northeast corner of the sixth share, running west eighteen degrees, south one hundred & thirty seven rod to the northwest corner of the sixth share, then running north twenty six rod and an half to a stake and stones, thence east eighteen degrees, north one hundred and thirty one rod to a stake and stones standing by the way, then to the bounds first mentioned, containing abt. twenty two acres. Also a piece of cedar swamp at Beaver Brook about five rod wide, and twenty six rod long, also the eighth part of Beaver

Brook Mill, during the whole term of time it is to stand by a former agreement and one half of the pew in the Meeting House.

"Seventhly:—The seventh share being one seventh part, we assign to Silence, containing near fourteen acres, beginning at a stake and stones by the road at the northwest corner of the sixth, thence running west eighteen degrees, south one hundred and twenty eight rod, thence running north eighteen rod, to the south west corner of the second share, then east eighteen degrees, north by said share to the way by a stake and stones, then by the way to the bounds first mentioned. Also five rod on the southerly side of a cedar swamp in Streams Swamp, and a quarter part of Tirrell's Mill.

Dated at Abington, Oct. 27th, 1755.

Christopher Dyer,
Josiah Torrey,
Jacob Porter,
Samuel Pool, Junr.
William Tirrell, Junr."

CHILDREN

148. William, b. Feb. 24, 1732.
149. Mary, b. March 27, 1734; m. Feb. 1, 1755, Joseph Hersey, Jr.
150. Sarah, b. March 29, 1736; m. July 10, 1755, Elijah Reed.
151. Obadiah, b. May 15, 1738; m. 1st. Content Lincoln; m. 2d. in 1770, Elizabeth Shaw.
152. Silence, b. June 7, 1741.
153. Matthew, b. Feb. 21, 1750.
154. Silas, b. Oct. 27, 1751; m. in 1772, Experience (Reed) Josselyn, of Middleborough.

A 48

Ebenezer Reed, son of William and Alice (Nash) Reed.

b. July 13, 1709.

m. Feb. 21, 1732, Hannah Thompson, of Middleborough.

They lived in Abington.

WILL

"In the name of God, Amen.—I Ebenezer Reed of Abington in the County of Plymouth and Commonwealth of Massachusetts Bay, gentleman being of sound and disposing mind (praised be God) do make this my last will and testament, as follows, Viz:—

"I give to my three children, David & Barnabas Reed & Abigail Dyer, all my right in a saw mill known by the name of Tirrell's Mill in equal shares,

"Item. I give to my two sons David & Barnabas all my wearing apparel in equal halves.

"I give to three children of my son Jonathan Reed deceased, six shillings each.

"I give to my son David Reed a state of three pounds seven shillings, likewise two thirds of all my notes of hand.

"The other third of my notes, together with all my household furniture at Mr. Jacob Dyer's, I give to my daughter Abigail Dyer, my will is that my debts and funeral charges shall be paid out of my notes of hand.

"I constitute Capt. Luke Bicknell of the town and County aforesaid sole executor of this my last will and testament. In Witness whereof I have hereunto set my hand and seal this fourteenth day of April in the year of our Lord, One thousand seven hundred and ninety.

"N. B.—The interlineation above was made prior to the signing and sealing of this will and testament.

"Sealed, published & declared by the above named Ebenezer Reed for and as his last will & testament in the presence of

Joseph Pool. Ebenezer Reed (Seal)."
John Norton.
Seth Porter.

CHILDREN

155. Ebenezer, b. Dec. 11, 1733; d. June 4, 1740.
156. William, b. Oct. 28, 1735; m. Dec. 27, 1759, Ruth Shaw.
157. Ichabod, b. April 26, 1738; d. in service during the French and English War. (See His. of Abington, p. 207.)

158. David, b. July 9, 1740; d. May 10, 1808; m. 1st. April 22, 1762, Mercy Ford; m. 2d. Jan. 9, 1788, Hannah (Reed) Bates.
159. Jonathan, b. July 9, 1740; d. 1769; m. April 28, 1763, Mary Tirrel.
160. Paul, b. March 3, 1743; d. June 4, 1743.
161. Silas, b. March 3, 1743; d. Aug. 3, 1797; m. 1st. Rebecca; m. 2d. Mary.
162. Abigail, b. April 10, 1745; m. Feb. 2, 1766, Jacob Dyer.
163. Barnabas, b. April 5, 1748; m. Silence Sprague.
164. Ebenezer, b. Dec. 18, 1751.

A 50

Daniel Reed, son of William and Alice (Nash) Reed.
b. Dec. 6, 1713; d. Apr. 5, 1781.
m. 1st. Sept. 15, 1739, Ruth White, she d. in 1775.
m. 2nd. Feb. 7, 1776, Sarah Hamlyn.

He was one of the first settlers of Cummington. He was a captain.

According to tradition, Mr. Reed, while on a visit to Abington, at the time of the death of his first wife, had a presentiment that she was dead, an apparition appearing at his bedside in the night. He told his friends that his wife was dead, and as soon as it could be ascertained, his apprehension proved true.

While riding through a wood a tree fell upon and killed her. His daughter-in-law, Thankful Whitmarsh, was killed in the same accident.

WILL

"In the name of God Amen:—I, Daniel Reed of a place called number five in the County of Hampshire and province of the Massachusetts Bay in New England, Gentleman. Now in the enjoyment of a good degree of bodily health and possest of a sound mind and perfect memory blessed be God for the same, do make and publish this my last will and testament, in manner and form following (that is to say) I order all my just debts to be paid by my executor hereafter named.

"First:—I also give and bequeath to my beloved wife, Sarah Reed one room, Viz. that which lies on the southwest corner of my dwelling house or in other words the Southwest room below in the front of said house, a privilege of performing that business that is proper to be done in the kitchen, also a privilege of using a buttery in said kitchen to be improved by her in person not allowing her to improve it by tenanting or leasing of it to any other person whatever, so long as she shall continue my widow, and no longer shall she have the improvement or use of the above mentioned room privilege in the kitchen and buttery. Further I order my executor hereafter named to pay out to my beloved wife Sarah Reed and do by her agreeable to a certain written contract which I made with her before marriage, in every respect it is my will that it be fulfilled by him in every respect that he fail not under any pretense whatever without her consent thereto.

"I also give and bequeath to my third son Enoch Reed who is now absent from me upon his return if ever it should be, two Hundred pounds lawful money.

"I also give and bequeath to my youngest daughter Ruth Gannett, the sum of seventy three pounds, six shillings, and eight pence lawful money.

"I also give and bequeath to my eldest daughter Rachel Porter Sixty pounds lawful money.

"I also give and bequeath to my youngest son, Noah Reed, my home farm, consisting of one hundred acres of land, the house and barn upon said land, together with my saw mill, excepting one half of said saw mill which I give and bequeath to my fourth son Seth Reed, I also except from the enjoyment of my youngest son so much of the house as I have given to my wife in this my will above during the time she continues my widow, after which he is to be in full possession of my said house.

"I also give and bequeath to my fourth son Seth Reed, and to my youngest son Noah Reed, my waggon and the furniture belonging to the same, Viz., chains, irons, plows,

and their furniture, and I order that these be equally divided between these my two sons.

"Further I will and order that my wearing apparel the whole of it be equally divided amongst my several sons, my sons in law, excepted or excluded from the same.

"Further I will and order that the remains from my real and personal estate be divided amongst my sons and daughters, an equal share to each son, excepting my youngest son Noah Reed, I exclude from a share in this having above given him what I suppose is proper and sufficient. My daughters I order to draw but half shares or but half so much as my sons, or in other words I will to them so much each as I do to each individual son of the said remainder of my real and personal estate.

"And I do appoint my youngest son Noah Reed, sole executor to this my last will and testament, hereby revoking all former wills testaments by me made.

"In witness whereof I have hereunto set my hand and seal this ninth day of December, in the year of our Lord Christ, one thousand seven hundred and seventy six.

Daniel Reed Seal."

"Signed, sealed and published and delivered by the above named Daniel Reed to be his last will and testament in presence of us who have hereunto subscribed our names.

Micah White.
Asa Joy.
Aaron Reed."

Hampshire County, ss.
Registry of Probate.

Northampton, Mass., May 12, A. D. 1899.

A true copy of record.

Attest: Hubbard M. Abbott, Register.

CHILDREN OF DANIEL AND RUTH

165. Rachel, b. Dec. 20, 1740; m. June 6, 1763, Jacob Porter, Jr.
166. Micah, b. Feb. 1, 1742; m. Oct. 20, 1767, Deborah Thompson.
167. Jesse, b. March 16, 1745; m. Nov. 18, 1781, Mrs. Ruth Whitman.

168. Enoch, b. Dec. 23, 1747; d. at sea, on board of a British man-of-war. He was a lieutenant in the British Navy.
169. Seth, b. July 16, 1750; m. 1st. in 1773, Thankful Whitmarsh; m. 2d in 1776, Mary Lazell.
170. Ruth, b. Dec. 4, 1752; m. Aug. 12, 1774, Jacob Gannet.
171. Noah, b. Dec. 10, 1754; d. Jan. 19, 1832; m. July 12, 1784, Abigail Rice.

A **51**

James Reed, son of William and Alice (Nash) Reed.

b. March 3, 1716; d. ———.

m. May 10, 1739, Abigail Nash, she d. in 1808 in the 91st year of her age, she was a daughter of Ensign James Nash of Weymouth (see History of Abington).

Of Abington.

WILL

"In the name of God Amen:—I, James Reed of Abington, in the County of Plymouth, & the Province of the Massachusetts Bay, in New England, husbandman, being years & competent health of body & sound in my understanding & memory (blessed be God therefor) considering the uncertainty of my life here on earth, do make & ordain this my last will & testament, (Viz.) principally & first of all I commit my soul into the hands of God my Creator, hoping and trusting in Jesus Christ my Redeemer for pardon & eternal life, my body I commit to the earth to receive such a decent & Christianlike funeral as my executor, hereafter named shall think fit. And my worldly goods & estate (my just debts & funeral charges being first pd.) I give & bequeath in the following manner.

"Imprimis:—I give & bequeath unto my beloved wife Abigail, the improvement of all my estate, both real and personal, till and as the children come of age, and also one half of my dwelling house so long as she continues my widow, but in case my wife should marry again after my decease, then my will is that the children shall come into possession of it or have the profit and advantage of it.

"Item:—I give unto my sons, Solomon, Adam, Stephen, & Abel, my buildings and all my homestead and part of lands adjoining, Viz. all that part of it that lays easterly of a stream, which is westerly of what is called Huckleberry Plain, and also forty rods in length of the said tract of land at the westerly end of the said lot, also all my right and interest that I own in the meadow called the Mill Pond Meadow to be divided equally among them excepting my wife (who is with child) be delivered of another son then for it to be entitled to the above specified buildings and lands equally with the rest of the sons but if a daughter to share equally with the rest of the daughters hereafter mentioned.

"Item. I give to my daughters Tabitha, Experience, Huldah and Molly, the remaining part of the lot of land I have not disposed of which is adjoining to the homestead, also one-half of a lot of land called Mitchell's lot, likewise I give unto my daughters, my land at the head of the Mill Pond, called the New Mill or Beaver Brook Stream, which I bought of Colonel Lincoln to be divided equally among them.

"And I do hereby appoint and ordain my brother Daniel and my beloved wife Abigail to be my executors of this my last will and testament, and I do hereby make void and of none effect all and every other will or wills whether by word or writing, ratifying and confirming this and no other to be my last Will and Testament, In witness whereof I have hereunto set my hand and seal this fifth day of May, A. D. 1758.

James Reed (Seal)."

"Signed, sealed and delivered by the testator to be his last will and testament.

John Noyes.
Jacob Noyes.
Samuel Noyes, Jr."

Will proved September 5th, 1762.

CHILDREN

172. Tabitha, b. March 3, 1740; m. Oct. 5, 1779, Elisha Lincoln.
173. Experience, b. Oct. 28, 1741; m. 1st. Oct., 1767, Josiah Josselyn; m. 2d. 1772, Silas Reed.
174. Solomon, b. Oct. 25, 1743; m. Sept. 28, 1765, Mercy Tirrell.
175. Adam, b. Aug. 19, 1745; m. July 14, 1768, Silence Reed.
176. Stephen, b. July 5, 1748.
177. Huldah, b. April 25, 1751; d. unmarried. (See her father's will.)
178. Abel, b. April 15, 1754; d. in service in Revolutionary Army. (See His. of Abington, p. 269.)
179. Molly, b. March 3, 1756.
180. James, b. June 24, 1758; m. May 19, 1779, Susannah Niles.

A 52

Rev. Solomon Reed, son of William and Alice (Nash) Reed.
b. Oct. 22, 1719; d. in spring of 1785, aged 66 years.
m. 1st. in 1748, Abigail Stoughton of Conn.
m. 2nd. Sarah Reed, the daughter of Jacob, his father's youngest brother.

Of Titicut Parish, Middleborough, Mass.

In his will executed in 1785, it will be noticed he mentions all the children except Sarah. She must have died earlier than that.

WILL

"In the name of God, Amen—the twenty sixth day of April A. Domini 1785 I Solomon Reed of Middleborough, in the County of Plymouth, clerk, being of sound and disposing mind and memory, & calling to mind that it is appointed for all men once to die, do proceed to make & ordain this my last will & testament. In the first place I recommend my soul into the hands of God who gave it, hoping through the merits, mediation & intercession of Jesus Christ to obtain a full and free pardon of all my sins & inherit eternal life and my body I commit to the earth, to be decently buried at the discretion of my executor hereafter named, believing that at the resurrection I shall receive the same again by the

power of God Almighty, and as touching my worldly interest, I give and dispose of it in the following manner Viz:—

"In the first place my will is that all my real estate should be sold as soon as there may be a convenient time after my decease, and that all my debts should be paid out of the same, & after the sum of all my debts are deducted, I give and bequeath a fifth part of what remains to my well beloved wife Sarah Reed, to be paid her in two years after my decease—I also give her all the notes that are given in her name, with all the household furniture she brought with her & what is wasted is to be made good.

"Item: I give and bequeath to my four sons, Viz:—John, Solomon, Samuel and Timothy Reed, the whole of my estate, both real and personal besides what is before disposed of, excepting the household provisions, which are to be spent for the use of the family.

"Finally:—I constitute & appoint my son Timothy, to be my sole executor of this my last will & testament. In witness whereof I have hereunto set my hand and seal the day and year aforesaid.

Solomon Reed (Seal)."

"Signed, sealed, delivered, pronounced, & declared by the said Solomon Reed to be his last will & testament in the presence of us.

Isaac Perkins
Joseph Hathaway
Jona. Crane."

Will allowed June 6, 1785.

Rev. Solomon Reed graduated at Harvard College in 1739. There is no record informing us under whose instruction he pursued his studies for the ministry; though it was probably with the Rev. Mr. Brown, the minister of his native town. That he entered the profession from a conviction of duty, and with an earnest purpose to promote the religious well-being of his fellowmen, is very manifest from such of his manuscript writings as have come down to us, as well as from the direct tradition of those who knew him intimately.

During the first few years of Mr. Reed's ministry, and afterwards as we have reason to suppose, he was very earnest and devoted in his labors for the spiritual good of others, both by religious conversation and preaching, as well in neighborhoods on week-days as in the regular ministrations on Sunday.

Among the precious antiquarian treasures in the archives of the Pilgrim Society of Plymouth are a few manuscript sermons of Mr. Reed, written in a fine clear hand in an easy flow of style of composition and indicating decided ability. With those documents there is also an original manuscript journal kept by him from Oct. 3, 1743, to Jan. 9, 1745. This journal indicates often a great tenderness of religious feeling; and often too a sadly morbid sensitiveness of conscience, evidently arising from the mingled influence of his uncheerful religious views, and a diseased physical constitution, of which he often speaks.

It was during the period when Mr. Whitefield was preaching in New England that Mr. Reed was keeping his journal, and was so self-scrutinizing as to his spiritual state. The following passages from the journal, relating to Mr. Whitefield, cannot fail to be read with interest:

"Abington, Sunday, Dec. 23, 1744. Heard Mr. Brown in the afternoon. Monday I travelled to Duxbury, and heard Mr. Whitefield preach in the evening; and then I travelled with him, and heard him every day, all the week, Sunday Dec. 30, preached at Titicut and we had some token of the divine presence. I heard Mr. Whitefield again on Monday, Tuesday, and Wednesday, at Bridgewater, Easton and Taunton, N. B. Mr. Whitefield is exceedingly filled with the spirit of Jesus, and not afraid of Christ his cause or children; and a wonderful power attended his administrations. The assemblies seem much quickened, melted down; and sometimes many were overpowered with the sense of divine things and crying out. Sometimes when I have been with Mr. Whitefield, I have felt guilty, low and dull; sometimes I have been sweetly revived and refreshed."

In 1746 Mr. Reed was ordained as minister of the second Congregational Church in Framingham; he remained there until 1756, when he dissolved his connection with that church, and was installed as minister of Titicut, a parish embracing the northwestern border of Middleborough and the southwest part of Bridgewater.

His health, never firm, sensibly declined in 1784, and he died in the spring of 1785, at a little past the age of sixty-five.

Notwithstanding the limited support given to clergymen in those days, Mr. Reed gave to each of his four sons a collegiate education.

We have been permitted to copy the following interesting notice of his funeral. It is from a coarse half-sheet of manuscript, broken and yellow with age, but clearly written in a homely hand. It had been carefully kept, probably from near that time to the present, in an old bible of his cousin William, son of Jacob, which recently came into the hands of a grandson:

"Died at his house in Titicut Parish of a lingering illness; on the seventh inst. (month not named) the Rev. Solomon Reed, Pastor of a Church in Middleborough; and was interred on the 10th, age sixty-five. The interment was attended by a numerous concourse, in the procession to the meeting house, and a sermon suited to the occasion, from Isa. xxxiii 20, was delivered by the Rev. Mr. Shaw of Bridgewater. The whole was concluded by a pertinent and pathetic prayer by the Rev. Mr. Porter; while an effusion of tears marked the affliction of the church and the people, and testified the respect they bore his memory. The character of Mr. Reed as a disciple of Jesus Christ, and a luminary in the candle stick in which Providence had placed him, was respectable. The advancement of Christ's kingdom in the hearts of his flock, and among mankind in general, was a subject, in which he was much engaged. He was a workman that needed not to be ashamed; for he rightly divided the work of truth, and gave to every one his portion in due season."

CHILDREN

181. Sarah, b. 1750.
182. John, b. Nov. 11, 1751; m. 1st. in 1780, Hannah Sampson; m. 2d. in 1822, Mrs. Phoebe Sampson Paddock.
183. Solomon, b. March 18, 1753; d. Feb. 2, 1808; m. March 14, 1781, Susannah Willard.
184. Samuel, b. 1754; d. July 13, 1812; m. in 1780, Anna Shaw.
185. Timothy, b. 1756; m. in 1788, Hannah Kingman.

A 54

Moses Reed, son of William and Alice (Nash) Reed.
b. Jan. 15, 1723, at Abington.
m. ———, Phoebe.

Order of court dividing estate annexed, mentions his children Moses, Aaron and Miriam.

DIVISION OF THE ESTATE OF MOSES REED DECEASED

"Pursuant to a warrant from the Honorable John Cushing Esq., Judge of Probate of Wills for the County of Plymouth in the province of the Massachusetts Bay, in New England, directed to us the subscribers for the division of the real estate of Moses Reed late of Abington, deceased, which we have done in manner as followeth, Viz:—

"We have divided the said estate into four equal shares, the first share we assign and set off to Moses Reed the eldest son of the said deceased, containing thirty two acres and one hundred and thirty six rod, bounded as followeth, beginning at a stake and stones standing by the road, being the north west corner of Micah Samson's land, thence running east, seven degrees, south by said Samson's land to a stake and stones standing in William Norton's line, thence north ten degrees, east fifty four rods to a black oak tree, thence west five degrees, north to a stake and stones standing by the road, thence southerly by the road to the bounds first mentioned.

"The second share we assign and set off to the said Moses

Reed containing thirty acres bounded as followeth, beginning at a stake and stones standing by the road, being the north west corner of the first share, thence east five degrees, south to a black oak tree before mentioned, thence east twenty six degrees, north to a river, thence by a river to a maple tree in the four mile line so called, thence west seven degrees and a half south to a stake and stones standing by the road, thence southerly by said road twenty three rods to the bounds first mentioned, and the one half of two pews in the Abington Meeting house.

"The third share we assign and set off to Aaron Reed, containing fourteen acres and twenty four rods, bounded as followeth, beginning at a stake and stones standing by the road, being the north west corner of the second share thence running east seven degrees and a half north to a maple tree before mentioned, thence north thirty two degrees and half west sixteen rods and thirteen feet to a stake and stones, thence west six degrees, south to a stake and stones by the Road, thence southerly by said road to the bounds first mentioned, said share hath a dwelling house and barn thereon belonging to it, and a quarter part in two pews in Abington Meeting House.

"The fourth share we assign and set off to Miriam Reed, containing twenty eight acres, one hundred and forty four rods, bounded as followeth, beginning at a stake and stones standing by the road, being the north west corner of the third share, thence running by the road to Obadiah Reed's land, thence easterly by said Obadiah and Jacob Reed's land to a stake standing by the river, near Isaac Hobart's dam, thence running north sixteen degrees, east to a stake standing by said Hobart's dam, thence running easterly by said Hobart's land to his south east corner, thence running southerly by Benoni Gurney's land to a stake and stones standing in the four mile line so called thence by the four mile line to a maple before mentioned thence north thirty two degrees and a half west sixteen rod, thirteen feet to a stake and stones, thence west six degrees, south to the

bounds first mentioned, and one quarter of two pews in Abington Meeting House.

"Dated at Abington, September 16th, 1771.

Eleazer Whitman.
James Hersey.
Daniel Shaw."

CHILDREN

186. Moses, b. March 22, 1751.
187. Aaron, b. June 30, 1754.
188. Miriam, b. Jan. 15, 1757; d. May 24, 1804; m. April 21, 1778, Jonathan Marsh; d. Nov. 6, 1822, aged 70.

A 56

John Reed, son of John and Sarah (Hersey) Reed.

b. Aug. 10, 1713; d. 1784.

m. June 20, 1734, Mary Torrey. They were married by the Rev. James Bayley. Moved to Weymouth and lived and died there. She died Feb. 3, 1790.

Extracts from his will:

"John Reed (Gentleman) and wife Mary Torrey, will Apr. 6, 1768, gives wife one third-part of all real and personal estate, speaks of dau. Mary. Grandson Robert Pratt when of age gives thirteen pounds six shillings and eight pence. Son Samuel all Real Estate, Stock except that part to wife, and whole to son Samuel at last. Will proved May 4, 1784. James Humphrey, Elnathan Bates, Urban Bates witnesses."

He lived near King Oak Hill and was probably a school teacher. Was a descendant of William Reed and Esther Thompson, and was probably born in Abington.

CHILDREN

189. Mary, b. April 7, 1735; m. ———.
190. Hannah, b. May 16, 1738; m. (prob. m. Ebenezer Pratt, April 14, 1757).
191. Samuel, b. Nov. 10, 1740; m. Nov. 29, 1764, Mary Torrey.
192. Sarah, b. June 14, 1744.
193. John, b. Feb. 9, or 17, 1748.

A 57

James Reed, son of John and Mary (Whitmarsh) Reed.

b. Oct. 12, 1716; d. at the age of 37.

m. Ruth Ford Pool, widow of Joseph Pool; her maiden name was Ford, daughter of Hezekiah and Ruth (Whitmarsh) Ford; after her husband's death she married Samuel Porter.

Order of court dividing estate mentions his wife Ruth and children Hezekiah, Jeremiah, Joseph and Naomi.

DIVISION OF THE ESTATE OF JAMES REED, DECEASED

"Pursuant to, a warrant from John Cushing, Esq., Judge of Probate of wills in the County of Plymouth in New England, to us the subscribers, for the dividing of the real estate of James, Junr. late of Abington, dec'd accordingly:

"We have divided and set off first to Ruth Porter the wife of Samuel Porter & late widow of sd. decd. her thirds or dower & is bounded as follows, beginning at a stake and stones in the line of Benj. Bates Jun'r land from thence west five degrees south to the south east corner of the barn, thence from the southwest corner of the barn west five degrees, south to the brook thence down the Brook to Edson's meadow, thence east fourteen degrees south to Thomas Torrey's land, thence north to the northwest corner of sd. Thos. Torrey's thence running eastly by sd. Thomas Torrey's land to sd. Bates and so bounded by sd. Bates land to the bounds first mentioned, together with the house and half of the barn. All which land lies in Bridgewater.

"2ndly. We have set off to Hezekiah Reed, son of the said James Reed thirty one acres more or less, laying in Bridgewater and is bounded as follows, beginning at a stake and stones, which is the south east corner of the seventh lot in the fourth share from thence south one degree, east in the line of Bates land thirty six rods to a stake and stones, from thence west seven degrees, south forty six rods to a stake and stones, from thence west ten degrees, and half

north thirteen rods and half to a stone wall, thence west eleven degrees north by said wall, twenty eight rods to a stake, thence west twenty degrees & half north to a white oak tree the north west corner of Edson's land, thence west twenty one degrees, south forty seven rods to a white oak tree the southwest corner of the fourth share, thence north thirty seven rods to the southwest corner of the seventh lot in the fourth share, together with about two acres and three quarters of meadow, bounded as follows—begin at the north west corner of James Edson's Meadow lot, from thence north about twelve degrees, east twenty rods to a stake and stones, thence east fourteen degrees, south to a stake by the brook, thence down the brook to Edson's meadow thence west fourteen degrees, north to the bounds first mentioned.

"3rdly. We have set off to Jeremiah Reed son of the said James Reed, about fourteen acres more or less, laying in Bridgewater and is bounded as follows—Beginning at a stake and stones the southeast corner of the land set off to Hezekiah Reed, from thence westerly by said Hezekiah's land to a white oak tree, the northeast corner of Joseph Edson's land thence south twelve degrees, west about sixty nine rods, to the northwest corner of Hezekiah's meadow lot, thence east fourteen degrees, south to the brook, thence up the brook till it comes to the northwest Corner of the land set off to Ruth the wife of Samuel Porter, thence running easterly by the land set off to said Ruth to Bates land, thence north one degree west eight rods, to the bounds first mentioned, with nine acres more or less, lying the seventh lot in the fourth share, with three acres and thirty rods more, lying in Abington, lying on the east side of Beaver Brook in the Old Mens shares, so called, and is bounded as follows, Beginning at a stake and stones in the north line of the fourth lot of said share, thence north one degree, west twenty five rods and an half to a stake and stones, thence west one degree and half south twenty rods to a stake and stones, thence south one degree east twenty five rods and an half to a stake and stones, thence east one de-

gree and half north twenty rods to the bounds first mentioned.

"4thly. And we have set off to Joseph Reed son of said James Reed fifty acres more or less lying partly in Abington and partly in Bridgewater, and in the Old Mens Shares and is bounded as follows, beginning at a stake and stones the southwest corner of the land set off to Jeremiah Reed, Thence running west one degree and a half, south one mile more or less, to the north west corner of the fourth lot in said share being a stake and stones thence north twenty five and a half rods to a stake and stones, thence east one degree and half north, one mile more or less to the north west corner of Jeremiah's land, thence south one degree, east twenty five and a half rods to the bounds first mentioned.

"5thly. We have set off to Naomi Reed daughter of said James Reed thirteen acres more or less, lying in Abington partly and partly in Bridgewater and is bounded as follows, beginning at a stake and stones, the northwest corner of the land of Jacob Porter, thence west in the four mile line sixteen rods and a half to a stake and stones, thence south two degrees, east 132 rods to Whitman's land, thence east one degree & an half, north sixteen rods and an half to the southwest corner of said Porter's land, thence north two degrees, west to the bounds first mentioned, also fourteen acres more or less lying in Abington & bounded as follows, beginning at the south east corner of the land set off to Jeremiah Reed, in the Old Men's Shares thence east one degree, & half north 88 rods to a stake & stones the corner of Saml. Noyes land, thence north one degree, west on said Noyes line 25 1/2 rods to a stake, thence west one degree, an half south 88 rods to a stakes and stones the northeast corner of said Jeremiah's land thence south one degree east 25 rods to the bounds first mentioned. Also more we set off to the said widow, three quarters of a pew in the Meeting House in Abington on the back side—& more we set off to Hezekiah Reed one half of a pew in the south end of the above said house—more we set off to Jeremiah, the

other half of the above sd. pew more we set off to Joseph, three quarters of a pew in the south Gallery in the above said house, More we set off to Naomi, one quarter of the above said pew in the South Gallery and one quarter of the pew set off to the said widow.

June 14th, 1765. Christopher Dyer.
Samuel Pool.
Eleazer Whitman."

"Plymouth ss—To Messrs. Daniel Shaw, Jacob Pool and Samuel Pool all of Abington in the County aforesaid—Gentlemen—Greeting.

(Seal) You are hereby empowered and directed to take a view of the part of the real estate whereof James Reed late of Abington in said County yeoman decd. died seized, which was assigned and set off to to Ruth Reed, the widow of said decd. as her thirds or right of dower in said decd. estate—and you are to assign and set off to Deborah Reed the widow of Hezekiah Reed late of Bridgewater decd. her thirds or right of dower therein, and you are to assign and set off the same by metes & bounds (quantity and quality considered) so that she may hold & improve the same in severalty during her life—and you are to make return of the Warrant with your doings thereon, under your hands, & upon your oaths, as soon as conveniently may be. Given under my hand & seal of Office at Plymouth in sd. County this 13th day of March 1792."

Joshua Thomas Judge of Probt.

"To the Honorable Joshua Thomas Esq., Judge of Probate of wills for the County of Plymouth—Sir—In compliance to the directions of your Warrant to us directed we the subscribers have taken a view of that part of the real estate whereof James Reed late of Abington in said County, yeoman decd. died seized, which was assigned and set off to Ruth Reed the widow of said deceased, as her thirds or right of dower in sd. decd. estate, and have assigned and set off

to Deborah Reed the widow of Hezekiah Reed late of Bridgewater decd. her thirds or right of dower therein by metes & bounds, (quantity & quality considered) viz—one acre & a half of land lying in Bridgewater, bounded as follows viz—beginning at a stake & stones by a stone wall thence running east 7 degrees 1/2 north ten rods & four feet to a stake & stones, then south 6 degrees east, twenty three rods & 7 feet to a stone wall by Thomas Torrey's land, then westerly by sd. Torrey's land, ten rods & four feet to a wall then north 6 degrees west by said wall, twenty three rods & seven feet to the corner first mentioned—said acre 1/2 half of land being the orchard that formerly belonged to the abovesaid James Reed deceased.

Bridgewater April 2d, 1792. Daniel Shaw
Saml. Pool
Jacob Pool"

CHILDREN

194. Joseph, b. Aug. 9, 1742; d. unmarried; his will mentions his two brothers and sister Naomi.
195. Hezekiah, b. Feb. 23, 1744; m. May 16, 1766, Deborah Tirrell.
196. Jeremiah, b. April 11, 1747; m. Sarah Tirrel.
197. Olive, b. Feb. 2, 1748.
198. Naomi, b. 1751; m. 1777, Obadiah Hersey, of Abington.

A 60

Ezekiel Reed, son of John and Mary (Whitmarsh) Reed.
b. Nov. 14, 1721; d. in 1763.
m. in 1742, Hannah Beal, after the death of her husband she married Samuel Bates.

He served in the French and Indian War and died in the service. He served with his brother under Capt. Johnson in 1754, Capt. Slocomb's Company, Col. Joseph Williams' Regiment, in 1758; also under Capt. Dunbar 1759-62. He died in 1763, on the return passage, of fever, and was buried at sea near Boston. 273 persons embarked on this voyage and when discharged at Boston only 77 were alive. It is supposed that yellow fever broke out on board.

CHILDREN

199. Ezekiel, b. March 3, 1744; m. April 2, 1768, Mary Rogers.
200. Hannah, b. Nov. 1, 1746; m. April, 1766, Luke Ford.
201. Squire, b. Nov. 1, 1748.
202. Mary, b. Jan. 1, 1751; d. young.
203. Zebulon, b. March 31, 1752.
204. Mary, b. Nov. 20, 1754; m. in 1775, Simeon Gannett.
205. Samuel, b. Dec. 25, 1756; m. June 18, 1881, Betsey Smith, of Grafton.
206. Issachar, b. Aug. 9, 1759; m. ———.
207. Deborah, b. Dec. 6, 1762; m. Dec. 18, 1783, J. Gurney.

A 61

Peter Reed, son of John and Mary (Whitmarsh) Reed.

b. Mar. 29, 1723; d. Feb. 18, 1780.

m. Mar. 25, 1748, Lucy Hugens in Abington, Mass.

The widow Lucy moved to Cummington, Mass., soon after the death of Peter, where her son Benjamin already resided.

Of Abington, Mass.

FROM NASH MANUSCRIPT

"Cyrus Nash 1780-1850

"Peter Reed lived near the line between Abington and N. Bridgewater, where he died. His house stood about 40 rods S. W. of the old Abner Porter place and 1/4 mile S. W. from old Mr. John Fullertons.

"He married Lucy Hugens in Abington. Her father Mr. Hugens was from Ireland and lived in Bridgewater, and was a neighbor of old Dea. E. Whitman and of Mr. Macomber from Ireland. They lived on the old road that passed Snell's meadow so called and upon the south side of it. The wife of Mr. Hugens was from Ireland. At the age of 17 for some reason she left home and shipped for Pennsylvania where an Aunt of hers resided, but for some reason the ship came to Boston and the young girl was sold to pay her passage. Mr. Macomber before mentioned, bought her, and she went to live in his house at Abington. Later she

married Mr. Hugens who was considerably older than his wife. It is said that she was a very sprightly girl, brought up at home in fine style. She said she was not obliged to wet her hands only to wash them. At the birth of her first child she said, 'The finest of her small clothes were coarser than the poorest of her sisters at home.' Their children were John, Lucy and Mrs. Hosiah Porter of Weymouth, also another daughter who married Lot Randall, who had two daughters."

Peter Reed of Abington according to the Massachusetts State Archives served in the French and Indian Wars, the Record is, "Peter Reed (of Bridgewater) Sentinel in Capt. Johnson's Co. in 1754 also Peter Reed of Abington, Private in Capt. Slocomb's Co., Col. Joseph Williams' Regiment in 1758. Also in Dunbar's Co. at Halifax 1759-62."

Peter's brother Ezekiel (2 years older, b. Nov. 14, 1721) who married Hannah Beal, served at the same time and died on the return passage in 1762 of consumption and homesickness, 273 persons embarked on this voyage and when discharged at Boston only 77 were alive. It is supposed that yellow fever broke out on board.

The Nash MS. states that "At the death of Peter (1780) his widow (Lucy) removed to the westward probably to Cummington, and Samuel to the same place, where she died."

CHILDREN

208. Eunice, bapt. April 9, 1749 (her father owning the covenant), at 1st Church in Abington. She died previous to her father.

209. Benjamin, b. March 3, 1752, probably in Abington; d. July 10, 1835; m. Dec. 3, 1778, Huldah Pratt, of Bridgewater, Mass.; b. May 10, 1760; d. May 17, 1842.

210. Sarah, b. Aug. 26, 1757; bapt. Oct. 23, 1757; d. Dec. 29, 1836; m. Joel Hill at Cummington.

211. Samuel, b. Nov. 30, 1760; bapt. Jan. 29, 1761.

212. Joanna, b. Sept. 8, 1763; m. Nov. 27, 1788, Jacob Nash at Cummington, Mass.

All born in Abington.

A 67

Jacob Reed, son of Jacob and Sarah (Hersey) Reed.

b. July 7, 1720; d. Oct. 11, 1806, at Easton, Mass.

m. 1st. Nov. 26, 1741, Mary Ford, b. in 1719, daughter of Andrew and Mercy (Whitmarsh) Ford.

m. 2nd. Dec. 1, 1748, Alice Reed, daughter of Capt. William Reed.

m. 3rd. Widow Harden, relative of Capt. John Harden, she d. 1799.

He removed late in life to Easton where his children Abigail, Alice, and Bela resided, and died there Oct. 11, 1806, at the age of 86.

Of Abington.

CHILDREN OF JACOB AND MARY FORD

213. Marcia, b. Aug. 31, 1742; m. 1st. 1773, William Tirrell; m. 2d. Dec. 20, 1776, Benjamin Wood.
214. Abijah, b. Aug. 14, 1744; d. June 16, 1816; m. Oct. 29, 1768, Sarah Bates.

CHILDREN OF JACOB AND ALICE REED

215. Alice, b. in 1752; d. at Easton in 1841, aged 89; unmarried.
216. Jacob, b. May 6, 1757; m. Feb. 21, 1782, Sarah Noyes, daughter of Ebenezer Noyes.
217. Mary, bapt. July 23, 1758; d. at Easton, 1816; m. 2d. 1795, Joshua Pool.
218. Lydia, bapt. Aug. 12, 1759; m. 1791, Eliphalet Packard, of N. Bridgewater.
219. Phoebe, bapt. Feb. 14, 1762; m. 1790, Joshua Shaw, Jr.
220. Nathan, bapt. March 4, 1764; m. 1st. Widow Bartlett, of Plymouth, Mass.; m. 2d. Rebecca Morton.
221. Bela, b. Sept. 2, 1769; m. Aug. 20, 1795, Mehetable Reed, daughter of Obadiah Reed.
222. Besa, b. ———; d. young.

A 69

William Reed, son of Jacob and Sarah (Hersey) Reed.

b. Sept. 20, 1725; d. Dec. 4, 1807.

m. in 1750, Silence Nash, daughter of Ensign James Nash, grandson of James Nash of Weymouth; b. Apr. 19, 1726; d. Mar. 9, 1807.

He was an earnest, religious man and for many years a leader in the neighborhood religious meeting of that time.

Mrs. W. D. Taylor of Cleveland, O., has the old family bible with the following inscription: "November 25th, 1795. William Reed's Book the gift of Silence Reed." Mrs. Taylor also states that she was born in the old house in South Abington, which William and Silence Reed occupied in 1807 at the time of their death. Her father, grandfather and great-grandfather were all born in and occupied the same house, making five out of eight generations up to her day, who were born in or occupied this old family residence, which was bought by William Reed the ancestor mentioned above in 1799 or 1800.

CHILDREN

223. Silence, b. Aug. 6, 1753; d. July 10, 1794; unmarried.
224. William, b. June 8, 1755; d. Nov. 16, 1809; m. May, 1784, Olive Pool.
225. Jane, b. June 23, 1757; d. Jan. 2, 1842; m. 1787, Rev. David Gurney, of Titicut Parish, Middleborough, Mass.
226. Betsy, b. Feb. 23, 1760; m. Jan. 12, 1792, Ebenezer Porter, of Abington.
227. Susannah, b. July 26, 1762; m. 1789, Benjamin Bates.
228. James, b. Oct. 6, 1764; d. Oct. 30, 1855; m. Ruth Porter, of Bridgewater.
229. Timothy, b. May 29, 1767; d. Sept. 8, 1775.
230. Mehetable, b. Jan. 29, 1770; d. Jan. 6, 1773.

A **70**

Elijah Reed, son of Jacob and Sarah (Hersey) Reed.

b. Feb. 14, 1727.

m. July 10, 1755, Sarah Reed, daughter of Obadiah, son of William and Alice Reed.

CHILDREN

231. Hannah, b. Aug. 22, 1756.
232. Elijah, b. Sept. 20, 1758; d. Aug. 31, 1816; m. July 3, 1779, Lucy Washburn.
233. Luke, b. April 28, 1763; m. Oct. 19, 1786, Keziah Leonard.
234. Paul, b. Dec. 20, 1765; m. Feb. 7, 1788, Mercy Noyes.
235. Joshua, b. July 25, 1768; m. Feb. 7, 1788, Deborah Noyes.
236. Jacob, b. June 25, 1771; m. Sarah ———.

W 74

Daniel Reed, son of Thomas and Hannah (Randall) Reed.
b. Sept. 10, 1704.
m. 1st. Feb. 22, 1728, Ruth Torrey.
m. 2nd. Oct. 15, 1765, Sarah Howland Dawes, widow of Samuel Dawes of Bridgewater.

See his will annexed. Selectman 15 years in Abington. He was called Capt. Daniel Reed.

WILL

"In the name of God, Amen, This twenty seventh day of February Anno Domini one thousand seven hundred and seventy six, I Daniel Reed of Abington in the County of Plymouth, Gentleman, being weak of body but of sound and perfect memory praised be God, do make and ordain this my last will and testament in manner and form following. First & principally I commit my Soul into the hands of God that gave it hoping for pardon of all my sins the salvation of my Soul thro' the alone merits of Jesus Christ my Redeemer & my body to the earth to be buried in such decent manner as to my executors hereafter in this my will named shall be thought meet.

"Imprimis I will that all my just debts & funeral charges be paid by my executors in convenient season after my decease.

"Item I give & I bequeath to my wife ten dollars or three pounds yearly according to my agreement with her before marriage, as also two cords of wood to be delivered her yearly while she remains my widow & I will that my two sons pay each their half of the above legacy during the term above mentioned & further I will that my wife improve one dwelling house for the time above mentioned.

"Item I give devise & bequeath to my son Daniel his heirs & assigns forever all my field lying south of the road including the mowing tilling & also the barn & corn barn on said field, more to my son Daniel all the land I own north-

ward of the road leading by my house & west of the road commonly called Backstreet as also the dwelling house on said piece, more to my son Daniel a piece of pasture land bounded as follows, Viz:—west on the field first mentioned north on the road leading by my dwelling house east on the road above called Back Road running south with said road to a large white oak tree standing in the pasture marked D on the north side & T on the south from thence running a west course to another white oak tree with the abovesaid mark I to the field first mentioned. More to my son Daniel one half of the width of my land on the east side of the road till it comes to the east end of the land I purchased of Ezekiel Reed & also one half of the width of what I purchased of Moses Cushing & Joshua Lovell that lies east of the land I purchased of the above said Ezekiel Reed & I will that my son shall have the north side of the abovesaid division more to my son Daniel one half the lot I purchased of Moses Cushing lying east of the river called Frenches Mill River & that he shall have the north side of that lot also more to my son Daniel half my lot fronting upon the road against Whitcomb Pratt's dwelling house & I will he shall have the north side of that likewise, more to my son Daniel one half of a piece of Meadow I purchased of Deacon Samuel Pool at a place called the Old Mill Pond & I will that he shall have the west end of said meadow.

"Item To my son Thomas Reed I give & bequeath to him his heirs & assigns all my lands on the east and south of the two roads aforementioned not before disposed of bounded as follows, Viz:—south on Samuel Nash's land east on the road running to the white oak tree near the road marked as above mentioned then running west to the other marked tree & so to the field first disposed of which is its western bounds and also the house standing on said piece of land, more to my son Thomas one half of the width of my lands on the east side of the road which I purchased of Ezekiel Reed & others till it comes to the east end of the lot I purchased of said Ezekiel Reed as also one half of the

lots I purchased of Moses Cushing & Joshua Lovell that runs further east than the lot last mentioned & I will he shall have the south side of said lot with the barn on the same.— More to my son Thomas, one half my lot fronting on the road against Whitcomb Pratt's dwelling house & I will to him the south side of said lot, more to my son Thomas, the one half of a piece of meadow I purchased of Deacon Samuel Pool at a place called the Old Mill Pond &. I will that he shall have the east end of said meadow. More to my sons Daniel & Thomas Reed all my lands lying at a place called Mattakees Plain purchased of John Torrey, John Chubbuck, Amos Shaw, Joshua Lovell, Nath'l Bailey & John Hollis to be equally divided between them two.

"Item To my grandson Daniel I give and bequeath to him & his heirs all my real and personal estate in the township of Weymouth & further my will is that my just debts and funeral charges shall be paid out of my personal estate in the township of Abington & the rest to be equally divided between my two sons & I will that my son Daniel shall have the improvement of my interest at Weymouth until my grandson arrives at the age of twenty one years.

"Item I do hereby nominate and apoint my son Daniel Reed sole Executor of this my last will and testament.

"In witness whereof I the said Daniel Reed have hereunto set my hand and seal the day and year above written.

"Signed, sealed and published by the abovesaid Daniel Reed to be his last will & testament in presence of us witnesses.

Daniel Reed (Seal)."

"Mathew Nash.
Barnabas Reed.
Jacob Smith Jun'r."

CHILDREN

237. Daniel, b. Nov. 10, 1729; m. 1st. Feb. 1, 1755, Mary Turner; m. 2d. Anna Dawes; b. in 1735.

238. Thomas, b. April 17, 1732; m. 1st. July 10, 1755, Mary (Hobart) White; m. 2d. Sarah Thaxter Pulling.

239. Ruth, b. April 3, 1735.

W 81

John Reed, son of John and Sarah (Whitmarsh) Reed.
b. June 22, 1728; d. 1780.
m. Dec. 26, 1745, Mary Bates; b. Feb. 3, 1728; d. Oct. 3, 1811. (They were married by the Rev. William Smith.)

Mary Bates was the daughter of Samuel and Hannah (Ward) Bates. He was the son of Increase and Mary (Whitmarsh) Bates, who was born Dec. 23, 1641, and died Feb. 20, 1717 o. s. His wife Mary Whitmarsh died Dec. 21, 1715. (They had nine children.) Increase Bates was the son of Elder Edward Bates, born in 1606, and who died March 25, 1686, aged 80, who probably came over in the "Griffin" and landed in Boston Sept. 14, 1633. He joined the first church in Boston in Nov. 1638, and was made a freeman March 13, 1638-9.

On May 22, 1839, we find him one of the deputies of the General Court sitting at Boston, evidently from Weymouth. He was again elected a deputy from Weymouth Dec. 19, 1660. He held the important position of elder in the church of Weymouth for more than thirty years, and was mentioned by that title as early as Feb. 3, 1651-2, and he was also chosen to many important positions, as the records of Weymouth show. He was buried in the cemetery at Burying Hill, where may be found his gravestone suitably inscribed.

Mary Bates' maternal grandfather was John Ward who lived to the age of ninety years, son of Henry, son of Samuel Ward who was born in 1593, and was a representative to the General Court in 1637 and 1638 (see His. of Hingham, p. 275).

CHILDREN

240. Frederick, b. July 26, 1746; m. 1st. Dec. 6, 1770, Rebecca or Jane Ayers; m. 2d. Hannah Pool.

241. William, b. May 9, 1748; d. March 29, 1833; m. 1st. Sept. 3, 1768, Elizabeth Stammers; m. 2d. June 16, 1824, Bethia White (widow).

242. Jane, b. July 13, 1750; m. Sept. 20, 1770, Thos. Webb.

243. Mary, b. Aug. 12, 1752; m. April, 1781, Jonathan Trufant, Jr.

244. John, b. Feb. 13, 1755; m. Jan. 5, 1779, Rachel Clark.
245. Asa, b. Feb. 12, 1757. Town Treasurer's account of Weymouth shows that he was killed or died a soldier of the Revolution.
246. Noah, b. Nov. 18, 1759; m. July 6, 1788, Mehetable Wild.
247. Ezra, b. Nov. 24, 1762; m. 1st. Nov. 6, 1787, Mary Lovell; m. 2d. May 1, 1823, Hannah Tirrell.
248. Deborah, b. March 16, 1765; m. Oct. 21, 1798, James Gould Jeffers.
249. Salome, b. Nov. 5, 1767; m. Sept. 9, 1792, Robert Burrell.

T 86

George Reed, son of John and Bethiah (Cobb) Reed.

b. May, 1704; d. 1735.

m. Jan. 1, 1730, Abigail Woodward, daughter of James Woodward of Barrington, R. I. She died Feb. 1, 1791.

He was a farmer and removed from Taunton to Rehoboth. On his death, his widow and son returned to Taunton.

CHILD

250. George, b. Oct., 1733; d. Jan. 3, 1820; m. Elizabeth Harvey.

T 87

William Reed (Barrington, R. I)., son of John and Bethiah (Cobb) Reed.

b. Feb. 28, 1712-3.

m. Elizabeth ———.

Of Barrington, R. I.

CHILDREN

251. Bethia, b. Sept. 12, 1741, at Barrington.
252. Jonathan, b. ———. He lived near Shepherd's factory, in Newport, R. I.

T 91

John Reed, son of William and Mary (Richmond) Reed.

b. in 1722; d. in 1788.

m. 1st. Dec. 30, 1746, Dorothy Pinneo, daughter of James and Dorothy Pinneo. She was born Dec. 6, 1725, in Lebanon, Conn.

m. 2nd. Jan. 9, 1771, Mrs. Hannah Andrews.

He was a blacksmith by trade and a man of considerable business. He was a constable in 1767; selectman in 1775. Was a captain in the army and one of the committee of inspection and correspondence in the Revolution; and was a pious man. He was above middle stature, and rather stern in manner. His first wife was the daughter of James Pinneo, a French Huguenot, who escaped from France about the year 1685, at the date Louis revoked the edict of Nantes, and during the persecutions of that pious and devoted band. After having been secreted in dens and caves in France, he finally made his way to America; settled in Lebanon, Conn., and brought up a family of children, one of whom was Dorothy the wife of John Reed. His estate was valued at his decease, realty in silver money at 990 pounds sterling, and personalty 450 pounds sterling. The following poem was delivered by Hodges Reed before the Reed Association or Annual Gathering, at the old homestead, Aug. 24, 1847. The verses are so unique and full of historic interest, that I consider them worthy to be inserted here.

DOROTHY PINNEO

(1)

It was a cold December day,
  A hundred years ago,
The purling brooks had ceased their play,
The hill, the rock, the meadow lay
  All covered o'er with snow.

(2)

The withered leaves, the withered flowers,
  Their last cold sleep had come;
The snow it was their winding sheet,
The pelting rain, the rattling sleet,
  Consign them to their home.

(3)

Hark! Joyful sounds are on the air,
  From yonder ruins breaking,
For John has brought him a fair
Young bride, and all the neighbors there,
  Are met and merry making.

(4)

Her name was Dorothy—why smile?
  T'is no unworthy name!
Since many a maid, tradition says,
Renowned in Puritanic days,
  Was proud to bear the same.

(5)

Perhaps some, less fair, may have thought,
  T'would be a good idea,
Her name to modernize somewhat,
To suit politer ears, why not?
  We'll call her Dorothea.

(6)

No! let her name unaltered be,
  You cannot make it better;
John liked it well, " Sweet Dorothy,"
He rung it on his anvil, he
  Would never change a letter.

(7)

Her father was a Huguenot,
  A Frenchman, full of zeal,
In self-denying doctrines taught,
Who oft in caves his Savior sought,
  Secure from Romish steel.

(8)

But Popish eyes that never sleep,
  Found out the heretic
And Pinneo fled across the deep,
Trusting in God that he would keep,
  His promise to the meek.

(9)

The Huguenots were men whose faith,
  Soared on sublimest wings;
Their Standard, what the Bible saith,
Their March, onward in duty's path,
  In spite of Popes or Kings.

(10)

Is there, my kin, upon your crown,
  An elevated spot;
That stirs you up, to trample down,
All obstacles that cluster round?
  T'is that old Huguenot.

(11)

Within doth some electric spark,
  Play volatile as thought;
Up soaring like the morning lark,
Though present prospects may be dark?
  T'is that young Huguenot.

(12)

That spirit grim that bids you mope,
  When troubles are astir,
Fixing a feeble grasp on hope,
Too listless e'en to seize the rope,
  It never came from her.

(13)

Yon Horseblock,—she ne'er felt the lack,
  Of such dumb helpers near;
For she could spring up in a crack,
From the ground to the highest horse's back,
  Quick as the frighted deer.

(14)

And once, ere life had lost its tone,
  I've heard my mother say,
Mounted and spurred, and all alone,
She started off for Lebanon,
  Upon a summer's day.

(15)

It was a hundred miles or more,
  To her loved native place;
In her fond arms a child she bore,
And never a dog to trot before,
  Even so tradition says.

(16)

The way was long and dark the woods,
  The wolf howl pierced her ear;
But on, with child and traveling goods,
She sped o'er hills and plains and floods,
  With a heart that knew no fear.

(17)

Still joyful sounds are on the air,
  From yonder ruins breaking;
For John has brought him home a fair
Young bride, and all the neighbors there
  Are met and merry making.

(18)

A hazel laughing eye she had,
  Her dark curls flowing free;
Fairer I ween than fairest maid,
That sports beneath this Locust shade,
  If a thing *can* be.

(19)

I hear the hammer ringing loud,
  Through those cold wintry days;
The shop[1] is gone; but there it stood,
On yonder hillock near the wood,
  The cinders mark the place.

(20)

The sparks upon the evening air,
  Are dancing far and wide;
And well they may, for John is there
With thought intent upon his fair,
  Young Huguenotic bride.

(21)

Blow, happy smith! The steel thrust swift,
  Into the sputtering trough;
Heat the huge bar, the sledge uplift.
With such an argument for thrift,
  Thou'lt soon be better off.

---

[1] The first blacksmith shop stood on the east side of the road between the present shop and the ruins.

(22)

And thou, sweet Dorothy, meanwhile,
  Speed on the merry wheel;
With song and tardy hours beguile,
Till he return with wonted smile,
  To taste the frugal meal.

(23)

So played the sparks on the wintry sky,
  So formed the smith his shoe;
So swung his vigorous arm on high,
While the short months went gaily by,
  For love the bellows blew.

(24)

So whirred the merry wheel within,
  So blithely sung the fair
Young bride, so swift the knitting pin,
So welcome pots and kettles din,
  For answering love was there.

(25)

Now come the summer months, ah, where,
  Those fruit trees, hanging low?
The rosy peach, the lucious pear,
The seek no further that hung there,
  A hundred years ago.

(26)

A hundred years! what now, of all
They saw, have seen our days?
The ground, the river, that old wall,
The deep blue vault o'er arching all,
  The rest have gone their ways.

(27)

Not so! Who cometh there? T'is he!
  John and his fair young bride;
Now, underneath that spreading tree,
Look! Look! My kin why don't you see,
Upon that rock, how lovingly,
  They're seated side by side?

(28)

Sweet Dorothy,[1] behold her now;
  That eye; those glossy curls,
Parted so neatly on her brow,
Those lips, just like the peach just dropping now,
  Is'nt she a beauty, girls?

(29)

Her smile, like ripples in the sun,
  When gentlest breezes blow,
Her skin transparent doth not shun,
To tell you what is going on,
  In the loving heart below.

(30)

But still, her cheek is slightly pale,
  And a slight shade in her eye,
They tell us an unwelcome tale,
Sickness hath marked that body "*frail*"
  And one day it must die.

(31)

John marks it too, and on his face,
  The coming shadows fall;
Fear not,[2] She shall live many days.
The mother of a numerous race,
  The mother of us all.

---

[1] Concerning her, John Dudley writes by the dictation of his mother, now in her eighty-ninth year, daughter of Dorothy: "She was very mild in her disposition. When she was well she was full of animation and life. She was short and rather thick set; her hair was dark brown, her eyes dark grey, her complexion rather light. She was a Christian; belonged to the Presbyterian Church, and was esteemed a very good woman."

[2] Dorothy was about twenty years old when she was married. "She was sick a good deal," says my Aunt Dudley, but she lived after this long enough to become the mother of eight children, two of whom are alive this day, viz.: Dorothy, the widow of Paul Dudley, and Hannah, the widow of Stephen Dean.

(32)

Hark! Now he speaks! My kin draw near,
  Listen and you shall know,
That true and loving hearts were here,
Where strangers might not interfere,
  A hundred years ago.

(33)

Fair Dorothy, how good with thee
  To seek this calm retreat;
From the heated hearth and anvil free,
Beneath this overshadowing tree,
  To breathe the zephyrs sweet.

(34)

Come, sing the martyr's song my bride,
  First taught thee by thy sire;
Sweetly the moments ever glide,
Charmed by thy music, she replied,
  "To please thee, my desire."

THE MARTYR'S SONG.

(1)

Give me the parting hand,
  And when my spirit's flown;
Rejoice that I am going up where,
  No martyr fires are known.

(2)

I see the fagots piled,
  The martyr stake around;
O Jesus own me as thy child,
  When there I shall be bound.

(3)

They call me "Huguenot,"
  And hurl envenomed stings;
The fires are set, Ye Angels wait,
  And take me on thy wings.

(35)

She ceased, but still a tear is found,
To dim the visual ray;
That iron man is melted down,
He threw his stalwart arm around,
And kissed the pearl away.

(36)

The vision's fled, t'was but the lift,
Of time's o'ershadowing pall;
Go to thy shop thou man of thrift,
And thou, sweet Dorothy, not miffed,
That tear drop did not fall.

(37)

Aye, happy pair, on your ways,
You've a great work still to do;
Go train up a numerous race,
To serve God in the latter days,
And bless the Lord for you.

CHILDREN OF JOHN AND DOROTHY

253. Ruth, b. Nov. 20, 1747; m. Capt. Joseph Knapp.

254. Lois, b. ———; m. Oct. 4, 1764, Daniel Drake.

255. John, b. March 29, 1752; d. Feb. 24, 1841; m. Nov. 21, 1775, Mary Godfrey.

256. Mary, b. June 4, 1754; d. Aug. 9, 1822; m. in 1776, Richard Cobb.

257. Dorothy, b. March 1, 1759; d. Sept. 20, 1847; m. July 16, 1782, Paul Dudley, of Douglass.

258. Hannah, b. April 4, 1761; m. 1st. May 24, 1787, Abiah Hall, of Raynham.; m. 2d. in 1804, Stephen Deane, of Raynham.

259. Zilpah, b. Dec. 1, 1763; d. March 7, 1841; m. March 8, 1803, Gershom Gulliver.

260. Enos, b. Nov. 22, 1765; d. unmarried.

261. Lydia, b. May 30, 1768; m. March 8, 1891, Ebenezer Deane, of Raynham.

CHILDREN OF JOHN AND HANNAH

262. Nathan, b. Oct. 8, 1771; d. about 1809; m. Dec. 13, 1796, Ascah Gilmore.

263. Phebe, b. July 16, 1773; m. Bassett Dean Norton, of Avon, Me.

264. David, b. Oct. 11, 1775; d. June 24, 1850; m. May 22, 1803, Phebe Blake.

265. Jonathan, b. Oct. 11, 1775; d. Jan. 30, 1849. Was a farmer.

T 92

William Reed, son of William and Mary (Richmond) Reed.

b. ———.

m. Mar. 27, 1755, Mary Perce.

He removed to Rochester, Mass., about 1744.

CHILDREN

266. William, b. ———; m. Sept. 3, 1801, Sally Crocker.
267. Abigail, b. ———.
268. Margaret, b. ———.
269. Lydia, b. ———.

T 96

Thomas Reed (of Dighton), son of Thomas and Sarah (Tisdale) Reed.

b. Aug. 20, 1718.

m. in 1746, Rebecca Talbot.

Of Dighton.

CHILDREN

270. Rebecca, b. Nov. 1, 1747.
271. Thomas, b. Oct. 7, 1749; m. Sept. 8, 1773, Mary Briggs, of Dighton.
272. Sarah, b. June 3, 1751.

T 97

Joseph Reed, son of Thomas and Sarah (Tisdale) Reed.

b. Nov. —, 1725; d. Apr. 5, 1801.

m. Oct. 31, 1747, Elizabeth Elliot; b. ———; d. Feb. 15, 1801, in the 82nd year of her age.

Of Dighton.

CHILDREN

Taken from Probate Records, will of Joseph Reed, dated Jan. 20, 1801.

273. Elizabeth, b. ———.
274. Thomas, b. ———.
275. Joseph, b. Dec. 14, 1751; m. April 18, 1776, Abigail Barney.
276. Uriah, b. Nov. 27, 1756; d. Oct. 30, 1838; m. Jan. 1, 1783, Polly Pratt.
277. Ebenezer, b. 1759; m. Oct. 10, 1782, Lydia Hoskins, of Berkley.
278. Job, b. ———.
279. Rhoda, b. ———.
280. Josiah, b. ———; d. of smallpox, Feb. 1, 1777.

T 98

Seth Reed, son of Thomas and Sarah (Tisdale) Reed.
b. Nov. 7, 1726.
m. ———, Peddy Pool.

Of Dighton.

CHILD

281. A daughter, b. April 23, 1748.

T 102

Job Reed (of Dighton), son of Thomas and Sarah (Tisdale) Reed.
b. Mar. 13, 1731; d. at Dighton.
m. Feb. 17, 1750; Jemima Talbot.

Removed to Brookfield, Vt.

CHILDREN

282. Job, b. about 1751; m. Sally Troop.
283. Ruth, b. about 1753; m. April, 1776, Joseph Allen, of Middleborough.

T 103

Simeon Reed, son of Thomas and Sarah (Tisdale) Reed.
b. Apr. 17, 1733; d. July 10, 1804, aged 72.
m. ———, Deborah Codding; d. July 7, 1804, aged 70.

He was a deacon in the church.

Of Dighton.

CHILDREN

284. Phebe, b. Feb. 25, 1757; m. May, 1777, Jonathan Williams, of Dighton.
285. Hannah, b. Jan. 30, 1758; m. Nathaniel Fisher, of Dighton.
286. Simeon, b. July 28, 1763; m. 1st. Hannah Wheeler; m. 2d Elizabeth ——— (widow).
287. Elijah Augustus, b. (at Dighton) Sept. 20, 1769; m. 1st April 26, 1796, Delight Brown; m. 2d Sarah (Durfee) Borden.
288. Zebulon Leonard, b. in 1773 (lived in Warren, R. I.); m. Mary Brown, who d. Dec. 24, 1849, aged 72 years.

T 109

John Reed, son of George and Sarah (Whitmarsh) Reed.
b. Mar. 30, 1724; d. Sept. 14, 1776.
m. 1st. May 11, 1749, Miriam Talbot; she d. Dec. 11, 1749.
m. 2nd. Mar. 27, 1752, Mary Perry.

Spells his name Read in the Bible.
He was in the army at Lake Champlain, and died soon after his return home, in Vermont.

Of Townshend, Vt.

CHILDREN OF JOHN AND MARY PERRY

289. Miriam, b. June 6, 1753; m. Oct. 19, 1772, Joseph Horton.
290. Mary, b. July 6, 1755; d. July 28, 1756.
291. John, b. April 28, 1757; d. June 24, 1840; m. 1st. July 15, 1780, Deborah Baldwin; m. 2d. Elizabeth Cudworth.
292. Sarah, b. March 13, 1759; m. Feb. 20, 1783, Nathaniel Bodsworth.
293. William, b. March 7, 1761; m. Dee., 1786, Betsy Cartee.
294. Mary, b. May 1, 1763; m. ——— Harris.
295. Celia, b. March 25, 1765; m. Sept. 4, 1785, Matthew Briggs.
296. Elizabeth, b. June 7, 1767; d. young.
297. Ruth, b. April 10, 1768; m. Oct. 20, 1784, Capt. Adams Bailey, of Scituate, Mass.
298. Nancy, b. July 26, 1770; m. ———.
299. Evans, b. Feb. 25, 1772; d. July 9, 1854; m. June 6, 1796, Lydia Haven.
300. Seabury, b. July 1, 1774.
301. George, b. Jan. 12, 1776.

T 110

Samuel Reed (of Dighton), son of George and Sarah (Whitmarsh) Reed.
b. Nov. 29, 1725.
m. in 1748, Rachel Williams.

Of Dighton.

CHILDREN

302. Rachel, b. Jan. 28, 1752; d. March 30, 1756.
303. Samuel, b. Dec. 23, 1754; m. April 17, 1788, Mercy Gilmore.
304. Mary, b. Jan. 4, 1757.

305. Rachel, b. April 20, 1762; m. March 3, 1781, Jonathan Whitman.
306. Seth, b. May 14, 1765; d. 1844; m. May 18, 1788, Cassandra Dean, of Raynham.

T 114

George Reed (of Dighton), son of George and Abigail (Woodward) Reed.

b. Dec. 29, 1731; d. ——, 1758.

m. Dec. 25, 1756, Mercy Phillips.

CHILD

307. George, b. July 29, 1757; d. Aug. 10, 1842; m. May 7, 1782, Elizabeth Pitts.

T 117

Loved Reed (of Dighton), son of George and Abigail (Woodward) Reed.

b. Feb. 26, 1741.

m. 1st. Sept. 22, 1763, Charity Phillips. } Of Berkley.
m. 2nd. Oct. 15, 1786, Mary French. }

He was of Dighton.

CHILDREN OF LOVED AND CHARITY

308. Loved, b. May 22, 1764; d. young.
309. Charity, b. June 11, 1765; m. Oct. 3, 1784, Samuel Lewis, of Swansey.
310. Lydia, b. Sept. 19, 1766; m. Sept. 10, 1785, Peleg Lewis, of Swansey.
311. Phebe, b. July 22, 1768; m. March 3, 1786, Enoch Chase, Jr., of Swansey.
312. Phylene, b. March 24, 1770.
313. Mary, b. April 22, 1772; d. young.
314. Betsy, b. April 12, 1774.
315. Joshua, b. April 17, 1776.
316. Loved, b. Jan. 17, 1778.
317. Sarah, b. July 13, 1780; d. 1795.
318. John, b. April 13, 1782; m. Polly ——.

CHILDREN OF LOVED AND MARY FRENCH

319. Rebecca, b. Oct. 27, 1787.
320. David, b. Dec. 26, 1789; m. Jemima ——.
321. Mary, b. June 2, 1793.

T 119

Jonathan Reed, son of George and Abigail (Woodward) Reed.

b. Oct. 13, 1745.

m. ———, Miss Sheppard.

Of Dighton.

M 121

William Reed, son of William and Elizabeth (———) Reed.

b. July 18, 1715.

m. June 24, 1740, Sarah Warren, daughter of Samuel and Eleanor (Billington) Warren.

Richard Warren, first of the name in America, sailed from Plymouth, England, in the historic "Mayflower," 6th September, 1620. He was not one of the Leyden Company, but joined the Pilgrims from London, and was one of the signers of the compact, framed in the cabin of the "Mayflower," while in Cape Cod harbor. He was one of the third exploring party surprised by the Indians, 18th December, 1620, at the spot since known as "The First Encounter." In the land division of 1623, he received land as one of the "Mayflower" passengers; his was in the north side of town, with Edward Winslow, Myles Standish and others. He was one of the nineteen signers who survived the first winter. His wife Elizabeth followed him in the "Ann" in 1623. They had eight children. Nathaniel, the seventh child, was born at Plymouth. The last land granted him, June 5th, 1662, was in consideration of his being one of the first children born in the Colony. He owned lot 5 in Middleboro. Was Representative to General Court, 1657-58-59-60-63-64-65. He married Sarah Walker. They had twelve children. Richard, the first child of Nathaniel, married Sarah ———. He died at Middleboro, January 23d, 1696-97, where he moved after King Philip's War. They had six children; second son, Samuel, born in Middleboro, 7th March, 1682; died January, 1750; married January 26th, 1703, Eleanor, daughter of Isaac Billington; they had eleven children. Sarah, the tenth child, married William Reed, as above mentioned.

Of Middleborough.

CHILDREN

322. Priscilla, b. Dec. 8, 1742.
323. William, b. Jan. 4, 1744; m. Sept. 22, 1763, Mrs. Alice Richards.
√ 324. Benjamin, b. Jan. 29, 1746; m. Oct. 23, 1763, Mrs. Abiah Macomber.
325. Sarah, b. Jan. 15, 1748.
326. Elizabeth, b. May 4, 1750; d. young.
327. Israel, b. March 7, 1752.
328. Elizabeth, b. Sept. 9, 1759.
329. Abner, b. Aug. 12, 1764.

M 126

Peter Reed, son of William and Elizabeth (———) Reed.

b. May 7, 1729.

m. Aug. 21, 1751, Mercy Turner, of Raynham; d. Nov. 17, 1774.

Of Middleborough.

CHILD

330. Lydia, b. May 31, 1752; m. Oct. 20, 1768, Josiah Wilbore, of Raynham.

M 129

Samuel Reed, son of William and Elizabeth Reed.

b. Sept. 17, 1750; d. Mar. 9, 1822.

m. Nov. 5, 1780, Rebecca Knowlton; she d. Sept. 19, 1831, aged 71.

Of Middleborough.

CHILDREN

331. Bethiah, b. April 23, 1782.
332. Lucy, b. July 16, 1784.
333. Samuel William, b. Dec. 11, 1786; m. Ruth ———.
334. Eunice, b. Jan. 21, 1789.
335. Polly, b. Aug. 4, 1791.
336. John, b. July 21, 1793.
337. Nathaniel, b. Nov. 27, 1796.
338. Watson, b. April 19, 1804; m. Sylvia Lamson.

M 132

Ichabod Reed, son of William and Elizabeth Reed.

b. Dec. 20, 1755; d. at Middleborough.

m. Dec. 3, 1778, Sarah Vaughan.

Of Middleborough and Rochester.

WILL

"In the name of God, Amen. I, Ichabod Reed of Rochester in the County of Plymouth and Commonwealth of Massachusetts, yeoman, being weak of body, yet of sound mind & memory, blessed be God for the same, yet considering the mortality of the body, that it is appointed for all men once to die, do make & ordain this my last will & testament in manner following, Viz:—first I give & bequeath to my well beloved wife, Sarah Reed one third of all my real estate during her natural life, and one third of my personal estate to her forever to dispose of as she shall think proper and also my clock for her use during her natural life, and also my horse to her use and her unmarried daughters as much as they shall need and the other part of the time to use of the farm.

"Item:—I give & bequeath to my son Ichabod Reed one piece of fresh meadow which is called the middle lot, which I had of William, which is about three quarters of an acre and also one other piece of meadow and swamp which is the lowermost piece down stream on Black Brook, so called beginning at a ditch by the upland at the lower end of said meadow, ranging by said ditch to Black Brook, down said Black Brook until it comes to the pond, then by said pond to the upland, and then by upland to the first mentioned bound, and also a lot of cedar swamp which lays on Black Brook and also one half lot of cedar swamp I had of the Mortons, laying in Freetown, and also five hundred dollars in notes, and also one third part of two notes which I hold against Joshua W. Hall if ever collected, to him & his heirs forever.

"Item:—I give & bequeath to my son Josiah Reed all my real estate which I have not other ways disposed of, by his paying out such sums as I shall hereafter order to him & his heirs forever.

"Item:—I give & bequeath to my daughter, Betsey Neal, two hundred and thirty dollars to be paid to her by my executors hereafter named, to her & her heirs forever.

"Item:—I give & bequeath to my daughter Susanna Reed two hundred and eighty dollars to be paid to her by my executors hereafter named & also a privilege of living in my house as long as she shall remain unmarried, & also one cow to her & heirs forever.

"Item:—I give & bequeath to my daughter Sarah Reed two hundred and sixty dollars, to be paid to her by my executors hereafter named & also a privilege of living in my house so long as she shall remain unmarried, to her & heirs forever.

"Item:—I give & bequeath to my daughter Huldah Shaw two hundred and thirty dollars, to be paid to her by my executors hereafter named, to her & heirs forever.

"Item:—I give & bequeath to my daughter Loues * Reed two hundred and thirty dollars to be paid to her by my executors hereafter named, also a privilege of living in my house so long as she shall remain unmarried, and also one cow to her and her heirs forever.

"Item:—And my will is that my three daughters, unmarried, viz:—Susanna Reed Sarah Reed & Loues * Reed have two thirds of my indoor movables equally divided among them and also my will is that my three daughters if they should remain unmarried after my wife's decease, that they shall have a privilege of keeping one cow and also a privilege of fire wood if needed and also my will is that my son Josiah Reed shall have my clock after my wife has done with it.

"Item:—I do appoint my son Josiah Reed to be my executor to this my last will & testament, thus hoping that this my last will & testament will be kept and performed according to the true intent in meaning thereof. In witness whereof I the said Ichabod Reed have hereunto set my hand and seal this twenty-fifth day of April, in the year of our Lord one thousand eight hundred and eighteen.

Ichabod Reed (Seal)"

*Recorded "Lois."

"Signed and sealed, published and declared to be the last will and testament by the said Ichabod Reed in presence of us.

John Bennet,
John Bennet, Jr.
Galon Bennet."

Will proved June 27, 1818.

CHILDREN

339. Ichabod, b. July 6, 1789; m. Lucy ———.
340. Thomas V., b. ———. Settled at Middleborough.
341. Josiah V., b. ———. Settled at Rochester, Mass.
342. Susannah, b. ———.
343. Huldah, b. ———; m. ——— Shaw.
344. Sarah, b. ———. Settled in Brookfield, Vt.
345. Priscilla, b. ———.
346. Lois, b. ———.
347. Betsy, b. ———; m. ——— Neal.

M **144**

Benjamin Reed, son of Benjamin and Hannah (Chase) Reed.
b. May 21, 1721; d. Feb. 12. ———.
m. ———, Elizabeth, ———.

Of Middleborough.

CHILDREN

348. Elizabeth, b. Sept. 3, 1750.
349. Anna, b. April 16, 1754.
350. Benjamin, b. Nov. 13, 1757.

FIFTH GENERATION

A **151**

Obadiah Reed, son of Obadiah and Mary (Nash) Reed.
b. May 15, 1738.
m. 1st. ———, Content Lincoln.
m. 2nd in 1770, Elizabeth Shaw, daughter of Zachariah and Sarah (Packard) Shaw of Bridgewater, Mass.

Of Abington, Mass.

CHILD OF OBADIAH AND CONTENT

351. Obadiah, b. Jan. 4, 1760; m. Elizabeth Richmond.

CHILDREN OF OBADIAH AND ELIZABETH

352. Joel, b. Oct. 26, 1771; m. 1st. July 4, 1793, Ruth Gurney; m. 2d. Widow Jane Raymond.

353. Mehetable, b. Jan. 24, 1775; m. Bela Reed, son of Jacob.

A 154

Silas Reed, son of Obadiah and Mary (Nash) Reed.

b. Oct. 27, 1751; d. Mar. 1, 1800.

m. Dec. 6, 1772, Experience Reed Josselyn, widow of Joseph Josselyn, daughter of James and Abigail (Nash) Reed. She died June 28, 1811.

WILL OF EXPERIENCE REED

"In the name of God Amen, I Experience Reed of the town of Abington in the County of Plymouth & Commonwealth of Massachusetts, widow & relict of Silas Reed of said Abington deceased, considering the uncertainty of life, and though weak in body yet of perfect mind and memory (blessed be God for it) do make and publish this my last Will & Testament in manner & form following, that is to say principally & firstly of all, I commend my Soul into the hands of God who gave it my body I commit to the dust to be interred or buried at the discretion of my executor—

"The small property remaining in my possession after the payment of my just debts & funeral charges by my executors hereafter appointed I give & bequeath in the following manner—

"Item—I give and bequeath to my brother James Reed about one acre & an half of land lying in the Town of Abington aforesaid, which land was set to me, as my part of my sister Molly Reed's estate in her father's land given her before his decease, also my poorest feather bed a coverlet a pair of sheets under bed & a bedstead made to run under a high or common bedstead—

"Item—I give and bequeath to Goddard Reed son of my brother James Reed, about five acres & an half of land lying

in said Abington bounded northerly on the land that was formerly Adam Reed deceased's reference being had to my deed for the boundaries of said land—Also the whole of my right in the pew in Abington Meeting House of which my father died seized, also the whole of my household furniture not before & hereafter disposed of together with the whole of my wearing apparel, also the whole of the Notes of hand I hold against different persons that have not been paid to my executor for the payment of my just debts & funeral charges, & my will is that as I have given him the said Goddard Reed so much of my property, he should be kind to his father & help him under his needy circumstances so far as his father's prudence in improving what he gives him lays a foundation for his son's generosity.

"Item—I give & bequeath to Harriet Burrell daughter of Robert Burrell my gold necklace, my bed in the chamber, under bed, one pair of sheets a coverlet, bedstead & bedcord & a brass kettle holding about seven or eight gallons to be delivered to her by my executor, when she shall arrive at the age of eighteen years—

"And I do hereby constitute & appoint Philip Pratt of said Abington the sole executor of this my last Will & Testament hereby revoking & disannuling all other & former wills by me made, & I do hereby order & direct my executor to pay all my just debts & funeral charges, & set up grave stones at my grave, hereby ratifying and confirming this to be my last Will and Testament—In witness whereof I have hereunto set my hand & seal this nineteenth day of June in the year of our Lord 1811.

Experience Reed (Seal)"

"Signed sealed published & declared by the above named Experience Reed to be her last Will & Testament in the presence of us who have hereunto subscribed our names as witnesses in the presence of the testator.

Robert Burrell
Salome Burrell
Daniel Shaw."

A 156

William Reed, son of Ebenezer and Hannah (Thompson) Reed.

b. Oct. 28, 1735.

m. Dec. 27, 1759, Ruth Shaw.

Of Abington, Mass.

Immediately after the battle of Bunker Hill, a Company of 58 non-commissioned officers and privates enlisted for eight months and served at Roxbury. The officers were Capt., William Reed; Lieut., Samuel Brown; Ensign, David Cobb.

Capt. William Reed represented the town of Abington at the General Court in 1777.

He was a Revolutionary soldier, and lies buried in the old family burying ground of William Reed who married Silence Nash, the father of James Reed, who married Ruth Porter, who was the father of Marcus who married Mehetable Jenkins.

Jan. 11th, 1773, a Committee of Safety and correspondence was chosen, consisting of Mr. David Jenkins, Capt. Daniel Noyes, Lieut. Nathaniel Pratt, Dr. David Jones, Capt. Edward Cobb, Capt. William Reed, Jr., and Mr. Thomas Wilks.

The family burying ground is still held by representatives of the family, and the tombstone of this William is still standing in the old burying ground and bears this inscription:

"In memory of Capt. William Reed, who died of ye Small
Pox March ye 29th 1778, in the 43rd year of his age
Not long after his return from the Continental Service."

My Country Strong for you I've stood.
have fought & ventured my blood.
But now I'm seized by Deaths Arrest.
Farewell my friends may you be Blest."

A 157

Ichabod Reed, son of Ebenezer and Hannah (Thompson) Reed.

b. Apr. 26, 1738.

Died in the service during the French and English War (see Hobart's History of Abington, p. 267). He was killed by the Indians while crossing Lake Ontario in a batteau.

A 158

David Reed, son of Ebenezer and Hannah (Thompson) Reed.

b. July 9, 1740; d. May 10, 1808, at Cummington.

m. 1st. Apr. 22, 1762, Mercy Ford.

m. 2nd. Jan. 9, 1788, Hannah (Reed) Bates, daughter of Ezekiel Reed of Abington and widow of Samuel Bates.

WILL

"In the name of God Amen, I David Reed of Cummington in the County of Hampshire and Commonwealth of Massachusetts, Yeoman, being weak in body but of sound and perfect mind and memory blessed be God for the same, do make and publish this my last will and testament in manner and form as following, that is to say.

"First:—I give and bequeath unto my beloved wife Hannah Reed, a right for her to sit in my pew in the meeting house in said Cummington during her natural life and also one third part of my personal estate excepting my farming tools and outdoor moveables after paying my just debts and funeral charges which I order my executor to pay.

"I also give and bequeath unto my sons David Reed, Ebenezer Reed, Paul Reed, William Reed, Barnabas Reed, each of them six dollars which I hereby order my executor to pay to them in one year after my decease which sums together with what they have already received I consider to be their full share of my estate.

"I also give and bequeath to my son Thaxter Reed, Five hundred dollars to be paid by my executor who is here-

after named one half of said sum to be paid in one year after my decease, unless that time should be before the time the said Thaxter should arrive at the age of twenty one years, and if that should be the case the first half is to be paid to the said Thaxter at the time he shall be twenty one years of age and the other half of said Five hundred dollars to be paid in one year from the time the first half shall become due and interest on the last payment from the time the first payment shall become due.

"And lastly as to the rest residue and remainder of my personal estate goods and chattels of what kind or nature soever and also my pew in the meeting house excepting a right to my said wife in said pew during her natural life. I give and bequeath to my son Ichabod Reed who I hereby appoint sole executor of this my last will and testament, hereby revoking all former wills by me made.

"In witness whereof I have hereunto set my hand and seal this twenty fifth day of April in the year of our Lord one thousand eight hundred and eight.

"Signed, sealed, published, and declared by the above said David Reed to be his last will and testament in the presence of us who have hereunto subscribed our names as witnesses in the presence of the testator.

Adam Packard, David Reed (Seal)"
Dan'l Dawes,
Mitchel Dawes,

Hampshire County ss.
Registry of Probate.

Northampton, Mass, May 12, A. D. 1898.

A true copy: Attest.

Hubbard M. Abbott, Register.

CHILDREN OF DAVID AND MERCY

354. Ichabod, b. Nov. 25, 1763, at Abington; d. Jan. 12, 1778, at Cummington.
355. Abigail, b. June 4, 1765; d. April 13, 1781.
356. David, b. May 3, 1767; m. Sept. 10, 1810, Elizabeth T. Brown.
357. Ebenezer, b. March 27, 1769.

358. Andrew, b. June 25, 1771.
359. Paul, b. Oct. 12, 1773.
360. William, b. May 7, 1777.
361. Barnabas, b. Oct. 16, 1779.
362. Ichabod, b. May 12, 1782; m. Nov. 9, 1804, Betsy Robbins.
363. Thaxter, b. ———. Mentioned in his father's will, supposed to be the son of his second wife, Hannah (Reed) Bates.

A 159

Jonathan Reed, son of Ebenezer and Hannah (Thompson) Reed.
b. July 9, 1740; d. ———, 1769.
m. Apr. 28, 1763, Mary Tirrel.

His children are mentioned in their grandfather's (Ebenezer Reed), will.

Of Abington, Mass.

CHILDREN

364. Hannah, b. July 13, 1764.
365. Jonathan, b. Feb. 2, 1767; m. April 23, 1788, Deborah Porter.
366. Molly, b. May 6, 1769.

A 161

Silas Reed, son of Ebenezer and Hannah (Thompson) Reed.
b. at Abington Mar. 3, 1743; d. Aug. 3, 1797.
m. 1st. ———, Rebecca ———.
m. 2nd. ———, Mary ———.

Of Abington, Mass.

CHILDREN OF SILAS AND REBECCA

367. Abigail, b. (at Cummington), Nov. 2, 1768; m. Aug. 6, 1789, George Cole.
368. Patience, b. June 21, 1770; m. Jan. 2, 1791, Joel Randall.
369. Hannah, b. Feb. 18, 1772; m. Dec. 1, 1799, N. Tower.
370. John, b. Aug. 14, 1773; m. 1st. Jan. 1, 1798, Hannah Waters; m. 2d. Jerusha ———.

CHILDREN OF SILAS AND MARY

371. Eunice, b. Jan. 21, 1779.
372. Rebecca, b. Nov. 2, 1780.
373. Mary, b. Jan. 14, 1782.
374. Asa, b. Nov. 1, 1784.

A 163

Barnabas Reed, son of Ebenezer and Hannah (Thompson) Reed.

b. (at Abington) Apr. 5, 1748.

m. ———, Silence Sprague; after her husband's death she moved to Plainfield, Mass.

Lived at Abington, Mass.

CHILDREN

375. Polly, b. March 6, 1775; m. Sept. 3, 1796, Oliver Tirrell, of Plainfield, Hampshire Co., Mass.
376. Sarah, b. Oct. 14, 1776; m. April 14, 1799, John Ford, of Ashfield, Mass.
377. Barnabas, b. May 22, 1780; d. in 1835, in Abington, Mass., unmarried.
378. Wealthy, b. March 9, 1782; d. in Plainfield, Mass., in 1831.
379. William, b. May 6, 1783; d. Sept. 20, 1860; m. Jan. 11, 1814, Lovisa Beals.
380. Elizabeth, b. Dec. 23, 1785; d. May 17, 1849; m. May 13, 1802, Joseph Beals.
381. Joshua, b. March 6, 1788; d. March 1, 1835; m. Nov. 6, 1817, Susannah Noyes, of Plainfield.
382. Annis, b. in 1790; m. Benjamin Towne.

A 166

Micah Reed, son of Daniel and Ruth (White) Reed.

b. Feb. 1, 1742.

m. Oct. 20, 1767, Deborah Thompson of Halifax, Mass.

Of Weymouth, Mass.

WILL OF DEBORAH REED

"In the name of God Amen,—I Deborah Reed of Weymouth, in the County of Norfolk & Commonwealth of Massachusetts, Spinster, considering the uncertainty of this mortal life, and being of sound and perfect mind and memory, blessed be Almighty God for the same, do make and publish this my last will and testament in manner and form following Viz:—

"First—I give to my son Seth Reed one dollar and the same to be paid him in one year after my decease.

"Item:—I give to my son Noah Reed one dollar and the same to be paid him in one year after my decease.

"Item:—I give to my daughter Nabby Reed my best bed bed stead & a full set of the best bedding I have, also one cow I give her.

"Item:—I give and bequeath to my five daughters (viz) Susanna Gloyd the wife of David Gloyd, Hitty Hunt the wife of Seth Hunt, Mercy Noyes the wife of Benjamin Noyes, Ruth Blanchard the wife of Bela Blanchard & Nabby Reed all my wearing apperel after my decease.

"Item:—I give and bequeath to my daughter Susanna Gloyd one fifth part of all my estate both real & personal, wherever it may be found after the payment of my just debts & funeral charges to her & her heirs and assigns forever.

"Item:—I give and bequeath to my daughter Hitty Hunt one fifth part of all my estate real & personal wherever it may be found after the payment of my just debts and funeral charges to her, her & heirs & assigns forever.

"Item:—I give and bequeath to my daughter Nabby Reed one fifth part of all my estate real & personal wherever it may be found after the payment of my just debts and funeral charges & to her heirs & assigns forever.

"Item:—I give and bequeath to my daughter Mercy Noyes the wife of Benjamin Noyes the improvement of one fifth part of all my estate real and personal after the payment of my just debts & funeral charges & it is my will that the same shall not be disposed of in any way or manner whereby the principal may be lessened & that she hold the improvement during her life time, after which it is my will that the same go to her heirs as a free estate & inheritance forever that is to say one fifth part of my estate.

"Item:—I give and bequeath to my daughter Ruth Blanchard the wife of Bela Blanchard the improvement of one fifth part of all my estate, real & personal wherever it may be found after the payment of my just debts & funeral charges & it is my will that the same shall not be disposed of in any way or manner, whereby the principal may be lessened, & that she hold the improvement during her

lifetime, after which time it is my will that the one fifth part go to her heirs as a free estate & inheritance forever.

"And I hereby appoint Seth Hunt and David Gloyd joint & sole executors of this my last will and testament, ordering them to pay my just debts & funeral charges and the several legacies mentioned in this will, & I hereby revoke and disannul all other wills by me made and establish this as my last will and testament. In witness whereof I have hereunto set my hand & seal this eleventh day of April in the year of our Lord one thousand eight hundred & four.

"Signed, sealed published & declared by the above named Deborah Reed to be her last will & testament in the presence of us who have hereunto subscribed our names as witnesses in the presence of the testatrix.

Eliphalet Loud — Deborah Reed (Seal)"
Asa White 2nd.
Benjamin Derby

CHILDREN

383. Susannah, b. Sept. 6, 1770; m. Oct. 20, 1797, David Gloyd.
384. Mehetable, b. Dec. 23, 1771; m. Seth Hunt.
385. Mercy, b. April 21, 1772; m. Dec. 3, 1793, Benjamin Noyes.
386. Enoch, b. Feb. 11, 1773.
387. Seth, b. Jan. 9, 1776; d. Dec. 19, 1853; m. July 4, 1804, Hannah Shaw.
388. Ruth, b. July 3, 1778; m. Jan. 23, 1800, Bela Blanchard, of Weymouth, Mass.
389. Noah, b. April 22, 1781; m. Susannah White.
390. Abigail, b. Nov. 13, 1784; d. unmarried.

A 167

Jesse Reed, son of Daniel and Ruth (White) Reed.

b. Mar. 16, 1745.

m. Nov. 18, 1781, Mrs. Ruth Whitman of Weymouth.

They were married by Rev. Simeon Williams.

After the death of her husband, she married a Mr. Johnson.

He was of Charlemont, and was a minister of the Congregational Church. He graduated from Princeton College in 1769.

ABSTRACTS FROM RECORDS OF HAMPSHIRE COUNTY, MASS.

"Power of Administration of all and singular the Goods and Chattels Rights, and Credits which were of Jesse Reed late of Charlemont in the County of Hampshire, Deceased, is this day granted unto Ruth Reed and bond is taken for her faithful performance of said trust.

March 6th, 1792."

"On petition of Ruth Reed administratrix on the estate of Jesse Reed late of Charlemont in the County of Hampshire, deceased, representing said estate as insolvent and insufficient to discharge the debts due therefrom Commissions on insolvency are granted unto Messers Artemas Rice, Moses Heaton and Calvin Rice all of said Charlemont and 12 months are allowed the creditors to said estate to bring in and support their claim.

E. Porter

March 6th, 1792— Judge of Probate."

Hampshire County, ss.
Registry of Probate.

Northampton, Mass, May 12th, A. D. 1899.

A true copy. Attest:

Hubbard M. Abbott,
Register.

CHILDREN

391. Jesse, b. ———; m. ———. Was in Plainfield.
392. Lorenzo, b. ———; m. ———. Was in Plainfield.
393. Ruth, b. ———; m. ———. Settled in Clairmont.
394. Sarah, b. ———; m. ———. Settled in Clairmont.

A 169

Seth Reed, son of Daniel and Ruth (White) Reed.

b. July 16, 1750.

m. 1st in 1773, Thankful Whitmarsh, she died in Cummington June 2, 1775.

m. 2nd in 1776, Mary Lazell of Bridgewater; b. in 1754, daughter of Isaiah and Bathia (Alger) Lazell.

Of Cummington, Mass.

CHILDREN

395. Olive, b. in 1774; d. Jan. 2, 1775, in Cummington, Mass.
396. Seth, b. in 1777; d. Dec. 19, 1853; m. Jan. 10, 1801, Catherine Brown.

A 171

Noah Reed, son of Daniel and Ruth (White) Reed.

b. Dec. 10, 1754; d. Jan. 19, 1832.

m. July 12, 1784, Abigail Rice, daughter of Sylvanus Rice of Charlemont; she d. Oct. 9, 1837.

Settled in Cummington, Mass.

CHILDREN

397. Abigail, b. April 16, 1785; d. Feb. 14, 1853, at Plainfield; m. Feb., 1812, Salem Streeter.
398. Daniel, b. Nov. 5, 1786; d. (at Cummington) Nov. 29, 1854; m. Oct. 20, 1814, Cynthia Warner.
399. Ruth, b. June 21, 1789; m. Oct. 10, 1825, Josiah Shaw, settled in Cummington.
400. Nancy, b. April 30, 1791. Lived at Sharon, Mass.
401. Olive, b. Dec. 15, 1793; m. Nov., 1840, Joseph Tolman, lived at Sharon.
402. Jesse, b. March 25, 1796; m. Feb. 19, 1829, Mary (Davis) Griswold.
403. Orpha, b. June 12, 1805; m. Jan. 25, 1825, Alonzo Gurney.

A 174

Solomon Reed, son of James and Abigail (Nash) Reed.

b. Oct. 25, 1743.

m. Sept. 28, 1765, Mercy Tirrel.

Of Abington, Mass.

CHILD

404. Molly Gurney, b. Nov. 22, 1766. Mentioned in her Aunt Huldah's will.

A 175

Adam Reed, son of James and Abigail (Nash) Reed.

b. Aug. 17, 1745.

m. July 14, 1768, Silence Reed.

Of Abington, Mass.

WILL

"In the name of God Amen—This twenty sixth day of May A. D. 1791—I Adam Reed of Abington in the County of Plymouth & Commonwealth of Massachusetts Bay in New England, yeoman, being apprehensive of my approaching change, but of perfect mind and memory thanks be given to God therefor calling to mind the mortality of my body, and knowing that it is appointed for all once to die, do make and ordain this my last will and testament, that is to say, principally and first of all, I give and recommend my soul to God who made it, and my body I recommend to the earth to be buried in Christian decent burial at the discretion of my executrix nothing doubting but at the general resurrection, I shall receive the same again by ye mighty power of God, and as touching such worldly estate, wherewith it has pleased God to bless me with in this life, I give devise and dispose of the same after my just debts & funeral charges are paid in the following manner and form—

"Imprimis:—I give and bequeath to my well beloved wife to improve all my housing & lands (that is to say) during the time of her remaining my widow, also my will is that my wife shall have all my household moveables, and all outdoor moveables, as likewise all notes obligations, my will is that the above said moveables, be to her own disposal to whom she will, it is also my will that my wife shall be sole executrix of this my last will & testament, and do hereby constitute, ordain & appoint my well beloved wife to be sole executrix of this my last will & testament, also it is my will that after the death of my wife my real estate be disposed of in the following manner, and it is my will that my beloved wife to have & hold & dispose of as she sees fit all the lands she has deed of—I give to my sister Tabitha Lincoln's son David the eighth part of all my lands and real estate, to him, his heirs & assigns forever (excepting the improvement) of the same which shall be to his mother to improve during her life.

"Item:—I give my brother James Reed's son Abel Reed

the eighth part of all my lands and real estate, to him his heirs and assigns forever.

"Item:—I give unto Paul Reed one fourth part of all my lands & real estate, to him his heirs and assigns forever.

"Item:—I give Thomas Hearsey the eighth part of my real estate and lands, to him his heirs & assigns forever.

"Item:—I give unto Joel Reed the eighth part of all my lands & real estate, to him his heirs and assigns forever.

"Item:—I give unto Adam son of Obadiah Reed Junr. the eighth part of all my lands & real estate, to him his heirs & assigns forever.

"Item:—I give unto my beloved wife all the lands and real estate in Abington and Bridgewater, and all my other estate both real & personal that I have not disposed of already as expressed above to her & her heirs and assigns forever, and I hereby disallow disannul and revoke all and every other testament, legacies and bequests & executors by me before named, willed or bequeathed, ratifying and confirming this and no other to be my last will & testament.

"In witness whereof I the said Adam Reed have hereunto set my hand & seal the year and day above written.

Adam Reed (Seal)"

"Signed sealed published and pronounced & declared by the said Adam Reed to be his last will & testament in the presence of us the subscribers.

Obadiah Reed
Jonathan Noyes
Samuel Noyes."

CHILD

405. Adam, b. ———; m. Feb. 25, 1819, Mary Porter.

A 178

Abel Reed, son of James and Abigail (Nash) Reed.
b. Apr. 15, 1754.

Died in service of the Revolutionary Army (see Hobart's His. of Abington, p. 269).

A 180

James Reed, son of James and Abigail (Nash) Reed.
b. June 24, 1758; d. Feb. 16, 1827.
m. May 19, 1779, Susannah Niles.

CHILDREN

406. Abel, b. Sept. 5, 1780; d. 1817; m. Lydia Loud, of Plymouth.
407. Susannah, b. Feb. 18, 1782.
408. Ruth Porter, b. Dec. 14, 1783.
409. Goddard, b. ———; m. and lived in Randolph.
410. Abigail, b. ———. See Huldah Reed's will.

A 182

Rev. John Reed, son of Rev. Solomon and Abigail (Stoughton) Reed of Conn.
b. Nov. 11, 1751; d. Feb. 17, 1831.
m. 1st in 1780, Hannah Sampson; she died in 1815.
m. 2nd. in 1822, Mrs. Phoebe (Sampson) Paddock, sister of his first wife (see J. W. R. extended account, p. 361).
Of West Bridgewater.

Rev. John Reed graduated at Yale College in 1772. He prepared for the ministry under the instruction of his father, in Titicut; and after the Declaration of Independence, was for some time chaplain in the United States Navy. On the 7th of January, 1780, he was ordained as pastor of the Congregational Church and Society in West Bridgewater; being the third minister in that ancient parish.

Mr. Reed was a man of remarkably clear and discriminating intellect; was known and acknowledged by the strong minds of his time as a master of logic—of the great art of thinking and reasoning correctly. In the earnest theological discussions between the Hopkinsians and the Arminians at the large clerical gatherings of fifty years ago, he always stood forward as the champion of the liberal doctrine. By his ready exposure of sophistry and his clear and forcible statements, the success of his argument was generally triumphant and crushing.

Soon after the adoption of the Federal Constitution, the

almost unanimous sentiment of his Congressional District, pointed to him as eminently qualified, by his ardent patriotism, his sound judgment, his readiness and power in debate, for the office of representative in Congress; and in 1794, he was elected to fill the office which he held for six years, through three successive Congressional terms; at the close of which time he declined a re-election. In 1803, he received the degree of Doctor of Divinity from Brown University. Several of his discourses were published; and about the year 1805, he published a duodecimo volume on the subject of infant baptism.

In his intercourse with men, Mr. Reed's manner, notwithstanding his high intellectual claims, was always marked with great modesty and evident humility of spirit. His public discourses, always clear and convincing, were most noticeable, perhaps for their strength and pathos. In his devotional performance, his manner was most devout and reverential, and indicated unusual absorption of mind. He had the entire confidence and respect of his people, and performed among them, with great discretion and faithfulness, the duties of the Christian ministry for upwards of fifty years. Near the close of his life, he became entirely blind; but continued still to preach, and to perform other duties of his profession. He died Feb. 17, 1831, in his eightieth year. It is to be regretted that there is no print of his remarkably fine head.

Children of John and Hannah

411. John, b. Sept. 2, 1781; m. Olive Alger, daughter of Aliezer Alger, of W. Bridgewater, Mass.
412. Daniel, b. Aug. 29, 1783; m. in 1812, Nancy Foster.
413. Hannah, b. Dec. 15, 1785; d. Feb. 20, 1786.
414. Solomon, b. March 22, 1788; m. in 1811, Abigail Howard, daughter of Geo. Howard.
415. Hannah, b. July 7, 1790; m. in 1818, Jonathan Copeland, 3d.
416. Sally, b. March 21, 1793; d. April 27, 1797.
417. Caleb, b. April 22, 1797; d. Oct. 14, 1854; m. 1st. July, 1838, Mary E. Minot; m. 2d. Nov., 1847, Ruth Cobb.
418. Sampson, b. June 10, 1800; m. Dec. 25, 1832, Catherine Clark.

A 183

Rev. Solomon Reed, son of Rev. Solomon and Abigail (Stoughton) Reed of Conn.

b. Mar. 18, 1753; d. Feb. 2, 1808, at Petersham, Mass.; inscription on tombstone "Second pastor of Church of Christ who died in this town Feb. 2, 1808 ae. 55."

m. Mar. 14, 1781, Susannah Willard, daughter of Col. Josiah and Hannah Willard of Winchester, N. H. (she was born June 2, 1757).

He graduated at Yale College in 1775; was ordained as minister of the Congregational Church of Petersham, Mass. He was represented to be a man of large frame and great physical power. His boldness and determination of character are illustrated by an incident at the time of Shay's rebellion, the account of which is from a reliable source. It relates that a party of Shay's troops came to Mr. Reed's house during a bad snow storm, one Sunday morning; turned Mr. Reed's cattle out of his barn and put their horses in; and at the same time took possession of his house, putting their camp kettles in the several fire places, and having things their own way. So great was the confusion that the Sabbath services were entirely interrupted; and when he had time to collect himself and determine his course of action, he went to the barn turned the horses out and put his own cattle back in their place; and in the house he passed from room to room manifesting such resolute determination that the troops were awed and restrained from violence. The result was that the report of the near approach of Genl. Bowdoin's troops induced the Shay party to decamp, in such haste as to leave several camp kettles behind them, and gave an opportunity of an uninterrupted afternoon service. (From J. W. R. Book, p. 370.) His widow married Asahel Pomeroy of Northampton, Mass., Feb. 24, 1763, and died Jan. 26, 1826, aged sixty-nine years.

The following inscription taken from his wife's father's tombstone, in Evergreen Cemetery, Winchester, N. H., will be of interest to their descendants:

"Col. Josiah Willard, who died April ye 19th, 1786, in the 72nd year of his age. His birth and education which were honorable he dishonored not in his youth. At an early period of his existence he began to figure on the stage of life, his disposition and manners were engaging, his connections numerous and respectable. His vocations various and important, his influence and usefullness equally extensive, and ye present populous and flourishing state of these western territories may be attributed in a great measure to his vigorous and laudable exertions in promoting ye settlement and cultivating of ye wilderness. His principles and morals were unimpeachable his faith and practice truly evangelical, sensible, sociable and benevolent. His heart and doors were always open to his friends in general and to ye learned regular and reputable among ye clergy in particular. He lived and died in a firm belief of ye Gospel, supported and animated to ye end of his course by ye hope and prospect of an immortal crown. His family and friends in his death sustain a loss irreparable. He will be had long in remembrance.

"The wise will imitate his virtue, and fools will lament they did not when he shall rise immoral."

CHILDREN

419. Solomon, b. July 23, 1783; d. May 15, 1846; m. Lucy Ward, of Petersham, June, 1811.

420. Susannah Willard, b. Dec. 8, 1781; d. 1854; m. Dec., 1813, John Drury, of Colrain, Mass.

421. Mary, b. March 5, 1785; d. Jan. 16, 1835, at Rowe, Mass., unmarried.

422. Josiah Willard, b. Sept. 7, 1790; d. Oct. 29, 1835; m. 1st. Fanny Hunt, of Northampton, Oct. 8, 1821; m. 2d. March 25, 1833, Lucina Warner, of Charlemont.

423. Hannah Willard, b. Jan. 14, 1787; d. 1821; m. Dr. Joseph H. Flint, of Petersham, Sept., 1811.

424. Sarah, b. March 6, 1788; d. 1844; m. Jan. 20, 1811, Col. Noah Wells, of Rowe.

425. Samuel Horton, b. Oct. 27, 1794; d. 1874; m. 1st. Elizabeth Foster, of Rowe, Sept. 17, 1818; m. 2d. Hannah Foster, of Rowe, May 3, 1825.

426. John, b. Dec. 24, 1792; d. Oct. 9, 1802, at Petersham, Mass.
427. William, b. Jan. 12, 1797; d. Jan. 25, 1814; attended Williams College.
428. Catherine, b. March 28, 1799; d. Oct. 18, 1802, at Petersham, Mass.

A 184

Rev. Samuel Reed, son of Rev. Solomon and Abigail (Stoughton) Reed of Conn.

b. ———, 1754; d. July 13, 1812, aged 57 and in the 33rd year of his ministry.

m. 1780, Anna Shaw.

Of Warwick, Mass. (see J. W. R. extended acct., p. 370).

Samuel Reed graduated at Yale College in 1777; ordained over the church and society of Warwick, Mass., in 1779. He was a man of sound sense; a devoted Christian, and much beloved by his people, and the community generally. After his death his bereaved flock erected a monument to his memory. It is a marble tablet, supported by four pillars over his grave with the following inscription:

REV. SAMUEL REED.

Second minister in Warwick,
Died July 31st. 1812, aged 57.

He had strong powers of mind; was bold in defense of the truth; severe against wickedness; mild towards the humble; pitiful to the distressed; affectionate towards his friends.

Frank and sincere in all his professions; rational and fervent in his piety; faithful in his pastoral duties.

He taught the Christian doctrine in its simplicity and truth; he maintained the freedom of the human mind, the unchangeable obligations of moral duty, the impartial justice of God, and future retribution.

Under the vital impression of this faith, he felt, and communicated the cheering entertainments of life, and enjoyed the richest solace and triumph in death.

CHILDREN

429. Samuel, b. March 23, 1781; d. young.
430. Anna, b. April 19, 1784; d. 1835 (in Warwick); m. Dec., 1813, Deacon Joseph Wilson.
431. Abigail, b. Feb. 17, 1786; m. Dec., 1805, Joel Mayo.
432. Samuel, b. April 25, 1788; m. Melinda Wheelock.
433. Stephen, b. Nov. 5, 1790; d. 1847; m. Jerusha Moor.
434. Timothy, b. July 10, 1793; d. 1853; m. Susan Kingsley.

A 185

Timothy Reed, son of Rev. Solomon and Abigail (Stoughton) Reed of Conn.

b. in Framingham, 1756; d. ———, 1813.

m. in 1788, Hannah Kingman; she died May 7, 1849, daughter of Caleb and Freelove (Fenno) Kingman.

Graduated at Yale College in 1782, was a lawyer and resided at West Bridgewater.

CHILDREN

435. Caleb Kingman, b. 1789; d. 1796.
436. Caleb Kingman, b. 1799; d. 1837, unmarried.

A 191

Samuel Reed (of Abington), son of John and Mary (Torrey) Reed.

b. Nov. 10, 1740.

m. Nov. 29, 1764, Mary Torrey, both of Weymouth. Married by Rev. Wm. Smith.

He was a school teacher, selectman, &c. Was residuary legatee to his father, inheriting the bulk of his estate.

CHILDREN

437. Samuel, b. Sept. 16, 1765; d. Feb. 28, 1853, m. Nov. 17, 1793, Mary Greenleaf.
438. John, b. May 9, 1767; d. March 5, 1852; m. 1st. Nov. 29, 1792, Elizabeth Gould; m. 2d. Martha (Gould) Swain.

439. Hannah, b. Oct. 4, 1769; m. Feb. 9, 1795, Alexander Arnold, of Weymouth.
440. Thomas, b. Dec. 10, 1771; d. Jan. 12, 1843; m. Sept. 12, 1792, Sarah White.
441. Mary, b. July 17, 1774; d. unmarried.
442. Philip, b. July 31, 1777; m. Polly Taylor, of Hanover.
443. Sarah, b. April 20, 1780; m. Jonas Halstrom.
444. William, b. Aug. 12, 1783; m. ———.

A 194

Joseph Reed, son of James and widow Ruth Ford (Pool) Reed.

b. Aug. 9, 1742.

Was unmarried.

Of East Bridgewater, Mass.

WILL

"In the name of God Amen—ye first day of September in the year of our Lord one thousand, seven hundred & seventy six—

"I Joseph Reed of Bridgewater in the County of Plymouth & Province of the Massachusetts Bay in New England, yeoman, being in declining state of Bodily health, but of perfect mind & memory thanks be to God therefore, & calling to mind the mortality of my body, knowing that it is appointed for all men once to die, do make & ordain this my last will & testament, that is to say, principally & first of all I give & recommend my soul into the hands of God that gave it & my body I recommend to the Earth to be buried in decent burial & as touching such worldly estate wherewith it has pleased God to bless me in this life, I give & dispose of the same in the following manner & form.

"I give to my well beloved brother Hezekiah ten dollars & to his children when come of age twenty six pounds, thirteen shillings & four pence & of the rest I give to my well beloved brother Jeremiah for him to settle all my accounts & concerns whatever & of what there may be left for him to let my well beloved sister Naomi, have one third part

of it & the two thirds I give to my well beloved brother Jeremiah, whom I constitute & ordain my sole executor of this my last will & testament—

"In witness whereof I have hereunto set my hand & seal the day & year first & fore written—signed sealed & declared by ye sd. Joseph Reed as his last will & testament in the presence of us.

Anthony Dike his
Isaac Otis Joseph (X) Reed (Seal)"
mark

A 195

Hezekiah Reed, son of James and (Widow) Ruth Ford (Pool) Reed.

b. Feb. 23, 1744.

m. May 16, 1766, Deborah Tirrel of Abington; she died in 1820, aged seventy-three.

Settled in East Bridgewater, Mass.

Record at Plymouth setting off to his wife Deborah her dower. He left no will.

ORDER OF COURT

"Plymouth ss—To Messrs. Daniel Shaw, Jacob Pool and Samuel Pool all of Abington in the county aforesaid—Gentlemen—Greeting—

"(Seal) You are hereby empowered and directed to take a view of that part of the real estate whereof James Reed late of Abington, in said county yeoman, decd. died seized, which was assigned and set off to Ruth Reed, the widow of said decd. as her thirds or right of dower in said decd. estate and you are to assign and set off to Deborah Reed the widow of Hezekiah Reed, late of Bridgewater decd. her thirds or right of dower therein, and you are to assign and set off the same by metes & bounds (quantity and quality considered) so that she may hold & improve the same in severalty during her life—and you are to make return of the warrant with

your doings thereon, under your hand & upon your oaths, as soon as conveniently may be.

"Given under my hand & seal of Office at Plymouth in sd. County this 13th day of March 1792.

Joshua Thomas, Judge of Probt."

"To the Honorable Joshua Thomas Esq. Judge of Probate of wills for the County of Plymouth—Sir—In compliance to the directions of your warrant to us directed, we the subscribers have taken a view of that part of the real estate whereof James Reed late of Abington, in sd. County, yeoman decd. died seized, which was assigned and set off to Ruth Reed the widow of said deceased as her thirds or right of dower in sd. decd. estate and have assigned and set off to Deborah Reed the widow of Hezekiah Reed late of Bridgewater decd. her thirds or right of dower therein by metes & bounds, (quantity & quality considered) Viz.—one acre & a half of land lying in Bridgewater, bounded as follows, viz—

"Beginning at a stake & stones by a stone wall, thence running east 7 degrees 1/2 north ten rods & four feet to a stake & stones, then south six degrees, east twenty three rods & 7 feet to a stone wall by Thomas Torrey's land, then westerly by sd. Torrey's land, ten rods & four feet to a wall, then north six degrees west by said wall, twenty three rods & seven feet to the corner first mentioned—said acre 1/2 half of land being the orchard that formerly belonged to the above said James Reed deceased.

"Bridgewater, April 2, 1792.

Daniel Shaw.
Samuel Pool.
Jacob Pool."

CHILDREN

445. Deborah, b. 1768.
446. Olive, b. 1770.
447. James, b. 1772; d. young.
448. Isaac, b. 1774; m. in 1803, Sally Stetson.
449. Jeremiah, b. 1777; m. March 3, 1803, Rebecca Jenkins.
450. Calvin, b. 1780; m. Oct. 15, 1807, Hannah Ludden.
451. Joseph, b. Oct. 18, 1782; m. in 1807, Charlotte Stetson.

452. Jared, b. 1785; d. 1855; m. 1st. in 1811, Mehetable Gardner; m. 2d. Nov. 25, 1832, Electa Phillips.
453. Nancy, b. 1789.

A 196

Jeremiah Reed, son of James and (widow) Ruth (Pool) Reed.
b. Apr. 11, 1747.
m. ———, Sarah Tirrel.
Of East Bridgewater, Mass.

CHILDREN

454. Obadiah, b. ———.
455. Olive, b. ———.

A 199

Ezekiel Reed, son of Ezekiel and Hannah (Beal) Reed.
b. Mar. 3, 1744 in Abington.
m. Apr. 2, 1768, Mary Rogers of Marshfield.
Of Abington, Mass.

Hayward's Gazetteer of Mass., says: "Another important manufacture took its rise early in this town, (Abington), viz. the manufacture of cut nails and brads. The making of tacks by hand commenced early. But the mode of making by hand was much improved upon by moveable dies placed in an frame like an ox-bow, and brought together by the pressure of the foot. This was a great improvement and the inventor, Mr. Ezekiel Reed was entitled to a patent. In 1815 and 1816 a machine was invented by Jesse Reed, son of Ezekiel Reed, to make tacks in one operation. They were soon after much improved by Thomas Blanchard and others. For the exclusive patent rights of these inventions Elihu and Benj. Hobart paid thirty thousand dollars. The price of tacks was reduced 50% immediately. When they had just got their machines in operation they learned that a large consignment of tacks had been received in this country from England, and their tacks sent over here for sale. Under these circumstances they were led to look to our Government for relief and protection. A Bill was im-

mediately passed in Congress fixing the duty on imported tacks at five cents per hundred, up to 16 oz. tacks and after that at 5 cents per pound, and also including brads and sparables. Without this tax the business must have been given up in this country.

It is also claimed for Ezekiel Reed that he made the first wooden clocks made in the United States. His brother Samuel is reported to have owned one of them with maker's name on the face. Cyrus M. Reed the grandson of Samuel Reed, wrote that he had seen it many times.

CHILDREN

456. Polly, b. 1769.
457. Zelotes, b. 1771.
458. Ezekiel, b. Sept. 16, 1772; m. 1st. in 1794, Rebecca Edson; m. 2d. Oct. 27, 1808, Hannah Littlefield; m. 3d. Dec. 10, 1845, Polly Luddens.
459. Zebulon, b. 1774.
460. Hannah, b. 1776.
461. Olive, b. 1777.
462. Jesse, b. 1778; m. 1st. in 1800, Hannah Howard; m. 2d. May 28, 1850, Lovisa Lindsey.
463. Charles, b. ———.
464. Abraham, b. ———.
465. Briggs Rogers, b. May 2, 1784; d. Sept. 28, 1835; m. May 21, 1809, Betsy Hutchinson, of Danvers.
466. Samuel Licander, b. July 24, 1786; m. Feb. 27, 1817, Nancy Gray, of Watertown, Mass.

A 205

Samuel Reed, son of Ezekiel and Hannah (Beal) Reed.
b. Dec. 25' 1756, in Abington; d. Apr. 24, 1826.
m. June 18, 1781, Betsy Smith of Grafton.

His father having died when he was about seven years of age he was bound to Deacon Whitmarsh, a shoemaker.

When the war of the Revolution broke out everybody went to war; and Deacon Whitmarsh turned out his bound boy to go to the war, he being about twenty years of age.

All of their children were born in Chesterfield, Mass.

Cyrus M. Reed, son of Simeon Reed, says, "In searching the town records of Chesterfield, Mass., I find Samuel Reed came from Abington and settled in Chesterfield about 1778 or 1780."

Hobart's History of Abington says of the old French War, "This war was waged between England and France, continued seven years and terminated in 1763. Abington contributed largely of her strength to carry on this war. The following persons were in the service and died therein or on their way home at the close of that war." Then follows a list of nineteen and among them is Ezekiel son of John Reed. "This substantiates the testimony of Nelson K. and Ellen R. Reed, that their grandfather was a soldier in the French and English war, and died on shipboard and was buried at sea at the close of the war of 1763."

Ellen R. Reed of Brockport copies some records left her by her father, Daniel Reed, to the effect that Samuel Reed (our grandfather), was bound to one Dea. Whitmarsh a shoemaker. "When the Revolutionary War broke out everybody went to war, including Samuel Reed our grandfather, then not quite twenty years old. He served three years. At one time while out on a scout with twelve others they suddenly came upon a company of Red Coats who fired upon them. Some threw down their arms and fled. Grandfather ran but the straps of his knapsack caught in a bush. While trying to disentangle himself the bullets flew thick around him. He thus became separated from his comrades and it was several weeks before he could find his command, as they had moved and he could get no trace of them in that sparsely settled country." Hobart's History of Abington substantiates all this by saying:

"Ebenezer Whitmarsh and family were probably in Abington some time before 1712." He says further in speaking of the war of the Revolution: "Almost every man capable of bearing arms was in the war for a shorter or longer period." This explains why Dea. Whitmarsh was called on to turn out his bound boy.

CHILDREN

467. Samuel, Jr., b. Sept. 1, 1782; d. April 13, 1869; m. 1st. March 7, 1805, Sally Bates, of Worthington; m. 2d. Feb. 16, 1823, Sarah Teasiear, who died Oct. 16, 1849.
468. Betsy, b. March 13, 1784; d. Aug. 14, 1850; m. Feb. 22, 1804, Joseph Nash, of Cummington, Mass.
469. Daniel, b. July 26, 1786; d. Feb. 28, 1874; m. 1st. in 1804, Lucy Bates; m. 2d. Mercy Nash; m. 3d. Marrilla Knapp.
470. Simeon, b. March 30, 1789; d. Nov. 3, 1865; m. 1st. Feb. 14, 1814, Bersheba Thayer; m. 2d. May 4, 1820, Mary Whitton; m. 3d. Nov. 22, 1851, Mrs. Eunice (Swan) Reed.
471. Hannah, b. July 29, 1791; d. April 5, 1794.
472. Joseph, b. May 26, 1793; d. Nov. 25, 1866; m. Sept. 9, 1813, Wealthy Williams. Were married in New York.
473. Olive, b. July 19, 1795; d. May 22, 1807.
474. Solomon, b. May 22, 1797; d. Oct. 5, 1800.
475. Sally, b. June 6, 1799; d. July 11, 1882; m. June 16, 1815, Luther Tower.
476. Susan, b. June 30, 1801; d. May 15, 1875; m. 1st. Josiah Pettingill, Jan. 2, 1822; m. 2d. May 22, 1825, Thomas W. Stearns.
477. Polly E., b. July 27, 1803; d. May 5, 1866; m. ——— Bates.
478. Alanson, b. June 21, 1807; d. Aug. 29, 1837; m. Jane Everetts.

A 206

Issachar Reed, son Ezekiel and Hannah (Beal) Reed.

b. Aug. 9, 1759 (said to have lived to a great age, nearly one hundred years).

m. ———.

Lived in Rutland, Vt.

Was a merchant, the only one in the town at that time, and kept a hotel and resided about three miles east of what is now called Rutland. He belonged to the Free Masons and was a grandmaster. He was a Presbyterian. His only daughter, Marcia, married a gentleman named Green, a merchant, who was robbed and murdered one night on his way from his store.

CHILDREN

479. John, b. ———.
480. Freeman, b. ———.
481. Willard, b. ———.
482. Marcia, b. ———; m. ——— Green.

A 209

Benjamin Reed, son of Peter and Lucy (Hugens) Reed.

b. May 3, 1752, probably in Abington, Mass.; d. Jan. 10, 1835, in Putney, Vt.

m. Dec. 3, 1778, Huldah Pratt of Bridgewater, Mass., who was born May 10, 1760; died May 17, 1842, at the age of eighty-two.

Of Cummington, Mass.

The Abington Town Records read "Benj. Reed of No. 5 (which was Cummington, Mass.) and Miss Huldah Pratt of Bridgewater was married Dec. the 3rd. 1778."

The Pratt family attended church in Abington, nothing is yet known of the antecedents of Huldah, who died May 17, 1842, aged eighty-two, seven years after the death of Benjamin.

Huldah Pratt died in Putney, Vt., and lies buried beside her husband Benjamin, in the East Putney or Putney Falls Cemetery. The stone marking her grave reads "Huldah widow of Benjamin Reed died May 17, 1842, Aged 82—

'Adieu my friends and children daer,
Who in the worl remain;
May virtue be your practice here
Till wee do meet again.'"

Benjamin probably went to Cummington from Abington between 1770 and 1775, about the time that Daniel Reed, son of William and Alice (Nash) Reed, and who was first Moderator at Cummington, went there. At the age of twenty-three Benjamin enlisted at Cummington, April 21, 1775, as a minute man, at the Lexington Alarm. He served almost continuously in the Revolutionary struggle, from this date, until the final date of discharge, Nov. 29, 1777.

He was in the company commanded by Capt. Abel Thayer and Lt. Joseph Warner, from Cummington and Williamsborough. Was in the siege of Boston, in the Eighth Regt. of Foot, posted in Dorchester, commanded by Col. John Fel-

lows, Oct., 1775. His name is on the "Coat Rolls," Nov. 22, 1775; was at Morristown, March. 15, 1777, in Capt. Jonathan Wales' Co., Regt. commanded by Lt. Col. S. Williams.

In the northern army in Capt. Joseph Warner's Co. and Col. Ruggles' Woodbridge Regt. Aug. 18, 1777, to Nov. 29, 1777, being engaged in the battle of Saratoga, Oct. 7, 1777. These abstracts are from a certified copy from Mass. State (Revolutionary) Archives.

The Department of the Interior, Bureau of Pensions, at Washington, has this record of his application for a pension. "He first entered the service in the year 1775. Discharged finally sometime during the year 1777, having rendered nine months actual service as a private and eight months actual service as a corporal with the Massachusetts troops. He mentions the following as officers under whom he served: Capt. Thayer and Capt. Warner. Engaged at Saratoga. Residence at the time of enlistment Cummington, Mass. Date of application for pension July 24, 1832, residence at date of application Putney, Vt., age at date of application 80 years." His pension was allowed.

This was fifty-five years after his discharge, when old and infirm. He received only one payment, as he was placed on the pension rolls March, 1834. The amount of his pension was $60 18/100.

"Three months after his marriage he sold land at Cummington, Mass., Mar. 9, 1779" (Registry of deeds, Hampshire Co. Records, Springfield, Mass.); "Apr. 28, 1780, (two months after the death of Peter his father) Benjamin and Huldah sold 45 acres of land in Cummington, Mass., for 100 pounds, to one Jepthah Pool of Windsor." Benjamin is recorded as yeoman in the deed. (Registry of Deeds, Hampshire Co. Records, Springfield, Mass.)

There is no record of the family from this date until 1812 when his fifth child is said to have been living in Newfane, Vt., at the age of twenty-four. Benjamin was thus one of the youngest sons of Vermont, as Vermont was admitted into the Union in 1791.

He was a farmer owning a fine farm on the Connecticut river in East Putney. It was intersected by the Vermont Valley Railroad (afterward Central Vermont), in later years, and its value somewhat impaired. The farm is now owned by Geo. W. Leach (1899) and occupied by his son F. C. Leach. Mrs. Evans, granddaughter of Sarah (Benjamin's sister), remembers (1898) visiting the old house, still standing, and knew Benjamin and Huldah well. She says they were fine people, of good character and well beloved by all who knew them. They were members of the Congregational Church in Putney, Vt. Benjamin was living with his son Luther when he died. He lies buried in East Putney Cemetery. His stone is inscribed:

"Benjamin Read died Jan. 10, 1835, Aged 82 years." His farm went jointly to his sons Calvin and Luther at his death.

CHILDREN

483. Benjamin, b. Aug. 4, or 17, 1779; d. Oct., 1845; m. Fanny Granger.
484. John, b. July 20, or 21, 1781; (Mrs. Roane, of Springfield, Mass., in 1899, says he went to Sacketts Harbor, N. Y. and lived there.)
485. Huldah, b. Aug. 21, 1783; d. Dec. 13, 1813, or 1818.
486. Cyrus, b. Oct. 24, 1786; d. Oct. 14, or 19, 1804.
487. David, b. Nov. 19, 1788; d. July 13, 1842; m. 1st. March 29, 1810, Mary Martha Morse; m. 2d. Nov. 23, 1826, Lucy Keyes.
488. Betsey, b. Aug. 22, 1791; d. March 9, 1801.
489. Calvin, b. Dec. 2, 1793; d. July 26, 1850; m. 1st. Feb. 22, 1830, Mary Reynolds; m. 2d. March 1, 1834, Rebekah E. Jones.
490. Luther, b. April 16, 1796; d. Nov. 27, 1851; m. Feb. 24, 1831, Jerusha Wilson.
491. Nancy, b. Aug. 2, 1798; d. April 2, 1854; m. Truman Glynn.
492. Almira, b. Sept. 9, or 18, 1801; d. July 28, 1835.

A 214

Abijah Reed, son of Jacob and Mary (Ford) Reed.
b. Aug. 14, 1744; d. June 16, 1816, in Easton.
m. Oct. 29, 1768, Sarah Bates.

About 1790 he removed to Easton. He was Deacon of the Church of Rev. William Reed of Easton. He was a man of extraordinary biblical knowledge, an independent thinker, and an earnestly religious man.

Of Easton, Mass.

CHILDREN

493. Sarah, b. April 25, 1770; d. April 15, 1851; m. Lemuel Lothrop, of Bridgewater, Mass.
494. Hannah, b. June 17, 1774; d. young.
495. Abijah, b. Oct. 15, 1776; d. young.
496. Abijah, b. June 5, 1777; m. Catherine Lothrop, of Easton.
497. Noah, b. June 22, 1780; m. Lucy Hayward, of Easton.
498. Hannah, b. March 16, 1790; m. James Lothrop.

A 216

Jacob Reed, son of Jacob and Alice (Reed) Reed.

b. May 6, 1757.

m. Feb. 21, 1782, Sarah Noyes, daughter of Ebenezer Noyes.

He removed from Abington to Farmington, Me., and was a taxpayer in that town in 1798. He afterward removed to Springfield.

Of Springfield, Mass.

CHILDREN

499. Polly, b. Oct. 27, 1782; m. Amos Turner.
500. Sarah, b. April 12, 1784.
501. Alice, b. March 2, 1787.
502. Lucretia, b. June 1, 1789; m. ——— Carey, of North Bridgewater.
503. Jacob, b. June 30, 1791.
504. Nathan, b. ———.

A 221

Bela Reed, son of Jacob and Alice (Reed) Reed.

b. Sept. 2, 1769.

m. Aug. 20, 1795, Mehetable Reed, daughter of Obadiah Reed, of Abington.

He lived on what was called the Old Road, in Easton; was one of a company formed May 1, 1810, to provide machin-

ery for the manufacture of cotton yarn in that place. (See History of Easton, Mass.)

CHILDREN

505. Mehetable, b. Sept. 1, 1797; d. Jan. 11, 1835; m. Galen Sylvester.
506. Bela, b. Oct. 3, 1800; m. Caroline Caswell.
507. Elbridge Gerry, b. Jan. 22, 1809; d. July 13' 1857; m. Maria Keith.
508. Lydia, b. ———; m. ——— Drake.

A 224

Rev. William Reed, son of William and Silence (Nash) Reed.
b. June 8, 1755; d. Nov. 16, 1809.
m. May, 1784, Olive Pool; she died Mar. 26, 1850.
Of Easton.

Rev. William Reed, being in early life religiously disposed, desired a liberal education, with the purpose of entering the Christian ministry. He graduated at Harvard College in 1782; and in April, 1784, was ordained as pastor in the Congregational Church in Easton, Mass., where he remained for upwards of twenty-five years. His ministry, though not distinguished by unusual instances of religious excitement, was a successful one, considering its limited duration. The number of church members was much increased, and his labors were believed by disinterested observers to have had an important influence in effecting a decided reformation in the moral character of the town, whose reputation in the surrounding places had for some time been low. There is an interesting sketch of him in "The History of Easton" of eighteen pages, which the want of space prevents being repeated here.

CHILDREN

509. Mehetable, b. (in Easton) June 20, 1785; m. 1808, Jacob Deane, of Mansfield.
510. William, b. Dec. 12, 1787; m. 1st. Nov. 21, 1811, Betsy Drake; m. 2d. Nov., 1822, Abigail Howe, widow.
511. David, b. Feb. 6, 1790; m. May 2, 1836, Mary Ann Williams.
512. Olive, b. April, 1792; d. Aug., 1793.

513. Jason, b. Oct. 14, 1794; m. May 19, 1824, Nancy Elizabeth Coates.
514. Daniel, b. March 22, 1797; d. Oct. 2, 1879; m. 1st. Sept. 17, 1821, Sally Wild; m. 2d. Feb. 10, 1828, Persis C. Hammond: m. 3d. May 15, 1832, Betsy T. Hammond; m. 4th. Dec. 8, 1847, Mary Ann Richardson.
515. Seth, b. Aug. 22, 1799; m. July 22, 1827, Lucy Holden.
516. Lyman, b. Dec. 28, 1801; m. Oct. 22, 1832, Marcia Ann Harris.
517. Lucius, b. Oct. 27, 1805; d. Nov. 1, 1855; m. Aug. 19, 1831, Abba Sumner Harris.

A 228

James Reed, son of William and Silence (Nash) Reed.
b. Oct. 6, 1764; d. Oct. 30, 1855.
m. ——, Ruth Porter, daughter of Samuel and Hannah (Jackson) Porter of East Bridgewater. Samuel Porter was born Oct. 12, 1727; died Oct. 5, 1811. Hannah Jackson was the widow of Samuel Green. Ruth Porter was born Feb. 1, 1766; died Apr. 13, 1848.

Of Abington, Mass.

He was a man of modest and retiring disposition; an exemplary and practically good man; a lover of the Scriptures and of good men, but from the dislike of rigid church requirements, not a professor of religion. He died at peace with the world, and respected and beloved by all who knew him.

CHILDREN

518. Mehetable, b. May 10, 1784; d. Sept. 8, 1846; m. Samuel Porter.
519. Hannah, b. March 12, 1786; d. April 19, 1853; m. Jacob Fullarton, of Abington.
520. James, b. Aug. 13, 1788; d. Dec. 23, 1810; m. April 19, 1810, Mehetable Dyer.
521. Jane, b. June 10, 1791; d. Feb. 3, 1869; m. Jan. 10, 1811, Daniel Bates.
522. Samuel Porter, b. May 14, 1793; d. Sept. 9, 1815.
523. Timothy, b. March 22, 1796; d. Oct. 17, 1815.
524. Marcus, b. Aug. 23, 1798; d. Oct. 6, 1888; m. May 7, 1821, Mehetable Jenkins.
525. Cyrus, b. July 23, 1800; d. Oct. 2, 1850; m. Nov. 12, 1829, Mary Noyes.

A 232

Elijah Reed, son of Elijah and Sarah (Reed) Reed.
b. Sept. 20, 1758; d. Aug. 31, 1816.
m. July 3, 1779, Lucy Washburn.
Resided at Middleborough.

Of Middleborough.

WILL

"In the name of God, Amen. I, Elijah Reed, of Middleborough in the County of Plymouth & Commonwealth of Massachusetts, gentleman, being weak in body, but of sound and perfect mind and memory, blessed be Almighty God for the same, do make and publish this my last will and testament in manner and form following (that is to say).

"First, I give and bequeath to my beloved wife Lucy Reed and Allice Reed my daughter, one half of my dwelling house where I now live, the southerly part of said house, and the north buttery in said house during my wife's natural life, and after the decease of my wife, so long as my daughter Allice remains single I give and bequeath to her the south front room on the lower floor in said house and the chamber over it and a bed room in the south end of sd. house.

"I also give and devise to my said daughter Allice Reed a certain piece of land to her, her heirs and assigns forever sd. land lying on the easterly side of the road near my dwelling house where I now live, and bounded as follows (to wit) beginning at a stake & stones near the southeast corner of the barn, from thence east to a corner of the pasture by a pair of bars thence south by said bars and wall to Joseph Hathaway's line, thence in said Hathaway's line easterly to a corner, from thence northerly on sd. Hathaway's line to a corner, from thence on said Hathaway's line westerly to the road, from thence southerly by sd. road to a corner, from thence easterly running two rods distance from the north side of the barn two rods beyond the barn, thence southerly to the bounds first mentioned. I also give &

devise to my sons Solomon Reed & Elijah Reed all my buildings and lands not above disposed of, to them their heirs and assigns forever, to be equally divided between them, also after the decease of my daughter Allice Reed—I give and bequeath to my sons Solomon & Elijah to them, their heirs & assigns forever, that part of my dwelling house which I have given to my said wife and daughter to occupy, to be equally divided between them. But if my sons Solomon & Elijah do not live until the decease of my wife & the marriage and decease of my daughter Allice, I give the same to their heirs forever.

"Also to my beloved wife, I give & bequeath one half of my indoor moveables. Also I give and bequeath to my daughter Allice the other half of my indoor moveables. I hereby order my sons Solomon & Elijah to pay all my just debts and also to pay to my son Beezar Reed four hundred and fifty dollars in two years after my decease and four hundred & fifty dollars more in two years after the decease of my wife, also, I order my two sons Solomon & Elijah to pay my daughter Sarah Keith one hundred and fifty dollars in two years after my decease, and one hundred & fifty dollars more in two years after the decease of my wife—I also order my sons Solomon and Elijah to pay my daughter Parnal Edson, one hundred and fifty dollars in two years after my decease, and one hundred & fifty dollars more in two years after the decease of my wife—Also I order my sons Solomon & Elijah to pay my daughter Lucy Eaton one hundred and fifty dollars in two years after my decease & one hundred & fifty dollars more in two years after the decease of my wife. I also give and bequeath to my beloved wife one cow which I order my sons Solomon & Elijah to keep for her or some other in the room of it free from any expense to her during her natural life, also I give and bequeath to my wife & daughter Allice Reed one heifer a year old last Spring. I hereby order my two sons Solomon & Elijah to be at one half of the expense of keeping said heifer for their mother—also I give & bequeath to my daughter Allice one cow.

"I hereby appoint my two sons Solomon & Elijah sole executors of this my last will & testament, hereby revoking all former wills by me made. In witness whereof I have hereunto set my hand & seal this twenty-eighth day of August in the year of our Lord one thousand eight hundred & sixteen.

Elijah Reed (Seal)"

"Signed, sealed, published & declared by the above named Elijah Reed to be his last will & testament in the presence of us who have hereunto subscribed our names as witnesses in the presence of the testator.

Paul Hathaway
Luke Reed
David Richmond"

Will proved September 28, 1816.

CHILDREN

526. Bezaleel, b. Feb. 10, 1780, at Middleborough; m. Oct. 10, 1798, Ruth Edson.
527. Sarah (or Sally), b. Oct. 26, 1782; m. Amos Keith.
528. Solomon, b. April 26, 1785; m. Feb. 23, 1809, Delancy Shaw.
529. Parnel, b. Sept. 11, 1787; m. N. Edson.
530. Elijah, b. Dec. 28, 1790; m. Jane Thomas.
531. Lucy, b. Jan. 4, 1793; m. ——— Eaton.
532. Alice, b. July 5, 1797; m. John Tripp.

A 233

Luke Reed, son of Elijah and Sarah (Reed) Reed.

b. Apr. 28, 1763.

m. Oct. 19, 1786, Keziah Leonard; she died Aug. 26, 1831, aged eighty-one.

Of Middleborough.

CHILDREN

533. Mehetable, b. May 19, 1787, at Middleborough.
534. Luke, b. Aug. 18, 1788; m. Ann Leach.
535. Keziah, b. May 8, 1791; m. Jacob Perkins.
536. Paul, b. ———.
537. Joshua, b. ———.
538. Jacob, b. ———.

A 234

Paul Reed, son of Elijah and Sarah (Reed) Reed.

b. Dec. 20, 1765; d. ———, in Vermont.

m. Mercy Noyes, daughter of Capt. Daniel Noyes; died a widow in Abington.

Of Abington or Middleborough.

CHILDREN

539. Adam, b. May 11, 1793; d. in 1813, aged about 20. Member of Middlebury College, Vt.
540. Paul Adam, b. in 1820.

A 235

Joshua Reed, son of Elijah and Sarah (Reed) Reed.

b. July 25, 1768.

m. Feb. 7, 1788, Deborah Noyes, daughter of Capt. Daniel Noyes.

He settled in East Bridgewater.

CHILDREN

541 Deborah, b. May 30, 1790.
542. Joshua, b. July 24, 1792.
543. Samuel P., b. ———.
544. Silence, b. Oct. 19, 1796.
545. Daniel Noyes, b. Aug. 13, 1799.
546. John, b. Jan. 29, 1802; m. Nov., 1833, Hannah G. Barrel.
547. Mary F., b. ———.

A 236

Jacob Reed, son of Elijah and Sarah (Reed) Reed.

b. June 25, 1771.

m. ———, Sarah ———.

Of Abington, Mass.

CHILDREN

548. David, b. Dec. 1, 1800. Settled in Cummington, Mass.
549. Cyrus, b. ———; lived in New York City; m. Cynthia ———.

W 237

Daniel Reed, son of Daniel and Ruth (Torrey) Reed.

b. Nov. 10, 1729.

m. 1st. Feb., 1755, Mary Turner, of Weymouth.

m. 2nd. Anna Dawes, daughter of Samuel and Sarah (Howland) Dawes. She was born in 1735.

Of Abington, Mass.

WILL

"In the name of God Amen. I Daniel Reed of Abington in the County of Plymouth, and Commonwealth of Massachusetts, yeoman, being advanced in years, but being in free exercise of reason & memory, calling to mind the mortality of my body and knowing that it is appointed for man once to die—do make & ordain this my last will & testament—that is to say principally & first of all I give and recommend my Soul into the hands of God that gave it, hoping for a full & free pardon of all my sins through the merits of Jesus Christ my only redeemer & Savior—and my body I recommend to the earth to be buried with Christian burial nothing doubting but at the general resurrection I shall receive the same by the mighty power of God—And as touching such worldly estate wherewith it hath pleased God to bless me with in this life, I give & dispose of the same in the following manner, viz:—

"Imprimis:—I give and bequeath to my son, Daniel Reed, a piece of land lying on the westerly side of the road near John Chamberlain's dwelling house—also the homestead farm I bought of Benjamin Townsend with the buildings standing thereon—Likewise one other piece of land lying on the road leading to Hanover near Ezekiel Townsend's dwelling house called Mattakees Plain—also the one half of a lot of timber & pasture land lying on the east side of my mill river—likewise the north mowing field of my homestead farm, north of my small farm, bounded northerly by the land that formerly belonged to Samuel Nash, easterly by the road, southerly as the stone wall now stands across said lot—Also a piece of woodland lying north of the schoolhouse on the easterly side of the road, bounded northerly by the land of my son Daniel Reed then Westerly by the

road, to run southerly so far by said road as to bring it on a straight line with the wall mentioned on the other side of said road, then to run easterly on a straight line with said wall, until it extends so far as by turning & running northerly shall bring it on a straight line with the boundary line between John Tolman's and my son Daniel.

"Daniel Reed.—Likewise a piece of meadow land, lying in the Old Mill Pond (so called) also one third part of a saw mill formerly known by the name of French's Mill with all the privileges & appurtenances thereunto belonging. Also the one half of a pew in the Abington Meeting House, which pew the said Daniel now occupies.

"Item.—I give and bequeath to my son Jacob Reed the whole of my homestead farm, excepting that which I have given to my son Daniel Reed, together with all the buildings standing thereon, also the one third of the saw mill before mentioned with all the privileges & appurtenances thereunto belonging, likewise the one half of a pew in Abington Meeting House which I now occupy—Also the lands which I bought of Robert Townsend & Benjamin Townsend lying near the saw mill above mentioned, with the dwelling house standing thereon, like wise a piece of salt meadow lying in Weymouth in the old Cedar Swamp (so called).

"Item:—I give to my son John Reed the improvement of two thirds of the Job House farm (so called) where he now lives with the buildings thereon during the term of his natural life & at his decease is given & bequeathed to my four grandchildren & children of my son John Reed (viz) John, Owen, Nancy & Ruth Reed, in the following manner, two thirds of the above described premises equally to my two grandchildren above mentioned John & Owen Reed & one third equally to my two granddaughters above mentioned Nancy & Ruth Reed I likewise give and bequeath to my son John Reed the other half of the last mentioned pew—

"Item:—I give and bequeath to my daughter Ruth Torrey the land & buildings that I bought of Job House,

which formerly belonged to Ezekiel Lincoln, which Nathaniel Wells Bennett now improves—

"Item:—I give and bequeath to my daughter Sarah Shaw seven hundred dollars to be paid equally by my two sons Daniel Reed & Jacob Reed in one year after my decease.

"Item:—I furthermore give & bequeath to my three sons Daniel Jacob & John Reed equally my money on hand & all securities for money of all kinds—I likewise give to my sons Daniel & John Reed all my wearing apparel equally.

"Also I give to my son Jacob Reed all my real estate that I have not otherwise disposed of with all my outdoor and indoor moveables—

"Item:—I appoint & ordain my son Jacob Reed my sole executor to this my last will & testament—

"Lastly it is my will & pleasure that my just debts & funeral charges be paid equally by my two sons Daniel & Jacob Reed.

"In witness whereof I have hereunto set my hand & seal this thirteenth day of June in the year of our Lord one thousand eight hundred & six.

Daniel Reed (Seal)"

"Signed sealed, published & declared by the said Daniel Reed to be his last will & testament in presence of us the subscribers.

Samuel Norton.
Noah Ford.
Jacob Gurney Junr."

CHILDREN OF DANIEL AND MARY

550. Ruth, b. Oct. 8, 1756; m. March 20, 1783, Josiah Torrey.
551. Daniel, b. July 11, 1759; m. April 4, 1782, Annie Blanchard.
552. Jacob, b. Sept. 12, 1762; d. Jan. 21, 1839; m. Nov. 18, 1799, Nancy Porter.
553. Molly, b. July 3, 1766.

CHILDREN OF DANIEL AND ANNA

554. John, b. Aug. 27, 1769; m. 1st. Dec. 1, 1789, Thankful Jenkins; m. 2d. March 1, 1805, Dorothy Brown.
555. Sarah, b. Aug. 17, 1772; m. Jacob Shaw.

W 238

Thomas Reed, son of Daniel and Ruth (Torrey) Reed.

b. Apr. 17, 1732.

m. 1st. July 10, 1755, Mary (Hobart) White, daughter of Isaac Hobart; she was born in 1735.

m. 2nd. Sarah (Thaxter) Pulling, widow of John Pulling of Boston. She was the daughter of Major Samuel and Abigail (Smith) Thaxter, a descendant of Thomas Thaxter, of Hingham. Dr. Gridley Thaxter of Abington was his brother.

His father by his will devised to him certain lands on the East and South of two roads mentioned.

He was a man of large frame, more than six feet in height, of great physical endurance and energy of character. He was possessed of large landed estates, and was one of the most wealthy men of that time. He lived in the place now occupied by Isaac Reed, on Plymouth street.

In 1776 a committee of Safety and correspondence was chosen, of which committee Thomas Reed was a member.

Of Abington, Mass.

CHILDREN OF THOMAS AND MARY

556. Mary, b. June 7, 1758; m. 1775, Simeon Gannet.
557. Hannah, b. Oct. 24, 1759; d. young.
558. Thomas, b. Dec. 12, 1761; m. May 24, 1783, Joanna Shaw.
559. Hannah, b. June 28, 1764; m. Oct. 25, 1780, Daniel Bicknell.
560. Samuel, b. March 11, 1766; d. June, 1805; m. Aug. 28, 1787, Mary Pool.
561. Huldah, b. April 27, 1768; m. Aug. 12, 1784, Dr. Richard Briggs.
562. Isaac, b. Aug. 4, 1770; m. 1st. May 12, 1793, Sarah Pulling, daughter of Sarah Thaxter Pulling; m. 2d. Nancy Lincoln.
563. Abiah, b. Nov. 22, 1773; m. in 1814, Jane Gurney.

W 240

Frederick Reed, son of John and Mary (Bates) Reed.

b. July 28, 1746.

m. 1st. Dec. 6, 1770, Rebecca Ayers of Weymouth; married by the Rev. Simeon Williams.

m. 2nd. 1781, Hannah Pool.

He lived in Boston at the time of the first marriage, he also lived at Abington and Weymouth.

Of Weymouth, Mass.

CHILDREN OF FREDERICK AND REBECCA

564. David, b. Sept. 30, 1771; d. May 12, 1822; m. Susan Spear.
565. Frederick, b. April 19, 1774; d. April 2, 1821; m. Sally Packard.
566. Asa, b. May 27, 1777; m. Esther Hobart.
567. Rebecca, b. Oct. 15, 1780; m. Sept. 19, 1802, Jonathan Trufant.

CHILDREN OF FREDERICK AND HANNAH

568. Hannah, b. April 2, 1782; m. Dec. 25, 1800, John Vining.
569. Lydia, b. June 13, 1788.
570. Isaac, b. June 23, 1795; m. May 24, 1819, Cynthia Pratt.

W 241

William Reed, son of John and Mary (Bates) Reed.

b. May 9, 1748; d. at Braintree, Mar. 29, 1833.

m. 1st. Sept. 3, 1768, Elizabeth Stammers, daughter of Capt. John Stammers of Boston, who was lost at sea. Born March 18, 1774, in England. Of Braintree. She died Oct. 2, 1821.

m. 2nd. June 16, 1824, Bethia White (widow), her maiden name was Bethia Turner; her first husband was Reuben Burrell, her next was a Mr. White. They were married by Rev. Wm. Tyler.

He lived at Weymouth, where six of his children were born, and at one time lived at Randolph; but at the close of his life lived in Braintree.

There was an estate in England to which Elizabeth Stammers was entitled. Nathaniel T. Holbrook of Neponset, one of her descendants spent considerable time and money looking it up, but found that it had reverted to the Queen.

CHILDREN

571. Elizabeth, b. June 14, 1770; d. Aug. 26, 1859; m. March 27, 1794, Pearson Wild, of Braintree.
572. William, b. Feb. 27, 1774; d. Sept. 14, 1813; m. Feb. 2, 1799, Relief Penniman, of Braintree, pub. Feb. 2, 1799.
573. Mary, b. May 14, 1776; d. Sept. 10, 1858; m. Dec. 5, 1795, Joshua Holbrook, pub. Dec. 5, 1795.
574. Sarah, b. Oct. 9, 1779; d. July 21, 1820; m. Nov. 28, 1816, Wm. Cabot.

575. Lydia, b. Sept. 21, 1782; d. July 31, 1877; m. Jan. 13, 1803, James Holbrook.
576. Ruth, b. Dec. 1, 1785; d. (over 90 years old); m. March 19, 1812, Silas Wild, Jr.
577. Anna, b. Jan. 21, 1789; d. Oct. 2, 1859; m. June 22, 1807, Elisha Thayer, of Braintree.

W 244

John Reed, son of John and Mary (Bates) Reed.

b. (Weymouth, Mass.) Feb. 13, 1755.

m. Jan. 5, 1779 (at Braintree), Rachel Clark, daughter of Ebenezer and Abigail (Ager) Clark. They resided in Bolton, Mass.; m. by Rev. Ezra Wild.

For trace of Rachel Clark's ancestry, see appendix.

He removed to Bolton about or a little before the year 1800.

He was one of the men who built the fortifications on Dorchester Heights, which caused the British to evacuate Boston. His military record was as follows: Private, Capt. Jacob Gould's Co., Col. Benjamin Lincoln's Regiment, April 19, 1775. Private, Capt. Joseph Trufant's Independent Co., May 9, 1775. Private, Capt. Thomas Nash's Co., Col. Solomon Lovell's Regiment, March 4, 1776. Private in Capt. Joseph Trufant's Co., Col. Josiah Whitney's Regiment, May 22, 1776, to Jan. 1, 1777. Sergeant, Independent Companies, March 1, 1777.

The explanation of his service in so many different companies is, that he was a minute man and only served when he was called out. He served altogether seventeen months and twenty-three days.

He drew a pension the latter part of his life. His wife was fair, blue eyes, and a very quick witted, bright woman.

The Col. Benjamin Lincoln mentioned above afterwards became quite a distinguished officer; was made Major General and had command of a division of Washington's army; was later Secretary of War, and after this war, had command of the Massachusetts troops who put down Shay's rebellion.

Old South 2nd Congregational Church
SOUTH WEYMOUTH

CHILDREN

578. John, b. June 21, 1780, supposed to have been lost at sea; m. in 1801, Lucy Houghton.
579. Rachel, b. May 19, 1781; d. Nov. 19, 1781.
580. Rachel, b. Jan. 3, 1782; d. April 2, 1858, unmarried.
581. Elias, b. Feb. 16, 1783; d. Jan. 10, 1854; m. 1814, Sally Block.
582. Elihu, b. Feb. 19, 1784; d. Aug., 1863; m. Nov. 28, 1805, Sabra Houghton.
583. Silas, b. June 13, 1786; d. July 13, 1847; m. Jan. 13, 1813, Betsy Whitcomb.
584. David, b. Oct. 2, 1787; d. Oct. 4, 1848; m. 1st. Nancy Nourse; m. 2d. Eliza Nourse.
585. Henry Ludovicus, b. Sept. 18, 1790; d. Sept. 16, 1886; m. March 14, 1826, Charlotte Stickney.
586. Charlotte, b. May 29, 1793; d. June 10, 1876; m. Nov. 3, 1813, Levi Houghton, of Bolton, and moved to Bath, Me.
587. Clarissa, b. Dec. 18, 1794; d. June 4, 1862; m. 1st. 1821, Joseph Hartwell.
588. Warren, b. May 27, 1803; d. (at Scottsville, Va.) July 2, 1838, unmarried.

W 246

Noah Reed, son of John and Mary (Bates) Reed.

b. Nov. 18, 1759; d. Sept. 20, 1837.

m. July 6, 1788, Mehetable Wild of Milton, whose father kept a tavern in the house once owned and occupied by C. L. Copeland, and later removed to Randolph avenue, near Pleasant. Noah Reed was a shoemaker by trade, but on account of feeble health came to Milton and bought of Daniel Vose, July 13, 1795, the homestead formerly owned by Capt. Samuel Wadsworth. The spot where the old house stood is opposite Geo. K. Gannet's residence between Randolph avenue and Highland street, the original house was burned in 1669. The second house was built by Capt. Wadsworth and was purchased by Noah Reed. It was taken down in 1803; its walls were packed with seaweed, a common custom in those early times. About 1801 Noah Reed bought of Joel Pratt the house built by John Gibbons on the corner of Highland and Reed streets where Mrs. Charlotte (Reed) Wadsworth resided.

Children

589. Betsy, b. March 28, 1789; d. June 18, 1840; m. Jesse Tucker.
590. Warren, b. Feb. 12, 1793; m. Jan. 15, 1837, Mary Howe Wadsworth, who d. Feb. 23, 1871.
591. Avis, b. July, 1795; d. Jan. 9, 1797.
592. Charlotte, b. Feb. 26, 1799; d. Dec. 31, 1887; m. June 18, 1829, Jason Wadsworth.
593. Rachel, b. July 8, 1803; d. unmarried. Lived with her sister Charlotte in the old Reed homestead, formerly the Gibbons house, which was owned and had been remodeled by her.

W 247

Ezra Reed, son of John and Mary (Bates) Reed.

b. Nov. 24, 1762; d. May 14, 1839.

m. 1st. Sept. 13, 1787, Mary Lovell; she died Nov. 20, 1821.

m. 2nd. May 1, 1823, Hannah Tirrell. Married by Rev. Wm. Tyler.

Ezra and John Reed lived together in an old mansion at Weymouth, and all their children were born there. Ezra Reed came into the possession of the old grist mill in 1811, which was situated where the old Plymouth road crosses the mill road. The mill was built by Jeremiah Shaw about the close of the eighteenth century, and it then became known as Reed's mill and was run as such until 1855.

Of Weymouth, Mass.

Children of Ezra and Mary

594. Ezra, b. May 28, 1788; m. June 16, 1816, Susanna Colson Richards.
595. Harvey, b. May 11, 1791; m. 1st. June 14, 1814, Lydia Dyer; m. 2d. Sept. 10, 1818, Jane Pratt.
596. Quincy, b. Nov. 11, 1793; m. Feb. 11, 1821, Lucy Loud.
597. Betsy, b. Aug. 15, 1796; m. Nov. 28, 1816, Seth S. Hersey, of Hingham.
598. Mary, b. May 17, 1799; d. Nov. 18, 1800.
599. Mary, b. 1802; m. Dec. 6, 1821, David Lovell.
600. John, b. Jan. 22, 1804; m. Nov. 10, 1825, Lydia B. Vining.
601. Alvan, b. ———; d. June 26, 1852; m. 1st. Phebe Arnold: m. 2d. Anna Titterton, an English lady from New Orleans; m. 3d. Lucy Vining.

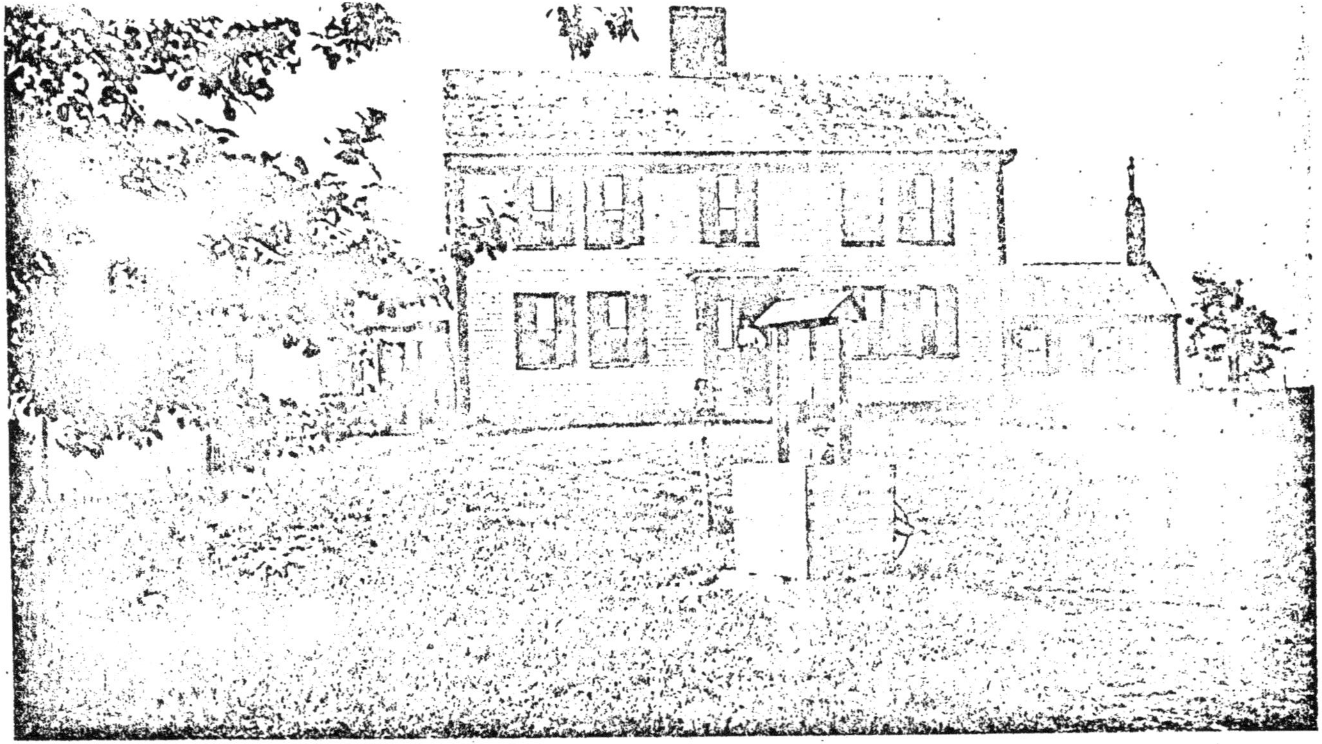

THE RESIDENCE OF JOHN AND EZRA REED, IN WHICH HENRY L. REED, SON OF JOHN REED,

T 250

George Reed, son of George and Abigail (Woodward) Reed of Barrington.

b. Oct., 1733; d. Jan. 3, 1820.

m. ———, Elizabeth Harvey; she died Dec. 19, 1822, aged eighty-nine years, daughter of Abigail Harvey, who died Feb. 1, 1771.

Resided in Taunton.

Of Taunton.

CHILDREN

602. Isaiah, b. Feb. 2, 1757; d. Oct. 13, 1814; m. Abigail Briggs.
603. George, b. Nov. 21, 1759; d. Sept. 4, 1830, m. Experience Blackman, of Canton, Mass.
604. Percy, b. ———.
605. Oliver, b. 1769; d. Dec. 27, 1849; m. March 13, 1788, Bethia Leonard, of Taunton, Mass.
606. Betsy, b. May, 1772; m. May 19, 1793, Jonah Thayer, Jr.; d. April 28, 1831.

T 252

Jonathan Reed, son of William and Elizabeth (———) Reed.

b. ———.

He lived near Sheppard's factory in Newport, R. I.

T 255

John Reed, son of John and Dorothy (Pinneo) Reed.

b. Mar. 29, 1752; d. Feb. 24, 1841.

m. Nov. 21, 1775, Mary Godfrey, born Nov. 19, 1751, daughter of Brig. Gen. George Godfrey; she died Oct. 12, 1843.

John Reed was a selectman from 1804 to 1809, representative to Gen. Court in 1813. He was above middle stature, athletic, and uncommonly regular in his habits. He was often chosen an arbitrator between parties, and was known as Esquire Reed. He was likewise distinguished for piety, and filled an important place in the society to which

he belonged. His wife was also a woman superior in sound sense and practical piety.

Of Taunton, Mass.

CHILDREN

607. John, b. Aug. 11, 1776; d. Nov. 7, 1864; m. May 13, 1804, Rebecca Gooding, who was b. Sept. 28, 1782; d. Jan. 31, 1872.
608. William, b. Oct. 6, 1778; m. 1st. April 24, 1804, Elizabeth Dennis; m. 2d. Feb. 14, 1825, Mary Dennis.
609. Polly, b. Aug. 31, 1782; d. Nov. 6, 1796.
610. Dolly, b. May 31, 1785; m. Oct. 1, 1809, Zephaniah L. Hodges.
611. Marshall, b. Jan. 17, 1788; m. Jan. 11, 1817, Clarissa C. Willis.
612 Hodges, b. June 3, 1790; d. April 15, 1864; m. May 13, 1813, Clarissa Hodges; d. Nov. 19, 1856, aged 68.
613. Sophia, b. Sept. 2, 1792; d. Nov. 19, 1847.
614. Zilpah, b. Dec. 22, 1796; d. May 24, 1798.

T 262

Nathan Reed, son of John and Hannah (Andrews) Reed.
b. Oct. 8, 1771; d. about 1809.
m. Dec. 13, 1796, Ascah Gilmore.

His wife had in all, three husbands. He lived at Norridgewock, Me.; they had children, Nathan and Ebenezer Wyman, who lived in Dexter, Me. She married Solomon Bixby of Norridgewock for third husband; she died in Aug., 1851.

Of Taunton, Mass.

CHILDREN

615. Sylvanus, b. ——.
616. John Gilmore, b. ——; d. at the age of 35; m. ——.
617. Florentius, b. 1801, or 1802; m. ——.

T 264

David Reed, son of John of Taunton and Hannah (Andrews) Reed.
b. Oct. 11, 1775; d. June 24, 1850.
m. May 22, 1803, Phebe Blake.

Farmer, lived at Taunton, Mass.

CHILDREN

618. Gilbert B., b. Sept. 30, 1804; d. Feb. 9, 1828.
619. Phebe H., b. April 3, 1808; m. May 12, 1831, Lloyd French, of Taunton.
620. Mary Adeline, b. Sept. 11, 1811; d. Oct. 12, 1887.
621. Hannah E., b. Jan. 29, 1823; m. Nov. 29, 1854, Jeremiah Whitmarsh, of Dighton, Mass.

T 265

Jonathan Reed, son of John and Hannah (Andrews) Reed.
b. Oct. 11, 1775; d. Jan. 30, 1849.
Was a farmer.

Of Taunton, Mass.

T 271

Thomas Reed, son of Thomas and Rebecca (Talbot) Reed.
b. Oct. 7, 1749.
m. Sept. 8, 1773, Mary Briggs of Dighton.

Of Dighton, Mass.

T 275

Joseph Reed, Jr., son of Joseph and Elizabeth (Elliot) Reed.
b. Dec. 14, 1751; d. July 16, 1823.
m. Apr. 18, 1776, Abigail Barney; b. Oct. 15, 1753; d. Dec. 11, 1828, of Dighton.

CHILDREN

622. Ephraim, b. Dec. 8, 1776.
623. Elizabeth, b. Feb. 2, 1779.
624. Abigail, b. June 3, 1781; d. Nov. 24; m. Gilbert Lincoln.
625. Lydia, b. June 13, 1784.
626. Capt. Joseph, b. June 5, 1786; d. Jan. 4, 1838; m. Sept. 15, 1810, Peddy Hunt.
627. Rhoda, b. April 21, 1789; d. May 19, 1816; m. Dier Pratt.
628. Sally, b. May 13, 1792; d. April, 1793.
629. Sally, b. Feb. 8, 1794; d. Sept. 15, 1829; m. Washington Lennets.

T 276

Uriah Reed, son of Joseph and Elizabeth (Elliot) Reed.
b. Nov. 27, 1756; d. Oct. 30, 1838.
m. Jan. 1, 1783, Polly Pratt; b. Oct. 19, 1762; d. Feb. 1, 1841.

Of Taunton, Mass.

CHILDREN

630. Mary, b. in 1783; d. at Taunton, Nov. 16, 1831, aged 48.
631. Laura, b. in 1810; d. at Taunton, April 20, 1858, aged 48, unmarried.

T 277

Ebenezer Reed, son of Joseph and Elizabeth (Elliot) Reed.

b. ———, 1759.

m. Oct. 10, 1782, Lydia Hoskins, of Berkley.

Of Dighton, Mass.

CHILDREN

632. Mercy, b. ———; d. about 1813; m. Ebenezer Briggs.
633. Josiah, b. ———; m. Mary Tripps.
634. Lydia, b. ———; m. Osmond Babbitt.
635. Ebenezer, b. ———; m. Mary Chase.
636. Isaac, b. ———; m. Nancy Babbitt.
637. Sallie, b. ———; m. Lewis Gay.
638. Abbie, b. ———; m. William Tripps.
639. Betsey, b. ———; m. Isaac Hathaway.
640. Deborah, b. ———; m. Peleg Drew.
641. Gilbert, b. March 10, 1811; m. Oct. 26, 1834, Delina Peck.

T 282

Job Reed, son of Job and Jemima (Talbot) Reed.

b. in 1751; d. Mar. 27, 1842; buried at Berlin, N. H.

m. ———, Sally Troop; b. in 1765; baptized Nov. 11, 1792; d. Jan. 28, 1849; buried at Berlin, N. H.

He was a soldier in the Revolution and died at Northfield, Vt.; he was a shoemaker. They were Congregationalists, and very strict in the observance of the Sabbath and other religious appointments.

CHILDREN

642. Job, b. April 30, 1785; d. in Williamstown, Vt.; m. March 4, 1811, Lovisa Andrews.
643. Sarah, b. in 1787; d. young.
644. Rhoda, b. March 2, 1789; d. April 21, 1819; m. March 8, 1810, Richard Hedges.
645. Polly, b. July 8, 1791; d. Oct. 15, 1825; m. July 25, 1813, James Hopkins.

646. Sally, b. May 28, 1793; m. Samuel Perrin.
647. Morton, b. July 11, 1795; m. Jan. 24, 1817, Lucy Whitney.
648. Betsy, b. Aug. 27, 1797; m. Philetus Robinson.
649. Clarissa, b. Aug. 14, 1799; m. Aneil Seaver.
650. Roxanna, bapt. Sept. 6, 1801: m. Snow Kellogg.
651. Rebecca, b. ———; m. Lyman Davenport.
652. Fanny, bapt. Sept. 11, 1803; d. young.
653. Elvira, b. ———.

T 286

Capt. Simeon Reed, son of Simeon and Deborah (———) Reed.

b. July 28, 1763.

m. 1st. Nov. 1, 1783, Hannah Wheeler; she died May 18, 1803, in the fortieth year of her age.

m. 2nd. Elizabeth ——— (widow); d. Mar. 9, 1852, aged eighty-seven.

Of Dighton, Mass.

CHILDREN OF SIMEON AND HANNAH

654. Simeon, b. June 10, 1784.
655. Hannah, b. Jan. 21, 1788.
656. Deborah, b. March 12, 1793.

CHILD OF SIMEON AND ELIZABETH

657. Eliza, b. Aug. 20, 1804.

T 287

Elijah Augustus Reed, son of Simeon and Deborah (———) Reed.

b. (at Dighton) Sept. 20, 1769.

m. 1st. April 26, 1796, Delight Brown.

m. 2nd. Sarah (Durfee) Borden, widow of William Borden, no children by her first marriage. She had two children, Melinda Borden, who married Rev. Augustus Brown Reed, and Mary Ann Borden, who married John Newton Reed.

He was a deacon of the Orthodox Congregational Church, Rehoboth, Mass. He removed from Dighton, Mass., to Re-

hoboth and married widow Brown. The children of this family changed the orthography from Reed to Read.

Of Rehoboth, Mass.

CHILDREN

658. Augustus Brown, b. Nov. 19, 1798; d. Sept. 30, 1838; m. Nov. 17, 1824, Melinda Borden, of Fall River, daughter of William and Sarah (Durfee) Borden.
659. Harriet A., b. March 1, 1802; d. Dec. 10, 1873; m. Nov. 28, 1819, Samuel Warson Remington.
660. Delight, b. April 26, 1804; d. ———.
661. John Newton (sea captain), b. Nov. 18, 1806; m. 1st. Mary Ann Borden; m. 2d. May 15, 1845, Jane Thompson. No children.
662. Gustavus Adolphus, b. Dec. 1811; d. April 22, 1889; m. March 16, 1836, Electa A. Miller.

T 288

Zebulon Leonard Reed, son of Simeon and Deborah Reed.

b. in 1773; d. Jan. 7, 1833 (sixty years of age).

m. ———, Mary Brown; d. Dec. 24, 1849, aged seventy-two.

Contractor and builder, lived in Warren, R. I.

CHILDREN

663. Mary Ann, b. Feb. 11, 1806; d. April 28, 1854. Founder of Ladies Seminary in Warren, R. I.
664. Lydia Brown, b. Aug. 9, 1808; d. Nov. 7, 1880; m. May 8, 1831, Chas. Randall, Editor of the "Northern Star."

T 291

John Reed, son of John and Mary (Perry) Reed.

b. (at Dighton) Apr. 28, 1757; d. (at Putney, Vt.), June 24, 1840.

m. 1st. July 15, 1780, Deborah Baldwin; b. Apr. 5, 1758; d. May 16, 1785.

m. 2nd. Nov. 27, 1785, Elizabeth Cudworth; b. Nov. 5, 1762; d. Dec. 18, 1850.

He had a common school education, and lived at Putney, West Hill, Putney, Vt. He was a farmer.

Of Dummerston, Vt.

CHILDREN OF JOHN AND DEBORAH

665. John, b. May 11, 1781; d. Dec. 19, 1868; m. March 15, 1803, Joanna Wilson.
666. Deborah, b. Aug. 13, 1783; d. Jan. 28, 1851; m. George Carey.

CHILDREN OF JOHN AND ELIZABETH

667. Mary, b. Sept. 20, 1786; d. Sept. 22, 1869; m. March 15, 1810, Daniel Hibbard.
668. Isaac, b. Sept. 19, 1788; d. Jan. 5, 1879; m. July 12, 1810, Lucretia Newton.
669. Simeon, b. Jan. 25, 1791; d. Oct. 24, 1876; m. Dec. 12, 1819, Betsy Joy.
670. Elizabeth, b. April 24, 1793; d. Feb. 28, 1873; m. March 10, 1818, Lewis D. Joy.
671. Sarah, b. Nov. 23, 1794; d. Oct. 17, 1879; m. Dec. 17, 1819, Samuel Bennett.
672. Hannah, b. Aug. 7, 1798; d. June 3, 1876; m. Dec. 5, 1871, Thomas Turner; m. 2d. June 12, 1852, Nathaniel Hills.
673. Perry, b. Aug. 9, 1800; d. Dec. 7, 1801.

T 293

William Reed, son of John and Mary (Perry) Reed.

b. Mar. 7, 1761.

m. Dec., 1786, Betsy Cartee. She was born June 14, 1767; died May 3, 1855. She came from Benecia, France.

He was a ship carpenter.

Of Townshend, Vt.

CHILDREN

674. George, b. Oct. 20, 1787, was drowned in 1806, aged 19.
675. Betsy, b. Nov. 5, 1789; d. in 1869; m. John Perry.
676. Sally, b. Oct. 20, 1791; d. 1876; m. Edward Blake.
677. William, b. Dec. 27, 1793; d. Nov., 1862; unmarried.
678. Charles Leonard, b. Feb. 15, 1796; d. July 25, 1854; m. May 8, 1820, Hannah N. Beetle.
679. John, b. Oct. 17, 1798; d. Aug. 26, 1861; m. 1st. May 6, 1824, Juliet Merrifield; m. 2d. Sept. 3, 1844, Charity Webb.
680. James, b. May 7, 1801; d. Aug. 23, 1820, unmarried.
681. Patty, b. Aug. 11, 1803; m. George Bowers.
682. Anthony, b. July 10, 1805; d. June 8, 1878; m. Dec. 4, 1828, Elizabeth Bliss, of Rehoboth.
683. Mary, b. Aug. 19, 1812; m. Cyrus Talbot.

T 299

Evans Reed, son of John and Mary (Perry) Reed.

b. Feb. 25, 1772; d. July 19, 1854, at Townshend, Vt.

m. June 6, 1796, Lydia Haven; b. June 24, 1774; d. June 6, 1828, at Townshend, Vt. She was born at Dighton and went to Putney when she was eight years old.

After his marriage, which took place in Dummerston, Vt., he settled in Townshend, Vt., and lived there the remainder of his days. All his children were born there. This family spelt their name Read. He and his wife were Baptists. He was a farmer, was five feet five inches in height, with light hair and complexion. She was light with dark hair and of a cheerful temperament.

Of Townshend, Vt.

CHILDREN

684. Evans Haven, b. May 7, 1797; d. Aug. 19, 1859; unmarried.
685. Lydia, b. Nov. 23, 1798; d. June 25, 1859; unmarried.
686. Lucinda, b. Oct. 18, 1800; d. March 27, 1840.
687. Philanda, b. March 24, 1803; d. Dec. 5, 1848.
688. Daniel, b. June 30, 1805; m. Jan. 1, 1835, Fanny Burr Barber.
689. Roswell, b. Sept. 28, 1808; d. July 8, 1811.
690. Fanny, b. Oct. 24, 1810; d. June 15, 1852; m. Feb. 4, 1835, Luke T. Barber, who d. May 31, 1849.
691. Luther, b. April 5, 1813; d. Oct. 19, 1845; m. Oct. 17, 1837, Harriet Heald.

T 301

George Reed, son of John and Mary (Perry) Reed.

b. Jan. 12, 1776.

m. ———.

Of Townshend, Vt.

He was a very capable man. He became a sea captain and was lost at sea.

T 303

Samuel Reed (of Dighton), son of Samuel and Rachel (Williams) Reed.

b. Dec. 23, 1754.

m. Apr. 17, 1788, Mercy Gilmore, of Raynham.

Of Dighton, Mass.

CHILD

692. Alpheus, b. March 21, 1790.

T 306

Seth Reed, son of Samuel and Rachel (Williams) Reed.

b. May 4, 1765 (at Dighton); d. ———, 1844.

m. May 18, 1788, Cassandra Dean of Raynham, who died in 1840.

He was a farmer and shoemaker, and choir leader in Dighton.

Of Dighton, Mass.

CHILDREN

693. Seth, b. Oct. 14, 1790; d. Nov. 22, 1863; m. May 14, 1823, Matilda Smith.
694. Salmon, b. Dec. 23, 1795.
695. Cassandra, b. Aug. 14, 1798.
696. Otis, b. Sept. 16, 1801; d. Jan. 15, 1854; m. 1st. Rosamond Chase; m. 2d, Oct. 28, 1832, Ann E. Colton; m. 3d. Feb. 25, 1844, Amanda Paul.
697. Stephen D., b. March 3, 1810; m. Emeline Lane.

T 307

George Reed (of Berkley), son of George and Mercy (Phillips) Reed.

b. July 29, 1757; d. Aug. 10, 1842.

m. May 7, 1782, Elizabeth Pitts of Taunton, who died March 9, 1852.

Lived in Berkley at the time of their marriage.

Of Berkley.

CHILDREN

698. Caleb, b. Feb., 1790.
699. William, b. July 16, 1791.
700. George W., b. May 19, 1796.

T 318

John Reed, son of Loved and Charity (Phillips) Reed.
b. Apr. 13, 1782.
m. ———, Polly ———.
Of Dighton, Mass.

CHILDREN

701. George, b. Nov. 20, 1805.
702. Betsy J., b. July 20, 1807.
703. John C., b. April 22, 1813.
704. Charles P., b. Aug. 21, 1814.

T 320

David Reed (of Dighton), son of Loved and Mary (French) Reed.
b. Dec. 26, 1789.
m. ———, Jemima ———.
Of Dighton, Mass.

CHILDREN

705. Clarinda, b. July 22, 1812.
706. Nancy, b. April, 1814.

M 323

William Reed, son of William and Sarah (Warren) Reed.
b. Jan. 4, 1744.
m. Sept. 22, 1763, Mrs. Alice Richards.
Of Middleborough, Mass.

M 324

Benjamin Reed, son of William and Sarah (Warren) Reed.
b. Jan. 29, 1746, at Middleborough.
m. Oct. 23, 1763, Mrs. Abiah Macomber.
Of Middleborough, Mass.

Removed to Shutesbury, Mass., where they died, and were buried. Their children settled in Connecticut river valley, at Deerfield, and other localities, a little south of Deerfield, and one son and daughter married in Cunningham, near Hamilton, and Cazenovia, in eastern New York.

Served as corporal in Capt. Nathaniel Wood's company, Col. Simeon Corey's regiment. On duty at Roxbury April 1, 1776; also served in 1776 and 1778 in Col. Sproat's regiment.

CHILDREN

707. Benjamin, b. ———; m. 1st. Anna Chubbick; m. 2d. ———.
708. Sarah, b. ———; m. Lorenzo Cunningham; resided at Cazenovia, N. Y.
709. John, b. ———; m. Sarah Atherton; resided at Cazenovia, N. Y.
710. Warren, b. July 6, 1780; m. May 25, 1805, Mary Atherton; resided in Chester, Mass.
711. Gideon, b. ———; m. ———; resided at near Whately, Mass.; m. ———, Eleanor Clifford.
712. James, b. Feb. 26, 1783; m. Sophronia Smith; resided at Deerfield, Mass., and Marion, Ohio.
713. Abiah, b. ———; m. ——— Cunningham, M. D., of Cazenovia, N. Y., a brother of Lorenzo Cunningham.
714. Simeon, b. 1789; d. Aug. 28, 1853; m. Aug. 2, 1814, Miranda Morton; resided at Whately, Mass.
715. Levi, b. 1791; m. Nancy Pratt; resided in Hamilton, N. Y.

M 329

Abner Reed, son of William and Sarah (Warren) Reed.
b. Aug. 12, 1764.

Of Middleborough, Mass.

M 333

Samuel William Reed, son of Samuel and Rebecca (Knowlton) Reed.
b. Dec. 11, 1786.
m. ———, Ruth ———.

CHILD

716. William, b. Dec. 7, 1819, at Middleborough, Mass.

M 338

Watson Reed, son of Samuel and Rebecca (Knowlton) Reed.
b. Apr. 19, 1804.
m. ———, Sylvia Lamson.

Of Middleborough, Mass.

M 339

Ichabod Reed, son of Ichabod and Sarah (Vaughan) Reed.
b. July 6, 1789.
m. ———, Lucy ———.

Lived at Middleborough, Mass.

CHILDREN

717. Huldah, b. April 5, 1814.
718. Sylvanus, b. Jan. 4, 1816; m. Olive P———.
719. Lucy, b. June 1, 1818.
720. Jeremiah, b. July 6, 1819; m. Mary G.; lived at Middleborough, Mass. Had no children.
721. Sarah, b. Aug. 11, 1821.
722. Ichabod, b. June 4, 1831; d. Sept. 3, 1854.

SIXTH GENERATION

A 351

Obadiah Reed, son of Obadiah and Content (Lincoln) Reed.
b. Jan. 4, 1760.
m. ———, Elizabeth Richmond; she is supposed to have died in 1857, aged ninety years.

Of Abington, Mass.

CHILDREN

723. Adam, b. 1787; m. Mary Porter.
724. Silas, b. Feb. 13, 1789; d. Jan. 9, 1856; m. April 13, 1818, Mahala Harris.
725. Abel Richmond, b. Sept. 27, 1791; m. April 3, 1828, Roxanna Willis. No children.
726. Obadiah, b. Jan. 1, 1796; m. Sept. 27, 1831, Deborah Tirrel Reed.
727. Elizabeth, b. March 25, 1797; m. Martin Drake.
728. Salmon, b. Oct. 25, 1798; drowned in 1823.
729. Isaac, b. June, 1801; m. Sallie Weeks.
730. Israel, b. Aug. 10, 1806; m. Nov. 18, 1838, Louisa Humble.
731. Emily, b. Oct. 23, 1809; m. Marshall Humble.

A 352

Joel Reed, son of Obadiah and Elizabeth (Shaw) Reed.
b. Oct. 26, 1771.
m. 1st. July 4, 1793, Ruth Gurney, daughter of Jacob, son of Nathan, son of John Gurney, who removed from Weymouth to Abington. (See His. of Abington, p. 384.)
m. 2nd. Widow Jane Raymond.

Of Abington, Mass.

CHILDREN OF JOEL AND RUTH

732. Joel, b. Feb. 8, 1794; m. 1st. ———; m. 2d. Nov. 16, 1837, Bethany Churchhill.
733. Ruth, b. ———; m. Samuel Snell.
734. Matthew, b. Jan. 4, 1798; m. Sept. 12, 1822, Thurza Harris.
735. Lydia, b. June 4, 1800; m. 1st. Zack Thayer; m. 2d. ——— Fish.
736. Albert, b. May 5, 1803; m. 1st. Aug. 26, 1840, Polly Reynolds.
737. Hervey, b. Feb. 27, 1806; m. 1st. Oct. 30, 1830, Sally Pool; m. 2d. Nov. 23, 1837, Mary Thaxter Nash.
738. Lucius, b. Sept. 25, 1808; m. Nov. 24, 1831, Lydia Shaw.
739. James M., b. May 25, 1815; d. unmarried.

CHILD OF JOEL AND JANE

740. George Washington, b. Feb. 21, 1827; d. unmarried.

A 356

David Reed, son of David and Mary or Mercy (Ford) Reed.
b. May 3, 1767.
m. Sept. 10, 1810, Elizabeth T. Brown.

Of Ware.

WILL

"I. David Reed of Ware in the County of Hampshire and Commonwealth of Massachusetts, being of sound and disposing mind and memory, but considering myself near the close of life, do make and publish this my last will and testament.

"I give to my wife Eliza Reed all the household furniture, clothing and other personal property in the house we now occupy.

"I also give to her all the notes I hold and whatever may be due me at my decease, for her own use, so long as she

shall remain my widow, enjoining it upon her to pay all my just debts, and in case of her intermarriage, or in case she shall not need the whole amount she shall receive from my estate for her comfortable support, it is my will that the rest and residue shall go to my son David H. Reed, his heirs.

"I nominate and appoint my wife Eliza Reed to be sole executrix of this my last will and testament, hereby revoking all former wills by me made.

"In witness whereof I have hereunto set my hand and seal this twenty first day of October, Eighteen Hundred and forty eight.

David Reed (Seal)"

"Signed sealed published and declared by the said David Reed as his last will and testament in the presence of us, who in his presence and in the presence of each other set our names as witnesses to the same.

Joel Rice
Sam' J. Dale
W. Hyde."

Hampshire County ss.
Registry of Probate.

Northampton, Mass., May 12, A. D. 1899.

A true copy,

Attest: Hubbard M. Abbott, Register.

CHILDREN

741. Charlotte, b. May 16, 1812.
742. Woodbridge Brown, b. Nov. 19, 1813; m. Orinda Neal.
743. Anson, b. Sept. 25, 1814.
744. Nancy, b. Dec. 5, 1815; m. Quincy Blanchard.
745. David H., b. ———; m. Nancy Smith.

A 362

Ichabod Reed, son of David and Mary or Mercy (Ford) Reed.
b. May 12, 1782.
m. Nov. 9, 1804, Betsy Robbins of Cummington.

He lived at Cummington.

CHILD

746. Betsy, b. ———; m. June 13, 1827, William Wilder, now living in Cummington, Mass.

A 365

Jonathan Reed, son of Jonathan and Mary (Tirrel) Reed.
b. Feb. 2, 1767.
m. April 13, 1788, Deborah Porter.

He settled in East Bridgewater.

CHILDREN

747. Mary B., b. 1788; m. Rev. Caleb Benson.
748. Jonathan L., b. 1791; m. 1st. Dec. 18, 1816, Charlotte Brown; m. 2d. Feb. 25, 1827, Lucy Champney.
749. John P., b. 1793; m. in 1816 Polly Ramsdale.
750. Deborah, b. 1795; m. in 1816, Jonathan R. Gurney.
751. Elizabeth M., b. 1797; d. unmarried.
752. Thaxter, b. 1800; m. 1st. Feb. 4, 1827, Mehetable Brown; m. 2d. July 30, 1837, Sophronia Barker.
752. Thaxter, b. 1800: m. July 30, 1837, Mehetable Brown. ? —
753. Ebenezer, b. 1801; m. Patience Penniman.
754. Clarissa, b. 1805; m. Ichabod Gurney.
755. Almira, b. 1806; m. Luther Keen.
756. David P., b. 1808; d. 45 years old; unmarried.

A 370

John Reed, son of Silas and Rebecca Reed.
b. Aug. 14, 1773, at Cummington.
m. 1st. Jan. 1, 1798, Hannah Waters at Worcester; d. April 22, 1811.
m. 2nd. ———, Jerusha ———.
Of Cummington, Mass.

CHILDREN OF JOHN AND HANNAH

757. Henry, b. April 5, 1799.
758. Charles, b. Sept. 27, 1800.
759. William, b. April 8, 1807.

CHILD OF JOHN AND JERUSHA

760. Theodore, b. Sept. 1, 1815, in Cummington.

A 379

William Reed, son of Barnabas and Silence (Sprague) Reed.
b. May 6, 1783, at Abington, Mass.; d. Sept. 20, 1860, at Albany, N. Y.

m. Jan. 11, 1814, Lovisa Beals; b. Jan. 4, 1792, at Plainfield, Mass.; d. Oct. 22, 1876, at Albany, N. Y. Daughter of Robt. and Lydia Porter Beals, of Plainfield, Mass. They were married by Rev. Albert Reed.

He had a common school education, was a Presbyterian and lived at Abington, Mass.

CHILDREN

761. Angelina, b. Nov. 13, 1814; d. May 23, 1860; m. May 19, 1835, Chester Driggs.
762. Cordelia, b. July 20, 1816; d. unmarried.
763. Lovisa, b. Nov. 24, 1818; d. Nov. 19, 1863; m. June 18, 1845, Ralzaemon Lucas Spelman.
764. William, b. Nov. 27, 1820; d. May 15, 1869; unmarried.
765. John Chester; b. July 7, 1823; d. May 11, 1825.
766. John S., b. Nov. 22, 1825; unmarried.
767. James Augustus, b. April 18, 1828; m. Oct. 23, 1850, Lydia M. Stockton.
768. Albert Chester, b. Aug. 31, 1832; m. May 8, 1865, Sarah M. Merriman.
769. A son, b. July 8, 1835; d. Aug. 4, 1835.
770. Mary, b. Sept. 2, 1838; d. unmarried.
771. Charles D., b. Dec. 24, 1843; d. June 7, 1886; unmarried.

A **381**

Joshua Reed, son of Barnabas and Silence (Sprague) Reed.

b. March 6, 1788, at Abington; d. March 1, 1835, at Plainfield, Mass.

m. Nov. 6, 1817 (at Abington), Susannah Noyes; b. Nov. 14, 1793, at Abington; d. Jan. 11, 1873, at Cummington, Mass.; daughter of Jonathan and Susannah (Eager) Noyes.

He had the advantages of the district schools of his day, but was eminently a self-made man. He was of fine appearance and pure moral character. His father died when he was but eight years old, and from that time until their death he was the mainstay of his widowed mother and invalid sister. In the war of 1812 he was for some time connected with the commissary department—taking stores to different points. At Plainfield, Mass., he owned and cultivated a

small farm. Susannah Noyes completed her education at Leicester Academy, Mass. She was a beautiful and talented woman. They were both good singers, and he was for many years the choir leader in the Congregational Church (Rev. Moses Hallock, pastor) with which they were connected.

CHILDREN

772. Rosanda, b. June 26, 1818; d. Sept. 20, 1843.
773. Susan Field, b. Nov. 2, 1819; d. June 10, 1855; m. May 12, 1841, Sumner Hyde, of Cummington, Mass.
774. Vesta Wales, b. Dec. 15, 1820; m. June 1, 1843, Franklin J. Warner.
775. Samuel Worcester, b. April 20, 1822; m. April 26, 1848, Adaline Norton.
776. Philomela Thurston, b. Oct. 21, 1823; m. 1st. April 6, 1844, Alden Barr Vining; m. 2d. Feb. 19, 1876, Lyman Burrell, of Oakland, Cal. She lives at Oakland, Cal.
777. Nancy Amanda, b. May 1, 1825; d. Sept. 10, 1830.
778. Lovinia Whiting, b. Nov. 27, 1826; d. Sept. 22, 1830.
779. Sarah Celestia, b. Sept. 16, 1828; d. Sept. 5, 1830.
780. Joshua Franklin, b. Nov. 25, 1830; d. Oct. 5, 1834.
781. Jonathan Edwards, b. July 4, 1833; unmarried, resides at 1358 West street, Oakland, Cal.

A 387

Seth Reed, son of Micah and Deborah (Thompson) Reed, of Halifax, Mass.

b. Jan. 9, 1776; d. Dec. 19, 1853.

m. July 4, 1804, Hannah Shaw, at Cummington.

CHILDREN

782. Allzida, b. April 3, 1805; d. April, 1805.
783. Olive, b. May 10, 1806; m. Oct. 28, 1824, Jonas Tirrell.
784. Betsy, b. Dec. 30, 1808.
785. Lucia, b. May 9, 1819; m. Sept. 1, 1839, Jonas F. Luce.
786. Robert, b. Oct. 4, 1822; m. Nancy ———.

A 389

Noah Reed, son of Micah and Deborah (Thompson) Reed.

b. April 22, 1781; d. Jan. 22, 1811.

m. ———, Susannah White, b. in Abington July 4, 1784; d. April 14, 1847. She was descended from Pere-

grine White. She was a daughter of Capt. John White, who served in the Revolutionary War.

Extract from Registry of Probate of Hampshire county, Mass.:

"Susannah Reed is appointed administratrix on the estate of Noah Reed, late of Plainfield, deceased.

"August 20th, 1811."

Hampshire County, ss.
Registry of Probate.

Northampton, Mass., May 12, A. D. 1899.

A true copy. Attest:

Hubbard M. Abbott, Register.

CHILDREN

787. Micah, b. in Abington, Jan. 23, 1803; d. in infancy.
788. Noah, b. in Abington, March 25, 1804; was in poor health; went south in a sailing vessel, which was never heard from afterwards.
789. Susan Clark, b. in Abington, March 22, 1806; d. in 1867; m. April 1, 1824, Emery Alden.
790. Malvina Fitzallen, b. May 26, 1807; d. July, 1884; m. Leonard Wood, of Leicester, Mass.

A 396

Seth Reed, son of Seth and Mary (Lazell) Reed.

b. ———; d. Dec. 19, 1853.

m. Jan. 10, 1801, Catherine Brown.

Of Weymouth.

CHILDREN

791. Lucy, b. July 20, 1802; m. 1819, Pliny Edson.
792. Seth, b. May 2, 1804; m. Sept. 13, 1826, Sally Blanchard.
793. Mehetable, b. June 4, 1806.
794. Noah, b. Feb. 20, 1810.

A 398

Daniel Reed, son of Noah and Abigail (Rice) Reed.

b. at Cummington, Nov. 5, 1786.

m. Oct. 20, 1814, Cynthia Warner; d. Sept. 10, 1849.

Of Cummington.

CHILDREN

795. Noah Warner, b. Nov. 25, 1815; m. Nancy ———.
796. Daniel E., b. March 17, 1818.
797. John C., b. July 4, 1820; m. Sarah ———.
798. Paul D., b. Feb. 24, 1823.
799. Lucius F., b. Sept. 24, 1829.

A 402

Jesse Reed, son of Noah and Abigail (Rice) Reed.
b. March 25, 1796.
m. Feb. 19, 1829, Mary (Davis) Griswold.

CHILDREN

800. Frances Jane, b. July 3, 1830.
801. William Lewis, b. May 5, 1832; m. Jan. 1, 1856, Julia Sampson.
802. Hiram Davis, b. Nov. 1, 1833.
803. Myron Winslow, b. Jan. 16, 1837.

A 405

Adam Reed, son of Adam and Silence Reed.
b. ———.
m. Feb. 25, 1819, Mary Porter.

Of Abington.

CHILD

804. Mary Porter, b. Sept. 16, 1823.

A 406

Abel Reed, son of James and Susannah (Niles) Reed.
b. Sept. 5, 1780; d. ———, 1817.
m. Lydia Loud of Plymouth.

He lived in Boston.

CHILDREN

805. William Cole, b. ———, who lived in Roxbury.
806. James Ward, b. ———, who lived in Roxbury.
807. Eliza, b. ———.
808. Lydia, b. ———.
809. Charles Thayer, b. ———; m. Feb. 3, 1828, Sophia E. Critston.

A 411

Hon. John Reed, son of Rev. John and Hannah (Sampson) Reed.

b. Sept. 2, 1781.

m. ———, Olive Alger, daughter of Abiezer Alger, Esq., of West Bridgewater.

(See extended account in J. W. R., p. 363.)

Of Yarmouth, Mass.

John Reed graduated at Brown University in 1803. The first two or three years after leaving college he devoted to teaching, first as preceptor of Plymouth Academy, Bridgewater, and then as tutor in Brown University. He chose the profession of law, and pursued his preparatory studies with the Hon. William Baylies, an eminent attorney of his town. He commenced the practice of law at Yarmouth, on Cape Cod. He soon attained eminence in his profession, and was elected a representative in Congress. This office he filled for twenty-eight years. By the impartiality of his course on all important questions, he early obtained in Congress the confidence of the members of both houses. His statements of facts and statistics relating to any subject of debate were always listened to as reliable and true. He thus exerted after the first years of his service, an important influence, especially in the settlement of all questions involving the interest of his district and state. There were instances indeed, particularly in the discussion of questions relating to the fisheries, when by a single speech he completely revolutionized the sentiment of the House, and changed the vote from a lean minority to a triumphant majority. In 1844 he was elected Lieutenant Governor, and was re-elected to that office each year during the administration of Gov. Briggs. In 1845 he received the degree of LL. D. from Brown University.

CHILDREN

810. Sarah, b. 1810; m. Caleb S. Hunt, of Bridgewater.

811. John, b. 1812; m. Amelia Crane, of Fair Haven.

812. Martha, b. 1816; d. Feb. 13, 1850; m. James F. Joy, Esq., of Detroit.
813. Edward, b. 1817; m. Nov. 6, 1848, Catherine Howard, of Boston.

A 412

Daniel Reed, son of Rev. John and Hannah (Sampson) Reed.
b. Aug. 29, 1783.
m. in 1812, Nancy Foster, daughter of Gershom Foster of Middleborough.

Of West Bridgewater.

CHILDREN

814. John Montgomery, b. Aug. 9, 1814; m. Elizabeth Broomfield.
815. Charles, b. Dec. 7, 1815; m. in 1843, Sophia Wilkins Clark.
816. Jane, b. Feb. 21, 1819.

A 414

Solomon Reed, son of Rev. John and Hannah (Sampson) Reed.
b. March 22, 1788; d. ——, 1822.
m. in 1811, Abigail Howard, daughter of George Howard.

Of West Bridgewater.

CHILDREN

817. Solomon, b. 1811; m. Sept. 7, 1838, Lydia Blanchard.
818. George Howard, b. 1814; m. April 19, 1838, Elizabeth Jeffery.
819. William Franklin, b. 1819; m. Adelaide Arnold.

A 417

Caleb Reed, son of Rev. John and Hannah (Sampson) Reed.
b. Apr. 22, 1797; d. Oct. 14, 1854, in Boston.
m. 1st. July, 1838, Mary E. Minot; she died in 1842.
m. 2nd. Nov. 1847, Ruth Cobb.

Of Boston.

The following is an account of Caleb's life and character selected from an obituary notice published in the "New Jerusalem Magazine" of Nov., 1854:

"He entered Harvard College in 1813, and was graduated

in 1817. After teaching school in Medford one year, he entered the office of his brother, the Hon. John Reed (recently Lieutenant Governor of this State), and there pursued the study of law for three years. He was then admitted to the bar, and practised his profession in Yarmouth, where he resided until 1827; when he removed to Boston for the purpose of entering into the firm of Cyrus Alger & Co., which was afterwards incorporated as the South-Boston Iron Co., and is widely known as one of the principal iron-founding establishments in the United States. He remained connected with this company until his death, which was caused by an attack of dysentery, with fever; and took place on Saturday, the 14th of October, 1854. During this fatal illness he was cheerful and child-like; not resigned (for this implies the subdual or suppression of some unwillingness); and to use his own expression, he had no choice, but was glad to leave the issues of life and death in the hands of his Father.

"He received the doctrine of the New Jerusalem while studying law; being one of a circle of young men, of about the same age, who were in college together, and received these doctrines nearly at the same time, and have since lived near to each other in a companionship, from which the late Mr. Hobart, and now Mr. Reed, are all that have been called away. The wish to be with the society of the Church in Boston was one of the motives which led him to remove to this city. He assumed at once the position that belonged to his character, and has ever held it; through all these years, aiding materially in promoting every good work, and in averting from us much evil.

"In 1832 Mr. Reed took charge of the Magazine, and has ever since been its editor. Of the manner in which he conducted this work, we need not speak to the readers of it. One thing however we cannot forbear saying: that during this long period, he has sustained the Magazine, sometimes with but little of the aid which might have been rendered, always when pressed by the urgent cares and duties of a

very extensive business, and always without pecuniary profit or compensation.

"The funeral services took place in the afternoon of Tuesday, the 17th of October, in the New Jerusalem Church in Boston, and were attended by a large assemblage."

CHILDREN OF CALEB AND MARY

820. Helen, b. ———.

821. Arthur, b. ———.

A **418**

Sampson Reed, son of Rev. John and Hannah (Sampson) Reed.

b. June 10, 1800.

m. Dec. 25, 1832, Catherine Clark, daughter of John Clark, Esq., of Waltham.

Of Boston.

Sampson graduated at Harvard College in 1818, where he held a high rank as a scholar. After graduating he remained at the university about two years as a theological student; but he finally removed to Boston, and adopted the profession of a merchant, a profession for which his honorable practice and example have uniformly tended to command respect.

Having early embraced the doctrines of the New Church, he has been one of the principal supporters of the society of this order in Boston, and of the General Convention of the New Church in America. His devotion to the interests of this church for a period of forty years has justly secured to him the confidence and respect of its members throughout the country. His literary tastes have led him to devote much time to books, and particularly to theological inquiries and studies. Besides his contributions to periodical literature, he has had the sole charge of the "New Church Magazine for Children" from its commencement in 1844; and also since the death of his brother Caleb, took a prominent part in the management of the "New Jerusalem Magazine." In 1826 he published a small work, entitled "Observations

on the growth of the mind," which has attracted much attention, and passed through five editions in this country, and one or more in England.

Unassuming in manners and of a retiring disposition, he has never sought place or influence in public affairs; though he has served two or three years in the office of alderman. The duties of this situation, as also those of membership of the public school committee, of bank director, and of various trusts, public and private, he has discharged in a manner to insure the general respect of his fellow citizens.

CHILDREN

822. James, b. June 8, 1834; m. Dec. 19, 1858, Emily E. Ripley.
823. Thomas, b. Feb. 3, 1837.
824. Elizabeth, b. July 10, 1838.
825. Joseph Sampson, b. Dec. 13, 1841.

A 419

Solomon Reed, son of Rev. Solomon and Susannah (Willard) Reed.

b. July 23, 1873, at Petersham; d. May 15, 1846, at Rowe, Mass.

m. June —, 1811, Lucy Ward of Petersham; she died June 24, 1867, aged eighty-one, at Onondaga Hollow, N. Y. Had no children.

Of Rowe, Mass.

A 422

Josiah Willard Reed, son of Rev. Solomon and Susannah (Willard) Reed.

b. Sept. 7, 1790; d. Oct. 29, 1835, at Rowe, Mass.

m. 1st. Oct. 8, 1821, Fanny Hunt of Northampton, Mass.; she died Aug. 27, 1822.

m. 2nd. March 25, 1833, Lucina Warner of Charlemont; died in 1860 or 1861.

CHILD OF JOSIAH AND FANNY

826. Josiah Hunt, b. Aug. 4, 1822; d. Aug. 1, 1898; m. July 19, 1845, Mary Elizabeth Chessman, of Auburn, N. Y.

CHILDREN OF JOSIAH AND LUCINA

827. John Newton, b. Feb. 20, 1834; d. in 1856, about 22 years of age.
828. Solomon Willard, b. Dec., 1835; d. Sept. 1, 1847.

A 425

Samuel Horton Reed, son Rev. Samuel and Susannah (Willard) Reed.

b. Oct. 27, 1794; d. July 14, 1874, in Greenfield, Mass.

m. 1st. Sept. 17, 1818, Elizabeth Foster of Rowe, Mass.; b. Feb. 18, 1796; d. Feb. 25, 1823.

m. 2nd. May 3, 1825, Hannah Foster; b. Jan. 15, 1802; d. Jan. 27, 1872; sister of Elizabeth.

He was associated with his brother Solomon, in Rowe, Mass., in manufacturing. He was a representative in the Legislature for five years, was postmaster twenty-five years. In 1847 was appointed high sheriff of Franklin county, which office he held for twenty years until he was afflicted with blindness, which continued until his death (six years after). His general health was good until within a few months of his death, and his intellectual vigor was remarkable for a man of his age.

Of Greenfield, Mass.

CHILDREN OF SAMUEL AND ELIZABETH

829. William, b. June 20, 1819; m. 1st. Sept. 14, 1846, Elizabeth Kent Sayer; m. 2d. Mrs. Elizabeth Newton Cleaver.
830. Elizabeth Foster, b. Aug. 2, 1821; d. Aug. 2, 1839; m. May 28, 1833, Dr. Edward M. Wheeler.

CHILDREN OF SAMUEL AND HANNAH

831. Samuel, b. Jan. 31, 1826; d. Dec. 12, 1849. He was a physician.
832. Susan Willard, b. May 28, 1828; d. Oct. 4, 1853.
833. Henry Augustus, b. June 9, 1832; d. Aug. 28, 1869.
834. Hannah Flint, b. June 7, 1838; d. Dec. 9, 1894.
835. Catherine Foster, b. Jan. 22, 1841, resides in Greenfield, Mass.

A 432

Samuel Reed, son of Rev. Samuel and Anna (Shaw) Reed.

b. April 25, 1788.

m. ———, Melinda Wheelock.

Lived in Greenfield. He died very suddenly and was interred in Warwick, where his widow afterward resided.

CHILDREN

836. John, b. Feb. 26, 1820; m. Delia Winter.
837. Melinda A., b. Oct. 12, 1824.

A 433

Stephen Reed, son of Rev. Samuel and Anna (Shaw) Reed.
b. Nov. 5, 1790; d. ——, 1847.
m. ——, Jerusha Moor.

They lived in Warwick, on the old homestead. He and his wife and all his children with one exception were teachers.

Of Warwick, Mass.

CHILDREN

838. Emily, b. March 1, 1821; m. May 18, 1843, Danford Tyler, of Warwick.
839. S. Chandler, b. April 22, 1822; m. 1st. Nov. 25, 1852, Lebiah H. Jones; m. 2d. Nov. 25, 1857, Rhoda G. Tyler.
840. Charles, b. Oct. 3, 1823.
841. Abby J., b. March 24, 1827; m. May 24, 1857, Nathan Kendall. of Laporte, Ind.
842. Samuel, b. March 22, 1829; m. Nov., 1853, Maria H. Barber.
843. Mary A., b. Sept. 29, 1830.

A 434

Timothy Reed, son of Rev. Samuel and Anna (Shaw) Reed.
b. July 10, 1793; d. ——, 1853, at Barnstable.
m. ——, Susan Kingsley.

He graduated at Dartmouth College, Hanover; adopted the profession of law, and was partner in a business with the Hon. John Reed in Yarmouth for many years. He was clerk of the court for Barnstable, register of deeds, register of probate, and cashier of a bank.

Of Barnstable.

CHILDREN

844. Helen, b. ——.
845. Eliza D., b. 1823.
846. Susan K., b. 1825; m. Nathaniel Wales, of Stoughton.

A 437

Samuel Reed, son of Samuel and Mary (Torrey) Reed.

b. Sept. 16, 1765; d. Feb. 28, 1853, at Hull.

m. Nov. 17, 1793, Mary Greenleaf of Hull, daughter of John and Mary (Gould) Greenleaf. She died May 22, 1857.

They lived at Hull.

CHILDREN

847. Mary, b. Aug. 26, 1794; d. Jan. 27, 1795.
848. Mary, b. Feb. 21, 1797; d. June 13, 1882.
849. Samuel, b. March 5, 1802; d. Feb. 20, 1869; m. Oct. 11, 1832, Caroline Nash, of Weymouth.
850. Elizabeth Greenleaf, b. March 17, 1809; d. July 14, 1869.

A 438

John Reed, son of Samuel and Mary (Torrey) Reed.

b. May 9, 1767; d. March 5, 1852.

m. 1st. Nov. 29, 1792, Elizabeth Gould of Hull, daughter of Elisha and Martha Louisa Gould of Hull; she died March 24, 1815.

m. 2nd. Nov. 21, 1816, Martha (Gould) Swain, widow of William Swain, a sister of his first wife; she died Dec. 29, 1838.

After the death of his second wife he moved to Scituate where he died and was buried at Hull.

Of Scituate, Mass.

CHILDREN OF JOHN AND ELIZABETH

851. Elizabeth, b. Nov. 30, 1793; d. Feb. 19, 1870; m. Nov. 22, 1812, James Marble, of Hingham.
852. John, b. March 3, 1797; d. April 17, 1828; m. Nov. 3, 1818, Emma Dill.
853. Elizabeth, b. Oct. 9, 1802; d. unmarried.
854. Martha Gould, b. Oct. 9, 1802; d. Oct. 9, 1829; m. Dec. 21, 1824, Nathaniel Fearing Lane, of Hingham.

A 440

Thomas Reed, son of Samuel and Mary (Torrey) Reed.

b. Dec. 10, 1771; d. Jan. 12, 1843.

m. Sept. 12, 1792, Sarah White; she died April 15, 1851, aged eighty years.

Of Weymouth.

CHILDREN

855. Sarah, b. Jan. 20, 1793; d. unmarried.
856. Hannah, b. Feb. 18, 1795; m. Elijah Pierce, of Weymouth.
857. Mary, b. Feb. 13, 1797; m. Capt. Joseph Elliot Clark.
858. Margaret, b. Dec. 16, 1798; m. Harry Harrington; lives at Quincy.
859. Mehetable, b. Feb. 8, 1801; d. young.
860. Loring W., b. Oct. 3, 1803; m. Ann Pool.
861. Thomas, b. in 1816; d. Feb. 19, 1859; m. Sept. 8, 1841, Elizabeth Hayward; she d. Sept. 8, 1855, aged 34.
862. Susannah, b. Jan. 16, 1807.
863. Rachel, b. ———; m. Sept. 17, 1833, Benjamin Newcomb.

A **442**

Philip Reed, son of Samuel and Polly (Greenleaf) Reed.
b. July 31, 1777.
m. ———, Polly Taylor, of Hanson.

Lived in South Abington, and was known as Dea. Reed of South Abington.

CHILDREN

864. Mary, b. Oct. 1, 1800.
865. Philip, b. Sept. 19, 1802; m. Dec. 15, 1825, Sapphira Howland.
866. Jane, b. Sept. 30, 1804.
867. Eliza, b. Oct. 31, 1806.
868. Phebe, b. April 16, 1809.

A **444**

William Reed, son of Samuel and Polly (Greenleaf) Reed.
b. ———.
m. ———.

Of Weymouth, Mass.

CHILD

869. Samuel, b. ———.

A **448**

Isaac Reed, son of Hezekiah and Deborah (Tirrel) Reed.
b. ———, 1774.

m. in 1803, Sally Stetson.

Lived in East Bridgewater, Mass.

CHILDREN

870. Sally, b. Oct. 22, 1803; d. Feb. 24, 1869.
871. Isaac, b. Jan. 26, 1805; m. 1st. Dec. 18, 1831; d. in 1844; m. 2d. in 1849, Sarah Porter.
872. Nahum, b. Dec. 15, 1806; m. Oct. 6, 1840, Maria Witherell.
873. Dexter, b. Jan. 21, 1809; m. in 1842, Lydia Wright.
874. James Thaxter, b. Oct. 8, 1815; m. 1st. in 1844, Eliza A. Keith; m. 2d. Mary A. Severance.
875. Calvin, b. April 3, 1819; m. in 1844, Mary S. Bates.
876. Diantha, b. April 21, 1821; m. Tolman French, from Maine.

A 449

Jeremiah Reed, son of Hezekiah and Deborah (Tirrel) Reed.

b. in 1777.

m. March 3, 1803, Rebecca Jenkins, daughter of David and Sarah (Spooner) Jenkins; she was born Feb. 15, 1781; died Aug. 19, 1848.

Of East Bridgewater.

CHILDREN

877. Albert, b. Aug. 23, 1803; m. in 1832, Almira Drake, of Hanson.
878. Melvin, b. March 30, 1806; m. Nov. 16, 1829, Emily Pool.
879. Nathaniel, b. Sept. 17, 1807; m. March 24, 1831, Betsy M. Bartlett.
880. David, b. July 2, 1812; m. 1st. in 1836, Nancy Smith; m. 2d. Oct. 9, 1839, Eliza Ann Bates.
881. Charles Spooner, b. Sept. 16, 1816; m. 1st. Clarissa S. Gurney; m. 2d. Rebecca T. Stetson.

A 450

Calvin Reed, son of Hezekiah and Deborah (Tirrel) Reed.

b. in 1780.

m. Oct. 15, 1807, Hannah Ludden.

Lived in Abington.

CHILDREN

882. Oakes, b. Sept. 11, 1808; m. in 1832, Letitia B. Hobart.
883. Deborah, b. Feb., 1810; m. in 1831, Obadiah Reed.
884. Hezekiah, b. July 12, 1812; m. Elizabeth Josselyn.
885. Susannah Pratt, b. Dec. 7, 1814; d. 1849; m. in 1831, Mark Dunbar, of E. Bridgewater.

A 451

Joseph Reed, son of Hezekiah and Deborah (Tirrel) Reed.
b. Oct. 18, 1782; d. Feb. 22, 1868.
m. in 1807, Charlotte Stetson, daughter of Peleg and Ruth Stetson; she died Jan. 19, 1874.

Lived in Whitman.

CHILDREN

886. Lucius, b. June 7, 1808; d. April 29, 1868; m. Jan. 7, 1833, Selina Dyer.
887. Aaron, b. Aug. 2, 1811; d. Jan. 22, 1892; m. Sept. 15, 1836, Hannah Fullerton.
888. Charlotte Tirrel, b. Sept. 14, 1814; d. June 27, 1863; unmarried.
889. Joseph, b. Sept. 12, 1817; d. Jan. 14, 1887; m. 1843, Mehetable Jenkins.
890. Daniel, b. June 18, 1820; m. 1st. Mary Ann Smith; m. 2d. Oct. 17, 1880, Sarah (Lewis) Poole, widow of ——— Poole.
891. Marcus Stetson, b. Jan. 3, 1824; d. ———; m. Susan M. Whitman (no children).
892. Quincy, b. June 5, 1826; d. unmarried.
893. Ruth G., b. Sept. 22, 1828; d. Nov. 3, 1837.

A 452

Jared Reed, son of Hezekiah and Deborah (Tirrel) Reed.
b. in 1785; d. in 1855.
m. 1st. in 1811, Mehetable Gardner.
m. 2nd. Nov. 25, 1832, Electa Phillips.

Settled in East Bridgewater.

CHILDREN OF JARED AND MEHETABLE

894. Samuel P., b. ———; m. in 1840, Lemira D. Hurd.
895. Timothy, b. ———.
896. Mehetable, b. ———; m. in 1844, Alvan Porter, of Marshfield.

A 458

Ezekiel Reed, son of Ezekiel and Mary (Rogers) Reed.
b. Sept. 16, 1772.
m. 1st. in 1794, Rebecca Edson, daughter of Jesse Edson.

m. 2nd. Oct. 27, 1808, Hannah Littlefield, by Rev. J. Briggs; she died Jan. 25, 1845.

m. 3rd. Dec. 10, 1845, Polly Luddens.

Settled in West Bridgewater.

CHILDREN OF EZEKIEL AND REBECCA

897. **Emma, b. Aug. 7, 1795; m. in 1813, Jacob Tirrel.**
898. **Lydia B., b. May 30, 1797.**
899. **Josiah, b. March 2, 1799; m. Jennet Keith, daughter of John Keith.**
900. **Edwin B., b. Jan. 20, 1804; m. Furosina Glass, of Duxbury.**
901. **Charles Briggs, b. May 21, 1806; d. May 3, 1836; m. Eunice B. Harden.**

A **462**

Col. Jesse Reed, son of Ezekiel and Mary (Rogers) Reed.

b. in 1778.

m. 1st. in 1800, Hannah Howard, daughter of Caleb Howard.

m. 2nd. May 28, 1850, Lovisa Lindsey, daughter of James Lindsey.

Hobart's Abington says, "Jesse Reed, son of Ezekiel and Mary, born in 1778, married Hannah Howard, daughter of Caleb Howard in 1800. He is known as Col. Reed and lives in Marshfield. He has probably been the author of more new inventions, and obtained more patents than any other man in the United States.

"Among his long lists of his new inventions are machines known as the 'Odiorne Tool' or 'Reed Tool'; the machine is now in almost universal use for making cut nails; and machines for steering vessels, as well as various kinds of pumps, treenail machines, cotton gins, &c. He is said to be a man of great industry and indomitable perseverance. He has made and lost several fortunes. Although poor, he has made many rich, and his name will be remembered by future generations with respect and gratitude. Though no towering monument shall be erected to his memory, yet every nail driven in our dwellings, will speak forth the benefits of his wonderful ingenuity."

Hobart's Abington, says farther, "The blacksmiths have been few." Among them he mentions Cyrus Stearns and Thomas W. Stearns.

Cyrus Stearns invented the circular claw to the modern nail or claw hammer. The claw was formerly at a right angle, and none others were in use until Cyrus Stearns made several with the circular claw, which soon became the universal pattern.

CHILDREN OF JESSE AND HANNAH

902. Eliza, b. ———; m. June 14, 1818, John Davenport.
903. Hannah Howard, b. March, 1803; d. 1841, at East Bridgewater; m. Martin McLauthlin, of Mansfield.
904. Horatio Gates, b. ———; m. Wealthy Walker.
905. Simeon R., b. Oct. 1804; d. young.
906. Thomas, b. ———.
907. Harriet W., b. ———; m. Joseph Parsons, of Marshfield.
908. Mary, b. ———.
909. Ann M., b. ———; m. Charles Walker; lives at Marshfield.
910. Roxanna, b. ———.
911. George W., b. ———; d. young.
912. Jesse, b. ———; d. ———.

CHILDREN OF JESSE AND LOVISA

913. Mary Louisa, b. Aug. 9, 1853.
914. Jesse Edwards, b. Jan. 17, 1857.

A 465

Briggs Rogers Reed, son of Ezekiel and Mary (Rogers) Reed.
b. May 2, 1784; d. Sept. 28, 1835, in Danvers.
m. May 21, 1809, Betsy Hutchinson, of Danvers; she died March 31, 1850.

His son, Joseph Warren, was killed by the explosion of a boiler on board the "Empire State" at Fall River, July 27, 1856. He was a Baptist minister, very pious and devoted; and his sudden and awful death spread a gloom over the Christian community where his devotion and zeal had been known.

CHILDREN

915. Mary Ann, b. in Boston, Jan. 1, 1810; m. Wm. E. Kimball, of Topsfield.

COL. JESSE REED.

916. Elizabeth, b. Dec. 17, 1811, at Weymouth; m. Richard Phillips, Esq., of Topsfield.
917. Susan Jane, b. May 11, 1814, at Pembroke; m. William Alley.
918. William Briggs, b. Dec. 15, 1816, at Danvers; m. Eliza Howard.
919. Edward Rogers, b. March 14, 1819.
920. Augustus, b. April 13, 1821; m. Laura Ann Leach.
921. George W., b. Aug. 5, 1823; m. 1st. Oct. 20, 1852, Ellen Howard; m. 2d. Oct. 29, 1857, Hannah Elizabeth Marston.
922. John, b. Aug. 13, 1825.
923. James Hervey, b. Jan. 28, 1828. He was a teacher in St. Louis.
924. Joseph Warren, b. May 7, 1830; d. July 27, 1856.
925. Cornelia H., b. Aug. 28, 1832.

A 466

Samuel Licander Reed, son of Ezekiel and Mary (Rogers) Reed.

b. July 24, 1786, in Bridgewater.

m. Feb. 27, 1817, Nancy Gray, of Watertown, Mass.

Settled in Gardiner, Me., where he carried on the manufacture of nails.

Of Gardiner, Me.

CHILDREN

926. Samuel Licander, b. Oct. 24, 1817.
927. Thomas Rogers, b. May 1, 1819.
928. Harriet Newell, b. Aug. 19, 1821; d. Aug. 28, 1822.
929. Alonzo, b. Jan. 20, 1824; d. Aug. 9, 1852; m. Adeline White, of Watertown, Mass.
930. Jesse, b. Feb. 8, 1826.
931. George William, b. April 24, 1831; d. ———; m. Hannah Augusta Currier, of Bath, Maine.

A 467

Samuel Reed, Jr., son of Samuel and Betsey (Smith) Reed.

b. Sept. 1, 1782; d. April 13, 1869.

m. 1st. March 7, 1805, Sally Bates; b. Jan. 1, 1780; d. Oct. 13, 1822.

m. 2nd. Feb. 16, 1823, Sarah Teasiear; d. Oct. 16, 1849.

CHILDREN OF SAMUEL AND SALLY BATES

932. William Q., b. July 24, 1806, in Jefferson Co., N. Y.; d. Jan. 28, 1877; m. Aug., 1827, Harriet Leach.
933. Prentice J., b. Oct. 18, 1807, in Jefferson Co., N. Y.; d. May 24, 1859; m. Sept. 19, 1833, Jedidah K. Kingsbury.
934. Lucy B., b. Jan. 20, 1810, in Lewis Co., N. Y.; d. Jan. 11, 1813.
935. Betsy S., b. Feb. 10, 1812, in Lewis Co., N. Y.; d. Oct. 18, 1883; m. Abiah H. Stevens.
936. Samuel C., b. Oct. 28, 1814, in Orleans Co., N. Y.; d. Aug. 30, 1847; m. ———.
937. Hiram B., b. Sept. 28, 1816, in Orleans Co., N. Y.; d. July 27, 1818.
938. Sally B., b. June 17, 1818, in Orleans Co., N. Y.; m. Manly C. St. John, April 28, 1838.
939. Annis B., b. March 30, 1820, in Orleans Co., N. Y.; d. March 12, 1882; m. April 19, 1846, Graves L. St. John.

CHILDREN OF SAMUEL AND SARAH

940. Hannah Jane, b. Nov. 12, 1823, in Orleans Co., N. Y.; d. Jan. 23, 1889; m. in 1844, Lovell Farr.
941. Maria A., b. March 9, 1825, in Orleans Co., N. Y.; d. April, 1893; m. July 26, 1843, Lewis Prentice; divorced and m. Aug. 24, 1853, Luther B. Allen.
942. Hiram Joseph, b. May 23, 1827, in Orleans Co., N. Y.: d. Sept. 1, 1857; m. Eliza Keyes, about 1846.
943. Rachel Rosina, b. June 16, 1829, in Orleans Co., N. Y.; d. July 8, 1851.

A 469

Daniel Reed, son of Samuel and Betsy (Smith) Reed.
b. July 26, 1786; d. Feb. 28, 1874.
m. 1st. in 1804, Lucy Bates; b. May 5, 1787; d. July 12, 1814. Both of Chesterfield, Mass.
m. 2nd. Mercy Nash; b. Oct. 6, 1790; d. May 2, 1821.
m. 3rd. Marrilla Knapp; b. March 11, 1804; d. June 2, 1862.

Children of the first wife all born in Chesterfield, Mass., except Horace, who was born in Orleans county, N. Y. By second wife, Mercy was born in Chesterfield and Napoleon B. was born in Orleans county, N. Y. All of the children of the third wife were born in Orleans county, N. Y.

CHILDREN OF DANIEL AND LUCY

944. Fordyce, b. June 20, 1807; d. Sept. 7, 1848; m. May 21, 1837, Eunice Swan, of Kingston, Vt.
945. Louisa, b. April, 1808; d. Oct., 1808.
946. Daniel W., b. Jan. 22, 1810; d. April 1, 1885; m. Aug. 7, 1833, Electa Hubbard.
947. Lucy B., b. Feb. 22, 1812; d. Jan. 17, 1867; m. in 1835, Cyrus Stearns.
948. Horace, b. May 31, 1814; d. Aug. 15, 1876; m. Mahalah Hitchcock.

CHILDREN OF DANIEL AND MERCY

949. Mercy, b. Nov. 21, 1816; d. July 7, 1878; m. May 29, 1840, Orrin Moffitt.
950. Napoleon B., b. Jan. 12, 1818; m. in Nov., 1838, Czarina Hall Glazier.

CHILDREN OF DANIEL AND MARILLA

951. Alonzo, b. Jan. 21, 1823; d. April 8, 1882; m. Jan. 21, 1845, Celia Ann Sprague.
952. Susan M., b. Nov. 11, 1824; m. Oct. 6, 1846, Amos Robinson Sprague.
953. Samuel, b. March 7, 1827; d. March 27, 1887; m. Nov. 8, 1850, Sarah M. Partridge.
954. Sylvester Franklin, b. Oct. 6, 1829; d. Jan. 26, 1884; m. July 4, 1853, Maria Louisa Underhill.
955. Nelson Knapp, b. Sept. 11, 1831; m. 1st. June, 1853, Julia Ann Weeks; m. 2d. Dec. 2, 1863, Julia Augusta Dikeman.
956. Juliaette, b. Jan. 12, 1835; d. Oct. 8, 1882; m. Oct. 23, 1853, Martin C. Dawes.
957. Ellen Rosalthia, b. June 19, 1841; m. ———.

A 470

Simeon Reed, son of Samuel and Betsy (Smith) Reed.
b. March 30, 1789; d. Nov. 3, 1865.
m. 1st. Feb. 14, 1814, Bersheba Thayer; d. Dec. 4, 1817.
m. 2nd. May 4, 1820, Mary Whitton; d. Nov. 1, 1850.
m. 3rd. Nov. 22, 1851, Mrs. Eunice (Swan) Reed, widow of Fordyce Reed (b. Oct. 10, 1808; d. Sept. 28, 1880).

Was chosen captain of Company "I" 4th Mass. State Militia in 1824, and served several years under Col. Austin Bryant. He was selectman in 1829 and 1830.

His children were all born in Chesterfield, Mass.

CHILDREN OF SIMEON AND BERSHEBA

958. Hiram Smith, b. Aug. 2, 1816; d. Dec. 23, 1864; m. Aug. 11, 1844, Amanda Noyes.
959. Stillman Sears, b. Dec. 1, 1817; d. Sept. 22, 1874; m. Pamelia Paden.

CHILDREN OF SIMEON AND MARY

960. Sylvester Simeon, b. Jan. 8, 1821; d. Oct. 27, 1823.
961. Cyrus Monroe, b. Jan. 27, 1823; m. June 18, 1846, Polly W. Bates.
962. Mary Maria, b. Sept. 15, 1825; d. Dec. 18, 1851; m. Oct. 19, 1845, Paul H. Cudworth.
963. Franklin W., b. Jan. 27, 1828; d. Oct. 22, 1847.
964. Alanson W., b. Jan. 8, 1831; d. Sept. 21, 1878.
965. Daniel Whitton, b. Sept. 10, 1835; d. March 20, 1876; m. Oct. 20, 1863, Marcella Gould.
966. Edwin Tripp, b. Feb. 17, 1840; d. Sept. 21, 1841.

A 472

Joseph Reed, son of Samuel and Betsy (Smith) Reed.
b. May 26, 1793; d. Nov. 25, 1866.
m. Sept. 9, 1813, Wealthy Williams, in New York.

He was a native of Chesterfield, Mass. Was but a short time in the war of 1812, for which he received in 1856, a land warrant for 160 acres of government land. Cyrus M. Reed, of West Springfield, Pa., writes: "I also found the name of Joseph Reed (in Records of Chesterfield, Mass.) as First Serg't of Co. I 4th Mass. State Militia: and saw several orders calling the Company out, signed Joseph Reed." He was both a fifer and a drummer.

The six eldest of his children were born in Orleans county, N. Y.; the three next were born in Chautauqua county, N. Y.; and the three youngest in Geauga county, Ohio.

CHILDREN

967. Simeon Smith, b. April 19, 1815; m. June 18, 1844, Adaline Olds.
968. Emily Mercy, b. Nov. 27, 1816; d. Feb. 8, 1899; m. April 2, 1840, E. Nelson Wetherell.
969. Lucy Wealthy, b. May 11, 1818; d. May 17, 1845; m. Oct. 1, 1840, Andrew J. Barrows.

970. Otis Elbridge, b. March 13, 1820; m. April 3, 1845, Huldah E. Snow.
971. Freeman Williams, b. Oct. 27, 1822; d. May 27, 1862; m. April 13, 1845, R. Lucina Cole.
972. Joseph Wiram, b. Oct. 21, 1824; d. ———; m. 1st. Dec. 27, 1844, Rachel Ann Wells; m. 2d. April 9, 1865, Martha Jane Howard.
973. Alanson, b. Oct. 5, 1826; d. Feb. 2, 1844.
974. Phebe Esther, b. Sept. 27, 1828; d. Feb. 9, 1897; m. April 21, 1853, Wendel Fockler.
975. Amanda Maria, b. Sept. 22, 1831; m. Dec. 9, 1847, Alvah Lewis Rowley.
976. Daniel, b. Aug. 18, 1833; m. Sept. 22, 1873, Huldah E. Dann.
977. Elisha Rice, b. Dec. 5, 1835; m. Feb. 13, 1866, Isabella Owen Brown.
978. Susan Louisa, b. March 19, 1839; m. Aug. 21, 1856, Edmund Davis.

A 478

Alanson Reed, son of Samuel and Betsy (Smith) Reed.
b. June 21, 1807; d. Aug. 29, 1837.
m. ———, Jane Everetts.

He sailed for China Sept. 22, 1835, to devote his life to missionary work. He mastered the language and had begun his life-work when he was stricken down by death, leaving a wife but no children. After his death his wife returned to America.

A 483

Benjamin Reed, son of Benjamin and Huldah (Pratt) Reed.
b. Aug. 4, or 17, 1779; d. Oct. 1845, in Somerset, Vt.
m. ———, Fanny Granger; d. at Somerset.

The following account of Benjamin Reed's family is given from memory by David Reed and his wife Lizzie (Hill) Reed.

Mrs. David of East Dummerston, Vt., says, "She has heard many say that 'They came over the mountain to Somerset, Vt., on horseback, and that she carried her infant daughter in her arms.'"

"Over the mountain" locally means from Bennington county.

She said there were no roads, and they made their way through the mountain forests by the "blazed" trees, cut by the axes of the pioneers, who had preceded them. Benjamin (2nd) died in Somerset, Vt., of typhoid fever, the large family were all sick with the same disease at the same time.

CHILDREN

979. Betsy, b. ———; m. a Grant. Lived near the mountain or in Hoosic; d. in Shaftsbury, Vt. Has a son, Newton Grant, living in Shaftsbury, Vt.
980. Benjamin, b. ———; d. in Somerset, also lived in Dummerston, Vt.
981. Fanny, b. ———; m. a Dotty.
982. William, b. ———; went to Ohio.
983. Huldah, b. ———; m. a Ward in Worcester.
984. Mary, b. ———; m. a Harrington; d. in New Braintree, Vt.
985. Cyrus, b. ———; d. in the army.
986. Luciny, b. ———; living in W. Brattleboro, Vt. (1898).
987. Franklin, b. ———; d. in Somerset, Vt.
988. David, b. about 1823; m. Aug. 1847, Lizzie A. Hill; living in E. Dummerston, Vt. (1898); came to Dummerston about 1844, about two years after the death of his grandfather.
989. Sarah, b. ———; living in Williamsville, Vt. (1898).
990. Charles, b. ———; d. in Somerset, Vt.

A 487

David Reed, son of Benjamin and Huldah (Pratt) Reed.

b. Nov. 19, 1788; d. July 13, 1842.

m. 1st. March 29, 1810, Mary Martha Morse, daughter of Ebenezer and Henrietta (Siverly) Morse who was born July 28, 1789; d. April 24, 1826.

m. 2nd Nov. 23, 1826, Lucy Keyes, daughter of Jonas and Bridget (Reed) Keyes of Putney, Vt.; b. Aug. 21, 1793; d. Jan. 19, 1880.; buried at Forest Hills, Roxbury, Mass.

According to an old record he was living in Newfane, Vt., sometime before 1812. He built a house that was called the Parrish, it was still standing and occupied in 1892, by a Mr. Betterly. He moved to Williamsville about 1816, and kept

the first hotel there. He is supposed to have removed to West Dummerston about 1829 and also kept the hotel there. It was on the main road from Williamsville to Brattleboro, the building was still standing in 1898.

David also at one time in his life and during later years lived for a time in Dracut, Mass., a suburb of Lowell, where he carried on a baking business. He afterwards removed to Williamsville, Vt., where he died July 13, 1842.

Bridget Keyes, mother of Lucy Keyes Reed, was the daughter of Samuel Reed and Hannah Underwood Reed of Westford, Mass. Samuel Reed being a descendant of Esdras Reed, one of the first settlers of Boston.

David, while living in Dracut, Mass., was injured by a carriage accident, which weakened his health and obliged him to give up a prosperous business and return with his family to Dummerston, Vt., where he died shortly afterwards. He lies buried in Williamsville, Vt., Cemetery, beside Mary Martha his first wife and their child Ransford. At the death of David, his widow Lucy and their three children, Lucy, Juliette, and David removed to Roxbury, Mass., where they all resided for many years. The widow Lucy was a member of the Warren street M. E. Church. She died in Roxbury, Jan. 19, 1880. She lies buried in the Forest Hills Cemetery.

Jonas Keyes, father of Lucy (Keyes) Reed, was son of Daniel Keyes, 1731-1814, and Abigail Porter, 1738-1830, both died in Putney, Vt., but came there from Westford and Chelmsford. The Reed and Keyes houses still stand in Westford (1898).

CHILDREN OF DAVID AND MARY

991. Ransford, b. Dec. 29, 1810; d. July 4, 1818.

992. Chas. Edson, b. Jan. 3, 1813; d. Aug. 19, ——; m. 1st. Matilda Billings; m. 2d. Emma ———.

993. Henrietta Morse, b. Aug. 29, 1815; d. Feb. 12, 1837.

994. William Nelson, b. Sept. 7, 1817; d. Dec. 13, 1855; m. Sept. 4, 1839, Lucy Maria Stevens, of Watertown, Mass.

995. Martha Ann, b. Aug. 26, 1820; d. May 2, 1890, in Omaha, Neb.; m. 1st. May 10, 1844, Matthew M. Loud; m. 2d. Elijah Ware.

996. Lucius Elliot, b. April 20, 1825; m. ———; Helen Graves.

CHILDREN OF DAVID AND LUCY

997. Lucy Priscilla, b. Oct. 25, 1827, in Williamsville, Vt.; d. March, 1860; was a member of the first Universalist Church in Roxbury; unmarried.

998. Juliette Emily, b. July 29, 1831, in Vt.; lived in Roxbury until 1898, now resides with her brother David in W. Newton.

999. David Keyes, b. Sept. 7, 1833; m. 1st. June 25, 1851, Fausta McElroy; m. 2d. June 2, 1858, Caroline A. Fernald, of Boston.

A 489

Calvin Reed, son of Benjamin and Huldah (Pratt) Reed.

b. Dec. 2, 1793; d. July 26, 1850.

m. Feb. 22, 1830, in Mandarin, Fla., Mary Reynolds, daughter of Benjamin Reynolds, of Putney, Vt.; d. Jan. 24, 1833.

m. 2nd. March 1, 1834, Rebekah E. Jones.

Calvin Reed was one of the parties who attended the meeting to give the town of Mandarin its name. He was magistrate, postmaster and kept a store. He did much to improve and build up the place.

In connection with a Mr. Lowell he bought a large tract of land on the St. John's river. The old home is still standing and occupied by his grandchildren. The parapet to protect the town from Seminole Indians (1835-40) was built on Calvin's property, the remains of the works can still be traced. He was accidentally drowned in the St. John's river.

CHILD

1000. Charles Franklin, b. April 11, 1831; d. Jan. 19, 1893; m. Feb. 15, 1852, Sarah James.

A 490

Luther Reed, son of Benjamin and Huldah (Pratt) Reed.

b. April 16, 1796; d. Nov. 27, 1851.

m. Feb. 24, 1831, Jerusha Wilson, daughter of Luke Wilson; she died May 24 and was buried in East Putney, Vt., Cemetery.

Lived in East Putney, Vt.

Luther Reed was a stage driver and did teaming between Boston and Putney, Vt., in the days before the railroads. He owned a small farm adjoining his father Benjamin's. The farm was sold to Chas. Campbell who sold it to Warren Leach, the father of the present owner and occupant. The house is still standing (1898) and is occupied by Geo. W. Leach, who points out the room where Luther Reed died. The house stands on the bank of the Connecticut river, and a gigantic maple, whose trunk touches the house, was planted by Harriet Reed, daughter of Luther Reed, who took a tiny shoot from the water's edge and planted it next to the house.

CHILDREN

1001. Warren, b. Dec. 10, 1831; d. May 17, 1832, buried in E. Putney, Vt., Cemetery.
1002. Mary E., b. Nov. 18, 1833; m. Sept. 1, 1856, Michael Roane, at Chicopee Falls, Mass.
1003. Harvey L., b. March 18, 1836; d. Dec. 22, 1859; he was buried in E. Putney, Vt., Cemetery, near his parents.
1004. Almira J., b. July 13, 1838; m. May 23, 1860, Warren R. Wilson, at Springfield, Mass.
1005. Helen M., b. Sept. 3, 1840; m. Jan., 1877, Chas. F. Brady.
1006. Harriet A., b. July 8, 1843; m. Nov. 22, 1887, James E. Davis in N. Y. City; she d. in Springfield, Mass., July 14, 1899.
1007. George E., b. July 1, 1846; d. March 19, 1848; buried at E. Putney, Vt., Cemetery.

A 496

Abijah Reed, son of Abijah and Sarah (Bates) Reed.

b. June 5, 1777.

m.———, Catherine Lothrop, daughter of Isaac Lothrop of Easton.

Of Easton.

CHILDREN

1008. Abijah, b. ———; d. young.
1009. Lydia, b. Feb. 3, 1800; d. July 1, 1859; m. Edmund Curtis.
1010. Mary, b. March 23, 1801; m. Benjamin Buck.
1011. Sarah, b. Dec. 7, 1804; d. July 23, 1829; m. Edward W. Dean.
1012. Abijah, b. March 14, 1813; d. Sept. 14, 1835.

A 497

Noah Reed, son of Abijah and Sarah (Bates) Reed.

b. June 22, 1780.

m. ——, Lucy Hayward, daughter of Joseph Hayward of Easton.

Of Easton.

Was captain of a military company, which went into service in the war of 1812 from Easton, Mass. Did service in 1814; made major. (See extended account of his service in History of Easton, Mass.)

CHILDREN

1013. Noah, b. March 25, 1804; m. Feb. 21, 1830, Mary Shaw.
1014. Susannah, b. March 22, 1806.
1015. Melvina, b. Aug. 26, 1807.
1016. Lucy, b. Jan. 24, 1809; m. Ebenezer Drake, of Stoughton.
1017. Rotheus, b. July 26, 1811; m. 1st. Miss Howard; m. 2d. Miss Lewis.

A 506

Lt. Bela Reed, Jr., son of Bela and Mehetable Reed.

b. Oct. 3, 1800; d. at Foxbury, Oct. 5, 1827.

m. ——, 1825, Caroline Caswell.

CHILDREN

1018. William Faunce, b. 1826.
1019. Bela, b. ——.

A 507

Elbridge Gerry Reed, son of Bela and Mehetable Reed.

b. Jan. 22, 1809; d. July 13, 1857, at Easton.

m. ——, Maria Keith; she died in 1832.

He was captain of a military company April 18, 1833.

CHILD

1020. William E. (Capt. William E.), b. ——.

A 510

William Reed, son of William and Olive (Pool) Reed.

b. Dec. 12, 1787.

m. 1st. Nov. 21, 1811, Betsy Drake, daughter of Bethuel Drake of Easton; she died at Milton, Aug. 9, 1821.

m. 2nd. Nov., 1822, Abigail Howe, widow of Calvin Howe, in Boston.

On leaving college he spent several years as a teacher, first in Plymouth, then in charge of Milton Academy, and was popular and successful. He afterwards completed a course of study at Divinity School, Cambridge, and preached for several years but never took permanent charge of a parish. In middle life he settled on the homestead of his father at Easton, where for many years he held the commission and performed the duties of a justice of the peace.

CHILDREN OF WILLIAM AND BETSY

1021. William Gurney, b. Sept. 25, 1812, in Plymouth; m. 1st. Sept. 17, 1834, Sophia Witherell, at Chesterfield; m. 2d. Feb. 24, 1859, Susan C. Hyde, of Charlestown; m. 3d. Feb. 21, 1871, Elizabeth Bradlee Pray, of Boston.

1022. Lieuphemia Eustatia, b. Sept. 30, 1815, in Easton; m. Oct. 19, 1836, John A. Hall, of Raynham.

1023. Charles Henry, b. Feb. 5, 1818, at Milton, Mass.; m. Nov. 26, 1840, Mary Brightman Davis, of Westford.

A 511

Rev. David Reed, son of William and Olive (Pool) Reed.

b. Feb. 6, 1790, at Easton, Mass.; d. June 7, 1870, at (Roxbury) Boston, Mass.

m. May 2, 1836, Mary Ann Williams; b. March 28, 1805, at Providence; daughter of Capt. Howell Williams and Dolly (Wheat) Williams.

He was a soldier in the war of 1812.

Of Roxbury, Mass.

David graduated from Brown University in 1810; being a classmate of his elder brother William. Immediately on leaving college he commenced teaching. In Sept., 1810, he took charge of the Plymouth Academy at Bridgewater, and continued this connection two years; in the meantime and during part of the following year, giving attention as

far as other duties permitted, to professional studies with Rev. Dr. Sanger, then minister of the Congregational Society in South Bridgewater. Early in 1813 he removed to Cambridge and pursued his studies at the Divinity School. He commenced preaching in 1814; and from that time until 1821, had charge of different parishes for considerably extended periods, in Maine, New Hampshire, and Connecticut, but was not ordained. The disturbed state of religious opinions in the parishes at that time, at the breaking out of the great controversy between the liberal and orthodox parties in the Congregational body, and his experiences of the privations to which a clergyman's family were liable from precarious and inadequate support, led him to decline a permanent parochial connection, till he should be able, without worldly anxiety or embarrassment, to devote himself fully to professional duty.

The opportunity which his mode of life gave him, in these years of learning the state of religious sentiment and inquiry in various communities, and the growing interest generally manifested in the religious discussions of the time, induced him to propose the publication of a religious newspaper, as an advocate of liberal Christian views; and, with the approbation of his clerical friends, Rev. Dr. Channing, Rev. Dr. Ware and others he commenced in Boston in April in 1821, the publication of the "Christian Register," taking himself its editorial management; and he continued for fifty years as its publisher and proprietor. In politics he was a republican.

CHILDREN

1024. William Howell, b. March 16, 1837; m. 1st. Feb. 13, 1873, Helen Messenger, of Boston; m. 2d. Jan. 12, 1887, Grace Evelyn Atkins.
1025. Eliza Williams, b. Sept. 1, 1838; d. Dec. 1, 1847.
1026. Sophia Henrietta, b. April 13, 1842; d. Oct. 14, 1843.

A 513

Jason Reed, son of William and Olive (Pool) Reed.

b. Oct. 14, 1794, at Easton, Mass.; d. July 13, 1873, at Milton, Mass.

JASON REED.

m. May 19, 1824, Nancy Elizabeth Coates; b. April 16, 1795, at Boston; d. Feb. 18, 1873. She was the daughter of Ezra and Elizabeth Tudor (Birchstead) Coates.

He was fitted for college by his uncle (by marriage) Rev. David Gurney of Middleborough, Mass. Graduated at Harvard University in 1816. He attended the Unitarian church, he being secretary and treasurer of the parish in Milton for many years. He was a lawyer, held many town offices, was for many years a member of the State Legislature. In 1836, on account of his failing health, he gave up practice of law and removed to Milton where he purchased the estate of his father-in-law, Mr. Ezra Coates, where he remained until his decease, in 1873. A public road was laid out through the old homestead a few years ago which at the request of his daughter and in honor of her father was called Reedsdale road.

CHILD

1027. Elizabeth Tudor Lyman, b. Feb. 14, 1828, at Milton, Mass.; d. unmarried.

A 514

Daniel Reed, son of William and Olive (Pool) Reed.
b. March 22, 1797; d. Oct. 2, 1879.
m. 1st. Sept. 17, 1821, Sally Wild.
m. 2nd. Feb. 10, 1828, Persis C. Hammond, daughter of Thomas Hammond, of Carver.
m. 3rd. May 15, 1832, Betsy T. Hammond; b. Dec. 1, 1803; d. Oct. 11, 1843.
m. 4th. Dec. 8, 1847, Mary Ann Richardson.
Of Easton, Mass.

CHILDREN OF DANIEL AND SALLY

1028. Fidelia, b. Aug. 13, 1822; lives at Perkins Place, Roxbury, Mass.; m. April 12, 1853, John Jay Heard.
1029. Sally Wild, b. July 30, 1825; d. Aug. 23, 1865; m. May 4, 1847, Henry Daily, of Easton; d. Nov. 4, 1862.

CHILDREN OF DANIEL AND PERSIS

1030. Persis H., b. June 26, 1829; d. unmarried.

CHILDREN OF DANIEL AND BETSY

1031. Charlotte Augusta, b. Feb. 21, 1833; d. March 2, 1835.
1032. Almira Hammond, b. Feb. 9, 1835; d. unmarried. Lived in Bridgewater, Mass.
1033. Melissa Cobb, b. Feb. 6, 1837; m. May 10, 1883, Samuel W. Mabry, of Halifax, N. C.
1034. Olive Janette, b. March 20, 1839; m. June 17, 1868, Francis E. Gilmore; he d. April 26, 1873.
1035. Thomas Hammond, b. March 25, 1841; d. Dec. 29, 1851.

CHILD OF DANIEL AND MARY

1036. Daniel Richardson, b. July 19, 1850; d. Oct. 9, 1850.

A 515

Seth Reed, son of William and Olive (Pool) Reed.

b. Aug. 22, 1799.

m. July 22, 1827, Lucy Holden; b. May 3, 1804; d. Nov. 13, 1885.

He was a merchant in Baltimore, and assisted in procuring data for J. Whittimore Reed's book in 1861, and later gave information relative to his branch of the family to the compiler of this work.

Of Baltimore, Md.

CHILDREN

1037. Olive Ann, b. in Boston, June 2, 1828; d. Sept. 8, 1828.
1038. William Edward, b. Nov. 16, 1829, in Boston; m. Dec. 8, 1853, Sarah E. Thomas.
1039. Samuel Payson, b. (in Baltimore) March 24, 1833; d. July 13, 1864; m. Aug. 23, 1855, Rachel Ann Brown.
1040. James Holden Lander, b. (in Baltimore) July 6, 1835; m. Jan. 27, 1869, Lulu J. Daupree.
1041. Wallace Willard, b. (in Baltimore) July 26, 1838; d. unmarried.
1042. Seth Gurney, b. (in Baltimore Co.) July 20, 1840; d. June 26, 1880; m. Sally McCurley.
1043. Lucy Holden, b. (in Baltimore Co.) July 24, 1842; d. Oct. 13, 1886, in Boston; unmarried.
1044. Charlotte Whipple, b. (in Baltimore Co.) Nov. 12, 1845; d. unmarried.
1045. Mary Laura, b. (in Baltimore Co.) July 2, 1849; m. July 12, 1875, Joseph H. Sherbert, who was a flour and grain merchant of the firm of Sherbert, Maxwell & Co., 227 South street, Baltimore.

A 516

Lyman Reed, son of William and Olive (Pool) Reed.

b. Dec. 28, 1801, at Easton, Mass.; d. Feb. 17, 1876, at Boston, Mass.

m. Oct. 22, 1832, Marcia Ann Harris; b. April 30, 1810, at Strafford, Vt.; d. July 24, 1872, at Boston, Mass. She was the daughter of Judge Jedediah Hyde and Judith (Young) Harris, of Strafford, Vt.

Educated at Milton (Mass.) Academy, of which his brother William was principal. He began his business career, in 1819, as a clerk in a commission house. He was engaged in business in Baltimore from 1832 to 1842, in Boston from 1842 to 1856, in Baltimore from 1856 to 1863, in New York from 1863 to 1872, and in Boston from 1872 to his death. He was a Unitarian. In politics he was a Democrat and served as alderman, in Boston, 1845-6. He was stout, with dark hair and eyes.

Of Boston.

In 1830, Lyman Reed delivered, before the Lyceum in Montpelier, Vt., a lecture on the then new subject of "Rail Roads," and as chairman of a committee presented a report, advocating the building of a railroad from Boston to Ogdensburg by the way of Concord, Montpelier and Burlington.

In his lecture he made the prediction, that the time would soon come when a person leaving Montpelier by the railroad would find himself walking in the streets of Boston in six hours, the time then in making the journey to Boston was fifty-four hours. He was considered crazy and called a lunatic.

In this lecture he used the following language which is without doubt, the first recorded conception of our modern Parlor and Sleeping Cars:

"A carriage can be so constructed that it shall possess every comfort and convenience of the modern steam-boat, the travellers then in this land barge will find themselves seated in a social circle, enjoying every comfort which an

elegant drawing-room can impart, amusing themselves in reading and writing and at the same time travelling at the rate of 20 or 30 miles an hour."

"The farmer of the valley of the Onion River can at evening place his products in the R. R. carriages, take his berth for the night and at sunrise find himself and his vegetables in Boston."

In Sept. 1851, the city of Boston, in appreciation of the benefit it was to derive from the completion of the railroad, proposed and advocated in 1830, held a "R. R. Jubilee," at which President Fillmore and his cabinet, Lord Elgin, Governor General of Canada and other distinguished persons were present. The festivities lasted three days. The feature of the last was the military and civic profession.

To show some of the results accomplished by the completion of the railroad, two wagons, loaded with flour, were, at the particular request of the railroad committee, brought into the procession, one of which was surmounted by a banner bearing the following inscription:

WESTERN VIRGINIA FLOUR
Via Ohio River, Great Lakes, Ogdensburg, and Vermont R. R.
772 Bbls. from one Mill consigned to
Lyman Reed & Co.
Distance 1000 miles in 12 days.
Freight $1.05 from Ohio River to Boston.

On the reverse of the banner were the resolutions presented by Lyman Reed at Montpelier in 1830, one of which reads: "That the public good requires vigorous and persevering efforts on the part of all intelligent and public spirited individuals, until by their enterprise the survey and completion of a R. R. is accomplished from the seaboard at Boston through Lowell, Concord, Montpelier to Lake Champlain and thence to Ogdensburg, N. Y."

Children

1046. Jedediah Harris, b. (in Baltimore) Aug. 2, 1833; d. ———; m. Feb. 20, 1861, Mary Sophia Corner, of Baltimore, Md.

1047. Ellen Jeannette, b. Feb. 8, 1836; unmarried.

1048. Lyman, b. June 9, 1838; d. Feb. 28, 1839 (in Baltimore).
1049. Charles Lewis, b. Aug. 4, 1840; d. Sept. 9, 1842 (in Strafford, Vt.).

A 517

Lucius Reed, son of William and Olive (Pool) Reed.
b. Oct. 27, 1805; d. Nov. 1, 1855.
m. Aug. 19, 1831, Abba Sumner Harris; d. Nov. 6, 1839.
Of Baltimore, Md.

CHILDREN

1050. William Harris, b. (in Baltimore) Aug. 19, 1832.
1051. Lucius, b. (in Baltimore) 1834; d. Nov. 4, 1857 (in Texas).

A 520

James Reed, son of James and Ruth (Porter) Reed.
b. Aug. 13, 1788; d. Dec. 23, 1810.
m. April 19, 1810, Mehetable Dyer, daughter of Christopher (3rd) and Deborah (Reed) Dyer.
Of Abington, Mass.

A 524

Major Marcus Reed, son of James and Ruth (Porter) Reed.
b. Aug. 23, 1798; d. Oct. 6, 1888.
m. May 17, 1821, Mehetable Jenkins, daughter of David and Sarah (Spooner) Jenkins; b. Sept. 21, 1798; d. Nov. 2, 1881.

Major Marcus Reed was a man of superior natural ability, which had been given the right direction by excellent parentage and by a good education in the schools of Abington. These abilities, his reliable honesty and faithfulness were soon taken notice of by his townsmen and he became one of the most popular and favored men of his town. He was called early to serve the town and to fill its offices, often serving in two and three at the same time. He held the position of selectman in the old town of Abington for twenty-four years. He was town clerk, assessor, overseer of the poor, etc. During the Rebellion he was enrolling officer for Abington. This imposed upon him the duty of looking

after the welfare of the families of those who volunteered in their country's service, providing for the needy, counseling and aiding all, in every way and on all occasions as best he could. His military title was obtained in 1827, when for several years he held the position of Major Commandant of the Plymouth county battalion of artillery.

CHILDREN

1052. Marcus, b. Nov. 29, 1823; d. Apr. 22, 1881; m. July 9, 1847, Janet Logan Sproul.
1053. Timothy, b. Sept. 25, 1826; d. July 11, 1890; m. April 21, 1847, Lydia Ann Bourne.
1054. James, b. Feb. 26, 1831; m. Sept. 7, 1851, Peddy W. Howland.

A 525

Cyrus Reed, son of James and Ruth (Porter) Reed.
b. July 23, 1800.
m. Nov. 12, 1829, Mary Noyes.

Son Cyrus was private in Company E 4th Volunteer Infantry.

Of Abington.

CHILDREN

1055. Cyrus, b. Dec. 16, 1834; d. unmarried.
1056. Samuel W., b. Dec. 15, 1837; d. March 29, 1899; m. Ada Norton.

A 526

Bezaleel Reed, son of Elijah and Lucy (Washburn) Reed.
b. Feb. 10, 1780, at Middleborough, Mass.
m. Oct. 10, 1798, Ruth Edson.

Of Middleborough, Mass.

CHILDREN

1057. Bezaleel b. ———.
1058. Paul, b. ———.

A 528

Solomon Reed, son of Elijah and Lucy (Washburn) Reed.
b. April 26, 1785.
m. Feb. 23, 1809, Delancy Shaw.

Of Middleborough, Mass.

CHILDREN

1059. Delaney S., b. March 31, 1814, at Middleborough.
1060. Elijah, b. Sept. 11, 1816.
1061. Reliance, b. Feb. 22, 1822.
1062. Iantha, b. ———.

A 530

Elijah Reed, son of Elijah and Lucy (Washburn) Reed.
b. Dec. 28, 1790.
m. ———, Jane Thomas.

Lived at Middleborough, Mass.

CHILDREN

1063. William T., b. March 31, 1814; m. Sept. 24, 1851, Ann M. Watson.
1064. Jane D., b. May 4, 1816.
1065. Henry W., b. Nov. 15, 1818; m. Oct. 30, 1842, Emily Howard.
1066. Franklin, b. March 30, 1821; m. Harriet Richards.
1067. Nathaniel T., b. ———.
1068. Alexander H., b. ———. Did he marry Abigail Knight Stickney, of Hampstead, N. H.? (See Stickney Family, p. 298.)

A 534

Luke Reed, son of Luke and Keziah (Leonard) Reed.
b. Aug. 18, 1788.
m. Ann Leach.

Lived at Middleborough, Mass.

CHILDREN

1069. Adam, b. May 26, 1818; m. Eliza Staples.
1070. Julia Ann, b. Sept. 3, 1822; m. James E. Watson.
1071. Archelaus, b. ———; m. Mary Ann Hilman.
1072. Cyrus P., b. Dec. 24, 1831; m. Nancy Clark.
1073. Luke, b. Feb. 22, 1838.
1074. Gustavus, b. Aug. 15, 1836.

A 546

John Reed, son of Joshua and Deborah (Noyes) Reed.
b. Jan. 29, 1802.
m. Nov. 1833, Hannah G. Barrell.

Lived in East Bridgewater and was a justice of the peace.

CHILDREN

1075. Deborah, b. April 8, 1837.
1076. Hannah G., b. Sept. 1, 1839.
1077. John W., b. Sept. 8, 1842.
1078. Joshua, b. Feb. 3, 1848.

A 549

Cyrus Reed, son of Jacob and Sarah Reed.
b. ———.
m. ———, Cynthia ———.

Moved from Pembroke to New York.

Of New York City.

CHILDREN

1079. James S., b. Dec. 3, 1836; m. Nancy B. Pierce.
1080. Cyrus H., b. June 27, 1844.
1081. Cynthia L., b. Sept. 5, 1847.
1082. Cynthia Henrietta, b. Sept. 5, 1847.

W 551

Daniel Reed, son of Daniel and Mary (Turner) Reed.
b. July 11, 1759.
m. April 4, 1782, Annie Blanchard.

It will be noticed by reference to the will of his grandfather, Daniel Reed, that he bequeathed him all the lands and personal property he possessed in the township of Weymouth.

Of Weymouth.

CHILDREN

1083. Turner, b. about 1782-83; d. April 10, 1806, in his 24th year.
1084. Daniel, b. Nov. 18, 1784; m. 1st. Jan. 1808, Hannah Gurney; m. 2d. Sally Snow.
1085. Deane, b. May 28, 1787; m. July 23, 1812, Elizabeth Norton.
1086. David, b. March 27, 1790; d. Sept. 19, 1869; m. 1st. Elizabeth T. Brown; m. 2d. Nov., 1840, Delia Smith.
1087. Jesse, b. June 20, 1793; m. Feb. 14, 1818, Lucy Johnston Reed.

1088. Anna, b. Jan. 10, 1795; m. March 16, 1815, Richard Holbrook.
1089. Josiah, b. July 28, 1798; d. Aug. 8, 1879; m. June, 1829, Abigail N. Bicknell; d. Aug. 17, 1847.
1090. Molly, b. Jan. 7, 1800; m. ——— Gifford, of South Weymouth, Mass.
1091. Katherine, b. April 10, 1802; d. Sept. 17, 1839; m. Jesse Pierce, of Skowhegan, Me.; d. May 6, 1854.
1092. Gridly, b. Sept. 6, 1804; d. March 21, 1875; m. Nov. 22, 1830, Clarissa Dyer.
1093. Lydia, b. July 2, 1807; m. Warren Blanchard; d. Dec. 28, 1881.
1094. Turner, b. ———.

W 552

Jacob Reed, son of Daniel and Mary (Turner) Reed.
b. Sept. 12, 1762; d. Jan. 21, 1839.
m. Nov. 18, 1799, Nancy Porter.

See his father's will, of which he is sole executor.

Of Abington.

CHILDREN

1095. Jacob, b. March 7, 1801; d. Aug. 1, 1819.
1096. Bela, b. Dec. 2, 1803; m. Joanna S. Lane.
1097. Ezekiel, b. Oct. 14, 1810; d. Oct. 27, 1885; m. Dec. 13, 1831, Cephisa Studley.

W 554

John Reed, son of Daniel and Ann (Dawes) Reed.
b. Aug. 27, 1769.

m. 1st. Dec. 1, 1789, Dorothy Brown, daughter of Samuel and Dorothy (Torrey) Brown; she was born April 8, 1772.

m. 2nd. March 1, 1805, Thankful Jenkins, daughter of David Jenkins, a descendant of Edward Jenkins, of Scituate.

It will be seen by reference to his father's (Daniel Reed) will, that John, Owen, Nancy and Ruth, four of the children of John are mentioned.

Of Abington.

CHILDREN OF JOHN AND DOROTHY

1098. Molly, b. March 31, 1790; d. young.
1099. Nancy, b. Sept. 26, 1792.
1100. John, b. Sept. 15, 1795.
1101. Owen, b. Dec. 5, 1797; m. in 1817, Charlotte Harden.
1102. Ruth, b. June 20, 1802.

CHILDREN OF JOHN AND THANKFUL

1103. Molly, b. Jan. 1, 1806.
1104. Rachel, b. March 25, 1808; m. Isaac Reed.

W 558

Thomas Reed, son of Thomas and Mary (White) Reed.
b. Dec. 12, 1761.
m. May 24, 1783, Joanna Shaw.
Of Rockland, Mass.

CHILDREN

1105. Elizabeth, b. March 13, 1784; m. in 1802, John Lane.
1106. Thomas, b. Nov. 16, 1786; m. Lydia Jenkins.
1107. Goddard, b. May 3, 1788; m. Nov. 13, 1814, Marcia Reed.
1108. (Deacon) Ebenezer, b. July 6, 1790; m. 1st. Nov. 30, 1815, Lucy Jenkins; m. 2d. Patience Penniman.
1109. Simeon Gannet, b. Sept. 29, 1793; d. Oct. 1, 1831; m. June 3, 1829, Rachel Burgess.
1110. Joanna, b. Dec. 3, 1795; m. Samuel Wales.
1111. Albert, b. Oct. 8, 1800; m. 1st. in 1829, Maria Colburn; m. 2d. Nov. 24, 1864, Francis A. Plumer.
1112. Amos Shaw, b. May 22, 1804; m. 1st. Nov. 9, 1826, Huldah B. Loud; m. 2d. Dec. 14, 1834, Rachel B. Reed.
1113. Adeline, b. April 22, 1806; d. ———; m. 1826, Brackley Shaw.
1114. Clarissa, b. June 7, 1808; d. ———; m. Dec. 4, 1828, David Hunt.
1115. Theodore, b. April 7, 1810; m. 1st. Dec. 26, 1830, Clarissa Jenkins; m. 2d. Dec. 31, 1840, Abigail Wilder; m. 3d. Lydia Gurney, widow of Melvin Gurney.
1116. Martha, b. Sept. 8, 1802; m. Dec. 3, 1824, Michael Sylvester, of Hanover.

W 560

Samuel Reed, son of Thomas and Mary (White) Reed.
b. March 11, 1766; d. June, 1805.
m. Aug. 28, 1787, Mary Pool; d. Sept. —, 1839; daughter of Joseph Pool.

Lived in East Abington on the premises now owned by his sons Samuel and Abiah, and gave a piece of land for a burying ground, the site of the present cemetery, on the shore of a pond known as Reed's Pond. He died in 1805, and was one of the first buried on the land he had thus appropriated. He was a man of energy and great physical power. He was a lieutenant of the company of which his brother Thomas was captain and his brother Isaac was ensign. He owned most of the land now in possession of his sons Samuel and Abiah.

Of East Abington.

CHILDREN

1117. Mary, b. March 3, 1789; d. Sept., 1864; m. Peter Ford; lived in Windsor.
1118. Samuel, b. Dec. 18, 1790; m. 1st. April 21, 1810, Polly Corthell; m. 2d. Sept. 15, 1833, Serissa Littlefield Bailey.
1119. Abiah, b. May 19, 1793; m. May 23, 1814, Jane Gurney.
1120. Hannah, b. March 24, 1795; d. young.
1121. Marcia, b. Jan. 19, 1798; m. Goddard Reed, and they live near the meeting house in E. Abington.
1122. Joseph, b. Oct. 28, 1799; m. 1st. Jane Stoddard; m. 2d. Elizabeth (Murch) Clough.
1123. Ruth, b. July 16, 1801; d. young.
1124. Charles, b. Nov. 2, 1802; moved to Ohio, where he still resides.
1125. Elias, b. in 1804; d. young.

W 562

Isaac Reed, son of Thomas and Mary (White) Reed.

b. Aug. 4, 1770.

m. 1st. May 12, 1793, Sarah Pulling, daughter of Sarah Thaxter Pulling, granddaughter of Major Samuel Thaxter.

m. 2nd. Nancy Lincoln.

He was a deacon of the church in South Abington, his widow lived at Taunton.

Of South Abington.

CHILDREN OF ISAAC AND SARAH

1126. John Pulling, b. Sept. 15, 1795; d. in 1802.
1127. Sarah, b. Sept. 19, 1797; m. Aug. 7, 1815, Charles Lane, Jr.
1128. Lucy Johnston, b. May 29, 1800; m. Feb. 14, 1818, Jesse Reed, son of Daniel.

1129. Martha Pulling, b. March 16, 1802; m. May 2, 1819, Seth Pratt.
1130. Mary Hobart, b. April 11, 1804; m. Aug. 1, 1824, Greenwood Cushing.
1131. Isaac, b. Jan. 22, 1806; m. 1st. Sept. 7, 1826, Rachel Reed; m. 2d. Dec. 17, 1829, Eliza F. Shaw.
1132. Betsy Gannet, b. Aug. 25, 1807; m. Oct. 4, 1825, Merrit Jenkins, of E. Bridgewater.
1133. Ruth Torrey, b. July 31, 1809; m. May, 1827, John W. Jenkins, of E. Bridgewater.
1134. Annis, b. Dec. 13, 1811; d. Dec., 1817.

CHILDREN OF ISAAC AND NANCY

1135. Horace, b. Nov. 26, 1820; m. Sept. 21, 1840, Lurana Howland Bates.
1136. William Lincoln, b. Oct. 5, 1825; m. 1st. June 6, 1847, Deborah Chessman; m. 2d. June, 1887, Mrs. Lyman Clark, of Brockton.
1137. Annis, b. Sept. 3, 1828; m. Oct., 1848, Charles H. Cook; lives in Taunton.

W 564

David Reed, son of Frederick and Rebecca (Ayers) Reed.
b. Sept. 30, 1771; d. May 12, 1822.
m. Susan Spear; d. Aug. 26, 1801.

Of Weymouth.

CHILDREN

1138. David A., b. Dec. 6, 1795; m. Aug. 6, 1818, Nancy Loud.
1139. Susan, b. Aug. 15, 1797.
1140. Thomas S., b. June 9, 1800; m. Nov. 5, 1823, Cynthia Shaw.

W 565

Frederick Reed, son of Frederick and Rebecca (Ayers) Reed.
b. April 19, 1774, bapt. April 27, 1774.
m. ———, 1797, Sally Packard.

Settled in New Bedford, had previously lived in Randolph.

Of New Bedford.

W 566

Asa Reed, son of Frederick and Rebecca (Ayers) Reed.
b. May 27, 1777.
m. Esther Hobart, of Brockton, Mass.

He was a butcher and kept a stall in Faneuil Hall Market for many years. He lived in East Randolph, Mass., what is now Holbrook.

CHILDREN

1141. Asa, b. in 1800; m. Sally Curtis, of East Randolph, Mass.
1142. Esther, b. ———; m. May 3, 1830, Lucius T. Packard, of Bridgewater, Mass.
1143. Rebecca Ayers, b. July 17, 1803; m. Nov. 9, 1823, Martin Porter, of North Bridgewater, Mass.
1144. Thomas Jefferson, b. Jan. 6, 1806; m. 1st. Aseneth White; m. 2d. Aug. 3, 1834, Clarissa Belcher by Rev. Mr. Hitchcock.
1145. Sabra, b. ———; m. Thomas West.
1146. George Washington, b. ———; unmarried.

W 570

Isaac Reed, son of Frederick and Hannah (Pool) Reed.

b. June 23, 1795; d. April 12, 1879.

m. May 24, 1819, Cynthia Pratt; m. by Rev. Jacob Norton.

Of Weymouth.

CHILDREN

1147. Eliza, b. Dec. 22, 1819; d. March 17, 1898; m. Benjamin Pratt.
1148. Cynthia P., b. Dec. 25, 1821; m. Sept. 26, 1849, at Weymouth, Silas Whiting.
1149. Mary Ann, b. Jan. 4, 1824; d. July 1, 1898; m. Thomas Holbrook.
1150. Asa T., b. Jan. 1, 1826; m. July 4, 1851, Catherine M. Johnson.
1151. Isaac, b. Feb. 13, 1828; must have died young.
1152. Isaac, Jr., b. Nov. 4, 1831; m. 1st. Sept. 24, 1854, Elizabeth Estelle Lincoln; m. 2d. Nov. 1, 1870, Mrs. Sarah Parker.
1153. Frederick, b. July 29, 1834; m. Aug. 18, 1861, Abbie L. Dyer, of Hingham.
1154. Stephen S., b. May 2, 1838; m. Aug. 17, 1859, Ruth Merritt Curtis.

W 572

William Reed, son of William and Elizabeth (Stammers) Reed.

b. Feb. 27, 1774; d. Sept. 14, 1813.

m. (pub.) Feb. 2, 1799, Relief Penniman, of Braintree; m. Dec. 31, 1779; d. Feb. 14, 1870; daughter of Maj. Stephen and Sarah Penniman.

Of Braintree.

CHILDREN

1155. Dorcas Elizabeth, b. July 10, 1799; m. in 1820, Thomas O. Penniman.
1156. William, b. May 2, 1801; m. Aug. 26, 1824, Susan French.

W 578

John Reed, son of John and Rachel (Clark) Reed.

b. June 21, 1780.

m. in 1801, Lucy Houghton, daughter of Jonas and Lucy (Johnson) Houghton; b. at Berlin, Mass., June 30, 1780; d. at Wyoming, Mass., June 5, 1864.

Of Bolton, Mass.

CHILDREN

1157. John Amory, b. Feb. 23, 1802; m. May 18, 1831, Ann Eliza Rogiers.
1158. Catherine Wood, b. Feb. 7, 1804; d. Feb. 10, 1898; m. Nov. 6, 1828, John Bosworth Swanton, of Bath, Me.
1159. Charlotte Houghton, b. Oct. 4, 1807; d. Feb. 22, 1882; m. in 1837, Joseph Downing Bass Eaton, of Boston.
1160. Maria Clark, b. ———; d. aged 23 or 24.
1161. Lucy Johnson, b. ———; d. aged 8 or 9 years.
1162. James Amory, b. ———; d. aged 1 or 2 years.

W 581

Elias Reed, son of John and Rachel (Clark) Reed.

b. Feb. 16, 1783; d. Jan. 10, 1854.

m. in 1814, Sally Block, of Richmond.

Of Richmond, Va.

He came to Virginia about the year 1807 or 1808. He settled in Petersburg under the patronage of Canterbury & Co., of Boston. After a few years he removed to Richmond and for many years was engaged largely in business. From there he removed to New Orleans and was very successful in his business operations. His health failing he returned to Richmond and was for many years a leading merchant of that city. He established a line of packets be-

tween Richmond and New Orleans, also one between Richmond and the West India Islands. His vessels were freighted with flour to many foreign ports and returned laden with fruits and wines. Being of an enterprising disposition he was the founder of a well known Fire and Marine Insurance Company, which is still in a flourishing condition in Richmond.

The family of Reeds have been noted as amateur musicians of fine taste. Elias Reed at the early age of 18 or 19 (1801-2) used to play in the "Old South" Boston on the violoncello before it could boast of an organ. The instrument used for many years was brought from Boston and is said to be the oldest in the country, and is now in the possession of Leonidas Coil, Washington, D. C.

David Reed, the brother, was a prominent singer in the Handel and Haydn Society of Boston; Elias Reed was in the Richmond theatre the night it was burned but did not remain to the conclusion of the play, a mysterious intuition seemed to prompt him to leave, though urged by his friends not to do so; before he reached home the building was in a blaze.

CHILDREN

1163. Susan, b. Nov. 28, 1815; m. Nov. 13, 1839, David H. Reed.

1164. Rachel, b. in 1816; d. June 6, 1841; m. Jan., 1840, John Bolling Bland.

1165. Elias, b. ———; d. in early manhood; unmarried.

1166. Sarah Ann, b. April 4, 1822; d. June 26, 1899; m. Nov. 22, 1852, Richard Dunn.

1167. Charlotte, b. June 6, 1825; d. June 24, 1897; m. June 6, 1843, Capt. Wm. P. Poythress.

1168. William Block, b. May 6, 1828; d. Sept. 15, 1889; m. 1st. Nov. 25, 1855, Lucie Claiborne Franklin; m. 2d. Feb. 21, 1861. Mary Ann Larus.

1169. Virginia C., b. ———.

1170. John H., b. ———; d. ———; m. Henrietta Gilliam, of Bristol, England.

W **582**

Elihu Reed, son of John and Rachel (Clark) Reed.

b. Feb. 19, 1784, at Weymouth, Mass.; d. Aug., 1863, at Bolton.

m. Nov. 28, 1805, Sabra Houghton, by Rev. Isaac Allen; b. in Bolton Nov. 30, 1786; d. in Bolton, 1848. She was a daughter of Jonas and Lucy (Johnson) Houghton.

Of Bolton.

CHILDREN

1171. Elihu Houghton, b. Jan., 1807; d. Dec., 1880; unmarried.
1172. Charles Warren, b. 1809; d. June 30, 1874; m. 1st. Elizabeth Hersey; m. 2d. Martha Bullard; m. 3d. Rachel Hinkley.
1173. Elizabeth, b. 1813; d. 1813.
1174. Francis Ludovicus, b. March, 1818; d. Feb. 1867; unmarried.
1175. William, b. Dec. 26, 1820; d. Aug., 1875; m. Sarah Sawyer.
1176. James Henry, b. April 28, 1823; m. Jan. 13, 1859, Martha A. Wesson.

W 583

Silas Reed, son of John and Rachel (Clark) Reed.

b. June 13, 1786; d. July 13, 1847, at Manchester, Scott county, Ill.

m. Jan. 13, 1813, Betsy Whitcomb; b. Nov. 18, 1789; d. Sept. 28, 1849, at Manchester, Ill.

Of Manchester, Ill.

CHILDREN

1177. Charlotte Whitcomb, b. Nov. 30, 1813; unmarried; lives in Manchester, Ill.
1178. Ludovicus Warren, b. March 31, 1816; lives in California.
1179. John Clark, b. June 23, 1818; m. Sept. 30, 1841, Caroline Kinsey; lives in Holden, Mo.
1180. Rachel Emily, b. Aug. 25, 1820; m. March 7, 1854, John Murray Haslip; lives in Ill.
1181. Sarah Elizabeth, b. Dec. 21, 1823; m. July 20, 1841, Joseph Haslip.
1182. Catherine B., b. Feb. 26, 1825; m. July 21, 1842, David Robb, of Illinois.
1183. Silas Amory, b. Dec. 4, 1827; m. June 18, 1867, Mary E. Miller; lives in California.
1184. Joseph Hartwell, b. Jan. 8, 1831; d. July 24, 1833, at Alexandria, Va.
1185. James Allen, b. Dec. 28, 1833; d. Sept. 27, 1844, at Manchester, Scott Co., Ill.

W 584

David Reed, son of John and Rachel (Clark) Reed.
b. Oct. 2, 1787; d. Oct. 4, 1848.
m. 1st. ———, Nancy Nourse.
m. 2nd. ———, Eliza Nourse.

Of Richmond, Va.

CHILDREN OF DAVID AND NANCY

1186. David Henry, b. 1816; d. April 17, 1855; m. Nov. 13, 1839, Susan Reed of Richmond, Va.

1187. Ann, b. ———; d. young.

W 585

Henry Ludovicus Reed, son of John and Rachel (Clark) Reed.
b. Sept. 18, 1790, at Weymouth, Mass.; d. Sept. 16, 1886, at Chambersburg, Pa.
m. March 14, 1826 (at Worcester) Charlotte Stickney, daughter of Thomas and Mary (Ward) Stickney; d. at Chambersburg, Pa., Nov. 27, 1891.

Of Chambersburg, Pa.

The following clipping from the daily "Repository" of Chambersburg written two years before his death gives the principal items of interest connected with his life:

"In Repository of June 17, 1884, we published an extensive article on the life of Mr. Reed, written by our postmaster, Mr. E. W. Curriden (who obtained the facts from Mr. Reed's lips), from which we take the following extracts:

"Mr. Reed was born at Weymouth, Massachusetts, some nine miles from Boston, on the 18th of September, 1790. He was next to the youngest of eleven children and the only member of the family who survives. His parents reached the age of 82 years. Of the large family of children but one brother attained advanced years. He died at 80.

"When our venerable citizen was fifteen years of age he entered the store of Jacob Canterbury, dealer in shoes and leather, at the city of Boston. He was there but a short time when he accepted a position in the establishment of his brother Elias, then one of the leading merchants in the city

of Richmond, Va. Some three years following, having occasion to return to Boston and falling into the company of his old friend and employer, Mr. Canterbury, he was prevailed upon to return to the Old Dominion in the interest of that gentleman. He was entrusted with a stock of goods consigned to Fredericksburg, then a town of some commercial importance. War with Great Britain being imminent and business as a consequence being paralyzed in Fredericksburg, Mr. Reed transferred the merchandise in his custody to a store Mr. Canterbury had at Petersburg at the same time.

"The feeling of Americans at that time towards the mother country was exceedingly bitter, and a merchant's reputation was injured by dealing in any article manufactured abroad. In the midst of the general gloom that everywhere prevailed in those tempestuous times, Mr. Reed united with Josephus Colton from his native State in the establishment of a domestic dry goods store at Richmond. The firm was immediately successful in their venture, despite the hard times with which they had to contend, the profits of their first year's business aggregating some seven thousand dollars. They dealt largely, not only in domestic goods, but as the war progressed handled merchandise of various kinds captured by American seamen upon the deep, and at various opportune times Mr. Reed and his partner invested profitably in goods taken from the enemy upon American waters.

"In 1814 Mr. Reed rode from Boston to Richmond on horseback and his journey thither and return was full of exciting incidents as the war with the British was then in progress. Upon reaching Philadelphia on his homeward ride he was arrested by the military authorities of the city upon suspicion of being a British spy and was confronted by the Mayor. Being readily able to have himself identified he was soon released from surveillance. When he approached Washington he learned of its capture by the British, and the destruction of the capitol by fire. Thence to Richmond he was besieged with inhabitants along the road seeking infor-

mation concerning the destruction of the public buildings. On the morning following his return to Richmond he donned the garb of a soldier, shouldered a musket and joined in the defense of the city. For twenty-eight days he lent himself to the 'pomp and circumstance of war,' but at the end of that time the emergency having passed he, together with many other militiamen, was relieved from duty, and was not summoned back into service.

"After the war closed an addition was made to the firm of Colton & Reed in the person of Henry Clark, and the style of the firm was changed to that of Colton, Reed & Clark. The firm established a commission house in Boston, the management of which was entrusted to Mr. Reed. While engaged in business there Mr. Reed was one who attended the corner stone laying of Bunker Hill monument, where he saw General Lafayette and listened to the oration of Daniel Webster, which has taken its place among American classics.

"On the 21st of November, 1820, Mr. Reed visited Plymouth, Mass., and participated in the ceremonies held there at the bi-centennial of the landing of the Pilgrims.

"On the 14th of March, 1826, Mr. Reed was united in marriage with Miss Charlotte Stickney of Worcester, Mass., who retains her faculties and enjoys life with as much zest as her patriarchal husband. Some years subsequently to this marriage Mr. Reed severed his connection with the firm with which he had been identified in Richmond, to accept the inspectorship of the James River and Kanawha Canal Company, and removed to Scottsville, Va., in the discharge of the duties of his position. The canal had been but fairly completed and was regarded as one of the grandest triumphs of the age, and destined to conduce incalculably to the development of the resources of Virginia.

"Mr. Reed remained fourteen years in the employ of the company and at his withdrawal was made the recipient of a series of resolutions passed by the company expressing regret at his withdrawal and generously recognizing the efficiency and integrity which had ever marked his conduct in the dis-

charge of the responsible position so long occupied by him, at Scottsville.

"From Scottsville Mr. Reed removed to the city of Wheeling where he engaged in business for himself. From thence he went to Woodstock in Va., when the 'Mother of Presidents' was in the throes of revolution. Mr. Reed had no sympathy for the mad revolt in which the State was ready to plunge and averred from the outset of the clamor against the ascendency of the Republican party, that should Virginia secede from the Union he would exercise his prerogative as an American citizen and secede from Virginia. The question of dissolving the ties which bound Virginia to the confederacy of States being submitted to a vote of the citizens of Shenandoah county, and a majority being claimed by those favoring secession, Mr. Reed broke away from his unfavorable environment and took up his abode in Chambersburg, where he has resided ever since and expects to spend the balance of his days."

He was a Presbyterian, and one of those who organized the Central Presbyterian Church of Chambersburg, Pa.

CHILDREN

1188. Henry Clark, b. (in Boston) Nov. 20, 1827; d. March 10, 1861; m. Kate King, of York, Pa.

1189. Thomas Denny, b. (in Boston) Feb. 9, 1830; d. July 7, 1877; unmarried.

1190. John William, b. (in Norfolk) Oct. 21, 1831; d. Aug. 16, 1832, at Old Point, Va.

1191. Mary Elizabeth, b. (in Norfolk), April 10, 1833; m. Sept. 15, 1859, Isaac Haas, of Woodstock, Va.

1192. John Ludovicus, b. June 25, 1836; m. Nov. 10, 1864, Elizabeth McKee Bigham.

1193. Charlotte Stickney, b. March 1, 1839; m. Wm. S. Everett, June 6, 1865.

1194. Julia Lyle, b. Sept. 15, 1841; unmarried.

W 590

Warren Reed, son of Noah and Mehetable (Wild) Reed.

b. (at Weymouth) Feb. 12, 1793; d. (at Milton) Dec. 8, 1866.

m. Jan. 15, 1837, Mary H. Wadsworth; b. March 5, 1801; d. Feb. 3, 1871, at Milton; she was the daughter of Dea. Wm. and Mary Ruggles (Vose) Wadsworth, who was a descendant of Capt. Samuel Wadsworth who was killed in the Indian war, at Sudbury, 1676. He bought in 1660 a large and beautiful tract of land in Milton, a part of which joins the Reed estate, and is now in possession of Reed Bros.

Of Milton.

CHILDREN

1195. Edward Warren, b. March 21, 1841; m. Kate Karcher, of Kansas.
1196. John Henry, b. April 16, 1843; d. April 23, 1888; unmarried.
1197. William Ruggles, b. Feb. 5, 1845; d. Dec. 30, 1890; m. Sept. 24, 1882, Margaret Ellen Whittemore, of Boston.

W **594**

Ezra Reed, son of Ezra and Mary (Lovell) Reed.

b. May 28, 1788; d. July 7, 1859.

m. June 16, 1816, Susanna Colson Richards. She was born March 29, 1794; died April 9, 1880; lived in South Weymouth; daughter of Jacob and Lydia Colson Richards. They were married by Rev. Jonas Perkins.

Ezra being the eldest son took the farm of his father, as was customary in those days. He was a man of good judgment, being very clear headed. He had a large shop south of his house where he manufactured brogans and sold them in Boston. He also owned and ran a grist mill. He was a soldier in the war of the Revolution, under the title of Cornet Ezra Reed.

Of South Weymouth.

CHILDREN

All born in Weymouth.

1198. James, b. May 25, 1817; d. June 29, 1821.
1199. Susan, b. March 24, 1821; d. June 2, 1892; m. Sept. 18, 1850, Winslow Blanchard; lives at Weymouth; went to New Orleans in 1834.

1200. Ezra, b. Oct. 11, 1822; d. Jan. 10, 1874; m. Feb. 11, 1849, Jane A. Wright.

1201. Mary Lovell, b. May 17, 1825; d. Sept. 3, 1885; m. April 14, 1845, Eleazer S. Wright.

1202. James Austin, b. March 22, 1832; m. 1st. Mary Jane Holbrook Pratt; m. 2d. Feb. 18, 1875, Sarah C. Jacobs, of Hingham.

W 595

Harvey Reed, son of Ezra and Mary (Lovell) Reed.
b. May 11, 1791; d. in Bangor Feb. 9, 1859.
m. 1st. June 14, 1814, Lydia Dyer, of Weymouth.
m. 2nd. Sept. 10, 1818, Jane Pratt.

He lived in Bangor, Me., moved there about 1833. He was an active business man, commenced business in Boston in partnership with his brother Quincy in the wholesale shoe business, when he was eighteen years of age. He was the opposite in character to his brother Quincy, who was slow in movement and very cautious. In 1833 he removed to Bangor, Me., and engaged in the lumber business, employing a large number of men. He was one of the old time lumber merchants. He died suddenly in his lumber camp one hundred miles from home, of congestion of the lungs.

Children of Harvey and Lydia

1203. Mehetable T., b. May 12, 1815; m. Nov. 14, 1835, Samuel B. Loud, of Weymouth; no children.

1204. Harvey, Jr., b. April 1, 1817.

Children of Harvey and Jane

1205. Harvey H., b. Aug., 1819; d. 1819, aged 5 days.

1206. Harvey H., b. June, 1820; d. 1820, aged 7 days.

1207. Jane P., b. May, 1821; d. 1821, aged 12 days.

1208. Harvey H., b. March 27, 1822; d. June 26, 1864; m. May, 1844, Ann Ripley.

1209. Jane P., b. Sept. 4, 1824; m. April 16, 1844, Charles E. Lyon.

1210. Ann F., b. April 5, 1827; unmarried.

1211. George H., b. Dec. 26, 1829; d. July 31, 1896; m. Aug. 6, 1863, Helen Curtis.

These children were all b. in Weymouth, Mass., but spent their lives in Bangor, Me.

W **596**

Quincy Reed, son of Ezra and Mary (Lovell) Reed.
b. Nov. 11, 1793; d. April 15, 1886.
m. Feb. 11, 1821, Lucy Loud; m. by Rev. William Tyler.

Was engaged in the wholesale shoe business in Boston with his brother Harvey, was a careful, cautious business man. He earned his father three thousand dollars before he was twenty-one years of age. He lived on a beautiful farm in the village of South Weymouth. His sons rendered assistance to J. Whittemore Reed in procuring the data for his genealogy published in 1861, and his sons Quincy L. Reed, and William H. have been of great assistance to the author of this work. (See obituary notice in appendix.)

Of South Weymouth, Mass.

CHILDREN

1212. Quincy Lovell, b. (S. Weymouth) April 6, 1822; m. March 22, 1860, Lucy E. Hall at Warwick.
1213. Lucy Ann, b. Sept. 25, 1825; m. Jan. 9, 1849, Joshua E. Crane, of Bridgewater.
1214. Maria Theresa, b. Aug. 30, 1830; d. July, 1860; unmarried.
1215. William Henry, b. June 16, 1832; m. April 25, 1860, Julia L. Andrews.
1216. Harriet Pauline, b. April 5, 1838; m. William A. Shaw, of Weymouth.

W **600**

John Reed, son of Ezra and Mary (Lovell) Reed.
b. Jan. 22, 1804.
m. Nov. 10, 1825, Lydia B. Vining; m. by Rev. Wm. Tyler.

Of Weymouth, Mass.

CHILDREN

1217. Augusta M., b. Aug. 23, 1826; m. Dana W. Barrows.
1218. John Bradford, b. Nov. 3, 1830; m. 1st. Nov. 29, 1850, Emily Jane Loud; m. 2d. Jan. 28, 1865, Frances C. Thayer.
1219. Henry, b. Jan. 27, 1833; d. young.
1220. Franklin, b. Jan. 30, 1835; m. June 8, 1852, Pamelia Thayer.
1221. Frederick, b. May 13, 1839; m. 1st. Aug. 3, 1862, Helen Mehetable Brown, of Abington; m. 2d. July 14, 1886, Mary Jane Whitman.

1222. Helen Annie Titterton, b. Nov. 5, 1844; m. Clinton Humphrey.

W 601

Alvan Reed, son of Ezra and Mary (Lovell) Reed.

b. ———; d. June 26, 1852.

m. 1st. Phebe Arnold (of South Weymouth); d. May 17, 1832.

m. 2nd. Anna Titterton, an English lady from New Orleans.

m. 3rd. Sept. 26, 1848, Lucy Vining.

Of Weymouth, Mass.

CHILD OF ALVAN AND ANNA

1223. William, b. July 11, 1844; d. July 14, 1844, in Weymouth.

CHILDREN OF ALVAN AND LUCY

1224. William Titterton, b. Sept. 9, 1849; m. Oct. 30, 1872, Ella J. Harlow, of Scituate.
1225. Lucianna, b. Aug. 31, 1851; d. aged about 18.

T 602

Isaiah Reed, son of George and Elizabeth (Harvey) Reed.

b. Feb. 2, 1757; d. Oct. 18, 1814.

m. ———, Abigail Briggs of Berkley; she died April 17, 1841.

Lived in Taunton, Mass.

CHILDREN

1226. Abigail, b. Aug. 21, 1781, at Taunton.
1227. Sylda, b. Oct. 25, 1783.
1228. Salome, b. May 15, 1784; d. Feb., 1815.
1229. Allen, b. June, 1788; d. Dec. 12, 1789, aged 18 months.
1230. Achsah, b. 1790; d. Dec. 1816.
1231. Lucretia, b. Jan., 1796.
1232. Sophronia, b. April, 1799.

T 603

George Reed, son of George and Elizabeth (Harvey) Reed.

b. Nov. 21, 1759; d. Sept. 4, 1830.

m. ———, Experience Blackman, of Canton, Mass.

He moved to Augusta, Me., with his family.

Of Augusta, Me.

CHILDREN

1233. George, b. Feb. 15, 1787; d. Feb. 3, 1820; m. Lucinda B. Sawtell.
1234. Luther, b. July 4, 1790; m. 1st. March 5, 1816, Betsy Hamilton; m. 2d. Nov. 21, 1839, Fanny Howard.
1235. Jason, b. June 28, 1796; d. Oct. 18, 1824.
1236. Experience, b. May 4, 1802; m. Dec. 2, 1824, John Cory.
1237. Betsy, b. ———; d. young.
1238. Olive, b. ———; d. young.

T 605

Oliver Reed, son of George and Elizabeth (Harvey) Reed.

b.———, 1769; d. Dec. 27, 1849.

m. March 13, 1788, Bethia Leonard of Taunton.

Of Taunton.

CHILDREN

1239. Oliver, b. June, 1789; d. Jan. 1834; m. Chloe Briggs.
1240. George L., b. June 9, 1791; m. Betsy Lincoln.
1241. Betsy H., b. 1794; d. Oct. 30, 1813.
1242. Barney, b. Dec. 4, 1797; m. 1st. Rachel Woodward; m. 2d. Charlotte ———.
1243. Isaiah, b. ———; m. Fanny Thomas.
1244. Stimson, b. Nov. 12, 1805; m. 1st. Sept. 8, 1837, Fanny H. Briggs; m. 2d. Dec. 26, 1857, Hannah L. Bassett.
1245. Barzillai, b. April 16, 1808; d. Oct. 20, 1860; m. Sept. 21, 1837, Deborah Churchill.
1246. William H., b. March 14, 1810; m. Amanda Goff.
1247. Bethiah, b. Nov. 13, 1813; m. Nov. 13, 1842, Dennis S. Boodry, of Rochester.

T 607

John Reed, son of Esqr. John and Mary (Godfrey) Reed.

b. Aug. 11, 1776; d. Nov. 7, 1864.

m. May 31, 1804, Rebecca Gooding, of Dighton (b. Sept. 28, 1782; d. Jan. 31, 1872).

Of Taunton.

CHILDREN

1248. Mary Ann, b. May 20, 1805; m. July 21, 1837, Rev. Martyn Cushman, of Shutusbury, Mass.

1249. John, b. June 17, 1808; died unmarried.

1250. Henry Gooding, b. July 23, 1810; m. 1st. Jan. 5, 1842, Clara White; m. 2d. June 2, 1851, Frances Lee Williams; m. 3d. Oct. 27, 1858, Delight R. Carpenter.

1251. Rebecca, b. April 12, 1813; m. Sept. 10, 1845, James H. Cushman.

1252. William Andrew, b. Sept. 2, 1816; d. March 2, 1862; unmarried.

1253. Sophia Jane, b. Nov. 9, 1818; d. unmarried.

1254. Elizabeth Gooding, b. Sept. 4, 1822; m. June 14, 1853, Dr. Samuel G. Tucker.

T 608

William Reed, son of Esqr. John and Mary (Godfrey) Reed. b. Oct. 6, 1778; d. Sept. 10, 1865.

m. 1st. April 24, 1804, Elizabeth Dennis; b. Dec. 26, 1784; d. Jan. 29, 1824.

m. 2nd. Feb. 14, 1825, Mary Dennis; b. Aug. 15, 1787; d. March 25, 1875.

Wm. Reed was a Representative at the General Court in 1819; Town Court in 1825-6; Deacon of the Congregational Church for many years.

CHILDREN OF WILLIAM AND ELIZABETH

1255. A daughter, b. Oct., 1805; d. at birth.

1256. Elizabeth Dennis, b. March 2, 1807; d. Feb. 13, 1836.

1257. Mary Godfrey, b. Jan. 10, 1809.

1258. Julia, b. Sept. 11, 1810; d. Feb. 2, 1901; m. March 7, 1838, Rev. S. H. Emery, D. D.

1259. William Cowper, b. July 16, 1812; d. Sept. 9, 1813.

1260. Anna Dennis Sproat, b. July 29, 1814.

1261. Eleanor Sherbourne, b. Jan. 14, 1817; lives in Taunton: m. Jan. 27, 1842, Joseph P. Deane.

1262. William, b. Feb. 17, 1819; m. Nov. 17, 1850, Eliza Deane.

1263. Amelia, b. Feb. 25, 1821; d. Aug. 11, 1825.

1264. A daughter, b. Jan. 27, 1823; d. the same day.

1265. Chester Isham, b. Nov. 25, 1823; d. Sept. 2, 1873; m. Feb. 24, 1851, Elizabeth Y. Allyne; she d. May 24, 1901.

CHILDREN OF WILLIAM AND MARY

1266. A son, b. Dec. 26, 1825; d. same day.

1267. John Dennis, b. March 15, 1827; m. July 11, 1865, Helen Frances Sproat.

WILLIAM REED.

1268. Charles Edward, b. Jan. 27, 1830; m. Sept. 18, 1861, Rebecca P. Paige, of Chelsea.
1269. Erastus Maltby, b. July 28, 1832; m. Aug. 21, 1857, Sarah Jane Crockett.

T 611

Marshall Reed, son of Esqr. John and Mary (Godfrey) Reed.
b. Jan. 17, 1788.
m. June 11, 1817, Clarissa Crossman Willis; b. Aug. 10, 1796.

Of Taunton.

CHILDREN

1270. Sarah Almy, b. Aug. 20, 1818; m. Sept. 18, 1861, Dea. Silas Dean, of Stoneham.
1271. Clarissa Willis, b. Aug. 13, 1820.
1272. Edwin, b. May 6, 1822; m. Nov. 21, 1862, Victoria Graham, she d. Dec. 14, 1887, aged 49 years.
1273. Philomela, b. Sept. 13, 1824.

T 612

Hodges Reed, son of Esqr. John and Mary (Godfrey) Reed.
b. June 3, 1790; d. April 15, 1864.
m. May 13, 1813, Clarissa Hodges; d. Dec. 19, 1856, aged sixty-eight; daughter of Capt. Joseph Hodges, of Norton.

Hodges Reed was a merchant in Boston and later in Taunton. He was a member of the Legislature and an author of some religious works. He was regarded as a most estimable citizen and a devoted Christian man with mental endowments of a high order and rare poetic gifts, a profound veneration and love for the Holy Scriptures which were his daily study; he was as some one has well said of him, "Deeply spiritual, endeared to the friends of Zion, wherever known honoring his profession."

His wife was quiet, reserved and domestic in her habits, of a sweet and lovable spirit, the joy of her household, honored and beloved by her intimate friends and associates.

Of Taunton, Mass.

CHILDREN

1274. Edgar Hodges, b. July 3, 1814; m. Aug. 30, 1837, Ellen Augusta Godfrey.
1275. Clarissa W., b. Jan. 6, 1817; d. Aug. 29, 1869; m. May 25, 1846, Benjamin W. Williams.
1276. William Frederick, b. Sept. 13, 1820; d. Nov. 20, 1820.
1277. Frederick Alonzo, b. Dec. 7, 1821; d. June 9, 1883; m. April 30, 1850, Mary C. Hubbard.
1278. Eveline, b. May 7, 1825; m. Oct. 10, 1849, James H. Deane.
1279. Charlotte Augusta, b. Oct. 1, 1828; m. Oct. 6, 1853, Robert S. Washburn.

T 616

John Gilmore Reed, son of Nathan and Ascah (Gilmore) Reed.

b. ———; d. ———, aged 35.

m. ———. Settled in North Yarmouth.

CHILDREN

1280. A son, b. ———.
1281. A daughter, b. ———.

T 617

Florentius Reed, son of Nathan and Ascah (Gilmore) Reed.

b. ———, 1801-2.

m. ———.

He lived in Windsor, Me.

CHILDREN

1282. John, b. 1830; m. ———.
1283. Josiah, b. ———.
1284. Nathan, b. ———.
1285. David, b. ———.
1286. A daughter, b. ———; who lived in Windsor, Me.

T 626

Capt. Joseph Reed, son of Joseph and Abigail (Barney) Reed.

b. (in Taunton) June 5, 1786; d. Jan. 4, 1838.

m. Sept. 15, 1810, Peddy Hunt of Taunton; b. April 22, 1787; d. Feb. 15, 1866.

Of Taunton.

CHILDREN

1287. Nancy R., b. July 13, 1811; d. young.
1288. Joseph, b. Jan. 9, 1813; m. 1st. April 17, 1839, Lydia Bryant; m. 2d. April 4, 1847, Phebe Briggs.
1289. Leonard, b. June 20, 1814; d. Sept. 16, 1814.
1290. Peddy, b. Sept. 20, 1815.
1291. Nancy, b. Oct. 20, 1817; m. April 7, 1842, Hodges Reed Lincoln.
1292. Leonard W., b. July 29, 1819; m. Fidelia Thayer.
1293. Simeon C., b. Aug. 15, 1821.
1294. William D., b. Aug. 23, 1823; m. March 23, 1846, Rachel Ann Tripp, of Dighton.
1295. John R., b. April 27, 1825; d. Sept. 14, 1863.
1296. Mary Jane, b. June 24, 1827; d. Dec. 22, 1849.
1297. Sally Maria, b. Oct. 18, 1829; d. Oct. 26, 1844.
1298. Betsy, b. Sept. 25, 1831; d. Jan. 29, 1833.

T 633

Josiah Reed, son of Ebenezer and Lydia (Hoskins) Reed.
b. ———, 1784; d. Nov. 29, 1848.
m. Mary Tripp. She died Sept. 24, 1861.

CHILDREN

1299. Mary T., b. ———.
1300. Louisa, b. ———.
1301. Sarah G., b. 1820; d. June 12, 1841.
1302. Alice P., b. 1822; d. March 29, 1844.
1303. Nancy A., b. 1823; d. Oct. 13, 1844.

T 635

Ebenezer Reed, son of Ebenezer and Lydia (Hoskins) Reed.
b. ———.
m. ———, Mary Chase.

CHILDREN

1304. Betsey Turner, b. ———.
1305. Lydia, b. ———.
1306. Orlando, b. ———; m. Abbie Williams.
1307. William, b. ———; m. Eliza Palmer.
1308. John, b. ———.
1309. Almira, b. ———.
1310. Jonathan, b. Nov. 28, 1835; m. Lydia Ann Hoskins.

T 636

Isaac Reed, son of Ebenezer and Lydia (Hoskins) Reed.
b. Jan. 18, 1791; d. June 29, 1865.
m. ——, Nancy Babbitt.

CHILDREN

1311. Mercey, b. Aug. 2, 1816; m. 1836, Joseph Whitney.
1312. Isaac Albert, b. March 31, 1838; m. March 9, 1858, Almira Bowen Reed; she d. Dec. 9, 1893.

T 641

Gilbert Reed, son of Ebenezer and Lydia (Hoskins) Reed.
b. March 10, 1811.
m. Oct. 26, 1834, Delina Peck.

CHILDREN

1313. Gilbert, b. Aug. 1, 1836; m. Aug. 27, 1859, Valaria Rounseville.
1314. Jane, b. ——.
1315. Ira Madison, b. ——; m. Adeline Pratt, of Taunton.
1316. Henry E., b. March 31, 1842; m. June 9, 1875, Lottie J. Lincoln.
1317. Susan, b. ——.
1318. Josiah B., b. Dec. 19, 1849; m. Aug. 29, 1870, Josephine Jossylin Presbury.
1319. Elizabeth Adelaide, b. ——.
1320. Helen Frances, b. ——.

T 642

Job Reed, son of Job and Sally (Troop) Reed.
b. April 30, 1785; d. July 4, 1836, in Williamstown, Vt.
m. March 4, 1811, Lovisa Andrews; she was born Nov. 22, 1792; died April, 1880, in Northfield, Vt., daughter of Elijah and Mabel (Fox) Andrews.

He was a farmer. Congregationalist. All the children were born in Williamstown, Vt., except Freeman, who was born in Berlin, Vt., and Lovina, who was born in Northfield, Vt.

CHILDREN

1321. Freeman, b. Nov. 29, 1811; m. March 26, 1834, Lamira W. Jones.

1322. Leonard, b. Sept. 14, 1813; d. same day.
1323. Lovina, b. Oct. 2, 1814; m. Nov., 1848, Abel Marsh.
1324. Russell, b. Feb. 5, 1817; d. Sept. 2, 1896; m. Nov. 6, 1842, Mary Ann Edson.
1325. Caroline, b. May 1, 1819; d. Feb. 17, 1892; m. Oct. 31, 1851, Roswell Dewey.
1326. Rhoda, b. July 29, 1821; d. April 8, 1896; m. July, 1854, John Wheaton.
1327. Benjamin Porter, b. Nov. 2, 1823; m. Feb. 8, 1846, Harriet Jones.
1328. Mary E., b. Feb. 16, 1826; d. May 19, 1875; m. 1st. Oscar Livingston; m. 2d. Charles R. Smith.
1329. Elijah A., b. July 15, 1828; d. unmarried.
1330. Mabel H., b. Jan. 2, 1831; m. Jan. 10, 1850, George M. Hill.
1331. Sarah L., b. April 24, 1833; m. Feb. 22, 1855, Charles Simons.

T 647

Morton Reed, son of Job and Sally (Troop) Reed.

b. July 11, 1795, in Northfield, Washington county, Vt.; d. Jan., 1862, at Brookfield, Vt.

m. Jan. 24, 1817, Lucy Whitney, daughter of Elijah and Lidia (McWayne) Whitney; she died Feb., 1861, aged 63.

He was a farmer, obtained a common school education. They were Universalists and lived at Northfield and at Williamstown and then removed to Brookfield, Vt.

CHILDREN

1332. Samuel, b. 1819; d. young.
1333. Juliette, b. 1821; m. Dec., 1844, Jeduthan Rice.
1334. Sarah, b. (at Northfield), Oct. 9, 1823; d. at Braintree, Vt., Dec. 5, 1874; m. at Braintree, Dec. 25, 1847, Andrew J. Kinney.
1335. Betsy, b. 1824.
1336. Elijah, b. 1826; d. young.
1337. George, b. 1827.
1338. Mary Ann, b. March 28, 1828; m. Dec. 24, 1841, Calvin Fullam.
1339. Maria, b. 1830; d. at Braintree, Vt., Dec., 1863; m. Frank Kellum, had son Perrin.
1340. Samuel Perrin, b. 1834; d. 1862. Was in the army and died in the service and was buried in Virginia.

T 658

Rev. Augustus Brown Reed, son of Elijah and Delight (Brown) Reed.

b. Nov. 19, 1798, at Rehoboth, Mass.; d. Sept. 30, 1838, at Ware, Mass.

m. Nov. 17, 1824, Melinda Borden of Fall River; b. Jan. 13, 1805; d. Dec. 24, 1894, age 89 years, at Westfield, Mass. She was a daughter of William and Sarah (Durfee) Borden. After the death of her husband she married a Mr. Eddy.

This Augustus Reed and family changed the orthography from Reed to Read. He graduated from Brown University in 1821, and was prepared for college under the instruction of his pastor, the Rev. Mr. Thompson, with whom, after his graduation, he read theology. On the 2nd day of June, 1823, just twenty years before the great fire, he was ordained and installed pastor of the first Congregational Church of Fall River, at a salary of $450 a year. Mr. Reed was dismissed from the pastorate Aug. 3, 1825. He then settled in Ware, Mass., where he died Sept. 30, 1838, aged 39 years.

He was a chairman of the school committee, a Whig, an anti-Mason, and temperance advocate. He was 5 ft. 10 ins. in height, light complexion, blue eyes, slender, considered honorable, social, benevolent according to slender means, of considerable influence.

Of Ware, Mass.

CHILDREN

1341. Theodora Cyania, b. July 23, 1825; d. March 8, 1886; m. Dec. 6, 1855, Judge Eliab Williams of Fall River.

1342. Delight Brown, b. June 4, 1828, at Ware; d. Oct. 29, 1849; unmarried.

1343. William Augustus, b. April 8, 1830; m. Mary Lucetta Breckenbridge.

1344. John Richard, b. March 25, 1832; m. 1st. May 8, 1861, Julia Priscilla Breckenridge; m. 2d. Jan. 19, 1876, Martha H. Dudman.

1345. Thomas, b. Dec. 27, 1834; d. Feb. 10, 1835.

1346. Theophilus, b. March 15, 1836, at Ware, Mass.; d. Aug. 23, 1843, at Westfield, Mass.

T 661

John Newton Reed, son of Elijah and Delight (Brown) Reed.
b. Nov. 18, 1806; d. Nov. 4, 1853.
m. 1st. Mary Ann Borden; d. Feb. 19, 1843, aged 33.
m. 2nd. May 15, 1845, Jane Thompson, now Mrs. Jane Thompson (Reed) Chase of Newport, R. I.

He was a sea captain. No children.

Of Rehoboth, Mass.

T 662

Gustavus Adolphus Reed, son of Elijah Augustus and Delight (Brown) Reed.
b. Dec. 23, 1811, at Rehoboth; d. April 22, 1889.
m. March 16, 1836, Electa A. Miller.

Lives in Rehoboth, Mass.; was a deacon in the Congregational Church of that place for twenty-five years. Taught singing and sang in the choir a number of years.

Of Rehoboth, Mass.

CHILDREN

1347. Charles Leonard, b. Sept. 30, 1837; m. April, 1865, Annie Matthewson.
1348. Electa Ann, b. June 13, 1839, at Rehoboth, Mass.; d. July 24, 1867; m. Aug. 24, 1863, William Collins, at Bennington, Vt.
1349. Mary Ann Borden, b. Jan. 24, 1843; m. Rev. Calvin Grout Hill.
1350. Almira Miller, b. Dec. 10, 1844; m. June 3, 1868, Moses Gardner Walker, of Providence, R. I.
1351. Almond Augustus, b. Dec. 2, 1848; m. Feb., 1880, Hattie Carpenter.
1352. Jane Amelia, b. Feb. 22, 1851; m. Sept. 29, 1874, Henry Stone Ide, of E. Providence, R. I.
1353. Delight Carpenter, b. Feb. 14, 1856; d. unmarried at Harris, Mass.

T 665

John Reed, son of John and Deborah (Baldwin) Reed.
b. (at Putney, Vt.) May 11, 1781; d. (at Cortland, N. Y.) Dec. 19, 1868.

m. March 15, 1803, Joanna Wilson; b. at Putney, Jan. 29, 1782; d. at Cortland, Sept. 23, 1866.

Moved from Vermont to Worcester, Otsego county, N. Y., from there to Cortland, N. Y. On March 5, 1812, which was before the forests of that section had felt the woodman's axe, he cleared the land and built a log house within two miles of where the beautiful town of Cortland now stands. In 1819 he built a frame house, which was the first one built in the town. He had a common school education. His occupation was farming and his religion Methodist. He was a stout, fine looking man 5 1/2 feet, with a florid complexion and blue eyes. Joanna was large and strong with blue eyes, she had a strong mind and was a devout woman. They were a quiet, energetic couple, and did their work well in that new and then frontier country. In her younger days she was a great weaver and made nearly or quite all the cloth used in their house, and wove many of those heavy coverlids for the bed which are now held in such high esteem as relics of the olden time. It can be said of John Reed and his descendants that they are not addicted to the use of tobacco or intoxicating drinks.

Of Cortland, N. Y.

CHILDREN

1354. David Wilson, b. Dec. 27, 1803; d. Jan. 1, 1873; m. 1st. Dec. 27, 1827, Esther Sanders; m. 2d. May 13, 1871, Catherine Williams, of Waukesha, Wis.

1355. Polly, b. Nov. 28, 1805; m. April 15, 1828, Henry Gillette.

1356. Artemas, b. June 10, 1807; m. April 7, 1830, Eunice G. Benham.

1357. Marvin, b. Aug. 29, 1809; d. March 27, 1882; m. 1st. Dec. 28, 1836, Eunice A. Heath; m. 2d. Dec. 17, 1867, Mary D. Rose.

1358. John, Jr., b. Aug. 2, 1813; d. Oct. 9, 1894; m. April 16, 1837, Hannah E. Nesmith.

1359. George Wesley, b. Aug. 2, 1817; d. Nov. 14, 1818; accidentally scalded to death.

T **668**

Isaac Reed, son of John and Elizabeth (Cudworth) Reed.

b. Sept. 19, 1788, at Putney, Windham county, Vt.; d. Jan. 5, 1849, at Berlin, Erie county, Ohio.

SIMEON REED.

m. July 12, 1810, Lucretia Newton; b. Feb. 14, 1790, at Keene, N. H.; d. March 8, 1855, at Berlin, Erie county, Ohio; daughter of Ebenezer and (Hubbard) Newton.

Of Berlin, Erie county, Ohio.

CHILDREN

1360. Isaac Newton, b. April 6, 1811; m. Jan. 6, 1835, Margaret Miles.
1361. Maria Lucretia, b. Sept. 23, 1812; d. Nov. 4, 1861; m. George Walker.
1362. George, b. June 30, 1815; d. Oct. 20, 1847; unmarried.
1363. Eliza, b. Feb. 25, 1817; m. 1st. Dr. Zalmon Jennings; m. 2d. Peter W. Van Nattan.
1364. Perry, b. June 27, 1820; m. Hester House.
1365. Mary Jane, b. April 19, 1822; d. Sept. 16, 1887; m. Jan. 19, 1852, Alanson Thomas.

T **669**

Simeon Reed, son of John and Elizabeth (Cudworth) Reed.

b. at Putney, Vt., Jan. 25, 1791; d. Oct. 24, 1875, at Dummerston, Vt.

m. Dec. 12, 1819, Betsy Joy; b. Oct. 6, 1795, at Putney, Vt., d. March 3, 1881, at Dummerston, Vt., daughter of Amos and Rachel (Fletcher) Joy.

He had a common school education, was a farmer, elected as representative to General Assembly of Vermont in 1860-61. They were members of the Baptist Church, and lived in Putney and Dummerston, Vt. He was a little above the average height, straight, and of a pleasing appearance.

Of Dummerston, Vt.

CHILDREN

1366. Elizabeth Fletcher, b. April 9, 1821; d. June 23, 1864; m. May 19, 1841, Ezekiel Butler Campbell.
1367. Simeon Hibbard, b. July 23, 1823; d. May 26, 1849.
1368. Martha Ann, b. July 16, 1826; d. Oct. 1, 1865; m. Nov. 20, 1850, Mason A. Higgins.
1369. Thomas Newton, b. Aug. 31, 1828; m. June 1, 1854, Ellen Jerusha Miller.
1370. Mary, b. Oct. 5, 1831; d. Aug. 8, 1833.

T 678

Charles Leonard Reed, son of William and Betsy (Cartee) Reed.

b. Feb. 15, 1796, in Dighton; d. July 25, 1854, in New Bedford.

m. May 8, 1820, Hannah N. Beetle; b. May 31, 1799; d. April 26, 1831; daughter of Henry and Grace (Brownell) Beetle of New Bedford.

Married and lived in New Bedford.

Charles L. Reed was a soldier in the war of 1812.

Of New Bedford.

CHILDREN

1371. Charles Covell, b. Aug. 2, 1824; d. unmarried; was Capt. Reed, of Friday Harbor, San Juan Island, Wash. Ty.
1372. A daughter, b. ———; d. in infancy.

T 679

John Reed, son of William and Betsy (Cartee) Reed.

b. Oct. 17, 1798, at Dighton, Mass.; d. Aug. 26, 1861, in Henderson county, Ill.

m. 1st. May 6, 1824, Juliet Merrifield; b. Nov. 11, 1807, in Hardin county, Ky.; d. Dec. 14, 1843, in Henderson county, Ill.; daughter of Alexander and Rachel (Boone) Merrifield.

m. 2nd. Sept. 3, 1844, Charity Webb; d. Aug. 2, 1862, in Taylor county, W. Va.; daughter of Thomas and Susan (Griffin) Webb.

He left Massachusetts when about eighteen years of age, went to Hardin county, Ky., where he married, thence to Illinois in 1839, where he engaged in farming, and threshed out with a flail the first crop of wheat which he hauled to market and received for it twenty-five cents per bushel. He was an official member and communicant of the M. E. Church. He was a Republican, was six feet in height, fair complexion, brown hair, gray eyes, strong and noted for his energy, industry and thrift.

Of Henderson county, Ill.

CHARLES LEONARD REED.

CHILDREN OF JOHN AND JULIET

1373. Rachel Boone, b. April 29, 1825; d. March 2, 1872; m. Andrew Richey.
1374. Elizabeth, b. Oct. 12, 1826; m. Nov. 1, 1849; James H. Woods.
1375. William Jefferson, b. March 17, 1828; m. Aug. 23, 1855, Sarah Davis.
1376. James, b. Nov. 8, 1829; d. Dec. 9, 1864; m. April 11, 1850, Margaret A. Hogue.
1377. Milton, b. Sept. 11, 1831; d. Feb. 4, 1860.
1378. George Washington, b. Feb. 10, 1833; d. March 24, 1854.
1379. Amanda Jane, b. Oct. 17, 1834; d. March 15, 1835.
1380. Amanda Summers, b. Jan. 8, 1836; d. Oct. 23, 1863; m. Oct. 30, 1856, Thomas Hogue.
1381. John Alexander, b. Oct. 7, 1837; d. Oct. 15, 1837.
1382. Samuel Merrifield, b. March 27, 1839; m. Feb. 13, 1871, Harriet Welch.
1383. Benjamin Franklin, b. Nov. 6, 1840; d. Aug. 24, 1869.

CHILDREN OF JOHN AND CHARITY

1384. Emily Frances, b. Oct. 14, 1846; d. in 1880; m. Isaac Shingleton in W. Va.
1385. John Henry, b. April 18, 1849; d. unmarried.
1386. Calistier Angeline, b. Dec. 7, 1850; m. Sept. 19, 1867, Richard Woods.
1387. David Anthony, b. Feb. 2, 1853; m. Sept. 29, 1880, Lucy E. Dungan.
1388. Aciel Elihu, b. Feb. 7, 1855; m. Feb. 22, 1882, Louisa Case.
1389. Joseph Nathaniel, b. Nov., 1858; m. Sept. 5, 1888, Cora Tullis.
1390. Annie Levancy, b. March 5, 1860.

T **682**

Anthony Reed, son of William and Betsy (Cartee) Reed.

b. July 10, 1805, at Dighton, Mass.; d. June 8, 1878, at Hastings, Minn.

m. Dec. 4, 1828, Elizabeth Bliss; b. Nov. 25, 1810, at Rehoboth, Mass.; daughter of William and Lucy (Briggs) Bliss.

Anthony Reed led a very active business life in his native town of Dighton, Mass., and was connected intimately with its prosperity from 1830 to 1854. In the latter year he re-

moved with his family to Milford, Mass., and in 1856, to Nininger Territory of Minnesota, where he engaged in building and manufacturing. He was one of the early white settlers of that territory. He held various county and town offices and maintained an unblemished record in every line of life, whether in business, politically or socially, and so imbued his children that the name continues untarnished in their lives.

In his every effort he was aided by an exceptionally good wife and helpmate, it is safe to assert that no one of the William Reed stock (his father) has ever failed to pay his debts dollar for dollar, support their families in comfort, nor has any one of their hundreds of descendants ever been accused of crime. The record ls clear.

He and his wife received a common school education, were Universalists. He was five feet eleven inches in height, light complexion, light blue eyes, curly auburn hair, weight 170 pounds, quick speaker, was a student in science and a great general reader. Was Free-Soil and a Republican.

CHILDREN

1391. James Anthony, b. Sept. 11, 1829; d. June 12, 1867.
1392. Elizabeth Alice, b. June 30, 1832; m. Aug. 22, 1857, James Alvin Dodge.
1393. Wm. Bayliss, b. Aug. 22, 1834; m. Jan. 22, 1859, Amanda Bunnell.
1394. George Bowers, b. March 12, 1837; m. Nov. 27, 1860, Sarah Zillah Sims.
1395. Sarah Frances, b. Oct. 11, 1838; d. Jan. 30, 1856; unmarried.
1396. Julia Martha, b. Aug. 30, 1840; d. July 19, 1841.
1397. Mary Emma, b. May 9, 1843; d. Oct. 12, 1844.
1398. Ann Amelia Perry, b. Dec. 10, 1846; m. 1st. March 25, 1855, James Brownell; m. 2d. April 12, 1870, Joseph Elliot Bolles.
1399. Lucy Adelaide, b. June 3, 1848; m. June 26, 1870, Capt. William Edward Hull.
1400. John Murray, b. June 10, 1852; d. Aug. 26, 1852.
1401. Charles Anthony, b. Nov. 20, 1854, at Dighton; d. Nov. 11, 1871, in Minnesota.

T 688

Daniel Reed, son of Evans and Lydia (Haven) Reed.
b. June 30, 1805.
m. Jan. 1, 1835, Fanny Burr Barber.
Of Townshend, Vt.

T 691

Luther Reed, son of Evans and Lydia (Haven) Reed.
b. April 5, 1813; d. Oct. 19, 1845.
m. Oct. 7, 1837, Harriet Heald.
Of Athens, Vt.

CHILDREN

1402. Mary Jane, b. Feb. 5, 1839, at Athens, Vt.; m. July 28, 1860, John Bartlett.
1403. Henry Lafayette, b. July 5, 1843; m. July 11, 1863, Lizzie A. Osgood.

T 693

Seth Reed, son of Seth and Cassandra (Deane) Reed.
b. Oct. 14, 1790, at Dighton, Mass.; d. Nov. 22, 1863, at Dighton, Mass.
m. May 14, 1823, Matilda Smith; b. July 14, 1790, at Dighton, Mass.; d. Aug. 22, 1882, in South Hanson, Mass.; daughter of Stephen and Rebecca (Simmons) Smith.

Seth Reed had a very limited education; his wife was well educated and taught school. They lived in Dighton, where he was a farmer and shoemaker; he was a Congregationalist, his wife was a Baptist and a member of the church for over sixty years. She was very good looking, a good conversationalist and had an uncommon memory. He had quite a musical talent and succeeded his father as choir leader. His voice was remarkably melodious and he was familiar with the church music that prevailed in New England, in the early years of this century, and was passionately fond of singing. His wife's ancestors in the male line had lived in Dighton from its early settlement and on the same farm.

CHILDREN

1404. Alfred Wood, b. Oct. 26, 1823; m. June 14, 1846, Eunice Edson Paul.

1405. Benjamin Franklin Deane, b. Aug. 11, 1825; d. Sept. 16, 1826.

1406. Clarinda Smith, b. Dec. 5, 1827; m. May 6, 1846, George W. Adams.

1407. Joseph Brown, b. May 12, 1830, in Dighton, Mass.; m. 1st. Nov. 27, 1856, Elizabeth E. J. Williams; m. 2d. Jan. 26, 1880, Mary Elizabeth Barker.

T 696

Otis Reed, son of Seth and Cassandra (Deane) Reed.
b. Sept. 16, 1801; d. Jan. 15, 1854.
m. 1st. Rosamond Chase.
m. 2nd. Oct. 28, 1832, Ann E. Colton.
m. 3rd. Feb. 25, 1844, Amanda Paul.

He had two children by his second wife who are now living.

Of Dighton.

CHILD OF OTIS AND ANN

1408. Phebe, of Dighton, b. ———; m. ——— Goff, of Dighton, Mass.

CHILDREN OF OTIS AND AMANDA

1409. James C., b. Jan. 21, 1845.

1410. Susan A., b. Aug 21, 1847.

1411. Sibyl, b. Aug. 21, 1847.

1412. William B., b. April 8, 1849.

T 697

Stephen D. Reed, son of Seth and Cassandra (Deane) Reed.
b. March 10, 1810, at Dighton.
m. Emiline Lane of Norton, Mass.

Of Dighton.

CHILDREN

1413. Clara, b. Oct. 24, 1849.

1414. Emma F., b. June 2, 1851.

1415. Caroline A., b. Sept. 21, 1853.

1416. George F., b. Sept. 16, 1856.

M 707

Benjamin Reed, Jr., son of Benjamin and Mrs. Abiah (Macomber) Reed.

b. ———; d. April 19, 1818.

m. 1st. ———, Anna Chubbick; she died Sept. 12, 1813.

m. 2nd. ———.

CHILDREN BY FIRST WIFE

1416a. Sally, b. ———; m. ———, Shepperd Cutting; had several children.

1416b. Lucy, b. May 10, 1793; d. Oct. 23, 1891; m. Nov. 29, 1814, Joel Darling.

1416c. Stillman, b. ———; d. unmarried at Westmoreland, N. H., about 1863.

1416d. Oliver, b. Sept. 4, 1796, in Shutesbury, Mass.; d. May 4, 1865; m. April 16, 1821, Lucy Sloan, of New Salem.

1416e. Deborah, b. ———; m. Harvey Cooley; one child; parents and child drowned in Lake Michigan.

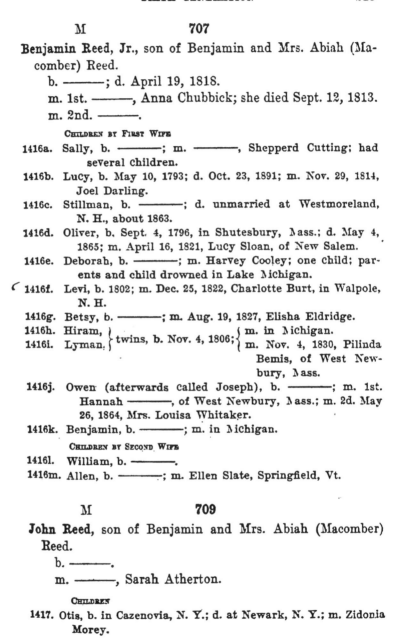

1416f. Levi, b. 1802; m. Dec. 25, 1822, Charlotte Burt, in Walpole, N. H.

1416g. Betsy, b. ———; m. Aug. 19, 1827, Elisha Eldridge.

1416h. Hiram, } twins, b. Nov. 4, 1806; m. in Michigan.

1416i. Lyman, } twins, b. Nov. 4, 1806; m. Nov. 4, 1830, Pilinda Bemis, of West Newbury, Mass.

1416j. Owen (afterwards called Joseph), b. ———; m. 1st. Hannah ———, of West Newbury, Mass.; m. 2d. May 26, 1864, Mrs. Louisa Whitaker.

1416k. Benjamin, b. ———; m. in Michigan.

CHILDREN BY SECOND WIFE

1416l. William, b. ———.

1416m. Allen, b. ———; m. Ellen Slate, Springfield, Vt.

M 709

John Reed, son of Benjamin and Mrs. Abiah (Macomber) Reed.

b. ———.

m. ———, Sarah Atherton.

CHILDREN

1417. Otis, b. in Cazenovia, N. Y.; d. at Newark, N. Y.; m. Zidonia Morey.

1418. Elizabeth, b. ———; unmarried.
1419. Mary, b. ———; m. ——— Webber.
1420. Simeon, b. ———; m. ——— Smith.
1421. Clarissa, b. ———.
1422. Harriet, b. ———; d. at Delphi, N. Y.; m. a preacher; were a musical family.

M 710

Warren Reed, son of Benjamin and Mrs. Abiah (Macomber) Reed.

b. July 6, 1780.

m. May 25, 1803, Mary Atherton; she died April 12, 1847.

Of Chester, Mass.

CHILDREN

1423. Sanford, b. June 13, 1804; d. Oct. 11, 1826.
1424. Sophronia, b. March 9, 1806; d. Oct. 4, 1886; m. May 28, 1828. George Wells, of Northampton, Mass.
1425. Infant daughter, b. Jan. 18, 1808; d. same day.
1426. Warren Atherton, b. Feb. 17, 1809; d. Sept. 10, 1345; m. Louisa Lyman.
1427. Edwin W., b. June 7, 1811: d. June 18, 1876; m. 1st. Julia Porter; m. 2d. Martha Bliss.
1428. James, b. Aug. 27, 1813; d. Nov. 14, 1873; m. Lydia Woods, resided at Savannah, Ga.
1429. Mary A., b. Sept. 23, 1817; d. June 22, 1859; m. Samuel Mather, of Troy, N. Y., and was one of the first settlers of Wyandotte, Kansas.
1430. Martha L., b. June 15, 1820; d. Oct. 15, 1855; m. William Frazer, of Troy, N. Y.
1431. Elizabeth W., b. July 6, 1823; d. Dec. 8, 1835.
1432. Henry M., b. Dec. 6, 1825; d. March 26, 1827.

M 712

James Reed, son of Benjamin and Mrs. Abiah (Macomber) Reed.

b. at Middleborough Feb. 26, 1783; d. Jan. 19, 1881.

m. Sophronia Smith, who was born Jan. 26, 1790; died June, 1853.

CHILDREN

1433. James Smith, b. at Deerfield, Mass., April 13, 1818; d. at Marion, O., Jan. 26, 1896; m. Dec. 7, 1841, Nancy A. Holmes.

1434. Elizabeth Pierce, b. at Deerfield, Mass., Jan. 7, 1821; m. Nov. 2, 1841, Dr. Henry A. True.

1435. Sarah Haskins, b. Oct. 11, 1824; m. Richard H. Johnson.

M 714

Simeon Reed, son of Benjamin and Mrs. Abiah (Macomber) Reed.

b. ———, 1789; d. Aug. 28, 1853, aged 64.

m. Aug. 2, 1814, Miranda Morton, daughter of Justin and Esther (Harding) Morton, of Whately. Resided on the west side of Chestnut Plain street, Whately.

The following abstracts are taken from the history of the town of Whately, Mass.:

"Simeon Reed owned the house and lot where David Callahan resides. There was a small house on the place, containing one room, pantry and bedroom, when he bought it, in 1823. He built a nice cottage house. He was a wheelwright and had a shop on the place, a progressive man and good workman."—p. 107.

"As a consequence of Governor Strong's position, the United States troops were withdrawn from Massachusetts, and the entire coast was left exposed to hostile invasion. In this emergency, early in the fall of 1814, the governor called out the chartered companies and made a requisition for troops to be drafted from the state militia.

"In answer to this call, the Whately Rifle Greens, under command of Capt. Amos Pratt, marched 15th September, 1814, for a three months' campaign. They were stationed, most of the time, 'On the South Boston shore opposite Fort Independence,' and were attached to the battalion in command of Maj. William Ward of Worthington. The company was discharged 28 October."—p. 240.

On the muster roll of the Whately Rifle Greens, who went

to Boston, September, 1814, appears the name of Simeon Reed, drummer.

CHILDREN

1436. Jeannette, b. Jan. 10, 1815; m. Alvin Sanderson, of Hatfield, Mass.
1437. Mary, b. Dec. 2, 1817, m. Sept. 28, 1893, Stephen G. Curtis, of Hatfield, Mass.
1438. Benjamin Franklin, b. Oct. 5, 1819; m. Nov. 26, 1845, Sarah W. Saunders, of Mason, N. H.
1439. George Washington, b. Feb. 23, 1825; m. Nov. 3, 1847, Helen M. Pease.
1440. Elizabeth, b. Oct. 26, 1826; m. Rufus W. Babcock.
1441. Martha W., b. Feb. 22, 1829; m. Henry J. Babcock.

M 715

Levi Reed, son of Benjamin and Abiah (Macomber) Reed.
b. ———, 1791; d. at Watertown, N. Y.
m. ———, Nancy Pratt,
Of Hamilton, N. Y.

CHILDREN

1442. Edwin Dwight, b. March 22, 1812; d. April 28, 1888, at Georgetown, N. Y.; m. Sophia Redfield.
1443. Franklin Levi, b. Nov. 7, 1814; d. Feb. 9, 1880; m. Harriet A. Bennett.
1444. Lucino, b. ———; d. young.
1445. David, b. ———; d. young.
1446. Sophia N., b. Jan. 12, 1823; unmarried; d. at Rome, N. Y., 1872.
1447. Lucinda M., b. June 22, 1825; m. Rev. H. H. Peabody, D. D.; reside in Rome, N. Y.

M 718

Sylvanus Reed, son of Ichabod and Lucy Reed.
b. Jan. 4, 1816.
m. ———, Olive P. ———.

Lived at Middleborough.

CHILDREN

1448. Lydia W., b. ———.
1449. Mary E., b. ———.

M 720

Jeremiah Reed, son of Ichabod and Lucy Reed.
b. July 6, 1819.
m. ———, Mary G. ———.

Lived at Middleborough, had no children.
Of Middleborough, Mass.

SEVENTH GENERATION

A 723

Adam Reed, son of Obadiah and Elizabeth (Richmond) Reed.
b. ———, 1787.
m. ———, Mary Porter.

CHILDREN

1450. A daughter, who died.
1451. Mary Porter, b. ———; d. Sept. 27, 1899; m. Edwin Harris Reed, son of Silas.

A 724

Silas Reed, son of Obadiah and Elizabeth (Richmond) Reed.
b. Feb. 13, 1789; d. Jan. 9, 1856.
m. April 13, 1818, Mahala Harris.
Of Abington.

CHILDREN

1452. Silas Richmond, b. Oct. 9, 1818; m. 1st. July 14, 1839, Josephine Baily; m. 2d. Aug. 22, 1841, Louisa Raymond.
1453. Edwin Harris, b. Aug. 30, 1822; d. July 30, 1899; m. Mary Porter Reed, daughter of Adam.
1454. Salmon, b. March 31, 1824; m. 1st. July 7, 1849, Maria Sanford; m. 2d. Lucia Kidder.
1455. Evander, b. May 27, 1827; m. 1st. June 3, 1849, Lucy C. Humble; m. 2d. Oct., 1851, Mary E. Jenkins.

A 725

Abel Richmond Reed, son of Obadiah and Elizabeth (Richmond) Reed.

b. Sept. 27, 1791.
m. April 3, 1828, Roxanna Willis.

Was a soldier in the war of 1812.
No children. Of Abington, Mass.

A 726

Obadiah Reed, son of Obadiah and Elizabeth (Richmond) Reed.
b. Jan 1, 1796; d. ———, 1887; lived to be 91 years old.
m. Sept. 27, 1831, Deborah Tirrell Reed, daughter of Calvin.

They lived at Abington.

Of Abington, Mass.

CHILDREN

1456. Obadiah, b. Jan. 30, 1832; m. Dec. 25, 1856, Sarah E. C. Noyes, of Ipswich, Mass.
1457. Deborah, b. July 26, 1832.
1458. Webster, b. March 4, 1834; d. unmarried.

A 729

Isaac Reed, son of Obadiah and Elizabeth (Richmond) Reed.
b. June, 1801.
m. ———, Sallie Weeks.

Of Abington, Mass.

CHILD

1459. Annie, b. Sept. 3, 1828; d. young.

A 730

Israel Reed, son of Obadiah and Elizabeth (Richmond) Reed.
b. Aug. 10, 1806.
m. Nov. 18, 1838, Louisa Humble.

Of Abington, Mass.

CHILDREN

1460. Edward Richmond, b. Aug. 19, 1839; m. June 6, 1869, Ella L. Wales, of Abington.
1461. Salmon Willson, b. Feb. 24, 1847; m. Aug. 11, 1873, Clara Ella Keene, of Abington.

A 732

Joel Reed, son of Joel and Ruth (Gurney) Reed.
b. Feb. 8, 1794.
m. Nov. 16, 1837, Bethany Churchill.
Of Abington, Mass.

CHILD

1462. Pauline Isabelle, b. May 19, 1840; d. Jan. 31, 1896; m. Dec. 29, 1858, Samuel S. Atwood.

A 734

Matthew Reed, son of Joel and Ruth (Gurney) Reed.
b. Jan. 4, 1798; d. Dec. 29, 1860.
m. Sept. 12, 1822, Thirza Harris, daughter of John and Abigail (Edson) Harris.

Settled in North Bridgewater (now Brockton).

CHILDREN

1463. Abigail Harris, b. March 6, 1823; d. April 13, 1882; m. March 29, 1840, Lebbews Alden.
1464. Eliza Ann, b. March 6, 1825; d. Jan. 31, 1879; m. Nov. 19, 1842, Daniel Soule.
1465. Thirza Maria, b. May 11, 1828; d. Dec. 16, 1885; m. May, 1848, Samuel Holmes Soule.
1466. Harvey Williams, b. Feb. 14, 1831; d. April 26, 1861; m. Feb. 16, 1860, Helen M. Tirrel.
1467. Hiram Farwell, b. April 29, 1833; m. 1st. April 25, 1857, Emily J. Loud Reed; m. 2d. June 11, 1874, Selina H. Nash.
1468. Lucinda Franklin, b. Jan. 17, 1835; d. Dec. 27, 1892; m. Jan. 9, 1863, Thomas F. Currier.
1469. Matthew Gordon, b. Feb. 11, 1837; d. April 17, 1896; m. May 1, 1861, Harriet Maria Bicknell, of Weymouth.
1470. Fidelia Amanda, b. Dec. 17, 1838; d. Feb. 20, 1839.
1471. Lucia Eleanor, b. Aug. 24, 1840; d. April 10, 1889; m. June 11, 1861, Joseph W. Brown.
1472. Henry Lendall, b. March 28, 1842; d. ———; m. Sept. 17, 1864, Susan Adelaide Pratt.
1473. Nahum Augustus, b. Feb. 4, 1844; m. 1st. June 7, 1868, Isabella Frances Bicknell, of E. Weymouth; m. 2d. April 1, 1888, Sarah Whitman Spilsted, of E. Weymouth.
1474. Martha Ella, b. April 20, 1846; d. ———; m. March 9, 1870, Geo. Augustus Brown, of Decatur, Ill.

A 736

Albert Reed, son of Joel and Ruth (Gurney) Reed.

b. May 5, 1803.

m. ———, Polly Reynolds.

Of Abington, Mass.

CHILDREN

1475. Charles Alonzo, b. April 29, 1850.
1476. Polly, b. ———.
1477. Alonzo H., b. ———; m. June 28, 1866, Olive Amelia Jacobs.
1478. Isaac Bradford, b. ———; m. Sarah Loud.

A 737

Hervey Reed, son of Joel and Ruth (Gurney) Reed.

b. Feb. 27, 1806; d. April 25, 1879.

m. 1st. Oct. 30, 1830, Sally Pool.

m. 2nd. Nov. 23, 1837, Mary Thaxter Nash, daughter of Micah and Sarah Thaxter Nash, who died in Rockland Dec. 25, 1898.

Of Abington, Mass.

CHILD OF HERVEY AND SALLY

1479. Sarah, b. June 29, 1833.

CHILDREN OF HERVEY AND MARY

1480. An infant, b. Oct. 1, 1838; d. young.
1481. Hervey Turner, b. March 29, 1840; d. unmarried.
1482. Mary Elizabeth, b. Aug. 13, 1842; m. Dec. 11, 1870, Dan. Packard.
1483. Francis Baylies, b. Dec. 30, 1844; m. May 28, 1879, Clara Raymond.
1484. Abigail Adelaide, b. May 14, 1847; m. Feb. 24, 1867, Howard Malcolm Shaw.
1485. Alsie Carsilla, b. Aug. 10, 1850; d. Aug. 28, 1872; m. Nov. 4, 1869, Willard W. Lewis (1 child; d. in infancy).
1486. Infant child; d. young.
1487. Sharlie Ettie, b. April 15, 1854; d. ———; m. Feb. 21, 1874, Nathan B. Foster; lives in Rockland.

A 738

Lucius Reed, son of Joel and Ruth (Gurney) Reed.

b. Sept. 25, 1808.

m. Nov. 24, 1831, Lydia Shaw; she died Dec. 1, 1899.

Of Abington, Mass.

CHILDREN

1488. Helen Maria, b. Feb. 3, 1833; m. Dec. 9, 1852, Geo. A. Beal.
1489. Lydia Frances, b. Nov. 10, 1836.
1490. Henry, b. Feb. 4, 1842.
1491. Lucretia Adelaide, b. May 24, 1843; m. Dec. 27, 1863, Geo. A. Beal; had two sons.
1492. Lucius Alston, b. Feb. 6, 1847; m. June 7, 1877, Emma Lincoln Reynolds.
1493. Florence Lorilla, b. Oct. 22, 1849; m. Geo. A. Beal.

A 742

Woodbridge Brown Reed, son of David and Elizabeth T. (Brown) Reed.

b. Nov. 19, 1813.

m. ———, Orinda Neal.

Of Cummington, Mass.

A 745

David H. Reed, son of David and Elizabeth T. (Brown) Reed.

b. ———.

m. ———, Nancy Smith.

Of Cummington, Mass.

CHILDREN

1494. Lucy Harris, b. Dec. 23, 1840.
1495. Nancy Smith, b. Feb. 8, 1846.
1496. Frank, b. Sept. 8, 1856.

A 748

Jonathan L. Reed, son of Jonathan and Deborah (Porter) Reed.

b. ———, 1791.

m. 1st. Dec. 18, 1816, Charlotte Brown.

m. 2nd. pub. Feb. 25, 1827, Lucy Champney of Brighton.

Was a soldier in the war of 1812.

Of East Bridgewater, Mass.

CHILD OF JONATHAN AND CHARLOTTE

1497. Charlotte, b. May 28, 1821.

CHILDREN OF JONATHAN AND LUCY

1498. Susan Champney, b. Dec. 30, 1827.
1499. Lucy Loring, b. Aug. 5, 1830.

A 749

John P. Reed, son of Jonathan and Deborah (Porter) Reed.
b. ———, 1793.
m. in 1816, Polly Ramsdale.

Resided in South Abington.

CHILDREN

1500. Mary Loring, b. Aug. 26, 1817; m. Nov. 30, 1837, Edwin Brown, of E. Bridgewater.
1501. John Porter, b. July 29, 1819; m. Adaline Brown.
1502. Lloyd Watson, b. Jan. 7, 1822; m. Lucy Bryant.
1503. Mehetable R. W., b. Sept. 15, 1824; m. Nov. 19, 1843, David Gurney.
1504. Thomas Baldwin, b. July 29, 1827; m. Olive B. Perkins.

A 752

Thaxter Reed, son of Jonathan and Deborah (Porter) Reed.
b. Feb. 7, 1800, in East Bridgewater; d. April 4, 1846, in South Abington.
m. 1st. Feb. 4, 1827, Mehetable Brown (b. in 1805, at Cummington, Mass.; d. Nov., 1833, in South Abington; daughter of Samuel Brown).
m. 2nd. pub. July 30, 1837, Sophronia Barker, b. 1804; d. 1883, in Hanson, Mass.

Both members of the Baptist Church at South Abington (now Whitman) of which Thaxter was one of the founders. He was a stone mason.

CHILDREN OF THAXTER AND MEHETABLE

1505. Mehetable, b. May 8, 1830.
1506. Homan Thaxter, b. Aug. 5, 1833; m. 1st. Nov., 1854, Caroline Jenkins; m. 2d. Dec. 25, 1857, Maria L. Soule.

A 753

Ebenezer Reed, son of Jonathan and Deborah (Porter) Reed.
b. ———, 1801; d. March 4, 1878.

m. Jan. 1, 1829, Patience Penniman.

Of East Bridgewater.

CHILDREN

All born in Abington, Mass.

1507. Ebenezer Franklin, b. Nov. 23, 1829.

1508. George Augustus, b. Oct. 3, 1831; m. Susan Maria Gurney.

1509. William Henry, b. April 12, 1833; m. Feb. 2, 1859, Lucy Ann Dyer.

1510. Elizabeth Thaxter, b. Dec. 4, 1834; m. Jan. 9, 1854, Samuel Norton.

1511. Emeline Frances, b. Sept. 29, 1837.

1512. Marie Frances, b. Aug. 25, 1840; m. Aug. 31, 1862, Henry A. Bates.

A **767**

James Augustus Reed, son of William and Lovisa (Beals) Reed.

b. April 18, 1828, at Albany, N. Y.

m. Oct. 23, 1850, Lydia M. Stockton (b. in London, Eng., Aug. 23, 1826; daughter of John and Lydia Ann Stockton; d. Feb. 11, 1878, in Albany, N. Y.).

He resided in Albany, N. Y. Was a man of fine musical talents; a manufacturer of pianos from 1855 to 1863, and later dealer in pianos. Was an able performer on the organ and held the position of organist in Presbyterian and other churches during forty years. His wife Lydia M. Reed, had a very powerful and mellow contralto voice, and sang in quartette and choirs until within a few months of her death.

Of Albany, N. Y.

CHILDREN

1513. August Beals, b. Sept. 24, 1851; d. March 4, 1859.

1514. William Stockton, b. July 30, 1855; d. April 21, 1856.

1515. Frederick, b. June 20, 1857; d. May 5, 1858.

1516. Newton Briggs, b. Aug. 22, 1861; m. May 28, 1885, Rachel Blessing.

1517. Cordelia Lovisa, b. June 2, 1864.

A **768**

Rev. Albert Chester Reed, son of William and Lovisa (Beals) Reed.

b. Aug. 31, 1832, at Albany, N. Y.

m. March 8, 1865, Sarah M. Merriman (b. Nov. 3, 1830, at Elbridge, N. Y., daughter of Ebenezer and Lovisa (Coleman) Merriman).

He was a clerk in Albany and New York from 1845-54. Graduated at Grove Hall, Conn., in 1849. They were both members of the Presbyterian Church, in Elbridge, N. Y., in 1863, he was ordained and installed pastor over the Presbyterian Church at Port Byron, N. Y., from 1866 to 1873; of Congregational Church, Flushing, L. I., from 1873 to 1878; of Congregational Church, at Manchester, Vt., from 1878 to 1884. At present at North Granville, N. Y.

Of North Granville.

CHILDREN

1518. William Ebenezer, b. Jan. 17, 1866. (He is now a member of the Class of 1889, Cornell University.)

1519. Harry Lathrop, b. Dec. 15, 1869. (He is now a member of Class of 1889 at Yale College.)

1520. Albert Merriman, b. March 14, 1870. (He is now a member of Class of 1891 at Yale College.)

1521. Maurice Coroydon, b. Dec. 11, 1872; d. Aug. 16, 1873.

A 775

Samuel Worcester Reed, son of Joshua and Susannah (Noyes) Reed.

b. April 20, 1822, at Plainfield, Mass.

m. April 26, 1848, Adaline Norton (b. Feb. 3, 1831, at East Machias, Me.; daughter of Capt. Jabez and Mary Fuller (Foster) Norton).

They enjoyed all the educational advantages which could be obtained in country towns at that period. They were members of the Congregational Church and prominent in every good work. They were of fine personal appearance and pure moral character. Occupation was fruit growing at Wright's Station, Santa Clara county, Cal., but has retired from the business, and removed to East Oakland, Cal.

Of East Oakland, Cal.

CHILDREN

1522. Sarah Keller, b. Feb. 8, 1849; d. Sept. 21, 1849.
1523. Charles Keller, b. April 20, 1851; d. ———; m. July 6, 1873, Carrie S. Bosworth.
1524. Ida May, b. Nov. 18, 1854, at Ashland, Mass. Music teacher, E. Oakland, Cal.
1525. Royal Vining, b. March 5, 1858, at Boston, Mass.; d. May 5, 1860.

A 781

Jonathan Edwards Reed, son of Joshua and Susannah (Noyes) Reed.

b. July 4, 1833. Lives at 1358 West street, Oakland, Cal., and is unmarried.

A 786

Robert Reed, son of Seth and Hannah (Shaw) Reed.

b. Oct. 4, 1822.

m. ———, Nancy ———.

Lived at Cummington, Mass.

CHILD

1526. Clara, b. Oct. 4, 1850.

A 792

Seth Reed, son of Seth and Catherine (Brown) Reed.

b. May 2, 1804; d. March 7, 1894.

m. Sept. 13, 1826, Sally Blanchard.

Of Weymouth, Mass.

CHILDREN

1527. Ann Merrill, b. Nov. 15, 1829; m. J. F. L. Whitmarsh, son of John Whitmarsh.
1528. Ruth Torrey, b. Dec. 24, 1833; m. Elephalet Ripley Bates, son of John and Mary (Ripley) Bates.
1529. Sarah Dean, b. April 17, 1839; d. May 25, 1839.
1530. Seth Dean, b. June 19, 1840; m. 1st. Sarah Isabelle McConihe; m. 2d. July 10, 1888, Annie V. Grant Bigelow.
1531. An infant, b. April 10, 1842; d. May 6, 1842.
1532. Sarah Weston, b. Oct. 9, 1847; m. Joseph W. Randall, son of Joseph Randall.

A 795

Noah Warner Reed, son of Daniel and Cynthia (Warner) Reed.

b. Nov. 25, 1815.

m. ———, Nancy ———.

He lived at Cummington, Mass.

CHILDREN

1533. Mary Jane, b. June 17, 1839.
1534. Cynthia W., b. March 20, 1841; m. Steeve ———.
1535. John S., b. March 31, 1843.
1536. Nancy E., b. Oct. 18, 1848.
1537. A son, b. Oct. 19, 1850.
1538. Horace E., b. May, 1855.

A 797

John C. Reed, son of Daniel and Cynthia (Warner) Reed.

b. July 4, 1820.

m. ———, Sarah ———.

He lived at Cummington, Mass.

CHILDREN

1539. A son, b. March, 1854.
1540. Mary A., b. Jan. 9, 1856.

A 801

William Lewis Reed, son of Jesse and Mary (Griswold) Reed.

b. May 5, 1832.

m. Jan. 1, 1856, Julia Sampson.

Lived at Cummington.

Of Cummington, Mass.

CHILD

1541. A daughter, b. Aug. 25, 1857.

A 805

William Cole Reed, son of Abel and Lydia (Loud) Reed.

b. ———.

Lived at Roxbury.

A 806

James Ward Reed, son of Abel and Lydia (Loud) Reed.
b. ———.

Lived in Roxbury.

A 809

Charles Thayer Reed, son of Abel and Lydia (Loud) Reed.
b. ———.
m. Feb. 3, 1828, Sophia E. Critston, of Nashua.

He lived in Boston.

Of Boston, Mass.

A 811

John Reed, son of John and Olive (Alger) Reed.
b. ———, 1812.
m. ———, Amelia Crane of Fair Haven.

He was Vice-Treasurer of the Boston Institution for Savings.

Of Boston, Mass.

A 813

Edward Reed, son of John and Olive (Alger) Reed.
b. ———, 1817.
m. Nov. 6, 1848, Catharine Howard, daughter of William Howard, Esq., of Boston, Mass.

Of Yarmouth, Mass.

CHILDREN

1542. John, b. ———.
1543. William, b. ———.
1544. Catharine, b. ———.

A 814

John Montgomery Reed, son of Daniel and Nancy (Foster) Reed.
b. Aug. 9, 1814.

m. Elizabeth Broomfield, of Falsom, Norfolk county, England.

Lived in New York City.

CHILDREN

1545. John M., b. 1849.
1546. Elizabeth B., b. 1850; d. 1852.
1547. Daniel W., b. 1852.
1548. Charles Edward, b. 1856.

A 815

Charles Reed, son of Daniel and Nancy (Foster) Reed.
b. Dec. 7, 1815.
m. in 1843, Sophia Wilkins Clarke.

Lived in New York, removed to Bridgewater, where his two youngest children were born.

Of West Bridgewater.

CHILDREN

1549. Caleb, b. Sept. 20, 1844.
1550. Charles Montgomery, b. 1846.
1551. Mary, b. 1848.
1552. Hubbard Wilkins, b. 1850.
1553. William Horton, b. 1852.
1554. Caleb, b. 1854.
1555. Samuel A., b. June 8, 1856.

A 817

Solomon Reed, son of Solomon and Abigail (Howard) Reed.
b. ———, 1811.
m. Sept. 7, 1838, Lydia Blanchard.

He lived at Newton.

CHILD

1556. Edmond, b. ———.

A 818

George Howard Reed, son of Solomon and Abigail (Howard) Reed.
b. ———, 1814.
m. April 19, 1838, Elizabeth Jeffrey.

He lived at Waltham.

CHILDREN

1557. Isadore, b. ———.
1558. Anna, b. ———.
1559. Walter, b. ———.
1560. Edgar, b. ———.
1561. Alice, b. ———.

A 819

William Franklin Reed, son of Solomon and Abigail (Howard) Reed.

b. ———, 1819.

m. ———, Adelaide Arnold.

Resided in Boston.

CHILDREN

1562. Frances Miriam, b. ———.
1563. Georgianna E., b. ———.
1564. John D., b. ———.
1565. William H., b. ———.
1566. Charles Frederick, b. ———.
1567. Abba Louise, b. ———.

A 822

Rev. James Reed, son of Sampson and Catherine (Clark) Reed.

b. June 8, 1834.

m. Dec. 19, 1858, Emily Elizabeth Ripley.

He graduated at Harvard University in 1855. After leaving college, he taught one year in the public Latin School in Boston, and then devoted his attention to theological studies, and in April, 1860, was ordained as a minister of the New Jerusalem Church, and installed as assistant pastor of the Boston Society. He will be remembered by the members of the Reed family who were present at the celebration of the two hundredth anniversary of the settlement of Bridgewater, as the gentleman who delivered the poem on that occasion.

Of Boston, Mass

CHILDREN

1568. Catherine Clark, b. Sept. 21, 1859; m. Nov. 8, 1887, Herbert Langford Warren.
1568a. John Sampson, b. April 4, 1861; m. Oct. 30, 1900, Jessie Estelle Burbank.
1568b. Gertrude, b. March 8, 1863; m. June 12, 1889, Harold Broadfield Warren.
1568c. Miriam, b. Nov. 17, 1864; d. March, 1876.

1568d. Josephine, b. Oct. 17, 1868; m. May 31, 1894, Thomas Worcester Thatcher.
1568e. Emily Elizabeth, b. Feb. 21, 1876.

A 826

Josiah Hunt Reed, son of Josiah Willard and Fanny (Hunt) Reed.

b. Aug. 4, 1822; d. Aug. 1, 1898.

m. July 19, 1845, Mary Elizabeth Chessman, of Auburn, N. Y.; she died Dec. 1894, in Orange, N. J.

In the spring of 1836, his father having died in Oct. of the year previous, he left home to live with his mother's brother, Thomas M. Hunt, of Auburn, N. Y. He was a member of his family, and a clerk in his drug store for a period of about ten years.

In Jan. 1845, when twenty-two years of age, he went to Chicago to establish a drug business for himself, assisted by way of capital and credit by his uncle and other friends. Chicago was then a city of about 10,000 inhabitants. He continued in the drug business there until 1867, his firm being J. H. Reed & Co. From a small beginning his business grew to be, at the time he left it, one of the largest of its kind in the United States. In 1858 he moved his residence to New York city, but continued active, however, in the management of his business, importing and purchasing supplies for the Chicago house. He retired from that business in 1867, and was out of business for the next eight years.

In 1875 he entered business again, forming a partnership with William H. Flagg, now located at 11 Pine street, New York City, dealers in railroad bonds of the highest grade. His business record has always been good, having always met promptly every obligation. During the last thirty-one years he has been a resident of Orange, N. J., and for nineteen years has been a regular communicant in the First Presbyterian Church, Orange, and for the best part of the time was also elder in that church. He has never been prominent in politics, but always exercised his rights as a citizen, voting with the Republican party.

Of East Orange, N. J.

CHILD

1569. Alice, b. April 20, 1846; d. Nov. 5. 1873; m. Nov. 1, 1866, Albert D. Smith, of W. Orange, N. J.

A 829

William Reed, son of Samuel H. and Elizabeth (Foster) Reed.
b. June 20, 1819.
m. 1st. Elizabeth Kent Sayer, Sept. 17, 1846 (she was b. April 17, 1826; d. Jan. 15, 1853).
m. 2nd. Mrs. Elizabeth Newton Cleaver.

Of Greenfield, Mass.

CHILDREN

1570. William Samuel, b. July, 1847; d. 1848.
1571. Elizabeth Kent, b. Jan. 7, 1849; m. Nov. 17, 1870, Harvey Sheldon Kitchel.
1572. Samuel A., b. Aug. 1, 1850; unmarried.
1573. Henry Lyman, b. Sept. 15, 1851; m. Oct. 14, 1875, Lizzie S. McLean.

A 836

John Reed, son of Samuel and Melinda (Wheelock) Reed.
b. Feb. 26, 1820.
m. ———, Delia Winter.

Lived in Worcester. He was a teacher of music.

Of Worcester, Mass.

CHILDREN

1574. Frederick E., b. March 1, 1847.
1575. Ella E., b. Aug. 7, 1856.

A 839

S. Chandler Reed, son of Stephen and Jerusha (Moor) Reed.
b. April 22, 1822.
m. 1st. Nov. 25, 1852, Lebiah H. Jones.
m. 2nd. Nov. 25, 1857, Rhoda G. Tyler.

He lived in Warwick, and was a school teacher.

Of Warwick, Mass.

A 842

Samuel Reed, son of Stephen and Jerusha (Moor) Reed.
b. March 22, 1829.
m. Nov., 1853, Maria H. Barber.

He lived in Warwick, Mass.

CHILDREN

1576. Almah M., b. 1855.
1577. Abby J., b. June 4, 1857.

A 849

Samuel Reed, son of Samuel and Polly (Greenleaf) Reed.
b. March 5, 1802; d. Feb. 20, 1869.
m. Oct. 11, 1832, Caroline Nash; she died June 24, 1889; married by Rev. Jonas Perkins.

Lived at Weymouth.

CHILDREN

1578. Charles Andrew, b. June 16, 1836; d. June 19, 1900; m. 1st. June 27, 1870, Wealthea Nolan Dean, of Taunton, Mass.; m. 2d. June, 1889, Myra L. Dean.
1579. Caroline Amelia, b. March 29, 1838; d. Feb. 27, 1877.
1580. George Milton, b. Jan. 8, 1840; d. ———.
1581. Samuel Willard, b. March 25, 1846; d. Sept. 11, 1848.
1582. Samuel Willard, b. Dec. 31, 1849; d. ———.

A 852

John Reed, son of John and Elizabeth (Gould) Reed.
b. March 3, 1797; d. April 17, 1828.
m. Nov. 3, 1818, Emma Dill, daughter of Daniel and Mary (Chubbock) Dill; b. Aug. 13, 1792; she died Aug. 6. 1884. After the death of her husband she lived at Hull.
Of Scituate.

CHILDREN

1583. Jane Binney, b. July 24, 1819; d. Aug. 3, 1866; m. Feb. 13, 1841, John Wesley Tower, of Hingham.
1584. John, b. Dec. 7, 1822; d. ———; m. Dec. 25, 1853, Mary Elizabeth Pope.
1585. Daniel Dill, b. Jan. 13, 1827; m. July 14, 1852, Esther B. L. Rachford.

A 860

Loring W. Reed, son of Thomas and Sarah (———) Reed.
b. Oct. 3, 1803.
m. Ann Pool of Abington.

Lived in Boston, 1334 Springfield street.

CHILDREN

1586. Anna F., b. Oct. 13, 1831; m. John W. Way.
1587. Charles Loring, b. Jan. 9, 1833.
1588. Sarah Lapham, b. Oct. 19, 1834; d. March 30, 1858; m. John M. Way, of Roxbury.
1589. Thomas Franklin, b. Oct. 6, 1836; d. about 1885.
1590. William Garrison, b. June 9, 1842. (25 Kelley St., Boston.)

A 861

Thomas Reed, son of Thomas and Sarah (———) Reed.
b. in 1816; d. Feb. 19, 1859.
m. Sept. 8, 1841, Elizabeth Hayward; she died Sept. 8, 1855, aged 34.

Of Weymouth, Mass.

CHILDREN

1591. Charles, b. ———; lives on Pacific coast, either Oregon or Washington.
1592. Herber A., b. ———; lives in Quincy.

A 865

Philip Reed, son of Philip and Polly (Taylor) Reed.
b. Sept. 19, 1802.
m. Dec. 15, 1825, Sapphira Howland.

Of South Abington, Mass.

CHILDREN

1593. George Williams, b. Sept. 29, 1826; m. June 18, 1846, Lucy Ann Cook.
1594. Lucy White, b. May 24, 1833.
1595. Charles Warren, b. Feb. 2, 1842.

A 871

Isaac Reed, son of Isaac and Sally (Stetson) Reed.
b. Jan. 26, 1805; d. 1870.
m. 1st. Dec. 18, 1831. 1st wife died in 1844.
m. 2nd. in 1849, Sarah Porter.

Lived in East Bridgewater, Mass.

CHILDREN BY FIRST WIFE

1596. George A., b. ———1832; m. Dec., 1858, Nancy Watson Brown.
1597. Nancy A., b. in 1836; m. Aug. 11, 1858, Joseph H. Cook.

CHILDREN OF ISAAC AND SARAH

1598. Isaac W., b. 1853; d. unmarried.
1599. Asa C., b. 1857; d. unmarried.

A 872

Nahum Reed, son of Isaac and Sally (Stetson) Reed.
b. Dec. 15, 1806; d. Oct. 27, 1872.
m. Oct. 6, 1840, Maria Wetherell.

He resided in Whitman, Mass.

CHILDREN

1600. Clinton W., b. Sept. 4, 1842; m. Jan. 1, 1868, Mehetable Nash Gurney.
1601. Nahum S., b. May 6, 1845; m. Nov. 4, 1869, Mary E. Ferris.
1602. Ezra A., b. Oct. 18, 1847; d. April 8, 1849.
1603. Frank Austin, b. July, 1852; m. Oct. 27, 1878, Alberta Thompson.

A 873

Dexter Reed, son of Isaac and Sally (Stetson) Reed.
b. Jan. 21, 1809.
m. in 1842, Lydia Wright.

Lived in East Bridgewater, Mass.

CHILDREN

1604. Samuel D., b. 1846.
1605. Franklin P., b. 1853.
1606. John B., b. 1856.

A 874

James Thaxter Reed, son of Isaac and Sally (Stetson) Reed.
b. Oct. 8, 1815; d. Feb. 22, 1875.
m. 1st. in 1844, Eliza Ann Keith; she died Feb. 16, 1851, aged 27 years and 7 months.
m. 2nd. Mary Ann Severance; she died Oct. 14, 1884, aged 63 years 2 months and 11 days.

He was a justice of the peace.

Of East Bridgewater, Mass.

CHILDREN OF JAMES AND ELIZA

1607. Lurana Thaxter, b. April 30, 1845; m. 1st. 1862, Nahum Poole, of Whitman, Mass.; m. 2d. June 3, 1880, Bela C. Josselyn, of Bridgeport, Conn.

1608. Sarah Scott, b. May 28, 1846; d. May 23, 1884; m. July 1, 1866, Henry C. Harding, of E. Bridgewater.

1609. James Lewis, b. Jan. 4, 1851; d. July 28, 1881; unmarried.

CHILD OF JAMES AND MARY

1610. Clarence Derwood, b. March 29, 1857; m. Dec. 25, 1889, Harriet Davis, of N. Easton, Mass.

A **875**

Calvin Reed, son of Isaac and Sally (Stetson) Reed.
b. April 3, 1819.
m. in 1844, Mary S. Bates.

He was a justice of the peace.

Of East Bridgewater, Mass.

CHILDREN

1611. Mary F., b. April 20, 1845.
1612. Benjamin C., b. Dec. 24, 1849.

A **877**

Albert Reed, son of Jeremiah and Rebecca (Jenkins) Reed.
b. Aug. 23, 1803.
m. in 1832, Almira Drake, of Hanson.

He lived in Abington, Mass.

Of Whitman or Hanson.

CHILDREN

1613. Albert Laurain, b. 1834; d. unmarried.
1614. Sarah Spooner, b. 1835; d. ———.
1615. Augusta, b. 1837; d. 1849.

A **878**

Melvin Reed, son of Jeremiah and Rebecca (Jenkins) Reed.
b. March 30, 1806; d. Aug. 7, 1891.
m. Nov. 16, 1829, Emily Poole; she was born at Abington, Feb. 19, 1810; died Nov., 1890. No children.

Of East Bridgewater, Mass.

A 879

Nathaniel Reed, son of Jeremiah and Rebecca (Jenkins) Reed.

b. Sept. 17, 1807; d. June 15, 1864.

m. March 24, 1831, Betsy M. Bartlett, daughter of Azel Bartlett; b. March 28, 1811, of Cummington; she died Dec. 11, 1849.

Son, Nathaniel L., was a private in 58th Regiment Massachusetts Volunteer Infantry.

Of East Bridgewater, Mass.

CHILDREN

All born in South Abington.

1616. Elizabeth M., b. July 1, 1832: d. March 4, 1833.
1617. Nathaniel L., b. June 14, 1834; d. June 18, 1864: killed in the Civil War.
1618. Edward F., b. May 15, 1837; d. Dec. 13, 1849.
1619. Marshall, b. Sept. 13, 1841; m. Sept. 28, 1863, Helen M. Penniman.
1620. Elizabeth B., b. Dec. 23, 1843; m. Jan. 11, 1870, Edwin B. Cook.

A 880

David Reed, son of Jeremiah and Rebecca (Jenkins) Reed.

b. July 2, 1812.

m. 1st. in 1836, Nancy Smith; she died in 1837.

m. 2nd. Oct. 9, 1839, Eliza Ann Bates, daughter of Daniel and Jane (Reed) Bates.

Of East Bridgewater, Mass.

CHILDREN OF DAVID AND ELIZA

1621. Lucy Harrison, b. Dec. 23, 1840; m. John Davis.
1622. David, b. March 7, 1843; d. same day.
1623. Daniel, b. March 7, 1843; d. same day.
1624. Nancy Smith, b. Feb. 8, 1846.
1625. Frank F., b. Sept. 8, 1855; d. Nov. 24, 1898; m. Alice Pickens.
1626. Edward S., b. Jan. 30, 1858; d. April 19, 1858.

A 881

Charles Spooner Reed, son of Jeremiah and Rebecca (Jenkins) Reed.

b. Oct. 12, 1816.

m. 1st. ———, Clarissa S. Gurney, of East Bridgewater; she died in 1849.

m. 2nd. Nov. 15, 1855, Rebecca T. Stetson, daughter of Zenas and Jane (Frank) Stetson.

Of East Bridgewater, Mass.

CHILDREN

1627. Mary Jane, b. Nov. 5, 1844; m. Charles Evans, of Haverhill, Mass.
1628. Charles Willis, b. 1846.
1629. Rebecca Jenkins, b. 1849.
1630. Clarissa Sophia, b. ———.

A 882

Oakes Reed, son of Calvin and Hannah (Ludden) Reed.

b. Sept. 11, 1808; d. March 1, 1848.

m. in 1832, Lettice Barker Hobart; she was born at Hanson, Mass., March 4, 1814, and died Sept. 11, 1885 Was daughter of Isaac and Lettice (Barker) Hobart.

CHILDREN

1631. Andrew Hobart, b. May 15, 1833; d. ———; m. 1856, Elizabeth E. Keene.
1632. Catharine Parris, b. March 10, 1837; d. March 10, 1854, at E. Bridgewater; unmarried.
1633. Eliza Attwood, b. June 19, 1840; m. Gilbert Shaw.
1634. Isaac Hobart, b. Aug. 28, 1842; d. Aug. 29, 1847, at E. Bridgewater.
1635. Calvin Payson, b. Nov. 2, 1844; m. Jan. 25, 1877, Cora Maria Beal.

A 884

Hezekiah Reed, son of Calvin and Hannah (Ludden) Reed.

b. July 12, 1812.

m. ———, Elizabeth Josselyn.

He lived in Hanover.

CHILD

1636. Herbert E., b. Dec. 19, 1845; d. May 12, 1883; buried in Hanover.

A 886

Lucius Reed, son of Joseph and Charlotte (Stetson) Reed.
b. June 7, 1808.
m. January 7, 1838, Selina Dyer.
Of East Bridgewater, Mass.

CHILDREN

1637. Lucius Franklin, b. May 6, 1840; d. unmarried, at Whitman.
1638. Henry Dyer, b. Feb. 4, 1842; m. January 21, 1875, Louisa Parker, of Whitman, Mass.

A 887

Aaron Reed, son of Joseph and Charlotte (Stetson) Reed.
b. Aug. 2, 1811; d. Jan. 22, 1892.
m. Sept. 15, 1836, Hannah Fullerton.

Lived in Abington.

CHILDREN

1639. Aaron Alden, b. April 25, 1839; m. July 23, 1876, Eunice Maria Slack.
1640. Hannah Maria, b. May 16, 1844; d. unmarried.

A 889

Joseph Reed, son of Joseph and Charlotte (Stetson) Reed.
b. Sept. 12, 1817.
m. in 1843, Mehetable Jenkins, daughter of Nathaniel and Eunice (Whitman) Jenkins; she was born April 18, 1822. (See Spooner's Acct.)

Lived in East Bridgewater.

Of Whitman.

A 890

Daniel Reed, son of Joseph and Charlotte (Stetson) Reed.
b. June 18, 1820.
m. 1st. ———, 1844, Mary Ann Smith, daughter of Lebbus and Polly (Bates) Smith.
m. 2nd. Oct. 17, 1880, Sarah (Lewis) Poole, widow of ——— Poole.

Of Whitman.

CHILDREN

1641. Daniel Lyman, b. April 7, 1847; m. 1st. Lucia Whitman (no children); m. 2d. Marcia Edson (no children).
1642. Forrest Samuel, b. Oct. 9, 1852; m. Louie Holbrook (no children).
1643. Mary Ann, b. Sept. 25, 1855; m. Harry A. Hill, of Stoneham, Mass. (no children).

A 891

Marcus Stetson Reed, son of Joseph and Charlotte (Stetson) Reed.

b. Jan. 3, 1824.

m. ———, Susan M. Whitman. No children.

Of Whitman.

A 894

Samuel P. Reed, son of Jared and Mehetable (Gardner) Reed.

b. ———.

m. in 1840, Lemira D. Hurd, of New Hampshire.

He lived in South Abington.

CHILD

1644. Lucina, b. Feb. 1, 1846.

A 899

Josiah Reed, son of Ezekiel and Rebecca (Edson) Reed.

b. March 2, 1799.

m. ———, Jennet Keith.

Lived in West Bridgewater.

Of West Bridgewater.

CHILD

1645. Ann, b. Sept. 10, 1848.

A 900

Edwin B. Reed, son of Ezekiel and Rebecca (Edson) Reed.

b. Jan. 20, 1804.

m. ———, Furosina Glass, of Duxbury.

Lived in Kingston, Mass.

Of Kingston, Mass.

CHILDREN

1646. Edwin Theodore, b. Sept. 26, 1823.
1647. Alphonso, b. Nov., 1830.
1648. Helen, b. April 30, 1837.

A 901

Charles Briggs Reed, son of Ezekiel and Rebecca (Edson) Reed.

b. May 21, 1806.

m. ———, Eunice B. Harden; d. Oct. 22, 1855, aged 50.

Of West Birdgewater.

CHILDREN

1649. Susan Frances, b. June 13, 1832; m. May 7, 1851, Simeon C. Keith.
1650. Emily Briggs, b. Dec. 17, 1833; m. Henry Copeland.
1651. Eunice Edson, b. Jan. 3, 1836; m. Charles F. Hicks.

A 904

Horatio G. Reed, son of Col. Jesse and Hannah (Howard) Reed.

b. Oct., 1804.

m. ———, Wealthy Walker; she was b. Nov., 1802.

Lived in Scituate and Marshfield.

Of Marshfield.

CHILDREN

1652. Horatio G. H., b. (in Marshfield) April 12, 1828; m. April 2, 1850, Esther M. Cole.
1653. Maria W., b. (in Scituate) Feb. 25, 1833; m. Henry L. Vinal.
1654. Ellen L., b. June 15, 1839; m. Charles D. West.
1655. Mary Forbes, b. Jan. 5, 1841; m. John E. O. Prouty.

A 918

William Briggs Reed, son of Briggs Rogers and Betsy (Hutchinson) Reed.

b. Dec. 15, 1816.

m. ———, Eliza Howard, of Salem.

In business at 134 Lincoln street, Boston, Mass. Residence 4 Winthrop street, Boston.

Of Boston, Mass.

CHILDREN

1656. William H., b. April 9, 1846.
1657. Benjamin C., b. Aug. 10, 1850.
1658. Isabel H., b. June 20, 1857.

A 920

Augustus Reed, son of Briggs Rogers and Betsy (Hutchinson) Reed.

b. April 13, 1821.

m. ——, Laura Ann Leach of Boston.

In business at East Boston (corner Mereton and Paris streets).

Of Boston, Mass.

CHILDREN

1659. Ann Eliza, b. ———.
1660. Emma Cornelia, b. ———.
1661. Warren Augustus, b. July 1, 1851; m. Dec. 3, 1878, Nellie A. Crocker.
1662. Alice Jane, b. ———.

A 921

George W. Reed, son of Briggs Rogers and Betsy (Hutchinson) Reed.

b. Aug. 5, 1823.

m. 1st. Oct. 20, 1852, Ellen Howard of Salem; d. May 6, 1855.

m. 2nd. Oct. 29, 1857, Hannah Elizabeth Marston of Salem.

He was of the firm of Reed and Hastings, Old State House.

Of Boston, Mass.

CHILDREN

1663. George Harvey, b. Sept. 7, 1853.
1664. Anna Josephine, b. Sept. 27, 1858.

A 929

Alonzo Reed, son of Samuel Licander and Nancy (Gray) Reed.

b. Jan. 20, 1824.

m. Aug. 9, 1852 (in Waterton, Mass) Adeline White.

Of Gardiner, Me.

A 931

George William Reed, son of Samuel Licander and Nancy (Gray) Reed.

b. April 24, 1831.

m. ———, Hannah Augusta Currier (daughter of Dr. Currier of Bath, Me.).

He was a dentist.

Of Bath, Me.

A 932

William Q. Reed, son of Samuel and Sally (Bates) Reed.

b. July 24, 1806; d. (in Jefferson county) Jan. 28, 1877.

m. Aug. —, 1827, Harriet Leach; b. Jan. 12, 1810; d. Jan. 31, 1871; m. in New York.

CHILDREN

1665. Almyra C., b. July 18, 1829, in Chautauqua Co., N. Y.; m. Oct. 12, 1849, Lucius M. Gilmore, in Kenosha Co., Wis.
1666. Marion A., b. Feb. 2, 1831, in Chautauqua Co., N. Y.; d. May 14, 1862; m. Oct. 15, 1847, Daniel Banker, in Chautauqua Co., N. Y.
1667. Harriet M., b. Dec. 25, 1833, in Chautauqua Co., N. Y.; m. Aug., 1853, Joel Farnsworth, in Kenosha Co., Wis.
1668. Sallie E., b. Sept. 19, 1838, in Borne Co., Ind.; d. Jan. 26, 1868; m. Bradshaw.
1669. William A., b. Oct. 21, 1841, in Borne Co., Ind.; m. March 11, 1869, Katie Hoyt.
1670. Rhoda J., b. Aug. 24, 1845, in Borne Co., Ind.; d. Aug. 18, 1861.

A 933

Prentice J. Reed, son of Samuel and Sally (Bates) Reed.

b. Oct. 18, 1807; d. May 24, 1859.

m. Sept. 19, 1833, Jedidah K. Kingsbury of Ohio; b. Aug. 17, 1813; d. Dec. 17, 1884.

CHILDREN

The five eldest children born in Geauga Co., Ohio; next three in Kenosha Co., Wisconsin; youngest in Littleton, Iowa.

1671. Caroline, b. Sept. 6, 1834; d. Feb. 2, 1835.
1672. Cyrus Joy, b. June 20, 1836; m. in 1864, Annette Smith.

1673. Samuel A., b. Dec. 2, 1838; d. July 1, 1890.
1674. Sarah Jane, b. March 8, 1840; d. June 5, 1862.
1675. Benjamin K., b. June 19, 1843; m. June 2, 1881, Philomenia Digman.
1676. Carrie L., b. Nov. 3, 1846; m. April 17, 1879, Geo. L. Marshall.
1677. Charles, b. April 2, 1849; d. March 11, 1851.
1678. William R., b. Dec. 11, 1851.
1679. Eva M., b. April 28, 1856.

A 942

Hiram Joseph Reed, son of Samuel and Sarah (Teasiear) Reed.

b. May 23, 1827, in Orleans county, N. Y.; d. Sept. 1, 1857.

m. about 1846, Eliza Keyes; she died Feb. 15, 1857.

CHILDREN

1680. Samuel Clark, b. Jan. 21, 1852; m. Oct. 17, 1884, Julia Baker.
1681. Clifford H., b. Feb. 20, 1855.

A 944

Fordyce Reed, son of Daniel and Lucy (Bates) Reed.

b. June 20, 1807, in Chesterfield, Mass.; d. Sept. 7, 1848.

m. May 21, 1837, Eunice Swan; b. Oct. 10, 1808; d. Sept. 28, 1880. Her native place was Kingston, Vt.

CHILD

1682. Amanda, b. Sept. 23, 1843, in Orleans Co., N. Y.; m. Nov. 4, 1880, Henry W. Latimer, of Utica, N. Y. He died March 13, 1895, his widow now of Holly, N. Y.

A 946

Daniel W. Reed, son of Daniel and Lucy (Bates) Reed.

b. Jan. 22, 1810; d. April 1, 1885.

m. Aug. 7, 1833, Electa Hubbard; b. May 19, 1812; d. Aug. 19, 1873.

CHILDREN

All born in Orleans Co., N. Y.

1683. George M., b. May 14, 1834; d. Aug. 2, 1835.
1684. Pamelia, b. Feb. 5, 1839; m. Oct. 9, 1861, John R. Seeley.
1685. Fordyce Daniel, b. Dec. 21, 1850; m. Feb. 8, 1875, Mina Zilpha Andrus.

A 948

Horace Reed, son of Daniel and Lucy (Bates) Reed.
b. May 31, 1814; d. Aug. 15, 1876.
m. ———, Mahala Hitchcock.

He was in Company "C," 105 N. Y. Infantry. His son Elijah also served in the same company.

CHILDREN

1686. Elijah, b. 1842; m. in Kansas and left two children.
1687. Lucy, b. Sept. 8, 1845; d. Jan., 1864.

A 950

Napoleon B. Reed, son of Daniel and Mercy (Nash) Reed.
b. Jan. 12, 1818, in Orleans county, N. Y.
m. Nov., 1838, Czarina Hall Glazier; b. Jan. 12, 1821; d. ———.

CHILDREN

All the children were born in Orleans Co., N. Y.

1688. Lyman A., b. Jan. 2, 1840; m. Jan. 28, 1858, Elizabeth M. Tutner.
1689. Czarina C., b. Aug. 14, 1841; d. July 18, 1854.
1690. Mercy A., b. Feb. 29, 1844.
1691. Napoleon B., Jr., b. Feb. 13, 1846; m. 1st. March 19, 1868, Marion Phillips; m. 2d. Sept. 13, 1885, Mrs. Nettie Sutherland.
1692. Daniel E., b. Feb. 8, 1851; m. April 2, 1871, Emeline Hayes.
1693. Elcena C., b. March 25, 1860; d. March 9, 1862.

A 951

Alonzo Reed, son of Daniel and Marrilla (Knapp) Reed.
b. Jan. 21, 1823, in Orleans county, N. Y.; d. April 8, 1882.
m. Jan. 21, 1845, Celia Ann Sprague in Orange county, N. Y.; b. Sept. 16, 1826; d. March 27, 1858.

CHILDREN

All the children born in State of New York.

1694. Celia Marrilla, b. Jan. 1, 1846; d. March 4, 1848.
1695. Celia Ann, b. Feb. 13, 1848; m. Jan. 1, 1873, Shively S. Mather.

1696. Phebe Belle, b. May 8, 1851; m. Dec. 25, 1874, Geo. W. Sisson.
1697. Helen May, b. May 6, 1853; m. Jan. 1, 1879, Fred. A. Richards.
1698. Cora Hattie, b. Feb. 21, 1858; m. Oct. 17, 1875, Eugene Morrill.

A 953

Samuel Reed, son of Daniel and Marrilla (Knapp) Reed.

b. March 7, 1827, in Orleans county, N. Y.; d. March 27, 1887.

m. Nov. 8, 1850, Sarah M. Partridge in Herkimer county, N. Y.; b. May 22, 1829; d. May 6, 1868.

Was in Company "C," 105 N. Y. Infantry.

CHILDREN

All born in Orleans Co., N. Y.

1699. Amer Alanson, b. Dec. 22, 1851; m. Sept. 16, 1875, Libbie Jessie Simmons.
1700. Orra Partridge, b. Dec. 22, 1853; m. Dec. 31, 1878, Ida B. Hall.
1701. Myron Samuel, b. June 4, 1860. Was reported in 1880 as studying for the ministry, and hopes to be sent on some foreign mission.

A 954

Sylvester Franklin Reed, son of Daniel and Marrilla (Knapp) Reed.

b. Oct. 6, 1829, in Orleans county, N. Y.; d. Jan. 26, 1884.

m. July 4, 1853, Maria Louisa Underhill, in Orleans county, N. Y.; b. Sept. 6, 1832.

CHILDREN

1702. Charles Martin, b. March 4, 1866, in Orleans Co., N. Y.; d. March 12, 1884.
1703. Ralph Underhill, b. Jan. 31, 1874, in Orleans Co., N. Y.

A 955

Nelson Knapp Reed, son of Daniel and Marrilla (Knapp) Reed.

b. Sept. 11, 1831.

m. 1st. June, 1853, Julia Ann Weeks, in Norway, Ind.; she died May 19, 1862.

m. 2nd. Dec. 2, 1863, Julia Augusta Dikeman, of Oneida county, N. Y.; b. March 21, 1841; d. Sept. 23, 1888.

CHILDREN OF NELSON AND JULIA AUGUSTA DIKEMAN

All born in Orleans Co., N. Y.

1704. Earnest R., b. Dec. 13, 1864; d. May 2, 1886.

1705. Rose Augusta, b. Feb. 16, 1866; m. Jan. 7, 1886, Benjamin F. Mayback.

1706. Florence Harriet, b. Sept. 30, 1867; m. March 9, 1887, Frank Benard.

1707. Dikeman D., b. March 12, 1870.

1708. Mary Belle, b. Nov. 23, 1871.

1709. Frances J., b. Feb. 16, 1875.

1710. Lulu Olive, b. Feb. 8, 1878.

A 958

Hiram Smith Reed, son of Capt. Simeon and Bersheba (Thayer) Reed.

b. Aug. 2, 1816, in Chesterfield, Mass.; d. Dec. 23, 1864.

m. Aug. 11, 1844, Amanda Noyes; b. May 16, 1818, in Cummington, Mass. Married in Oneida county, N. Y.

CHILDREN

Two eldest children born in Ashtabula Co., Ohio; three youngest born in Erie Co., Ohio.

1711. Waldo Simeon, b. Feb. 2, 1847; m. May 1, 1878, Luella Annette Miller.

1712. Cynthia Amelia, b. Dec. 31, 1848; m. Oct. 19, 1871, Anderson Hubbard.

1713. Hiram Elwin, b. Feb. 14, 1855; m. Hattie E. Allen.

1714. Noyes Williard, b. Sept. 25, 1857; m. Dec. 28, 1887, Addie Florence McHenry.

1715. Frank Rea, b. May 25, 1863.

A 959

Stillman Sears Reed, son of Capt. Simeon and Bersheba (Thayer) Reed.

b. Dec. 1, 1817; d. Sept. 22, 1874.

m. Pamelia Paden.

At the age of two years he was rendered deaf and dumb by an accident. His wife was a natural mute.

A 961

Cyrus Monroe Reed, son of Capt. Simeon and Mary (Whitton) Reed.

b. Jan. 27, 1823.

m. June 18, 1846, Polly W. Bates; b. May 21, 1823, in Westford, Vt. Married in Chesterfield, Mass.

CHILDREN

Two eldest born in Chesterfield, Mass.; youngest born in Erie Co., Pa.

1716. Marcia Angela, b. Feb. 2, 1848; m. May 19, 1868, Washington Irving Potter.

1717. Emma Augusta, b. July 27, 1852; m. Aug. 15, 1872, Charles C. French.

1718. Nellie Amanda, b. April 29, 1858; m. May 13, 1886, Willis Herbert Smith.

A 965

Daniel Whitton Reed, son of Capt. Simeon and Mary (Whitton) Reed.

b. Sept. 10, 1835, in Chesterfield, Mass.; d. March 20, 1876.

m. Oct. 20, 1863, Marcella Gould; b. Jan. 24, 1840, in Erie county, Penna.; d. Aug. 11, 1882.

He served nine months in Company "E," 52nd Mass. Infantry, and afterwards served until the close of the war in Battery "G," 1st Wis. Heavy Artillery at Fort Ellsworth, Va.

CHILDREN

1719. David Gould, b. Sept. 11, 1864, in Sheboygan Co., Wis.

1720. Freddie Alanson, b. Jan. 20, 1870, in Erie Co., Pa.; d. Nov. 15, 1871.

1721. Minerva May, b. Jan. 2, 1873, in Erie Co., Pa.

A 967

Simeon Smith Reed, son of Joseph and Wealthy (Williams) Reed.

b. April 19, 1815, in Orleans county, N. Y.

m. June 18, 1844, Adaline Olds; b. Nov. 23, 1817, in Cummington, Mass.; d. Jan. 29, 1887. Married in Geauga county, Ohio.

CHILDREN

1722. George H., b. May 19, 1845, in Geauga Co., Ohio; m. June 16, 1869, Ella S. Colton.
1723. Lucy Ann, b. July 18, 1848, in Rock Co., Wis.; m. April 26, 1868, Russell O. Chapel.
1724. Franklin Dwight, b. Sept. 24, 1851, in Rock Co., Wis.; m. Feb. 18, 1873, Mary E. Speelman.
1725. Charles Fremont, b. May 12, 1863, in Rock Co., Wis.; d. Oct. 28, 1864.

A 970

Otis Elbridge Reed, son of Joseph and Wealthy (Williams) Reed.

b. March 13, 1820, in Orleans county, N. Y.

m. April 3, 1845, Huldah E. Snow; b. Dec. 31, 1822, in Mass. Married in Geauga county, Ohio.

CHILDREN

All born in Dodge Co., Wis.

1726. Hattie Jane, b. Dec. 19, 1847; m. Oct. 24, 1866, Geo. S. Hazeltine.
1727. Albert E., b. April 12, 1851; d. April 28, 1872.
1728. Alanson H., b. Dec. 19, 1852; d. Jan. 2, 1853.
1729. May Emeline, b. Feb. 24, 1858; m. June 1, 1877, La Fayette M. Willis.
1730. Carrie Eudora, b. Dec. 19, 1861; m. Feb. 14, 1883, Irving P. Leigh.

A 971

Freeman Williams Reed, son of Joseph and Wealthy (Williams) Reed.

b. Oct. 27, 1822, in Orleans county, N. Y.; d. May 27, 1862.

m. April 13, 1845, R. Lucina Cole; b. Aug. 7, 1825, in Wayne county, N. Y. Married in Geauga county, Ohio.

CHILDREN

The eldest child born in Waukesha Co., Wis.; all the others born in Rock Co., Wis.

1731. Emma Jane, b. Feb. 15, 1846; m. May 27, 1866, Robt. Harrison Marsh.

1732. Mary Ann, b. March 23, 1847; m. July 3, 1864, Charles B. Roe.

1733. L. Joanna, b. Aug. 1, 1849; m. Dec. 29, 1867, Joseph H. Robinson.

1734. Elon Joseph, b. Oct. 6, 1852; m. Jan. 19, 1879, Isabella S. La Plant.

1735. Ella Ette, b. March 16, 1856; d. May 27, 1875; m. Sept. 15, 1874, Elihu Robinson.

1736. Fred. Elisha, b. Jan. 25, 1860.

A 972

Rev. Joseph Wiram Reed, son of Joseph and Wealthy (Williams) Reed.

b. Oct. 21, 1824, in Orleans county, N. Y.

m. 1st. Dec. 27, 1844, Rachel Ann Wells; b. Sept. 15, 1827, in Cattaraugus county, N. Y.; d. Jan. 6, 1865.

m. 2nd. April 9, 1865, Martha Jane Howard; b. Jan. 8, 1846, in Boone county, Ind. Married in Geauga county, Ohio.

CHILDREN OF JOSEPH AND RACHEL

1737. Alanson David, b. June 22, 1848, in Geauga Co., Ohio; d. Sept. 2, 1850.

1738. Mary Alvira, b. Aug. 21, 1851, in Dane Co., Wis.; m. April 10, 1870, Horace Greeley Hurd.

1739. Ellen, b. Dec. 2, 1859, in Rock Co., Wis.; m. Sept. 12, 1878, J. L. Malosh.

CHILD OF JOSEPH AND MARTHA

1740. Joseph Frank, b. Feb. 9, 1866, in Richmond Co., Wis.; m. Jan. 28, 1893, Sarepta E. Bundy.

A 976

Rev. Daniel Reed, son of Joseph and Wealthy (Williams) Reed.

b. Aug. 18, 1833, in Geauga county, Ohio.

m. Sept. 22, 1873, Huldah E. Dann; d. Aug. 2, 1848, in Golchester, N. J. Married in Le Sueur county, Minn.

CHILDREN

1741. Joseph E., b. Aug. 18, 1874, in Le Sueur Co., Minn.; m. Oct. 23, 1895, Augusta Marzinske.
1742. Eva Lula, b. July 9, 1876, in Twin Lakes, Minn.; d. Dec. 27, 1879.
1743. Ray Alanson, b. June 12, 1878, in Mapleton, Minn.; d. Jan. 8, 1880.
1744. Merta Luella, b. Jan. 26, 1881, in Mapleton, Minn.
1745. Nellei Louisa, b. May 23, 1882, in Mapleton, Minn.
1746. Mabel Edith, b. June 17, 1884, in Mapleton, Minn.

A 977

Elisha Rice Reed, son of Joseph and Wealthy (Williams) Reed.

b. Dec. 5, 1835, in Geauga county, Ohio.

m. Feb. 13, 1866, Isabelle Owen Brown; b. June 11, 1840, in Washington, D. C. Married in Washington, D. C.

He furnished the compiler of this work the data for tracing of the whole of the descendants of his ancestor Samuel Reed (205), son of Ezekiel and Hannah (Beal) Reed, of whom I had no record, and I desire here to make acknowledgment of his valuable assistance in the work. He furnishes the following brief sketch of his own career: "All men are proud of their military record, so am I. This is my only apology for the following and some other sketches that I have introduced. I enlisted in April, 1861; helped organize Co. 'H' 2nd Wis. Infantry. Was wounded and taken prisoner at first Bull Run battle. In prison ten and a half months in Libby Prison, and at Tuscaloosa, Ala., and Salisbury, N. C. In parole camp two months at St. Louis, Mo. Exchanged and returned to the front, was again wounded and taken prisoner at first day at Gettysburg, Pa., was so severely wounded that I could not be shipped South, and was paroled and left behind. On account of my wounds, was transferred to the Veteran Reserve Corps or 'Invalid Corps,' where I finished my three years and was discharged June 11, 1864. I went to Missouri and joined in the chase after Gen'l Ster-

ling Price, and was at the killing of the celebrated guerilla and bushwhacker 'Bill Anderson.'

"In 1866 I returned to Washington, D. C., and married Miss Belle Brown, daughter of Edmund F. Brown, U. S. Commissioner, &c. Father Brown wrote, but never published a genealogy on both his father's and mother's side dating back to 1625. I wish to state here, that his example in that effort is my inspiration to the enterprise of collecting the genealogy of my own family. A few will appreciate my labors, but many, many more will deem it time and labor wasted."

CHILDREN

1747. Edmund Hunt, b. April 26, 1867, in Doniphan Co., Kansas; d. Dec. 23, 1868.
1748. Frank De White, b. July 15, 1869, in Washington, D. C.; m. June 28, 1894, Sarah Storm.
1749. Marcia Wealthy, b. Dec. 22, 1870, in Madison, Wis.; m. March 21, 1895, Fred. M. Coulee.
1750. Lucius Fairchild, b. June 29, 1872, in Madison, Wis.
1751. Cora Main, b. Aug. 17, 1878, in Madison, Wis.; d. March 3, 1885.

A 992

Charles Edson Reed, son of David and Mary Martha (Morse) Reed.

b. Jan. 3, 1813; d. Aug. 19, ———.
m. 1st. Matilda Billings.
m. 2nd. Emma ———.

Lived in Boston. Business, caterer.

CHILDREN

1752. Cora, b. ———.
1753. Effie, b. ———; m. Joseph Weeth; lives in Omaha, Neb.
1754. Josie, b. ———.
1755. Charles, b. ———.
1756. Harry, b. ———.
1757. Blanche Imogene, b. ———; m. Jan. 1, 1898, J. Wardworth Carpenter; lives in Brooklyn, N. Y.
1758. Erwin, b. ———.

A 994

William Nelson Reed, son of David and Mary Martha (Morse) Reed.

b. Sept. 7, 1817, in Newfane, Vt.; d. Dec. 13, 1855, in Stoughton, Mass.

m. Sept. 4, 1839, Lucy Maria Stevens of Watertown, Mass., who was born May 7, 1816.

He was a baker and caterer, was a member of lodge 72, I. O. O. F. Their children were all born in Roxbury, Mass., except the two youngest, who were born in Boston, Mass.

CHILDREN

1759. Henrietta Maria, b. Dec. 30, 1841; m. in 1865, Horatio G. Littlefield, in Hamilton, O.; they lived later in Roxbury, on Parker Hill, and now at Wilmington, Mass.
1760. Melissa Almira, b. Sept. 24, 1843; d. Aug. 10, 1845, in Bedford, Mass.
1761. Adeline Louisa, b. July 13, 1845; m. Oct. 3, 1872, William Henry Kenyon, of Roxbury, Mass.
1762. Adelaide Lucy, b. July 13, 1845; d. March 31, 1847, at Roxbury, Mass.
1763. William Nelson, Jr., b. Jan. 31, 1848; m. April 27, 1871, Charlotte Louisa Daniels.
1764. Albert Henry, b. Jan. 9, 1851; d. May 12, 1875, in Roxbury, Mass.
1765. George Augustus, b. Sept. 10, 1853; d. Oct. 9, 1872, in Roxbury, Mass.

Geo. Augustus was a printer on Commercial Bulletin, and Daily Times, and a member of the Universalist Church in Roxbury, Mass.

A 996

Lucius Elliot Reed, son of David and Mary Martha (Morse) Reed.

b. April 20, 1825.

m. ——, Helen Graves.

Lived in Boston, Mass.

CHILDREN

1766. Helen M., b. ——; living in Burnham, Me. (1899).
1767. Howard, b. ——; living in Burnham, Me. (1899).

A 999

David Keyes Reed, son of David and Lucy (Keyes) Reed.

b. Sept. 7, 1833, in Dummerston, Vt.

m. 1st. June 25, 1851, Fausta McElroy of Roxbury, Mass., who died July 4, 1855.

m. 2nd. June 2, 1858, Caroline A. Fernald of Boston, Mass.

He came to Roxbury, Mass., with his mother and sisters when a boy of nine years of age. Attended old Washington school and other Boston schools.

He has been in business in Roxbury and Boston continuously since 1855, and is still in business (1899) under the firm name of D. K. Reed & Son. Both he and his son are members of the Boston Chamber of Commerce. David Keyes resided in Roxbury until 1898, and was an active member of the First Methodist Church of Roxbury, afterward the Winthrop St. Methodist Church, and was one of the original members of Warren St. M. E. Church with which he was prominently identified. He now resides at West Newton, Mass.

CHILD OF DAVID KEYES AND FAUSTA

1768. Henry Elliot, b. May 13, 1854; d. Oct. 1, 1854.

CHILDREN OF DAVID KEYES AND CAROLINE

1769. Laura Raymond, b. April 15, 1859; m. in Roxbury, Oct., 1891, J. Henry Dikeman. They live in New York City and have one child, Kenneth.

1770. George Fernald, b. Sept. 20, 1862; d. in Roxbury; m. Sept. 22, 1891, Rebecca Frances Hovey.

1771. Grace Adelaide, b. July 14, 1874, in Roxbury, Mass.

A 1000

Charles Franklin Reed, son of Calvin and Mary (Reynolds) Reed.

b. April 11, 1831; d. January 19, 1893.

m. Feb. 15, 1852, Sarah James.

Resided at Mandarin, Fla.

He was appointed postmaster soon after his marriage.

Kept a store and built the steamboat wharf which was burned during the war. He was an active member of the M. E. Church and a prominent man in the town.

CHILDREN

1772. Calvin James, b. Dec. 28, 1852; d. Feb. 15, 1853.
1773. Mary Almira, b. Jan. 18, 1854; m. Oct. 10, 1884, L. H. Tallman.
1774. Sadie S., b. Nov. 1, 1855.
1775. Alice Jane, b. Nov. 4, 1857; m. May 31, 1895, William Reet.
1776. Charles Calvin, b. March 15, 1860.
1777. Horace Luther, b. April 24, 1862; m. April 3, 1892, Annie L. Hamilton, of W. Va.
1778. Rosa Bell, b. Aug. 10, 1864; d. Sept. 26, 1867.
1779. Catherine Frances, b. July 7, 1867; m. June 4, 1892, H. D. De Grove.
1780. Ella May, b. June 9, 1870; d. Sept. 20, 1870.
1781. Arthur Herman, b. Sept. 3, 1874.
1782. Roxbury Maude, b. July 13, 1878.

A 1013

Noah Reed, son of Noah and Lucy (Hayward) Reed.
b. March 25, 1804.
m. Feb. 21, 1830, Mary Shaw.

Of Easton.

CHILDREN

1783. Lucy Catherine, b. Sept. 23, 1831.
1784. Catherine Frances, b. June 13, 1834.
1785. James Austin, b. ———.
1786. John Gurney, b. Oct. 6, 1841.

A 1017

Rotheus Reed, son of Noah and Lucy (Hayward) Reed.
b. July 26, 1811.
m. 1st. ———, Miss Howard.
m. 2nd. ———, Miss Lewis.

CHILD OF ROTHEUS AND FIRST WIFE

1787. Albert, b. ———.

CHILD OF ROTHEUS AND SECOND WIFE

1788. Elizabeth Lewis, b. ———.

A 1021

William Gurney Reed, son of William and Betsy (Drake) Reed.

b. Sept. 25, 1812, in Plymouth, Mass.

m. 1st. Sept. 17, 1834, Sophia Witherell; b. at Chesterfield; d. Oct. 31, 1855; daughter of Elisha Witherell.

m. 2nd. Feb. 24, 1859, Susan Coolridge Hyde, daughter of Enoch Hyde of Charlestown.

m. 3rd. Feb. 21, 1871, Elizabeth (Bradlee) Pray, widow of John H. Pray, daughter of Charles Bradlee of Boston.

He had a good English education, and was a Unitarian and lived in Massachusetts.

Of Easton, Mass.

CHILDREN OF WILLIAM AND SOPHIA

1789. Helen Sophia, b. June 7, 1835; d. Sept. 9, 1883; m. Nov. 17, 1853, Francis Copeland, of Bridgewater.

1790. William Elisha, b. June 17, 1837; d. Oct. 31, 1863; m. Annie Hyde, of Chestertown, Mass.

1791. Calvin Howe, b. March 25, 1842; d. Oct. 31, 1863.

1792. David Gurney, b. Jan. 29, 1844; d. Feb. 18, 1844.

1793. Horace Drake, b. July 20, 1847; d. Sept. 18, 1849.

1794. Maria Louisa, b. Feb. 19, 1849; m. Jan. 1, 1868, Lucius Howard, of S. Easton, Mass.

A 1023

Charles Henry Reed, son of William and Betsy (Drake) Reed.

b. Feb. 5, 1818, at Milton, Suffolk county, Mass.

m. Nov. 26, 1840, Mary Brightman Davis; b. May 8, 1815, at Westport; daughter of Joseph and Judith Brightman) Davis, all of Westport, Mass.

They had a common school education, were Unitarians, lived in Boston from 1838 to 1855, in Easton since 1855; occupation, house carpenter in younger days. In fire insurance business the last twenty-five years. Held a position as justice of the peace the past twenty-two years.

Of Easton.

CHILDREN

1795. Charles Davis, b. May 6, 1842; m. Aug. 19, 1867, Mary Clark.
1796. Henry Lyman, b. Dec. 3, 1843; d. Dec. 26, 1878; m. April 28, 1868, Ellen Farley Stearns.
1797. George William, b. Sept. 12, 1852; m. May 25, 1881, Fannie C. Wilbur.

A 1024

William Howell Reed, son of David and Mary Ann (Williams) Reed.

b. March 16, 1837, at Boston, Mass.

m. 1st. Feb. 13, 1873, Helen Messinger; b. in Boston, Feb. 10, 1837; d. May 16, 1876; daughter of Daniel and Mary Ann Messinger.

m. 2nd. Jan. 12, 1887, Grace Evelyn Atkins; b. March 1, 1851, in Boston; daughter of Elisha and Mary Elizabeth (Freeman) Atkins.

They were Unitarians. He was a Republican. Occupation: merchant and manufacturer; lived at Boston; connected with the sanitary commission during the war. Author of "Hospital Life in the Army of the Potomac."

Of Boston, Mass.

CHILD

1798. William Howell, b. April 30, 1876.

A 1038

William Edward Reed, son of Seth and Lucy (Holden) Reed.

b. Nov. 16, 1829, in Boston, Mass.

m. Dec. 8, 1853, Sarah Elizabeth Thomas.

Lived at Damascus, Montgomery county, Md.

Of Damascus, Montgomery county, Md.

CHILDREN

1799. Mary Emma, b. Nov. 7, 1855; d. unmarried.
1800. Lucy Holden, b. May 13, 1858; m. Oct. 15, 1885, Rev. Wm. A. Carroll.
1801. Elizabeth, b. Oct. 4, 1860; d. unmarried.
1802. John, b. Jan. 31, 1863; d. unmarried.
1803. Seth, b. July 12, 1876, d. Dec. 28, 1880.

A 1039

Samuel Payson Reed, son of Seth and Lucy (Holden) Reed.
b. (in Baltimore) March 24, 1833; d. July 13 or 18, 1864.
m. Aug. 23, 1855, Rachel Ann Brown.

Lived in Howard county, Md.

He died in the Finley Hospital, Washington. He was a soldier in the War of the Rebellion.

Of Howard county, Md.

CHILDREN

1804. Samuel Payson, b. May 20, 1856; m. Matilda Lydard.
1805. Olive Ann, b. May 7, 1857; m. June 1, 1881, William Edward Worthen.
1806. Charlotte Holden, b. April 9, 1859; m. Oct. 19, 1882, Jason Phillip Worthen.
1807. Fidelia Elizabeth, b. Aug. 1, 1862, in Long Corner, Howard Co., Md.; m. July 15, 1886, Darius F. Watkins.

A 1040

James Holden Lander Reed, son of Seth and Lucy (Holden) Reed.
b. July 6, 1835; d. Aug. 17, 1877, in Memphis, Tenn.
m. Jan. 27, 1869, Lulu J. Deupree of Bolivar, Miss.; b. July 14, 1850; d. Jan. 17, 1875, at Columbus, Miss.

Of Memphis, Tenn.

CHILD

1808. John Wallace, b. May 30, 1870.

A 1042

Seth Gurney Reed, son of Seth and Lucy (Holden) Reed.
b. July 20, 1840; d. June 26, 1880, in Baltimore.
m. ———, Sallie McCurley.

Of Baltimore county, Md.

CHILD

1809. Laura Graham, b. June 16, 1866.

A 1046

Jedidiah Harris Reed, son of Lyman and Marcia (Harris) Reed.

b. Aug. 2, 1833, in Baltimore, Md.; d. June 10, 1899, in Woodburn, Mass.

m. Feb. 20, 1861, Mary Sophronia Corner; b. April 20, 1839, in Baltimore, Md.; daughter of Solomon Corner; (d. Oct., 1886), and Sarah A. A. (Roszel) Corner (d. Aug., 1887).

J. H. Reed was educated at Roxbury Latin School, graduated from Dartmouth College, 1854. President of class and chief marshal at commencement. They lived in Baltimore until 1863, in New York until 1872, in Boston and vicinity since. His occupation was mercantile in Baltimore, insurance in New York. For six years secretary of Mt. Auburn Cemetery, Boston. Now secretary of manufacturing company, Boston, 1887. They were Unitarians and he was a democrat. Chairman of Democratic City Committee of Newton, Mass., 1855-6. He belonged to Alpha Delta Phi Society.

Of Boston.

CHILDREN

1810. Harris Corner, b. Nov. 22, 1861, at Baltimore; d. March 13, 1865, at New York.

1811. Charles Arthur, b. April 16, 1867, at New York; d. July 16, 1868, at New York.

1812. Willard, b. June 26, 1870, at Mt. Vernon, West Chester Co., N. Y.

Willard graduated at Newton (Mass.) High School in 1886; entered Harvard College in 1887, class of 1891; his great-grandfather graduated at Harvard College in 1782.

A 1052

Marcus Reed, son of Marcus and Mehetable (Jenkins) Reed.

b. Nov. 29, 1823, in Abington, Mass.; d. April 22, 1881, in Cleveland, Ohio; was buried in Abington, Mass.

m. July 9, 1847, Janet Logan Sproul, who was born in Paisley, Scotland, Feb. 23, 1827, daughter of Matthew and Janet Logan Sproul.

After the death of her husband she married Nathaniel Church of North Marshfield, Mass.

Marcus Reed removed in 1867, from Abington, Mass., to Cleveland, Ohio, and engaged in the manufacture of boots and shoes and slippers under the firm of Reed, Davis & Co. On his death in 1881, his remains were taken to Abington for interment in the family burying ground. He was a thoroughly honest man, and highly respected and beloved by all who knew him.

CHILDREN

1813. Jeannette Augusta, b. Oct. 22, 1849, in Abington; m. in Cleveland, Sept. 25, 1878, William Dean Taylor.

1814. Susan Mehetable, b. July 20, 1851, in Cleveland, O.; m. in Cleveland, Sept. 10, 1874, Valentine G. Swain.

1815. Marcus Webster, b. Oct. 6, 1856; d. unmarried; lived in Cincinnati, O.

1816. Amelia Frances, b. Oct. 2, 1858; d. young.

A 1053

Timothy Reed, son of Marcus and Mehetable (Jenkins) Reed.
b. Sept. 25, 1826; d. in Abington, July 11, 1890.
m. April 21, 1847, Lydia Ann Bourne, daughter of Francis W. and Jane Thompson Bourne.
Of South Abington, Mass.

Enlisted as a private and was made corporal and rose to the rank of captain in the 38th Mass. Volunteers. After the close of the war he was elected one of the selectmen of Abington and held other offices of trust.

He was highly esteemed in the community for his many virtues. He had seven children, only two of whom were living at the time of his decease.

CHILDREN

1817. Mary Ella, b. April 18, 1849; d. March 31, 1851.

1818. Eliza Ann, b. Sept. 22, 1853; m. Dec. 10, 1873, Walter E. Tribou, son of Chas. and Elizabeth Tribou.

1819. Hattie Frances, b. Dec. 8, 1857; m. Nov. 23, 1875, Charles D. Dyer.

A 1054

James Reed, son of Marcus and Mehetable (Jenkins) Reed.
b. Feb. 26, 1831; d. Sept. 3, 1879.

m. Sept. 7, 1851, Peddy W. Howland, daughter of Lewis and Pamelia T. Howland; she was born Jan. 18, 1833, and died Aug. 28, 1889.

Lived at Hanson.

Of Hanson, Mass.

CHILDREN

1820. James Lewis, b. (in Hanson) Jan. 10, 1853; m. Minnie (no children.)

1821. Alice Maria, b. Sept. 23, 1854; m. Norris Halcomb.

A 1056

Samuel W. Reed, son of Cyrus and Mary (Noyes) Reed.
b. Dec. 15, 1837; d. March 29, 1899, at Whitman.
m. ———, Ada Norton.

A soldier in 20th Unattached Company Aug. 11, 1864, to Nov., 1864, Mass. Vol. (See His. of Abington, p. 312.)

Of Abington, Mass.

CHILDREN

1822. Charles H., b. ———.

1823. Ada, b. ———.

A 1063

William T. Reed, son of Elijah and Jane (Thomas) Reed.
b. March 31, 1814.
m. Sept. 24, 1851, Ann M. Watson.

Of Middleborough, Mass.

CHILDREN

1824. Alexander H., b. ———.

1825. Ellen J., b. ———.

A 1065

Henry W. Reed, son of Elijah and Jane (Thomas) Reed.
b. Nov. 15, 1818.
m. Oct. 30, 1842, Emily Howard.

Of Middleborough, Mass.

CHILDREN

1826. Isabelle, b. ———.

1827. Jane, b. ———.

1828. Helen, b. ———.

1829. M. Shirley, b. ———.

A 1066

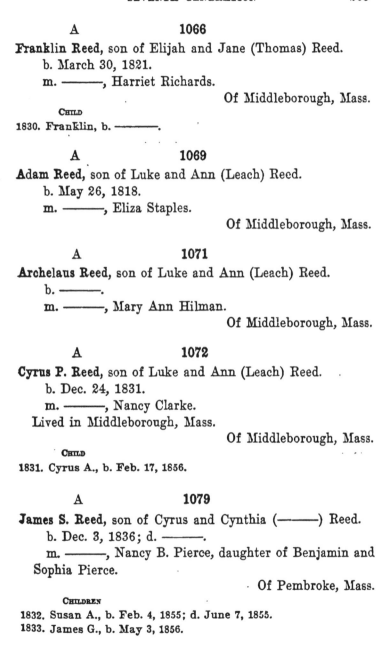

Franklin Reed, son of Elijah and Jane (Thomas) Reed.
b. March 30, 1821.
m. ———, Harriet Richards.
Of Middleborough, Mass.

CHILD

1830. Franklin, b. ———.

A 1069

Adam Reed, son of Luke and Ann (Leach) Reed.
b. May 26, 1818.
m. ———, Eliza Staples.
Of Middleborough, Mass.

A 1071

Archelaus Reed, son of Luke and Ann (Leach) Reed.
b. ———.
m. ———, Mary Ann Hilman.
Of Middleborough, Mass.

A 1072

Cyrus P. Reed, son of Luke and Ann (Leach) Reed.
b. Dec. 24, 1831.
m. ———, Nancy Clarke.
Lived in Middleborough, Mass.
Of Middleborough, Mass.

CHILD

1831. Cyrus A., b. Feb. 17, 1856.

A 1079

James S. Reed, son of Cyrus and Cynthia (———) Reed.
b. Dec. 3, 1836; d. ———.
m. ———, Nancy B. Pierce, daughter of Benjamin and Sophia Pierce.
Of Pembroke, Mass.

CHILDREN

1832. Susan A., b. Feb. 4, 1855; d. June 7, 1855.
1833. James G., b. May 3, 1856.

W 1084

Daniel Reed, son of Daniel and Annie (Blanchard) Reed.
b. Nov. 18, 1784; d. Dec. 30, 1886, at East Madison, Me., aged 102 years and 12 days.
m. 1st. Jan. —, 1808, Hannah Gurney; b. Sept. 18, 1784; d. April 3, 1837; daughter of John, son of Nathan, son of John Gurney who removed from Weymouth to Abington, Mass.
m. 2nd. ———, Sally Snow; d. Dec. 11, 1870. (See His. of Abington.)

He was a farmer, and lived in Abington for 32 years, he also lived in East Madison, Me. Communicant of Congregational Church, Republican. He had a very noble character, strong will, and unswerving fidelity to principles of right. His life is worthy of note not only that he attained the great age of 102 years; but to mention his life labors, the vigor and rectitude of all his acts, could they be written, could be worthily placed among the memories of the world's best men. His children and grandchildren inherit his strong will, and unswerving fidelity to principles of right, and abhorrence of vice and wrong doing in any form.

Of East Madison, Me.

Children of Daniel and Hannah

1834. Mary Gurney, b. Dec. 28, 1808; d. Feb. 16, 1869; unmarried.
1835. Martha, b. July 4, 1810; m. March 20, 1832, Theron Blanchard.
1836. Daniel Edward, b. Feb. 9, 1813; m. Dec. 28, 1843, Sophia L. Whittier.
1837. John Gurney, b. July 11, 1817; m. Jan. 16, 1851, Hannah French.
1838. Turner, b. Sept. 19, 1825; m. Anna C. Flower.

W 1085

Deane Reed, son of Daniel and Annie (Blanchard) Reed.
b. May 28, 1787; d. Oct. 28, 1863.
m. July 28, 1812, in Abington, Eliza Norton; b. April 11, 1790; d. March 14, 1864; 12 children.

Moved to Maine. Resided in Skowhegan, Me. Occupation, carpenter and farmer; was a church attendant.

Of Skowhegan, Me.

CHILDREN

1839. Deane Elbridge, b. Sept. 14, 1813; lives in Madison, Me.; m. 1st. Oct. 25, 1841, Electa Burns; m. 2d. Oct. 24, 1848, Hannah Spaulding.

1840. Samuel Norton, b. Oct. 1, 1817; d. Nov. 1, 1845; m. pub. Aug. 13, 1833, Jerusha Bailey.

1841. Sheldon, b. Nov. 17, 1820; lives in Aroostook region; m. 1st. June, 1849, Betsy D. Reed; m. 2d. Jan. 1, 1867, Martha R. Blanchard, of Madison, Me.

1842. Webster, b. June 10, 1822; lives in Aroostook region; m. 1st. in 1844, Sophia Cook; m. 2d. Sept. 13, 1855, Electa S. Howes; m. 3d. Nov., 1866, Louisa L. Reed; m. 4th. July 3, 1874, Annie E. Pratt.

1843. Elizabeth Norton, b. Feb. 26, 1824; m. July 20, 1850, Samuel S. Fuller, of Bridgeton, Me.

W 1086

David Reed, son of Daniel and Annie (Blanchard) Reed.
b. March 27, 1790; d. Sept. 19, 1869.
m. 1st. ———, Elizabeth T. Brown; d. March 6, 1839.
m. 2nd. Nov., 1840, Delia Smith.

He lived in Madison, Me., and was a farmer and hunter, church member, Republican.

Of Madison, Me.

CHILDREN OF DAVID AND ELIZABETH

1844. Woodbridge Brown, b. Nov. 19, 1810; m. Jan. 19, 1842, Orinda Neal.

1845. Charlotte, b. Sept. 7, 1812; d. April 4, 1877; m. John R. Morrison.

1846. Anson, b. Sept. 25, 1815; d. May 17, 1835.

1847. Nancy E., b. Dec. 6, 1816; m. W. Quincy Blanchard, of E. Madison, Me.

1848. Edson, b. Jan. 16, 1822; d. Sept. 2, 1863.

1849. Maria, b. Sept. 25, 1829; d. July 9, 1859; m. March 17, 1853, Joseph Wyman.

1850. Betsy T., b. Jan. 16, 1831; m. Oct. 31, 1860, Joseph Wyman.

CHILDREN OF DAVID AND DELIA

1851. Joseph N., b. Dec. 4, 1841; d. Oct. 5, 1853.
1852. Mary F., b. April 15, 1844; m. Oct. 24, 1868, Robert Goodman Bennett.
1853. Clara A., b. May 25, 1847; d. June 4, 1851.
1854. Abby M., b. May 25, 1847; d. June 19, 1868.
1855. Charles W., b. May 26, 1849; m. Dec. 25, 1871, Abbie A. Plummer.
1856. Anson, b. Aug. 20, 1853; m. Oct. 20, 1875, Augusta H. Plummer.

W 1087

Jesse Reed, son of Daniel and Annie (Blanchard) Reed.
b. June 20, 1793, at Abington, Mass.
m. Feb. 14, 1818, Lucy Johnston Reed; b. May 29, 1800; daughter of Jesse and Sarah (Pulling) Reed.

He was a farmer and resided in Abington and received a common school education, their church relations were with the Orthodox Congregational Church.

Of Abington, Mass.

CHILDREN

1857. Jesse, b. June 27, 1819; m. Oct. 23, 1842, Eliza Emeline Curtiss.
1858. Sally Thaxter, b. Feb. 9, 1822; d. Dec. 13, 1883; m. Oct. 27, 1843, Seth C. Everson.
1859. Turner, b. April 8, 1826; m. 1st. Oct. 3, 1848, Sarah H. Curtiss; m. 2d. April 23, 1862, Sarah Moulton.
1860. Lucy Ann, b. Feb. 9, 1829; m. Oct. 3, 1848, Calvin P. Powers.
1861. Clifford, b. ———.

W 1089

Josiah Reed, son of Daniel and Annie (Blanchard) Reed.
b. July 28, 1798, in Abington; d. Aug. 8, 1879.
m. June, 1829 (in Abington), Abigail W. Bicknell; b. Sept. 29, 1807, in Abington; d. Aug. 7, 1847.

He was a farmer in East Madison, Me.; church member.

Of East Madison, Me.

CHILD

1862. Abby L., b. Aug. 6, 1832; m. Feb. 5, 1850, Albert Lowell.

W 1092

Gridly Reed, son of Daniel and Annie (Blanchard) Reed.

b. Sept. 6, 1804; d. March 21, 1875, aged 70 years and 6 months.

m. Nov. 22, 1830 (at Skowhegan, Me.), Clarissa Dyer; d. July 23, 1877, aged 73.

No children, lived in East Madison, Me., engaged in farming, Baptist, Republican.

Of East Madison, Me.

W 1094

Turner Reed, son of Daniel and Annie (Blanchard) Reed.

b. ———.

m. ———.

Lived in Abington, and had children.

Of Abington, Mass.

W 1096

Bela Reed, son of Jacob and Nancy (Porter) Reed.

b. Dec. 2, 1803.

m. Sept. 27, 1826, Joanna S. Lane, daughter of John and Elizabeth (Reed) Lane.

Of Abington, Mass.

CHILDREN

1863. Jacob, b. April 5, 1827; lived in Abington; unmarried; d. 1899.
1864. Nancy, b. Jan. 31, 1832; d. young.
1865. Elizabeth Richmond, b. Oct. 8, 1835; living in Abington; unmarried.

W 1097

Ezekiel Reed, son of Jacob and Nancy (Porter) Reed.

b. Oct. 14, 1810; d. Oct. 27, 1885.

m. pub. Dec. 13, 1831, Cephisa Studley, of Hanover.

Lived at Abington Centre on the tract of land settled by his ancestors in 1708.

Of Abington, Mass.

CHILDREN

1866. Emily Cephisa, b. April 29, 1832; d. Oct. 25, 1856.
1867. George Fearing, b. May 31, 1834; m. May 31, 1855, Maria A. Faxon.
1868. Mary Turner, b. July 29, 1838; d. Feb. 7, 1840.
1869. Mary Augusta, b. Jan. 6, 1843; d. June 13, 1852.
1870. Charles, b. July 19, 1847; m. Nov. 28, 1878, Ellen M. H. Foote.

W 1101

Owen Reed, son of John and Dorothy (Brown) Reed.
b. Dec. 5, 1797.
m. in 1817, Charlotte Harden.

Of Abington, Mass.

CHILD

1871. Nancy, b. July 11, 1822.

W 1106

Thomas Reed, son of Thomas and Joanna (Shaw) Reed.
b. Nov. 16, 1786.
m. ———, Lydia Jenkins, daughter of Isaiah and Huldah (Gurney) Jenkins; b. April 25, 1787.

Of Abington, Mass.

CHILDREN

1872. Thomas, b. April 25, 1812; d. Nov. 30, 1844; m. 1st. Nancy Hunt; m. 2d. Achsah Wesson, June 12, 1840.
1873. Lydia Jenkins, b. June 14, 1814; d. Feb. 13, 1844; m. Dec. 17, 1834, Lysander Cushing.
1874. Henry Watson, b. Dec. 29, 1819; d. Sept., 1843; m. Emily Howard.
1875. Lucinda C., b. Dec. 11, 1834.

W 1107

Goddard Reed, son of Thomas and Joanna (Shaw) Reed.
b. May 3, 1788; d. Aug. 29, 1865.
m. Nov. 13, 1814, Marcia Reed (b. Jan. 19, 1798), daughter of Samuel and Mary (Pool) Reed.

They resided near the meeting house in East Abington. Was a soldier in the war of 1812.

Of East Abington, Mass.

CHILDREN

1876. Hannah, b. Feb. 18, 1816; d. young.
1877. Diana, b. Feb. 27, 1817; d. Jan. 21, 1838; m. June 14, 1835, Isaac Keene.
1878. Washington, b. July 6, 1820; m. June 2, 1839, Harriet R. Corthell.
1879. Charles Goddard, b. Jan. 18, 1823; d. Sept. 22, 1823.
1880. Marcia, b. July 22, 1828; d. Sept. 4, 1848.

W 1108

Deacon Ebenezer Reed, son of Thomas and Joanna (Shaw) Reed.

b. July 6, 1790.

m. 1st. Nov. 30, 1815, Lucy Jenkins, daughter of Isaiah and Huldah (Gurney) Jenkins; b. June 27, 1795.

m. 2nd. ———, Patience Penniman.

Of Abington, Mass.

CHILDREN

1881. Cleora, b. Nov. 3, 1816; d. Aug., 1868; m. Oct. 9, 1836, Sylvester Dawes.
1882. Lorenzo, b. May 26, 1818; d. Jan. 28, 1845; m. in 1841, Sarah P. Brockway, who afterwards m. Henry Weiderwax, of N. Chatham, N. Y.
1883. Egbert, b. June 10, 1821; d. Sept. 26, 1827 (drowned in a pond at Abington).
1884. Lucy, b. July 2, 1827; d. Sept. 30, 1884.
1885. Cordelia, b. July 10, 1830; d. April 26, 1832.
1886. Ebenezer A., b. Dec. 28, 1832; d. Oct. 9, 1834.

W 1109

Simeon Gannet Reed, son of Thomas and Joanna (Shaw) Reed.

b. Sept. 29, 1793; d. Oct. 1, 1831.

m. June 3, 1829, Rachel Burgess (she was of Harvard).

Of Abington, Mass.

CHILD

1887. Simeon Gannet, b. April 23, 1830; m. Oct. 17, 1850, Amanda Wood, of Quincy.

W **1111**

Albert Reed, son of Thomas and Joanna (Shaw) Reed.

b. Oct. 8, 1800, at East Abington, Mass.; d. in 1881, at East Orange, N. J.

m. 1st. Maria Colburn, daughter of Rev. Samuel W. Colburn, who for several years was pastor of the Congregational Church in East Abington. Her mother's maiden name was Cogswell; she was born in Boscawen, N. H.; she died Nov. 25, 1854, in New York City.

m. 2nd. Nov. 24, 1864, Frances A. Plumer, of Penacook, N. H.; she was born Nov. 17, 1837, and was a cousin of his first wife.

He lived in East Abington and Boston until 1851, when he moved to New York City, where he lived until 1875, when he removed to East Orange, N. J., where he lived until his death in 1881.

Of East Orange, N. J.

CHILDREN

1888. Samuel Colburn, b. June 2, 1832; m. April 22, 1893, Marguerite Bulkley.

1889. Frances Maria, b. June 9, 1866; unmarried; lives in Colorado.

W **1112**

Amos Shaw Reed, son of Thomas and Joanna (Shaw) Reed.

b. May 22, 1804; d. Sept. 26, 1886.

m. 1st. Nov. 9, 1826, Huldah B. Loud; b. April 1, 1805; d. Aug. 1, 1833.

m. 2nd. Dec. 14, 1834, Rachel Burgess Reed; b. June 4, 1803; d. Feb. 10, 1884; widow of Simeon Gannett Reed.

Of Abington, Mass.

CHILDREN OF AMOS AND HULDAH

1890. Amos Newton, b. May 21, 1829; m. Sept. 10, 1851, Sarah Elizabeth Boynton.

1891. Sarah Ann, b. June 14, 1832; d. Sept. 21, 1849.

CHILDREN OF AMOS AND RACHEL

1892. Edward Payson, b. Sept. 21, 1836; d. ———; m. Sept. 16, 1864, Georgiana Spencer Loud.

1893. Elizabeth Waldo, b. Aug. 4, 1839; d. Sept. 5, 1843.

1894. Marinda, b. April 26, 1843; d. Aug. 1, 1846.

W 1115

Theodore Reed, son of Thomas and Joanna (Shaw) Reed.

b. April 7, 1810.

m. 1st. Dec. 26, 1830, Clarissa Jenkins, daughter of Lemuel and Clarissa (Lovell) Jenkins.

m. 2nd. Dec. 31, 1840, Abigail Jacobs Wilder, of Hull; daughter of Edward and Abigail (Sylvester) Wilder; she died Oct. 30, 1845.

m. 3rd. ———, Lydia Gurney (widow of Melvin Gurney).

Of East Abington, Mass.

CHILDREN OF THEODORE AND CLARISSA

1895. Theodore W., b. Oct. 19, 1833.
1896. Martha, b. June 19, 1839.

CHILDREN OF THEODORE AND ABIGAIL

1897. Abigail, b. Sept. 8, 1843.
1898. Mary Franklin, b. Oct. 13, 1845.
1899. Lydia Maria, b. Dec. 31, 1847; d. young.
1900. Lydia Maria, b. Dec. 21, 1848.
1901. Thomas Henry, b. July 24, 1852.

W 1118

Samuel Reed, son of Samuel and Mary (Pool) Reed.

b. Dec. 18, 1790; d. June 23, 1870.

m. 1st. April 21, 1810, Polly Corthell; d. June 10, 1832, aged 44 years, daughter of Sherebiah and Lydia Whiton Corthell.

m. 2nd. Sept. 5, 1833, Serissa Litchfield Bailey (widow of Rowland Bailey, of Scituate), died Oct. 18, 1865.

Of East Abington, Mass.

CHILDREN OF SAMUEL AND POLLY

1902. Samuel, b. May 26, 1811; m. Elizabeth Wilkes.
1903. Mary, b. Jan. 16, 1813; d. June 10, 1889; m. John Burrill; lived at E. Abington.
1904. Levi, b. Dec. 31, 1814; m. April 20, 1837, Louisa C. Drake.
1905. Dexter, b. Nov. 10, 1816; m. Catherine Stetson.
1906. Mehetable, b. Sept. 14, 1818; d. Jan. 9, 1819.
1907. Mehetable, b. March 31, 1822; d. April 26, 1899; m. George Lewis.

CHILDREN OF SAMUEL AND SERISSA

1908. Serissa, b. June 27, 1834; d. July 11, 1890.
1909. Rowland, b. Oct. 13, 1836; d. Feb. 6, 1838.
1910. Martha, b. Nov. 13, 1838.
1911. Sophia, b. Oct. 3, 1840; m. 1866, Edward Peabody.
1912. Anna, b. Nov. 13, 1844; d. July 2, 1888.

W 1119

Abiah Reed, son of Samuel and Mary (Pool) Reed.
b. Nov. 22, 1793.
m. May 23, 1814, Jane Gurney.
He was a soldier in the war of 1812.

Of East Abington, Mass.

CHILDREN

1913. Abiah, b. Sept. 11, 1815; d. Dec. 7, 1835.
1914. Jane Gurney, b. Sept. 8, 1817; m. Jan. 22, 1844, Luther Josselyn, of Hanson.
1915. Roxanna, b. Aug. 24, 1819; m. May 13, 1835, George Totman, who lives in Abington.
1916. Walter, b. July 24, 1821; m. 1st. Sophronia Josselyn; m. 2d. April 1, 1849, Cordone Keen.
1917. Rebecca Packard, b. Aug. 29, 1823; m. Sept. 14, 1851, Augustus N. Warren.
1918. Hannah Perkins, b. July 6, 1827; m. Jan. 22, 1855, Horace Ames, of N. Bridgewater.
1919. Clarissa, b. June 17, 1830; m. May 2, 1847, Augustus N. Warren.
1920. Lucinda Dyke, b. Sept. 21, 1832; d. Aug. 18, 1834.
1921. Elias, b. Sept. 12, 1834; d. Sept. 14, 1834.
1922. Diana, b. Jan. 12, 1839; m. April 29, 1858, Benjamin S. Pratt.

W 1122

Joseph Reed, son of Samuel and Mary (Pool) Reed.
b. Oct. 28, 1799.
m. 1st. ———, Jane Stoddard.
m. 2nd. ———, Elizabeth (Murch) Clough.

Of Rockland, Mass.

CHILD OF JOSEPH AND JANE

1923. Marcia Jane, b. June 15, 1826; d. Jan. 17, 1896; m. Nov. 22, 1845, Baldwin Bradford Burgess.

W 1131

Isaac Reed, son of Isaac and Sarah (Pulling) Reed.

b. Jan 22, 1806; d. ———, 1882.

m. 1st. Sept. 7, 1826, Rachel Reed, daughter of John and Thankful Reed.

m. 2nd. Dec. 17, 1829, Eliza F. Shaw of Middleborough, Mass.

Of South Abington, Mass.

CHILDREN OF ISAAC AND ELIZA

1924. Isaac Thaxter, b. March 15, 1834, in Roxbury; d. ———; m. Susannah Jones, of Whitman.
1925. Eliza Shaw, b. April 2, 1836, in Bridgewater, Mass.; d. ———; m. Lemuel Freeman.
1926. Sarah E., b. Sept. 15, 1838; d. unmarried.
1927. Ellen Maria, b. Dec. 2, 1840; d. young.
1928. Henry Wallace, b. Jan. 15, 1843; m. ———.
1929. Rachel J., b. March 13, 1845; m. Feb. 15, 1863, Nelson Corthell, of Wollaston.
1930. Hannah, b. Sept. 12, 1848; m. Alonzo Cook, of Whitman.
1931. Mary Francina, b. Oct. 17, 1850; m. Charles W. Rice, of E. Weymouth, Mass. They had a daughter, Jennie Wesley Rice, b. Dec. 11, 1870, who married, Oct. 17, 1894, Leavitt Winthrop Bates, and they had a son Reginald Winthrop Bates, b. July 22, 1897.

W 1135

Horace Reed, son of Isaac and Nancy (Lincoln) Reed.

b. Nov. 26, 1820.

m. Sept. 21, 1840, Lurana Howland Bates; b. May 23, 1819, at Richmond, Va.; daughter of Christopher and Mary (Howland) Bates.

They had a common school and academic education, were Orthodox Congregational, lived in South Abington (now Whitman). He was a clerk and general manager in a boot and shoe factory until 1885. Member of school committee for several years. In House of Representatives in 1862 and 1863, and in Senate in 1884 and 1885 (State of Mass.). Treasurer of Whitman Savings Bank since 1888.

Of South Abington, Mass.

CHILDREN

1932. Helen Augusta, b. Aug. 19, 1842; m. Sept. 10, 1867, Jacob P. Bates.
1933. Emma Lurana, b. Dec. 28, 1845; d. Dec. 16, 1879; m. July 16, 1868, Gustavus H. Burrows.
1934. Horace Richmond, b. Aug. 12, 1852; d. Dec. 4, 1881; m. Jan. 16, 1879, Susan Hersey.
1935. Arthur Elsworth, b. April 8, 1861; m. Oct. 6, 1887, Nellie F. M. Bunting.

W 1136

William Lincoln Reed, son of Isaac and Sarah (Pulling) Reed.

b. Oct. 5, 1825, at Abington.

m. 1st. June 6, 1847, Deborah Chessman; b. 1827, at Weymouth; d. 1884, at Whitman; daughter of I. A. Chessman and Deborah (Blanchard) Chessman.

m. 2nd. June, 1887, Mrs. Lyman Clark of Brockton, Mass.

They had a common school and academic education, were Orthodox Congregational, lived in Whitman (S. Abington), now in Brockton, Mass. Was engaged in boot and shoe business (see His. of Abington, p. 291), now retired. In Mass. House of Representatives for two years. In Mass. Senate for two years. In Governor's Council for three years.

Of Brockton, Mass.

CHILDREN

1936. An infant, b. March 22, 1848.
1937. William Bradford, b. Feb. 25, 1852; d. Jan. 4, 1858.
1938. Anna Gertrude, b. Aug. 24, 1855; m. Oct. 23, 1877, Geo. E. Keith.
1939. Sarah Chessman, b. July 30, 1857; m. Oct. 17, 1883, John T. Blades.
1940. Walter Lincoln, b. Nov. 5, 1859; m. Alice Rose.

W 1138

David A. Reed, son of David and Susan (Spear) Reed.

b. Dec. 6, 1795.

m. Aug. 6, 1818, Nancy Loud.

His son Geo. W. was a Capt. in Co. K, 7th Reg., Mass. Vol.

Of Weymouth, Mass.

CHILDREN

1941. Susan S., b. Nov. 9, 1818; m. April 19, 1839, John Osburne.
1942. Mary Ann, b. Oct. 16, 1820; m. Feb. 24, 1844, Samuel O. Breed, of Lynn.
1943. David Augustus, b. Jan. 12, 1831; m. Nov. 3, 1850, Betsy D. Keith.
1944. Daniel Franklin. b. May 10, 1834; d. ———; lived in New Bedford; m. Joanna Cushing.
1945. George W., b. March 22, 1838.
1946. Nancy Maria, b. April 22, 1842; d. Jan., 1849.

W 1140

Thomas S. Reed, son of David and Susan (Spear) Reed.

b. June 9, 1800.

m. Nov. 5, 1823, Cynthia Shaw; m. by Rev. Wm. Tyler.

Of Weymouth, Mass.

CHILDREN

1947. George, b. April 19, 1824; m. Maria H. Vinal.
1948. Josiah, b. April 18, 1826; lives in S. Weymouth; m. 1st. Sept. 3, 1845, Sarah C. Fogg; m. 2nd. Oct. 25, 1864, M. Jennie Ainsworth.
1949. Ellen, b. (at Weymouth) March 25, 1828; d. Oct. 11, 1841.
1950. Adeline, b. Oct. 23, 1830; d. Nov. 29, 1869; m. Sept. 13, 1849, Oliver Loud.
1951. Jane Ellen, b. Sept. 26, 1841.

W 1141

Asa Reed, Jr., son of Asa and Esther (Hobart) Reed.

b. in 1800; d. in 1828, buried in East Randolph, Mass.

m. June 29, 1823, Sally Curtis, daughter of Capt. Samuel Curtis of East Randolph, Mass. They were married by Rev. David Brigham. She died Feb. 7, 1890, aged 84 years and 3 months; buried in Highland Cemetery, South Weymouth.

He also followed the trade of a butcher, like his father, and sold meat from house to house.

CHILDREN

1952. Abi T., b. Sept. 18, 1823; d. April 12, 1894; m. Lorenzo T. Brown, of E. Bridgewater.
1953. Sarah, b. ———; m. Joseph E. Ford, of Abington, Mass.
1954. Johannah Wales, b. April 1, 1827; d. July 4, 1860; m. Washington L. Bates, son of John and Nancy (Ripley) Bates (b. March 31, 1824; d. April 18, 1894).

W 1144

Thomas Jefferson Reed, son of Asa and Esther (Hobart) Reed.

b. Jan. 6, 1806.

m. 1st. ———, Aseneth White.

m. 2nd. Aug. 3, 1834, Clarissa Belcher of North Bridgewater, Mass.

CHILDREN OF THOMAS AND ASENETH

1955. Asa, b. ———; died young.
1956. Thomas, b. ———; died young.

CHILDREN OF THOMAS AND CLARISSA

1957. Asa, b. June 3, 1835; m. Oct. 18, 1857, Elizabeth Bunker, of North Bridgewater, Mass.
1958. Thomas, b. 1837; m. Abby Fish.
1959. Ebenezer, b. Oct., 1840; d. 1856.
1960. Sabra, b. ———; d. young.
1961. Edwin, b. April 24, 1842; m. Alma Jennie Ford, of Hardwick, Vermont.
1962. George Minot, b. Nov. 24, 1849; m. June 16, 1874, Martha Belcher.

W 1150

Asa T. Reed, son of Isaac and Cynthia (Pratt) Reed.

b. Jan. 1, 1826; d. Feb. 23, 1873.

m. July 4, 1851, Catherine M. Johnson, daughter of Jotham and Sarah (Jackson) Johnson; m. by Rev. Joshua Emery. She was born July 5, 1828.

Of Weymouth, Mass.

CHILDREN

1963. Sarah Jackson, b. May 8, 1853; m. Charles H. Delano.
1964. Eliza Emily, b. Jan. 28, 1855; m. Ellis P. Gay.
1965. Frank, b. May 25, 1861; d. March 13, 1891.

W 1152

Isaac Reed, Jr., son of Isaac and Cynthia (Pratt) Reed.

b. Nov. 4, 1831; d. Dec. 25, 1884, at East Weymouth.

m. 1st. Sept. 24, 1854, Elizabeth Estella Lincoln; b. Dec. 11, 1837, at Hingham; daughter of Daniel and Priscilla (Cain) Lincoln; she died Oct. 24, 1869.

m. 2nd. Nov. 1, 1870, Mrs. Sarah Parker of Groveland, Mass., daughter of Nathaniel and Mehetable Parker. She was born Sept. 24, 1835; died at East Weymouth, May 28, 1881.

Of Weymouth, Mass.

CHILDREN OF ISAAC AND ELIZABETH

1966. Estella, b. Feb. 25, 1855; d. Feb. 27, 1855.
1967. Ann Cynthia, b. March 18, 1859; m. June 20, 1878, Charles Sumner Stowell.
1968. Elizabeth Lincoln, b. May 1, 1862; m. July 19, 1883, Harry Winthrop Flagg Young.

W 1153

Frederick Reed, son of Isaac and Cynthia (Pratt) Reed.

b. July 29, 1834, at East Weymouth.

m. Aug. 18, 1861, Abbie Lovell Dyer of Hingham, Mass.; b. Feb. 23, 1841; daughter of Solomon and Sally (Stodder) Dyer of Melrose Highlands, Mass.

CHILDREN

1969. Lillian Spaulding, b. Jan. 18, 1866, at E. Weymouth, Mass.; m. April 3, 1889, Fred. T. Kimball, of Melrose, Mass.
1970. Nellie Harlow, b. April 11, 1869, at E. Weymouth, Mass.; d. Oct. 2, 1893.
1971. Grace Estelle, b. Feb. 20, 1870, at E. Weymouth, Mass.; d. Oct. 4, 1893.
1972. Charles Frederick, b. Jan. 14, 1877.
1973. Ralph Omer, b. Feb. 26, 1884.

W 1154

Stephen S. Reed, son of Isaac and Cynthia (Pratt) Reed.

b. May 2, 1838.

m. Aug. 17, 1859, Ruth Merritt Curtis, daughter of Luther and Sarah Rose Curtis.

CHILDREN

1974. Lulazine Anna, b. Feb. 17, 1861; m. Dec. 9, 1884, George Murray; no children.
1975. John Adams Spaulding, b. March 1, 1862; d. Aug. 3, 1862.
1976. Luther Adams, b. Dec. 21, 1863; d. Sept. 5, 1864.

W 1156

William Reed, son of William and Relief (Penniman) Reed.
b. May 2, 1801; d. March, 1872.
m. Aug. 26, 1824, Susan French (d. March 18, 1885).
Of Braintree, Mass.

CHILDREN

1977. Susan, b. Oct. 11, 1825; m. John Stoddard.
1978. William, b. March 10, 1828; d. young.
1979. Clarissa, b. Sept. 11, 1829; m. Gardner S. Penniman.
1980. William, b. Oct. 30, 1832; m. Jan. 12, 1859, Maria Louisa Derby, of S. Weymouth.

W 1157

John Amory Reed, son of John and Lucy (Houghton) Reed.
b. Feb. 23, 1802, in Boston; d. April 8, 1834, in St. Thomas.
m. May 18, 1831 (in St. Thomas, West Indies), Ann Eliza Rogiers; b. Aug. 29, 1813, in St. Croix; d. March 24, 1888, in Hamburg.

He was buried on the Smith's Bay Estate, Island of St. Thomas at a place selected by himself. His widow removed to Hamburg, Germany.

Of St. Thomas, West Indies.

CHILDREN

1981. Caroline Rogiers, b. Sept. 24, 1832, in St. Thomas; d. June 22, 1874, in Copenhagen; m. May 29, 1851, in St. Thomas, Jenz. Cecil August Hingelberg.
1982. Amory Charlotte Eveline, b. May 30, 1834, in St. Thomas; m. Sept. 28, 1850 (in St. Thomas), Carl George Heise; b. Dec. 18, 1817; d. June 30, 1886, in Hamburg.

W 1168

William Block Reed, son of Elias and Sally (Block) Reed.
b. May 6, 1828; d. Sept. 15, 1889.

m. 1st. Nov. 25, 1855, Lucie Claiborne Franklin (b. May 13, 1834; d. Oct. 12, 1858); daughter of David B. and Frances J. (Lipscomb) Franklin.

m. 2nd. Feb. 21, 1861, Mary Ann Larus (she was born May 13, 1834), daughter of Pleasant V. and Sally (Yarbrough) Larus.

He was a clerk in Richmond, Va., postoffice for twelve years. Ever since engaged as a machinist. He was a Baptist, Mary A. Larus was a Presbyterian, Lucie Franklin was a Baptist.

Of Richmond, Va.

CHILD OF WILLIAM AND LUCIE

1983. Welford Claiborne, b. Sept. 3, 1856; m. Nov. 18, 1885, Hattie Relay McGee.

CHILDREN OF WILLIAM AND MARY

1984. Arthur, b. Jan. 6, 1862; d. June 17, 1862.

1985. Sallie Larus, b. Dec. 15, 1862; d. April 16, 1864.

1986. William Thomas, b. Sept. 23, 1864; m. Alice Lewis Burwell. In the tobacco business.

1987. Pleasant Larus, b. Sept. 24, 1866. In the tobacco business.

1988. John Hobart, b. Feb. 9, 1870. In coal business.

1989. Charles Clinton, b. Jan. 13, 1873; m. Dec. 15, 1898, Lyllian Marie Hancock.

1990. Stanley, b. Oct. 10, 1875.

1991. Leslie Hartwell, b. May 13, 1878.

W **1170**

John H. Reed, son of Elias and Sally (Block) Reed.

b. in Richmond, Va.

m. ———, Henrietta Gilliam, of Bristol, Eng. (died in Cardiff, Wales).

John completed his education in Bath. At the age of twenty-one was put in charge of a fine sailing ship the "Kate Swanton." Under the auspices of his uncle Levi Houghton, a wealthy ship owner, he traded with most of the ports of Europe and the East Indies.

Of Richmond, Va.

CHILDREN

1992. Flora Europa, b. ———; m. Charles Knight, of England.

1993. Jennie, b. ———; m. James Langston, of England.

W 1172

Charles Warren Reed, son of Elihu and Sabra (Houghton) Reed.

b. in 1809; d. June 30, 1874, at Medford, Mass.

m. 1st. ———, 1838, Elizabeth Mary Ann Hersey, who was born Sept. 8, 1808; d. Sept. 24, 1843; daughter of Laban and Celia (Barnes) Hersey of Hingham.

m. 2nd. Oct. 20, 1853, Martha Ann Bullard.

m. 3rd. Dec. 24, 1868, Rachel Bearce Hinckley, of Truro, Mass.

Lived in Boston throughout his whole life; graduating from the English High School in class of 1822. He entered the china trade, making a number of voyages to Canton as supercargo of different vessels, notably the "Henry Tuke" and "Bombay." On one of the voyages an incident occurred that showed the quality of the young man. The vessel was returning from Canton with a valuable cargo on board when the crew of the vessel mutinied, murdering the captain and mates, but were overawed by the unflinching bravery and spirited action of young Reed, who took command of the vessel, bringing her with the valuable cargo safely into the port of Boston, and he was handsomely rewarded by the owners. During his life he occupied many positions of trust and responsibility; among others he was treasurer of the Massachusetts Nautical School, and Wharfinger of Commercial wharf for many years.

CHILD OF CHARLES AND ELIZABETH

1994. **Robert Hersey**, b. Feb. 15, 1839; m. 1st. March 1, 1861, Martha Augusta Fosgate, of Boston; m. 2d. June 21, 1882, Catherine Louisa Goodrich, of New York.

W 1174

Francis Ludovicus Reed, son of Elihu and Sabra (Houghton) Reed.

b. March, 1818; d. Feb., 1867.

Unmarried.

JAMES H. REED.

He was a merchant in the firm of Ross, Campbell & Co., of Baltimore.

Of Baltimore, Md.

W 1175

William Reed, son of Elihu and Sabra (Houghton) Reed.
b. Dec. 26, 1820; d. Aug. —, 1875.
m. ———, Sarah Sawyer.

Of Bolton.

W 1176

James Henry Reed, son of Elihu and Sabra (Houghton) Reed.
b. April 23, 1823, at Boston; d. Oct. 30, 1896, at Boston.
m. Jan. 13, 1859, Martha Ann Wesson (b. Feb. 8, 1837, at Charlestown); daughter of Charles Wesson and Mary S. Brown; she died Feb. 13, 1896.

He was engaged in the ice business in Boston. He and his family were Unitarians.

Mr. Reed was the owner of the old Reed farm in Bolton, which had been owned in the family for 150 years. The last deed dated back to 1805. It embraced 207 acres, equally divided into mowing, tillage, pasture and timber land, and is most eligibly located, being directly opposite the historic Wilder mansion. The property is the highest point of land between Boston and Mt. Wachusett; quality of soil the finest, with an abundance of fruit trees; purest of running spring water and the surroundings delightful. For a home it is unsurpassed. It was sold by his executors in Oct., 1897, to close the estate.

Of Boston, Mass.

CHILDREN

1995. John Wesson, b. Nov. 4, 1859; d. Sept. 16, 1870.
1996. Frank Elihu, b. Nov. 13, 1860; d. Nov. 15, 1861.
1997. Martha Houghton, b. Oct. 20, 1862; m. Charles Anthony Morss, Jr.
1998. Katherine Sabra, b. April 22, 1868; m. Jan. 13, 1890, John R. Bradlee.
1999. James Henry, b. Dec. 15, 1872; m. June 30, 1897, Mary Wade Page.

W 1179

John Clark Reed, son of Silas and Betsy (Whitcomb) Reed.

b. June 23, 1818, at Alexandria, Va., lives in Holden. Mo.

m. Sept. 30, 1841, Caroline Kinsey of Alexandria, Va., daughter of Zenas and Mary (Doxey) Kinsey.

Removed from Alexandria, Va., went west and settled at Holden, Mo.

Of Holden, Mo.

CHILDREN

2000. Mary Holman, b. April 11, 1843; d. Oct. 6, 1880; m. March 5, 1872, Harlan Feagan.
2001. Katie Ellery, b. Aug. 8, 1855; d. ———; m. Aug. 31, 1876, George W. McCabe, of Ohio.
2002. Charles Edwin, b. Feb. 7, 1845; d. Feb. 28, 1845.
2003. John Kinsey, b. April 18, 1846; m. Nov. 25, 1875, Kate Vance.
2004. James Leighton, b. May 23, 1848; m. Oct. 21, 1885, Emma Ellis, of Brazil, Mo.
2005. Silas Whitcomb, b. Oct. 2, 1852; d. Nov. 15, 1856.
2006. Alice, b. Oct. 26, 1858; d. Dec. 20, 1862.
2007. Warren, b. July 8, 1861; d. Jan. 1, 1862.
2008. Carrie H., b. Sept. 12, 1863; lives in Clarksville, Texas; unmarried.

W 1183

Silas Amory Reed, son of Silas and Betsy (Whitcomb) Reed.

b. Dec. 4, 1827; lives in California.

m. June 18, 1867, Mary E. Miller.

Lives in California.

W 1186

David Henry Reed, son of David and Nancy (Nourse) Reed.

b. ———, 1816; d. April 17, 1855.

m. Nov. 13, 1839, Susan Reed, his cousin; daughter of Elias and Sally (Block) Reed.

He was a man of great purity of character. Educated in Alexandria, Va., and removed to Richmond, Va., where he continued to reside until his death. He occupied the position of 1st Clerk of the Literary Department of Virginia,

up to the time of his death. He was also for many years Grand Secretary of the Odd Fellows of Virginia. He was a fine scholar. The compiler of this work had the pleasure of knowing him personally, and knew him as a man of singular purity and loveliness of character. His influence over his companions, his courtesy of manner and his spotless life all combined to make him a perfect man, a Christian gentleman. Being a fine musician and a person of literary pursuits and taste, he was an ornament to the most refined society. He was highly esteemed by the Odd Fellows of Virginia and their Grand Lodge passed the following resolutions of esteem at the time he was compelled by ill health to resign the active duties of the Grand Secretary:

"Whereas, P. G. David H. Reed, late Grand Secretary of the R. W. Grand Lodge of Virginia, in consequence of painful and lingering illness under which he is still suffering, has been unable to attend our sessions, and this Grand body has been compelled to transfer to another the important office so long and so ably filled by our Bro. Reed; and whereas it would be doing injustice to this body were it to close its session without giving expression to the feelings of deep sensibility with which it has heard of the illness of Bro. Reed, and its high appreciation as an officer and as an Odd Fellow; therefore be it Resolved, That the R. W. Grand Lodge of Virginia yields, with painful emotion and deep regret to the afflictive dispensation which has taken from it the most faithful, able and accomplished officer ever enlisted in its service.

"Resolved, That during the long period the office of Grand Secretary of this Grand Lodge has been held by our Bro. David H. Reed, he has exhibited a fidelity and ability, accompanied with a courtesy and fraternal kindness, which has won for him the confidence and love of the whole jurisdiction to an extent never heretofore enjoyed by any other man.

"Resolved, That a diploma upon which these resolutions shall be engrossed, shall be drawn up, signed by the Grand

Officers, and presented to Bro. Reed as a testimonial from this Grand Lodge of its sympathy with him in his suffering and its high appreciation of his character as an Odd Fellow and as an officer."

CHILDREN

2009. Nannie Eliza, b. ———.
2010. Susie St. Clair, b. ———; m. Philip G. Seay.

W 1188

Henry Clark Reed, son of Henry Ludovicus and Charlotte (Stickney) Reed.

b. Nov. 20, 1827, in Boston; d. March 10, 1861, at Woodstock, Va.

m. Oct. 11, 1853, Kate King (d. June 4, 1857); daughter of Geo. and ——— King of York, Pa.

No children. Of Baltimore, Md.

In early manhood he was induced by his uncle J. Henry Stickney, to come to Baltimore and accept a position in his counting house, and later he went to Chicago and remained there over winter, when Chicago was a small but growing place. He concluded however, not to locate there. He returned to Baltimore, and accepted a place as clerk with his uncle's firm, Stickney and Noyes and later with Stickney and Beatty. On the dissolution of the latter firm he was given an interest in the business, which was continued under the name of Stickney & Co. In the fall of 1860, his health having failed, he withdrew from the firm and went to Cuba to try and regain his health but returned no better, and died in the spring of 1861. He was a Presbyterian.

W 1192

John Ludovicus Reed, son of Henry Ludovicus and Charlotte (Stickney) Reed.

b. June 25, 1836, at Scottsville, Albemarle county, Va.

m. Nov. 10, 1864 (in Baltimore, where they reside), Elizabeth McKee Bigham, daughter of Samuel and Elizabeth (Lindsay) Bigham.

No children.

JOHN L. REED.

He is the author of this work, and was brought up at Scottsville, Va. Removed from there with his father and the family to Wheeling, W. Va., and thence to Baltimore, where he was employed by the firm of Stickney & Co., which comprised his uncle J. Henry Stickney and brother Henry C. Reed; upon the failure of his brother's health in 1860 he was given an interest in the firm. In 1872 upon the retirement of his uncle from active business the style of the firm was changed to Reed, Stickney & Co., comprising himself, with William Harvey and Geo. H. Stickney as general partners, and his uncle J. Henry Stickney as special partner. They did a coal shipping and iron commission business. He is a Presbyterian and has occupied many positions of prominence in connection with that denomination since his residence in Baltimore. Has filled the position of ruling elder in Westminster and later in the Boundary Ave. Churches. Has been treasurer of the Presbyterian Association for Church Extension in the city for twenty-six years, and is also treasurer for the Board of Governors of the Presbyterian Eye, Ear and Throat Charity Hospital. He was in the service for a short time during the Civil War as Sergeant in Capt. Ehler's Company, under Gen. Tyler, being a member of the Balto. City Guard, who offered their services when Maryland was invaded and Baltimore was threatened, which were accepted by the Government and the company assigned to the Relay House camp near Balto. to take the place of regular soldiers who had been stationed there and whom it was necessary to withdraw to meet the enemy then on Maryland soil.

W **1195**

Edward Warren Reed, son of Warren and Mary (Wadsworth) Reed.

b. March 21, 1841; d. ———, 1896.

m. Nov. 19, 1874, Kate Karcher of Kansas.

Peach Grove, Clay county, Kansas.

CHILDREN

2011. Nellie, b. ———; m. ———.

2012. Charlotte, b.———; m. ———.

W 1196

John Henry Reed, son of Warren and Mary (Wadsworth) Reed.

b. April 16, 1843; d. April 23, 1888.

Unmarried. Resided in Milton, Mass., and was engaged in business with his brother William under the firm name of "Reed Bros."

Of Milton, Mass.

W 1197

William Ruggles Reed, son of Warren and Mary (Wadsworth) Reed.

b. Feb. 5, 1845; d. Dec. 30, 1890.

m. Sept. 24, 1882, Margaret Ellen Whittemore of Boston.

Resided in Milton, Mass., and carried on a mercantile business with his brother John Henry under the firm name of Reed Bros. His widow now resides in Boston.

CHILD

2013. Warren Whittemore, b. Sept. 7, 1883.
2013a. Eliot Wadsworth, b. Jan. 19, 1889.

A 1200

Ezra Reed, son of Ezra and Susanna C. (Richards) Reed.

b. Oct. 11, 1822; d. Jan. 10, 1874, at South Weymouth.

m. Feb. 11, 1849, Jane A. Wright, of Weymouth, by Rev. M. Harding; she was born July 14, 1826, at Mansfield, Conn.; daughter of Stedman Huntington and Mary (Burrows) Wright.

Both he and his father lived at South Weymouth in the old Josiah Colson house, built about 1796, which was still standing in 1898, situated on the north side of the junction of Pleasant and Park streets.

Of South Weymouth.

CHILDREN

2014. Charles Stedman, b. Nov. 12, 1851, at S. Weymouth; m. Feb. 8, 1882, Ella Frances Colby, of Vasselborough, Me.
2015. Clara Jane, b. Nov. 28, 1849, at S. Weymouth; m. June 16, 1874, Irville Waterman, of Kingston, Mass.
2016. Ezra Walter, b. Feb. 15, 1872; d. May 9, 1882.

W 1202

James Austin Reed, son of Ezra and Susanna C. (Richards) Reed.

b. March 22, 1832; d. ———.

m. 1st. ———, Mary Jane Holbrook Pratt.

m. 2nd. Feb. 18, 1875, Sarah Caroline, daughter of Joseph and Esther C. Jacobs of Hingham; she was born Jan. 9, 1845.

He is a successful farmer, and lives on land that has been in his family for 150 years. He has no children.

Of South Weymouth, Mass.

W 1208

Harvey H. Reed, son of Harvey and Jane (Pratt) Reed.

b. March 27, 1822; d. June 26, 1864.

m. May ———, 1844, Ann Ripley.

Was a member of 1st Maine Heavy Artillery and died in hospital at City Point, Va., from wounds received in storming rifle pits, before Petersburg.

CHILDREN

2017. Alvan, b. ———.
2018. William F., b. ———; d. Oct. 1, 1895; m. ——— Danforth.
2019. Frederick, b. ———; d. aged 14 years.

W 1211

George H. Reed, son of Harvey and Jane (Pratt) Reed.

b. Dec. 26, 1829, at Weymouth; d. July 31, 1896, at Bangor, Me.

m. Aug. 6, 1863, Helen Curtis of Weymouth, who was born Feb. 10, 1840. She was the daughter of Ira and Elizabeth (Willis) Curtis.

They had no children. Of Bangor, Me.

W 1212

Quincy Lovell Reed, son of Quincy and Lucy (Loud) Reed.

b. April 6, 1822, in South Weymouth.

m. March 22, 1860 (at Providence, R. I.), Lucy Emeline Hall (she was born Aug. 8, 1828, at Warwick, R. I.), by Rev. Jonathan Leavitt, pastor of Richmond street church, Providence, R. I.

A surveyor and conveyancer. In his early life was engaged in mercantile business. Is highly esteemed in the community as a man of excellent judgment and strict integrity. Is a Vice-President of the Weymouth Historical Society, and has manifested a lively interest in the early history of his town and state, and has been of great assistance to the author of this work. He has written and published a great many valuable historical articles.

Of South Weymouth, Mass.

CHILDREN

2020. Harriet Loud, b. Dec. 19, 1860; m. Aug. 18, 1892, Albert Parker Worthen.
2021. Quincy, b. Sept. 22, 1864.
2022. Lucy Hall, b. Sept. 22, 1864.
2023. Abby Harris, b. Dec. 26, 1866.

W **1215**

William Henry Reed, son of Quincy and Lucy (Loud) Reed.
b. June 16, 1832, at South Weymouth, Mass.
m. April 25, 1860, Julia Leonard Andrews; b. Sept. 23, 1835, in Bridgewater, Mass.; she is a daughter of Manassah and Harriet (Leonard) Andrews and a sister of the late Gen'l George L. Andrews, Professor of Languages at the Military Academy, West Point, for about twenty-five years.

William H. Reed takes a great interest in the early history and families of Weymouth, Mass., and has rendered valuable assistance to the author of this work.

Of South Weymouth, Mass.

CHILDREN

2024. Julia Andrews, b. Feb. 18, 1861; d. ———; m. June 22, 1887, Frank Howard Wood, of E. Bridgewater. They have a daughter, Ivis, b. Weymouth, July 1, 1889.

QUINCY LOVELL REED.

2025. William Henry, Jr., b. Oct. 29, 1863; d. March 9, 1890; unmarried.

2026. Hepsie Hodges, b. Feb. 5, 1865; d. Sept. 6, 1885; unmarried.

2027. Grace Leonard, b. March 15, 1869; d. Aug. 21, 1869.

2028. Albert Hastings, b. Oct. 14, 1870.

2029. Mary Iris, b. June 12, 1872; d. Aug. 21, 1887.

2030. Helen, b. Aug. 26, 1873.

W 1218

John Bradford Reed, son of John and Lydia B. (Vining) Reed.

b. Nov. 3, 1830; d. Aug. 30, 1896.

m. 1st. Nov. 27, 1850, Emily Jane Loud of Weymouth; m. by Rev. Willard M. Harding.

m. 2nd. Jan. 28, 1865, Frances C. Thayer of Abington.

Of Weymouth, Mass.

CHILDREN

2031. Emily Bradford, b. Oct. 12, 1851; m. William W. Sampson, of Malden, Mass.

2032. Henry Horatio, b. Oct. 16, 1853; m. Nov. 12, 1885, Marion E. Crawford.

W 1220

Franklin Reed, son of John and Lydia B. (Vining) Reed.

b. Jan. 30, 1835; d. June 27, 1896.

m. June 8, 1852, Pamelia Thayer of Weymouth, Mass.; m. by Rev. James P. Terry; she was born May 20, 1835.

Of Weymouth, Mass.

He was a soldier in the War of the Rebellion; taken prisoner at one of the great battles, and was confined in Andersonville prison for over nine months, and returned home a wreck of his former self and died at the home of his daughter, Mrs. Dyer, in Whitman, June 27, 1896.

CHILDREN

2033. Jennie, b. Oct. 21, 1854, Weymouth; m. Charles Conant, of Whitman.

2034. Lizzie, b. May 13, 1858, Weymouth; m. Frank Dyer, of Braintree.

2035. Alvin, b. May 19, 1860, Weymouth; m. Irene Hollis, of Abington.

W 1221

Frederick Reed, son of John and Lydia B. (Vining) Reed.

b. May 13, 1839.

m. 1st. Aug. 3, 1862, Ellen Mehetable Brown of Abington.

m. 2nd. July 14, 1886, Mary Jane Whitman.

CHILDREN OF FREDERICK AND ELLEN

2036. Annie Estelle, b. at Abington, March 15, 1863; m. July 4, 1885, Charles Austin Brown.
2037. Frederick Livingston, b. July 24, 1864.
2038. John, b. July 31, 1871.
2039. Arthur Brown, b. Feb. 24, 1874; m. Oct. 7, 1896, Clara J. Warren, of Abington.

W 1224

William Titterton Reed, son of Alvan and Lucy (Vining) Reed.

b. Sept. 9, 1849, at South Weymouth, Norfolk county, Mass.

m. Oct. 30, 1872, Ella J. Harlow, daughter of James M. and Betsy J. (Clark) Harlow (b. at Scituate).

Of South Weymouth, Mass.

CHILDREN

2040. Alvan Tirrel, b. Sept. 23, 1874; m. June 26, 1901, Mary Emma Vining, daughter of A. Elliott Vining, and granddaughter of Hon. Benj. F. White and descendant of John Vining 1st who married Mary Read, daughter of Philip Read.
2041. Harvey Dennett, b. April 17, 1876; m. June 1, 1899, Eva Stewart Arnold.

T 1233

George Reed, son of George and Experience (Blackman) Reed.

b. Feb. 15, 1787; d. Feb. 3, 1820.

m. ———, Lucinda B. Sawtell.

Of Augusta, Me.

CHILDREN

2042. Lucinda S., b. May 9, 1813; m. Isaac Hilton.
2043. Eliza C., b. Oct. 13, 1814; m. Virgil Ballard.

T 1234

Luther Reed, son of George and Experience (Blackman) Reed.

b. July 4, 1790.

m. 1st. March 5, 1816, Betsy Hamilton.

m. 2nd. Nov. 21, 1839, Fanny Howard, daughter of Maj. Rewel Howard.

Of Augusta, Me.

CHILDREN OF LUTHER AND BETSY

2044. Betsy H., b. Feb. 28, 1818; m. Wm. A. Springer.
2045. Luther W., b. Feb. 25, 1822; m. Lucy D. Cummins.
2046. Julia A., b. Aug. 25, 1826; m. Oct. 3, 1841, James E. Watson.

T 1239

Oliver Reed, son of Oliver and Bethiah (Leonard) Reed.

b. June, 1789; d. Jan., 1834.

m. ———, Chloe Briggs.

Of Taunton, Mass.

CHILDREN

2047. Chloe, b. Jan. 9, 1816; m. Jan. 10, 1836, Charles H. Brown.
2048. Oliver Dean, b. April 9, 1817; m. Sally Wilber.
2049. Harriet Witherall, b. Nov. 10, 1819.
2050. George Leonard, b. Nov. 9, 1820; m. May 23, 1851, Hannah K. Field.
2051. Sarah Thayer, b. Feb. 8, 1823; m. April 25, 1861, Joseph Allen (New Bedford).
2052. Lydia Babbitt, b. Feb. 23, 1826; d. Dec. 21, 1848.
2053. Huldah W., b. Jan. 17, 1828; d. Dec. 28, 1829.
2054. Rebecca Leonard, b. Dec. 26, 1829; m. June 23, 1850, Wm. D. Newhall.
2055. Lorenzo Revelo, b. Sept. 16, 1832; m. Martha Hodges.

T 1240

George L. Reed, son of Oliver and Bethiah (Leonard) Reed.

b. June 9, 1791.

m. ———, Betsy Lincoln.

Of Taunton, Mass.

CHILDREN

2056. Betsy H., b. Oct. 30, 1815; m. April 19, 1854, Brazilia Briggs.
2057. Bethiah L., b. June 10, 1817.

T 1242

Barney Reed, son of Oliver and Bethiah (Leonard) Reed.
b. Dec. 4, 1797.
m. 1st. ———, Rachel Woodward (d. April 25, 1826).
m. 2nd. ———, Charlotte ———.

Of Taunton, Mass.

CHILDREN

2058. Jarvis Barney, b. March 14, 1821; m. May 2, 1847, Elizabeth W. Eddy.
2059. Salmon Leonard, b. Nov. 1, 1823; d. Jan. 20, 1881; m. ———.
2060. John Quincy Adams, b. Sept. 20, 1825; d. Feb. 26, 1853; m. Sept. 14, 1844, Arena C. Makepeace.
2061. Charlotte Lois, b. July 22, 1834.
2062. Isaiah, b. Aug., 1839; d. July 18, 1852.

T 1243

Isaiah Reed, son of Oliver and Bethiah (Leonard) Reed.
b. ———.
m. ———, Fanny Thomas.

Of Taunton, Mass.

CHILD

2063. Fanny M., b. Feb. 24, 1824; m. Aug. 22, 1841, Willard Johnson, of Providence, R. I.

T 1244

Stimson Reed, son of Oliver and Bethiah (Leonard) Reed.
b. Nov. 12, 1805.
m. 1st. Sept. 8, 1837, Fanny H. Briggs (d. May 8, 1848, aged 36).
m. 2nd. Dec. 26, 1857, Hannah L. Bassett.

Of Taunton, Mass.

CHILDREN

2064. Clarissa D., b. Aug. 26, 1838; m. Dec. 14, 1854, Wm. L. Wilbur.
2065. Stimson L., b. Oct. 6, 1840.

T 1245

Barzillai Reed, son of Oliver and Bethiah (Leonard) Reed.
b. April 16, 1808; d. Oct. 20, 1860.
m. Sept. 21, 1837, Deborah Churchill.

A farmer.

Of Taunton, Mass.

CHILDREN

2066. Deborah C., b. Aug. 20, 1838; m. June 30, 1859, Theron S. Sanford (Bristol, Conn.).
2067. Rachel J., b. June 28, 1840; d. June 24, 1844.
2068. Stephen O., b. ———.

T 1246

William Hodges Reed, son of Oliver and Bethiah (Leonard) Reed.

b. March 14, 1810.

m. ———, Amanda Goff.

Of Taunton, Mass.

CHILD

2069. William H., b. Dec. 2, 1843, at Rehoboth, Mass.

T 1250

Henry Gooding Reed, son of John and Rebecca (Gooding) Reed.

b. July 23, 1810; d. March 1, 1901.

m. 1st. Jan. 5, 1842, Clara White (b. Aug. 8, 1812; d. Sept. 27, 1847); daughter of Isaac White of Mansfield, Mass.

m. 2nd. June 2, 1851, Frances Lee Williams (b. June 10, 1834; d. May 9, 1857); daughter of Jared Williams of Dighton.

m. 3rd. Oct. 27, 1858, Delight R. Carpenter (b. Dec. 4, 1828; d. ———); daughter of Christopher Carpenter of Rehoboth.

Of Taunton, Mass.

Attended the public schools of Taunton and the academy. During vacation he would assist his father, as a clerk in his store. He early developed a marked mechanical taste and skill, making a collection of wood-working tools, and spending much of his leisure time in the use of them; planning and making useful articles for the family, and miniature vessels and toys for his schoolmates.

Thus early did he give promise of the distinguished career that was before him. When eighteen, he entered the shop

of Babbitt & Crossman, as an apprentice, continuing with them till 1831. When in 1835, the Taunton Britannia Manufacturing Company suspended operations, Henry G. Reed and Chas. E. Barton, two young men, who had been in its employ, with small capital but with abundant industry and considerable knowledge of the business, formed a partnership of Reed and Barton, which firm gained a reputation second to none in the country in that line of goods. Barton long since died, but the firm name, known in all parts of the civilized world, still survives, George Brabrook filling the place of Barton, and the holders of the estate of Henry H. Fish, deceased, being also represented in the corporation. They are now known as silversmiths and manufacturers of electro-plated nickel silver and white metal wares. Mr. Reed was the last survivor of the original firm, and the founder of the business.

No citizen of Taunton held a larger place in the esteem and confidence of the entire community. He had been director in the Taunton National Bank since 1851, trustee of the Taunton Savings Bank since its organization, an interested member and officer of the Associated Charities since their beginning, a liberal life member of the Old Colony Historical Society and president of the Reed family meetings, ever since the men of the former generations passed away.

CHILDREN OF HENRY G. AND CLARA

2070. Clara Isabel, b. Aug. 14, 1844; m. Dr. Chas. T. Hubbard, of Taunton, Mass.
2071. Henry Arthur, b. Oct. 15, 1846; d. Aug. 16, 1847.

CHILDREN OF HENRY G. AND FRANCES

2072. Ida Frances, b. May 12, 1852; d. Aug. 29, 1852.
2073. Fanny Lee, b. May 25, 1854; m. Wm. Bradford Homer Dowse, of Newton, Mass.
2074. Henry Francis, b. March 23, 1857.

T 1262

William Reed, son of William and Elizabeth (Dennis) Reed.
b. Feb. 17, 1819.
m. Nov. 17, 1850, Eliza Deane.

Of Taunton, Mass.

HENRY G. REED.

T 1265

Hon. Chester Isham Reed (of Dedham), son of William and Elizabeth (Dennis) Reed.

b. Nov. 25, 1823; d. Sept. 2, 1873, at White Sulphur Springs, W. Va.

m. Feb. 24, 1851, Elizabeth Allyne.

Chester Isham Reed was born in Taunton November 25, 1823. He was the son of William and Elizabeth Deane (Dennis) Reed. His ancestry on both sides can be traced back to the earlier settlers of the country. He received his early education in the Taunton High School and the Bristol Academy, then taught by Mr. Frederick Crafts. He entered Brown University in the class of 1845. With all his schoolmates he was a favorite. While he was a good scholar, no boy or young man was ever more fond of play when outside the schoolroom. Circumstances in his father's family prevented the completion of his college course, and he left Brown and commenced the study of law in the office of General David Bachelder in Gardiner, Me.

After being admitted to the bar in that State, he immediately returned to his old home in Taunton and commenced the practice of his profession. For a year or more he edited the "Old Colony Republican." In 1848, he formed a partnership with Anselm Bassett, Esq., then register of probate.

This partnership continued some fifteen years until Mr. Bassett's death. The firm of Bassett & Reed shortly acquired a very extensive practice throughout Bristol and Plymouth counties. At the age of twenty-six Mr. Reed represented Taunton in the Legislature. He was for several years judge of the Police Court. In 1858, and again in 1862, he served in the State Senate. But his time was given almost exclusively to his profession, in which he excelled.

Judge Bigelow of the Supreme Court writes to him, under date of February 23, 1857, Mr. Reed then being thirty-four years of age:

"There is no member of the bar, in any part of the State,

who prepares his cases with greater fidelity or who is listened to with greater attention or pleasure than yourself."

In the ninth volume of Allen's Reports he appears on one side or the other in eighteen cases before the Supreme Court.

In 1864, Mr. Reed, as a Republican, was elected attorney-general and held the office until his appointment to the Superior Court in 1867.

At this time he removed from Taunton to Dedham where he passed the remainder of his life. In 1870, he resigned from the Superior Court and resumed the practice of law in the various State and United States Courts, maintaining a high position as an advocate, and held in great esteem as a judicious counselor. He had filled many public stations with credit to himself and benefit to the public, and never was a shade cast upon his character for the strictest integrity. He had arrived at that age with his varied experience that made him one of the useful men of the Commonwealth.

In the maturity of his intellectual and with no apparent impairment of his physical powers, he had every reason to expect a long and pleasant autumn of life, where though the toil might be continuous it would be for those he loved and with the prospect of a golden harvest.

Although of an apparently robust physique he had been for some time afflicted with an obscure disease which medical science proved wholly unable to combat, and in 1873, his health failed before it. He died September 2, at the White Sulphur Springs in West Virginia, where he had gone with the hope of benefit from the waters. He was a learned and accomplished lawyer, an honorable and high-minded man. Some one writing at the time of his death said:

"In his feelings, conduct and conversation he was habitually as pure and gentle as a child. In his own family his presence was perpetual sunshine. In his personal friendships he was warm, disinterested, generous and if need be, heroic."

Said another:

"As a lawyer he was zealous for his clients but fair and

courteous to his opponents. He despised all trickery and never descended to low arts to gain a cause."

Hon. George Marston said of him:

"As a judge he was patient, faithful, competent and fearless. He was spotless in his integrity. In all his public and private relations he was without fear and without reproach."

Judge Pitman says:

"He was patient with most things but impatient of shams. In whatsoever sphere he moved he was one of the most genuine of men. As an advocate he had little of the art to make the worse appear the better reason. To dissemble was not in his nature."

Judge Reed married Elizabeth Y. Allyne, of New Bedford, Mass., February 24, 1851. They had two children: Sybil, born January 21, 1858, she was a sweet, lovely child who died in early youth; Chester Allyne, born April 28, 1860, a graduate of Harvard University in 1881, now practicing law in Boston, a resident of Dedham with his mother.

Prepared by his sister, Mrs. S. H. Emery.

CHILDREN

2075. Sybil Elizabeth, b. Jan. 21, 1858. in Taunton; d. Aug. 27, 1885.

2076. Chester Allyne, b. April 28, 1860, in Taunton.

T **1267**

John Dennis Reed, son of William and Mary (Dennis) Reed.

b. March 15, 1827.

m. July 11, 1865, Helen Frances Sproat of Taunton. They had no children.

He is a merchant at Taunton, grocer.

Of Taunton, Mass.

T **1268**

Charles Edward Reed, son of William and Mary (Dennis) Reed.

b. Jan. 27, 1830.

m. Sept. 18, 1861, Rebecca P. Page of Chelsea.

He is now a resident of Milwaukee, Wis.

Of Milwaukee, Wis.

CHILDREN

2077. Anna Nelson, b. } Dec. 25, 1864.
2078. William Dennis, b. }
2079. Katherine Fessenden, b. Feb. 12, 1868.

T 1269

Erastus Maltby Reed, son of William and Mary (Dennis) Reed.

b. July 28, 1832, at Taunton, Mass.

m. Aug. 21, 1857, Sarah Jane Crockett; b. March 30, 1835, in Middletown, Conn.; daughter of John W. and Mary (Pierce) Crockett. They were married at the family gathering of the Reeds in Taunton.

Had a common school education, was a member of the Orthodox Congregational Church, clerk of Society, was a lawyer in Mansfield, Mass., Judge of the District Court, Member of the Legislature, School Committee, Town Clerk, Member of St. James Lodge of Mason, and of the Royal Arcanum; Republican.

Of Mansfield, Mass.

CHILD

2080. Bertha Holden, b. March 10, 1868.

T 1272

Edwin Reed, son of Marshall and Clarissa C. (Willis) Reed.

b. May 6, 1822.

m. Nov. 21, 1862, Victoria Graham of Rumford, Me.; d. at Taunton, Dec. 14, 1887, aged 49 years.

He was a mechanic.

Of Taunton, Mass.

T 1274

Edgar Hodges Reed, son of Hodges and Clarissa (Hodges) Reed.

b. July 3, 1814; d. April ——, 1893.

m. Aug. 30, 1837, Ellen Augusta Godfrey, daughter of Chas. and Hannah (Shaw) Godfrey.

He was a member of the Winslow Church for 45 years, Supt. of the S. S. for 3 or 4 years, Pres. of the North Bristol Congregational Club for 3 years. Alderman in Taunton in 1865 and 1868, Rep. to General Court in 1869, Dea. of Congregational Church since 1862.

Of Taunton, Mass.

He took a just pride in his parentage (see the record of his father) and it was his delight to note and record all which related to the early history of the family, thereby creating and fostering a taste for genealogical research in general. Mr. Reed has long been known in the town and city of his birth as a most enthusiastic antiquarian and accurate genealogist. His search for dates and inscriptions on gravestones, records in registry was an unceasing work, a genuine labor of love, and his accumulation of valuable material for family and town history, as a consequence, is very large. His son-in-law, Geo. A. Washburn, Esq., in custody of this material, is often called upon to contribute of his stores for the benefit of anxious inquirers.

To such a man and such a mind, the Old Colony Historical Society, incorporated in Taunton in 1853, made a strong appeal and both he and his father were early and interested members, the father having been the first treasurer, and the son the first recording secretary and librarian. At the time of his death he was historiographer.

Lest it should be supposed the subject of our sketch confined himself to historical matters, it may be added, as a young man, he commenced business in Taunton, which he continued without interruption until he was quoted as the oldest merchant on Main street, a lifelong friend, Mr. George M. Woodward, saying of him:

"A man of marked individuality, of sterling integrity, of strong common sense and of sound practical judgment. Cautious, even timid perhaps in untried enterprises, prudent

and safe in all his business methods, he has been known for half a century as an honorable and successful merchant. Similar characteristics marked his religious life, quiet, cautious, with regard to new methods and new statements of doctrine, he had a genuine and experimental knowledge of the Lord Jesus Christ as a personal Saviour. The church of his choice was a part of his being. It did much for him because he did so much for it."

This sketch was prepared by Rev. S. Hopkins Emery, drawn in part from a notice prepared by him for collection of Old Colony Historical Society No. 5.

CHILDREN

2081. Ellen Dutton, b. Sept. 9, 1838; m. Nov. 14, 1866, Geo. A. Washburn, of Taunton, Mass.
2082. Eugene Godfrey, b. July 30, 1841; d. Aug. 13, 1841.
2083. Clarissa Maria, b. May 9, 1843; d. Aug. 6, 1843.
2084. Alice Maria, b. March 14, 1848; m. Nov. 3, 1869, Robert Elliott, of Hannibal, Missouri.

T 1277

Rev. Frederick Alonzo Reed, son of Hodges and Clarissa (Hodges) Reed.
b. Dec. 7, 1821; d. June 9, 1883, at Harvard.
m. April 30, 1850, Mary C. Hubbard of Concord.

Rev. F. A. Reed was a clergyman, settled over churches, East Taunton and Harvard. Author of several religious books.

No children.

Of Harvard, Mass.

T 1282

John Reed, son of Florentine and ——— Reed.
b. ———, 1830.
m. ———.

He was of the firm of Reed and Russ in China, Me.

Of China, Me.

CHILD

2085. A daughter, b. ———.

EDGAR HODGES REED.

T 1288

Joseph Reed, son of Joseph and Peddy (Hunt) Reed.

b. Jan 9, 1813.

m. 1st. April 17, 1839, Lydia Bryant; b. at Kingston, Sept. 26, 1813; d. Jan. 30, 1845.

m. 2nd. April 4, 1847, Phebe Briggs; d. Sept. 8, 1862, aged 48 years.

Of Taunton, Mass.

CHILDREN OF JOSEPH AND LYDIA

2086. Lydia Ann, b. April 5, 1840.
2087. Mary Elizabeth, b. Aug. 19, 1841.
2088. George L., b. Aug. 18, 1843; d. Aug. 4, 1844.

CHILDREN OF JOSEPH AND PHEBE

2089. Charles L., b. Jan. 6, 1848.
2090. George L., b. March 22, 1849; d. Aug. 21, 1850.
2091. James L., b. March 22, 1849; d. April 13, 1849.
2092. Sally M., b. Jan. 10, 1854; d. Oct. 7, 1855.
2093. Annie D., b. June 19, 1856.
2094. Henry P., b. Aug. 12, 1859.

T 1292

Leonard W. Reed, son of Joseph and Peddy (Hunt) Reed.

b. July 29, 1819.

m. ———, Fidelia Thayer.

Machinist.

Of Taunton, Mass.

CHILD

2095. Delia Viola, b. ———; d. June 5, 1846.

T 1294

William D. Reed, son of Joseph and Peddy (Hunt) Reed.

b. Aug. 23, 1823.

m. March 23, 1846, Rachel Ann Tripp of Dighton, Mass.

Of Taunton, Mass.

T 1306

Orlando Reed, son of Ebenezer and Mary (Chase) Reed.

b. ———.

m. ———, Abbie Williams.

CHILDREN

2096. Joshua, b. ———.
2097. Walter, b. ———.

T 1307

William Reed, son of Ebenezer and Mary (Chase) Reed.
b. ———.
m. ———, Eliza Palmer.

CHILDREN

2098. John Palmer, b. ———.
2099. Charlotte, b. ———.

T 1310

Jonathan Reed, son of Ebenezer and Mary (Chase) Reed.
b. Nov. 28, 1835.
m. March 20, 1859, Lydia Ann Hoskins.

CHILDREN

2100. Carrie, b. April 19, 1860; d. Aug. 18, 1860.
2101. Charles, b. Aug. 31, 1866; m. Nov. 5, 1891, Sarah White.
2102. Mary, b. Nov. 9, 1862; d. Jan. 8, 1892.

T 1312

Isaac Albert Reed, son of Isaac and Nancy (Babbitt) Reed.
b. March 31, 1838.
m. March 9, 1858, Almira Bowen Reed; she died Dec. 9, 1893.

CHILDREN

2103. Annie A., b. Sept. 15, 1861; m. Jan. 28, 1891, John Thornby.
2104. Charles, b. Oct. 16, 1862; m. Oct., 1891, Emily Baylies.

T 1313

Gilbert Reed, son of Gilbert and Delina (Peck) Reed.
b. Aug. 1, 1836.
m. Aug. 27, 1859, Valaria Rounseville.
Of Taunton, Mass.

CHILDREN

2105. Lillian Velzora, b. Feb. 29, 1860.
2106. Gilbert Ellsworth, b. June 11, 1861.

2107. Ada Velzora, b. Jan. 15, 1863; m. Nov. 30, 1882, ——— Crossman, son of Elsie Reed Crossman, b. Dec. 20, 1888.
2108. Lizzie Charity, b. Dec. 22, 1873.

T 1315

Ira Madison Reed, son of Gilbert and Delina (Peck) Reed.

b. ———.

m. ———, Adeline Pratt, of Taunton, Mass.; she died April 8, 1885.

CHILDREN

2109. Curtis Henry, b. Feb. 15, 1862; d. Sept. 29, 1894; m. Ellen Grace Tyndale, of Taunton, Mass.
2110. William Dier, b. July 12, 1864; m. Sept. 28, 1887, Ida M. Porter, of Lakeville, Mass.
2111. Wallace Elmer, b. Feb. 11, 1867; m. June 5, 1895, Annie Louisa Fuller, of Middleborough, Mass.

T 1316

Henry E. Reed, son of Gilbert and Delina (Peck) Reed.

b. March 31, 1842.

m. June 9, 1875, Lottie J. Lincoln, of Taunton, Mass.

CHILDREN

2112. Ethel L., b. Nov. 17, 1877.
2113. Clara E., b. Nov. 1, 1879.

T 1318

Josiah B. Reed, son of Gilbert and Delina (Peck) Reed.

b. Dec. 19, 1849.

m. Aug. 29, 1870, Josephine Jossylin Presbury.

CHILD

2114. Charles Gilbert, b. June 13, 1872; m. June 9, 1898, Abbie Bailey.

T 1321

Freeman Reed, son of Job and Lovisa (Andrews) Reed.

b. Nov. 29, 1811.

m. March 26, 1834, Lamira W. Jones, daughter of William Jones; b. March 26, 1816; d. June 10, 1897.

Of Berlin, Vt.

CHILDREN

2115. George M., b. June 3, 1835; d. March 24, 1869; m. 1st. May 14, 1856, Elizabeth Howe, who was b. Nov., 1834; d. June 16, 1865; m. 2d. Dec. 7, 1869, Mary M. Adams.
2116. Louisa M., b. March 19, 1837; m. March 8, 1855, Chauncey L. Hayden, who was b. Sept. 19, 1832.
2117. Mary Ann E., b. Feb. 7, 1841; d. Dec. 16, 1892; unmarried.
2118. Ai M., b. Oct. 31, 1845; m. Dec. 1, 1868, Helen M. Henry.
2119. Mabel H., b. Dec. 27, 1859; m. May 14, 1883, Chas. A. Ordway, of Northfield Centre, Vt.; no children.

T 1324

Russell Reed, son of Job and Lovisa (Andrews) Reed.

b. Feb. 5, 1817; d. Sept. 2, 1895.

m. Nov. 6, 1842, Mary Ann Edson (daughter of Daniel and Mary White Edson of Freetown, Mass.).

Of Northfield, Mass.

CHILDREN

2120. Emma A., b. March 1, 1846; m. Sept. 23, 1872, John M. Temple, 36 Prospect street, Athol, Mass.
2121. Charles E., b. April 24, 1847; m. Feb. 25, 1872, Cora C. Andrews.

T 1327

Benjamin Porter Reed, son of Job and Lovisa (Andrews) Reed.

b. Nov. 2, 1823; d. Nov. 5, 1899.

m. Feb. 8, 1846, Harriet Jones (daughter of William and Sally Jones).

Of Berlin, Vt.

CHILDREN

2122. Guy M., b. Jan. 9, 1847; d. Feb. 22, 1880; m. Nov., 1870, Ellen Lea Rock; no children.
2123. Annette L., b. July 24, 1848; m. Nov., 1873, Solon Lawrence.
2124. Henry C., b. March 20, 1850; m. Feb. 8, 1876, Hattie M. Rowell (no children).
2125. Myra E., b. Sept. 13, 1852; m. March 12, 1883, Fred. L. Thresher (no children).
2126. Stebbins D., b. Sept. 21, 1854; d, April, 1856.
2127. William P., b. March 16, 1857; m. Jan. 1, 1884, Sarah Rowell.

2128. Ilda S., b. April 14, 1858; m. Jan. 30, 1877, Lewis Chatfield, Berlin, Vt.
2129. Infant son, b. June 17, 1860; d. July, 1860.
2130. Harriet J., b. Aug. 11, 1862; m. Jan. 1, 1884, Clarence Pierce.
2131. George D., b. Sept. 19, 1864; m. Nov. 27, 1887, Kate Friend.

T 1343

William Augustus Reed, son of Rev. Augustus and Melinda (Borden) Reed.

b. April 8, 1830.

m. Jan. 30, 1856, Mary Lucetta Breckenridge, daughter of William and Clarissa (Paige) Breckenridge, sister of Julia P. Breckenridge who married John Richard Reed.

CHILDREN

2132. Mary Delight, b. Jan. 17, 1857; d. Aug. 24, 1892; m. Aug. 28, 1891, Elmer Case.
2133. Alice Sinclair, b. May 4, 1858; d. June 3, 1862.
2134. William Breckenridge, b. Nov. 6, 1861; d. Aug. 9, 1862.
2135. Robert Brown, b. Dec. 24, 1862; d. Aug. 30, 1863.
2136. Lucy Paige, b. Feb. 9, 1864; d. Feb. 12, 1864.
2137. Theodore Williams, b. April 10, 1866; m. June 27, 1892, James William Drysdale, of Peace Dale, R. I.
2138. Annie Breckenridge, b. May 13, 1869; d. March 7, 1870.

T 1344

John Richard Reed, son of Rev. Augustus and Melinda (Borden) Reed.

b. March 25, 1832, at Ware, Mass.

m. 1st. May 8, 1861, Julia P. Breckenridge; b. at Westfield, Mass.; d. Dec. 14, 1874, at Westfield, Mass.; daughter of Wm. and Clarissa (Paige) Breckenridge, sister of Mary Lucetta Breckenridge, who married William Augustus Reed.

m. 2nd. Jan. 19, 1876, Martha Huntington Dudman of Yarmouth, Nova Scotia, daughter of William Kaines and Susan Martha (Star) Dudman.

John Richard Reed was educated in the common schools, one term at Westfield Academy, left school at 15 years of

age. Julia Breckenridge was educated at the common schools and Monson Academy. They were communicants of the First Congregational Church of Westfield, he was a deacon, and teacher of the bible class.

He was a manufacturer, president of the H. B. Smith Co., Westfield, Mass., Foundry and Machine Shop, manufactured steam heating apparatus, amount of business $450,000 per year. He was a Republican from Freemont to Garfield, declined to vote for J. G. Blaine, voted for St. John that year. He clerked in a store for 5 years, whaling 4 years, in store again 3 years, connected with business for 29 years.

Of Westfield, Mass.

CHILDREN OF JOHN AND JULIA

2139. Richard Durfee, b. Feb. 4, 1862; m. Sept. 16, 1891, Ethel W. Mallory.
2140. Clara Melinda, b. May 21, 1865.
2141. Wm. Breckenridge, b. March 3, 1869.
2142. Elizabeth Borden, b. Nov. 12, 1870; d. Sept. 23, 1887.

CHILDREN OF JOHN AND MARTHA

2143. Edith Huntington, b. May 21, 1878.
2144. Susan Martha, b. Aug. 16, 1884.

T 1347

Charles Leonard Reed, son of Gustavus and Electa (Miller) Reed.

b. Sept. 20, 1837, at Rehoboth, Mass.
m. April —, 1865, Annie Mathewson; b. ———, 1843.

He was a merchant and they lived in Providence, R. I. No children.

Of Providence, R. I.

T 1351

Almond Augustus Reed, son of Gustavus and Electa (Miller) Reed.

b. Dec. 2, 1848, at Rehoboth, Mass.
m. Feb. —, 1880, Hattie Carpenter (b. at Rehoboth); daughter of Thomas and ——— (Graves) Carpenter.

JOHN RICHARD REED.

They were communicants of Orthodox Congregational Church. He is a farmer and lives in Rehoboth.

Of Rehoboth, Mass.

CHILDREN

2145. Annie Brown, b. June 6, 1884.
2146. Marion, b. Aug. 9, 1887.

T 1354

David Wilson Reed, son of John and Joanna (Wilson) Reed.

b. Dec. 27, 1803; d. Jan. 1, 1873.

m. 1st. Dec. 27, 1827, Esther Sanders (in Homer, Cortland county, N. Y.); she was born April 3, 1807; died March 4, 1870.

m. 2nd. May 13, 1871, Catherine Williams of Waukesha, Wis.

He was a merchant and farmer. In 1840 he removed to Wisconsin.

Of Waukesha, Wis.

CHILDREN

2147. George Irving, b. Nov. 9, 1828; d. March 25, 1852.
2148. Romanzo Marvin, b. June 23, 1830; m. May 7, 1856, Cornelia White.
2149. Esther Ann, b. Feb. 18, 1836; m. Sept. 11, 1855, Randall Fuller, in Mayville, Dodge Co., Wis.
2150. Frances Elizabeth, b. Sept. 8, 1843; d. Nov. 17, 1866.

T 1356

Artemas Reed, son of John and Joanna (Wilson) Reed.

b. June 10, 1807; d. at Cortland, N. Y., Jan. 2, 1897.

m. April 7, 1830, Eunice G. Benham, at Dryden, Tompkins county, N. Y.; she was the daughter of Isaac and Sally (Baker) Benham; b. at Fleming, Cayuga county, N. Y., Oct. 7, 1810; d. May 17, 1873.

In early life he learned the cabinet-maker's trade, and followed that until he had to give it up on account of ill health. He then took up the carpenter's trade. Lived a number of years in Ontario county, but in 1843 purchased a farm in Cayuga county. Later sold the farm and removed to Cort-

land, where his wife died. He joined the Methodist Episcopal Church, July 3, 1829, and held prominent positions in that church, was educated in the district schools, was a Republican in politics.

Of Cortland, N. Y.

CHILDREN

2151. Sarah Jane, b. Feb. 7, 1847, in Fleming, N. Y.; m. May 12, 1875, John H. Sturtevant, at Cortland, N. Y. (no children.)
2152. Ellen Augusta, b. June 27, 1850, in Fleming Co., N. Y.; d April 24, 1860.

T **1357**

Marvin Reed, son of John and Joanna (Wilson) Reed.

b. (in Oswego county, N. Y.) Aug. 29, 1809; d. March 27, 1882.

m. 1st. Dec. 28, 1836, Eunice Ann Heath; b. Delaware county, N. Y., July 17, 1812; d. Dec. 13, 1866, at Cortland.

m. 2nd. Dec. 17, 1867, Mary D. Rose; b. Jan. 17, 1821; d. Aug. 13, 1888, at Cortland, N. Y.

He had a common school education, was fond of reading and acquiring knowledge. He was a farmer, owned land and a mine in Iowa. He lived in Cortland, N. Y., except five years in Seneca Falls, N. Y. He was a member of the M. E. Church, S. S. superintendent four years, and trustee of Cortland Academy, he was a kind neighbor and a good citizen. An obituary notice of him by his church reads "Brother Reed had been a resident of this valley for nearly seventy years, was a faithful and devoted member from the age of nineteen until his death. He was a quiet man, clear in his convictions, firm in his adhesion to principle and duty, and particularly demonstrative in his religious life, but even and constant in his experience. The few last years of his life he was enfeebled by disease, but able to attend public worship until within a few months of his death. He was a good man and has left to his children the precious legacy of an untarnished name."

Of Cortland, N. Y.

CHILDREN OF MARVIN AND EUNICE

2153. Sarah Ann, b. Nov. 24, 1837; d. Sept. 5, 1843.

2154. Jason Lee, b. Sept. 15, 1839; d. Jan. 11, 1863; m. Sept. 11, 1862, Mary Felicia Palmer.

2155. Mary Frances, b. Dec. 25, 1841; m. Virgil Wadham Mattoon.

2156. Martha Caroline, b. Aug. 13, 1843; d. Feb. 28, 1862.

2157. Milo Heath, b. Aug. 8, 1845; d. Jan. 12, 1854.

2158. Sarah Jane, b. June 7, 1848; d. June 28, 1862.

2159. Howard John, b. Feb. 1, 1852; m. June 7, 1881, Emma A. Sweetlove.

2160. Clara Heath, b. Oct. 5, 1855; d. May 26, 1893; m. Jan. 7, 1888, Fred. Washburn Everson.

T **1358**

John Reed, Jr., son of John and Joanna (Wilson) Reed.

b. Aug. 2, 1813, at Cortland, N. Y.; d. at Lansing, Iowa, Oct. 9, 1894.

m. (at Cortland N. Y.) April 16, 1837, Hannah E. Nesmith; b. Jan. 7, 1816, at Antrim, N. H.; d. May 17, 1877, at Waukon, Iowa; she was the daughter of James and Polly (Taylor) Nesmith.

They had a common school education, he was a farmer until 1876, when he retired from active business. They were active members of the M. E. Church. Lived in Cortland, N. Y., until March, 1855, afterwards near Waukon. John Reed was five feet six inches in height, with light complexion, blue eyes and brown hair. Both he and his wife were most excellent people, highly esteemed by all who knew them. As a friend remarked, "they were the salt of the earth."

Of Lansing, Iowa.

CHILDREN

2161. Mary Sophronia, b. June 23, 1839; m. July 4, 1861, Liberty Eaton Fellows.

2162. David Wilson, b. April 2, 1841; m. Sept. 20, 1866, Ellen E. Manson.

2163. Milton Taylor, b. June 23, 1843; enlisted in the U. S. service in 1862; d. Feb. 2, 1863, in Jackson, Tenn.

2164. Ella Joanna, b. June 13, 1854; m. Dec. 25, 1878, Henry J. Bently.

T 1360

Isaac Newton Reed, son of Isaac and Lucretia (Newton) Reed.

b. April 6, 1811, at Putney, Windham county, Vt.

m. Jan. 6, 1835, Margaret Miles; b. Sept. 3, 1816, at Geneva, N. Y.; d. Feb. 5, 1870, at Berlin Heights, Erie county, Ohio; daughter of Jasper and Betsy (Bailey) Miles.

Of Putney, Vt.

CHILDREN

2165. Howard Newton, b. Sept. 27, 1835; d. Oct. 20, 1836.
2166. Maria Calista, b. June 28, 1837; m. Curtis Nichols.
2167. Ellen Augusta, b. Aug. 19, 1839; m. Nov. 22, 1855, Theodore C. Pratt, of Weymouth.
2168. Charles Wayland, b. March 18, 1841; m. Annah C. Brown.
2169. Miles Newton, b. Aug. 8, 1844; m. Aug. 26, 1874, Katie Porter Chaffin.
2170. John Melvin, b. March 28, 1847; m. Lizzie Ross.
2171. Georgianna Margaret, b. Dec. 31, 1850; d. May 28, 1853.
2172. William Perry, b. May 23, 1852; d. Oct. 26, 1862.

T 1364

Perry Reed, son of Isaac and Lucretia (Newton) Reed.

b. June 27, 1820.

m. ———, Hester House.

Of Putney, Vt.

T 1369

Thomas Newton Reed, son of Simeon and Betsy (Joy) Reed.

b. (at Putney, Vt.) Aug. 31, 1828.

m. June 1, 1854, Ellen Jerusha Miller; b. Sept. 12, 1828, at Dummerston, Vt.; daughter of John B. and Phila (Knight) Miller.

He had a common school and academic education, he held many town offices and was representative to Legislature in 1876. He was principally engaged in farming at Dummerston, Vt.

Of Dummerston, Vt.

CHILDREN

2173. Edward Fulton, b. July 6, 1855; m. Sept. 18, 1878, Nettie L. Worden.
2174. Carlton Thomas, b. Jan. 25, 1857; m. Jan. 1, 1879, Hattie E. Worden.
2175. Burton Miller, b. March 13, 1863.
2176. Gertrude Ellen, b. June 17, 1867; m. Nov. 17, 1887, Carlos E. Newton.

T 1371

Charles Covell Reed, son of Charles L. and Hannah (Beetle) Reed.

b. Aug. 2, 1824.

Of Friday Harbor, San Juan Island, Washington.

T 1375

William Jefferson Reed, son of John and Juliet (Merrifield) Reed.

b. March 17, 1828.

m. Aug. 23, 1855, Sarah Davis; b. Jan. 23, 1838, in Champaign county, Ohio; daughter of William and Elizabeth (Sipes) Davis.

He came to Illinois with his father in 1839. He is a farmer, and he, with his family, are members of the M. E. Church.

Of Henderson county, Ill.

CHILDREN

2177. James Henry, b. May 30, 1856; d. Sept., 1856.
2178. Mary F.; d. young.
2179. Minnie, b. July 4, 1859; d. Feb. 28, 1887; m. Edward B. Mitchell.
2180. Alice, b. Feb. 7, 1861; m. Edward Salter.
2181. Adelia, b. Dec. 4, 1864; m. Sam'l Elwell.
2182. Lida, b. March 7, 1866.

T 1376

James Reed, son of John and Juliet (Merrifield) Reed.

b. Nov. 8, 1829, at Harding, Ky.; d. Dec., 1864, in Henderson county, Ill.

m. April 11, 1850, Margaret Angeline Hogue; b. March 28, 1831, in Gibson county, Ill.; daughter of Sam'l L. and Mary H. (Woods) Hogue.

He was a class leader in M. E. Church, was engaged in farming. He was slim, dark hair, gray eyes, lively, cheerful disposition.

Of Henderson county, Ill.

CHILDREN

2183. Mary Juliet, b. March 15, 1851; m. Oct. 17, 1872, Sam'l Findly.
2184. Samuel Park, b. May 8, 1853; m. Nov. 23, 1876, Sarah E. Fair.
2185. George Washington, b. Jan. 5, 1855; m. Nov. 19, 1876, Flora Longley.
2186. Jennie E., b. Nov. 7, 1856.
2187. Ella Amelia, b. May 22, 1859.
2188. Leona Frances, b. March 6, 1861; m. Aug. 25, 1887, Chas. C. McClung.
2189. Alvira Angeline, b. Oct. 23, 1863; d. Jan. 9, 1865.

T 1382

Samuel Merrifield Reed, son of John and Juliette (Merrifield) Reed.

b. March 27, 1839, in Harding county, Ky.

m. Feb. 13, 1871, Harriet Welch; b. Aug. 7, 1851, in Henderson county, Ill.; daughter of John H. and Mary (Lathrop) Welch.

They were Methodists, he was first a school teacher, afterwards a farmer, good size and height. Crippled since he was a boy.

Of Henderson county, Ill.

CHILDREN

2190. John Milton, b. Dec. 20, 1871; d. Nov. 15, 1872.
2191. Julia Adelaide, b. Oct. 29, 1873.
2192. Nelson Franklin, b. March 12, 1876.
2193. James Boon, b. April 25, 1878.
2194. Mabel Estelle, b. Oct. 7, 1880.
2195. Clara Evilina, b. Aug. 10, 1883; d. Sept. 18, 1884.
2196. Lela Floy, b. May 7, 1886.

JOHN H. REED.

T 1385

John Henry Reed, son of John and Charity (Webb) Reed.
b. April 18, 1849.
Unmarried.

Of Reed, Henderson county, Ill.

T 1387

David Anthony Reed, son of John and Charity (Webb) Reed.
b. Feb. 2, 1853.
m. Sept. 29, 1880, Lucy Ellen Dungan; b. June 13, 1859; d. in Clark county, Mo.; daughter of George and Ann Eliza (Johnson) Dungan.

Lived in Henderson county till 1883, when they moved to Holt county, Neb., from there to ——, Neb. His occupation was farming.

Of Holt county, Neb.

CHILDREN

2197. Bertha Amelia, b. Aug. 26, 1881.
2198. Jessie Lurena, b. Feb. 10, 1883.
2199. Effie Jennette, b. April 23, 1885.

T 1388

Aciel Elihu Reed, son of John and Charity (Webb) Reed.
b. Feb. 7, 1855, in Henderson county, Ill.
m. Feb. 22, 1882, Louisa Case, in Avon, Ill.

He was born on the old Reed farm in Henderson county, Ill., moved from there to Abington, Knox county, Ill., when about nineteen years of age. Attended Hedding College one year but did not remain long enough to graduate, attended Commercial College at Quincy, Ill. He afterwards removed to Helena, Mont., in 1880, and was employed as a clerk in the establishment of R. G. Wallace of that place. Was connected with the M. E. Church. Is a Republican in politics, and a Master Free Mason. Height five feet eleven inches, medium stout. Is said to be benevolent and values highly his reputation for honesty and integrity.

Of Helena, Mont.

T 1389

Joseph Nathaniel Reed, son of John and Charity (Webb) Reed.

b. Nov. —, 1858, in Henderson county, Ill.

m. Sept. 5, 1888, Cora Tullis, daughter of Rev. A. K. Tullis.

Of Henderson county, Ill.

T 1393

William Baylies Reed, son of Anthony and Elizabeth (Bliss) Reed.

b. Aug. 22, 1834, at Dighton, Mass.

m. Jan. 22, 1859, Amanda Bunnell; b. Dec. 10, 1833, at Hannibal, Orange county, N. Y.; daughter of Lemon and Thankful (Warner) Bunnell.

He received a common school and college education in Boston, Mass. They lived in Dakota county, Minn., since 1856, have had no church relations, were liberal Unitarians, non-resistant, anti-war, anti-capital, adhered permanently to no political party, were Prohibitionists and Woman Suffragist.

He was a master mechanic and merchant, retired since 1879, 5 feet 10 1/2 inches height, weight 165 pounds, light complexion, blue eyes.

Of Hastings, Minn.

CHILDREN

2200. Lemon Garrison, b. Jan. 10, 1861; d. Nov. 9, 1861.
2201. Albert Irving, b. Nov. 6, 1862.
2202. Melville Emerson, b. April 1, 1865.
2203. Charles Anthony, b. Feb. 2, 1872.

T 1394

George Bowers Reed, son of Anthony and Elizabeth (Bliss) Reed.

b. March 12, 1837, at Dighton, Mass.

m. Nov. 27, 1860, Sarah Zellah Sims; b. Feb. 10, 1841, at Waynesville, Ohio; daughter of Isaiah and Beulah Ann (Burr) Sims.

He removed west and lived in Minnesota.

Of Hastings, Minn.

CHILDREN

2204. Mary Emma, b. Oct. 20, 1861; d. Nov. 7, 1866.
2205. Elizabeth Beulah, b. March 17, 1864; m. April 26, 1883, Augustine Harris Owens.
2206. George Emerson, b. Sept. 30, 1865; m. May 15, 1887, Jennie Breed.
2207. Ralph Otho, b. March 14, 1871; d. Aug. 28, 1880.
2208. Alvin Bliss, b. Dec. 11, 1876.
2209. Zillah Mary, b. Sept. 20, 1878.

T 1403

Henry Lafayette Reed, son of Luther and Harriet (Heald) Reed.

b. July 5, 1843.

m. March 11, 1863, Lizzie A. Osgood.

Lives at present in Albany, N. Y.

Of Amsterdam, N. Y.

CHILDREN

2210. Hollie L., b. March 26, 1867; m. ———.
2211. Fred. Daniel, b. Oct. 25, 1869; m. ———.

T 1404

Alfred Wood Reed, son of Seth and Matilda (Smith) Reed.

b. Oct. 26, 1823, at Dighton, Mass.

m. June 14, 1846, Eunice Edson Paul; b. March 6, 1826, in Dighton, Mass.; daughter of Peter and Eunice Edson Paul.

Common school education, lived in Dighton until 1849, since then in New Boston, N. H., both members of the Baptist Church in New Boston; he was a man of strict integrity. Farmer and dealer in horses and cattle, also butcher, selectman in Dighton and in New Boston for several years, also assessor, Republican; all his children born in Dighton but Bertha, who was born in New Boston, N. H.

Of New Boston, N. H.

CHILDREN

2212. Clementine Eunice, b. June 26, 1847; m. June 19, 1867, Edwd. A. Hayden.
2213. Lucie Malvina Matilda, b. April 6, 1850; m. Sept. 28, 1870, John P. Briggs.
2214. Laura A., b. Sept. 17, 1853; d. Feb., 1896; m. Nov. 1, 1876, Daniel A. Stanley.
2215. Franklin Alfred, b. June 1, 1855; m. April 11, 1877, Georgia Church.
2216. Charles Warren Paul, b. June 17, 1857; d. ———; m. March 26, 1884, Annie B. Dolley.
2217. Wallace Chester, b. March 11, 1859; d. Sept. 26, 1859.
2218. Harris Herman Jackson, b. Aug. 31, 1865; m. April 27, 1887, Alice Kittredge.
2219. Nora Bertha Forbes, b. June 11, 1870; d. New Boston, N. H., unmarried.

T 1407

Joseph Brown Reed, son of Seth and Matilda (Brown) Reed.

b. May 12, 1830, at Dighton, Mass.

m. 1st. Nov. 27, 1856, Elizabeth E. T. Williams; b. Oct. 28, 1834, at Raynham, Mass.; d. Jan. 22, 1879, at South Hanson; daughter of Nathan and Lucy Hall Williams.

m. 2nd. Jan. 26, 1880, Mary Elizabeth Barker, daughter of Dea. Josiah Barker of South Hanson, Mass.

Claims that he and his father's family have always adhered to the original way of spelling the name (Read) only dropping the final e.

Joseph graduated at Bridgewater, Mass., Normal School in 1850, afterwards attended some higher institutions, but graduated at no other.

Elizabeth Williams was educated at Titicut Select School and Pierce Academy, Middleborough, Mass. They lived in Hingham, Fall River, Dighton, Providencetown, Middleborough, Brewster, Belchertown, and South Hanson, all in Massachusetts. They were members of the Baptist Church. He was a teacher for twenty years up to 1867, after that date he was pastor of Baptist churches in Brewster, Belcher-

town, South Hanson, Pueblo, Colo., and Lyme Centre, N. H. Has served in several towns on school boards, enlisted in the 58th Mass. Regiment Feb. 17, 1864, and served until that regiment was discharged July 26, 1865.

Ranked as a private, discharged as a sergeant. Accompanied the regiment through the Wilderness campaign and siege of Petersburg. Was one of the half dozen belonging to the 58th who kept with it at the front and was neither killed, wounded or taken prisoner, nor sent back to the hospital sick.

Witnessed all the important battles in that memorable campaign, and took part in most of them. Saw his regiment captured twice, but both times managed to escape capture himself. Was detailed or acted in various capacities, as clerk, chaplain, company commander, and once as commander of the remnant of the regiment. Was in the midst of more danger than can be described, but no harm came to him, for God chose to preserve him for his own purpose.

CHILD OF JOSEPH AND ELIZABETH

2220. **Frank Williams**, b. June 12, 1858; d. Aug. 3, 1875, at Fall River.

CHILDREN OF JOSEPH AND MARY

2221. **Joseph Barker**, b. Nov. 3, 1881, in S. Hanson.
2222. **William Alfred**, b. July 27, 1884, in Lyme Centre, N. H.
2223. **Albert Cushing**, b. March 29, 1887, in Lyme Centre, N. H.

M 1416d

Oliver Reed, son of Benjamin, Jr., and Anna (Chubbick) Reed.

b. Sept. 4, 1796, in Shutesbury, Mass.; d. May 4, 1865.
m. April 16, 1821, Lucy Sloan, of New Salem.

CHILDREN

2224. **Orphia A.**, b. Feb. 26, 1824; d. Oct. 11, 1844.
2225. **Laura E.**, b. Dec. 5, 1832; d. March 9, 1834.
2226. **Jannette A.**, b. April 23, 1838; m. Oct. 8, 1870, George G. Pratt.

M 1416f

Levi Reed, son of Benjamin, Jr., and Anna (Chubbick) Reed.

b. ———, 1802; d. April 14, 1870.

m. Dec. 25, 1822, Charlotte Burt, in Walpole, N. H.

CHILDREN

2227. Charlotte E., b. June 23, 1825; m. April 9, 1851, Andrew Burt.
2228. Levi J., b. May 27, 1827; m. Jane Watters.
2229. Benjamin B., b. May 29, 1829; unmarried.
2230. Lucy S., b. April 24, 1831; m. ——— Shaw.

M 1416i

Lyman Reed, son of Benjamin, Jr., and Anna (Chubbick) Reed.

b. Nov. 4, 1806.

m. Nov. 4, 1830, Philinda Bemis.

CHILDREN

2231. Charles Oliver, b. Aug. 14, 1831; m. March 20, 1867, Angeline B. Nash.
2232. Aaron Benjamin, b. Nov. 4, 1832; d. Dec. 21, 1895; m. Martha Swan.
2233. Stephen B., b. Aug. 13, 1834; m. Julia Dewey.
2234. Ellen A., b. Feb., 1837.
2235. Lyman F., b. July 5, 1839; m. Louisa Freedman.

M 1416j

Owen Reed (afterward called Joseph), son of Benjamin, Jr., and Anna (Chubbick) Reed.

b. ———.

m. 1st. Hannah ———, of West Newbury, Mass.

m. 2nd. May 26, 1864, Louisa Whittaker, of New Salem, Mass.

Was a soldier in the Civil War, and died at his home in Springfield, Vt., from disease contracted in the army.

Of Springfield, Vt.

CHILDREN BY SECOND WIFE

2236. William, b. ———; d. unmarried.
2237. Allen, b. ———; m. Ellen Slate; two daughters, one grandchild.

M 1426

Warren Atherton Reed, son of Warren and Mary (Atherton) Reed.

b. Feb. 17, 1809; d. Sept. 10, 1845.

m. May 1, 1831, Louisa Lyman; b. in Chester, Mass.; daughter of Timothy and Experience (Bardwell) Lyman.

CHILDREN

2238. Sarah Louisa, b. March 24, 1834; m. Jan. 31, 1856, Thomas Jefferson Dowty, of Fort Adams, Miss.
2239. Lyman Coleman, b. June 7, 1838, at New Orleans; m. July, 1870, Kate Bettison, of Louisville, Ky.
2240. George Sanford, b. 1841, in Northampton, Mass.; d. 1842.
2241. Ellen Loraine, b. July 19, 1843, at Northampton, Mass.; m. Aug. 30, 1864, Seth Lathrop, of South Hadley Falls, Mass.
2242. Elizabeth Warren, b. March 13, 1846; d. Nov. 13, 1876, at Dallas, Texas.

M 1427

Edwin Reed, son of Warren and Mary (Atherton) Reed.

b. June 7, 1811; d. June 18, 1876.

m. 1st. ———, Julia Porter.

m. 2nd. ———, Martha Bliss.

CHILDREN OF EDWIN AND JULIA

2243. Jane W., b. Feb. 26, 1832; m. Alonzo B. Reed.
2244. Frederick P., b. Feb. 26, 1836; m. Nov. 1, 1858, Emily W. Fenton; no children.
2245. Henry M., b. Feb. 16, 1838; m. Antoinette Pomeroy; no children.

CHILDREN OF EDWIN AND MARTHA

2246. Warren Atherton, b. Nov. 22, 1845; d. Jan. 2, 1899; m. Martha Dunklee.
2247. Frank, b. May 11, 1847; m. Katharine Morris.
2248. Martha I., b. Sept., 1843; d. 1891; m. William Cleveland.

M 1428

James Reed, son of Warren and Mary (Atherton) Reed.

b. Aug. 27, 1813; d. Nov. 14, 1873, at Savannah, Ga.

m. Lydia Woods, daughter of Martin Woods, of Whately, Mass.

Resided at Savannah, Ga.

CHILDREN

2249. Fanny, b. Feb. 25, 1836; d. Dec. 27, 1879; m. Sept. 7, 1854, Benoni G. Carpenter, of Brooklyn, N. Y.
2250. Mary Elizabeth, b. ———; d. young.
2251. Mary Elizabeth, b. 1840; m. 1859, Omar Holden, of San Diego, Cal.
2252. Martha, b. June 2, 1847; m. 1867, Capt. Eben Fenton.

M 1433

James Smith Reed, son of James and Sophronia (Smith) Reed.

b. at Deerfield, Mass., April 13, 1818; d. at Marion, Ohio, Jan. 26, 1896.

m. Dec. 7, 1841, Nancey A. Holmes.

CHILDREN

2253. Sophronia, b. Oct. 10, 1842, in Marion, O.; m. John Williams, of Chicago, Ill.
2254. James H., b. Oct. 6, 1844; d. April 21, 1900; m. 1st. Elizabeth Pardee; m. 2d. Elizabeth Pickering.
2255. Sarah Elizabeth, b. Feb. 14, 1852; m. James Delano, of New Bedford, Mass.

M 1438

Benjamin Franklin Reed, son of Simeon and Miranda (Morton) Reed.

b. Oct. 5, 1819, in Whately.

m. Nov. 26, 1845, Sarah W. Saunders, daughter of Deacon David Saunders of Whately. They resided in Whately until they separated, when he removed to Atlanta, Ga.

CHILDREN

2256. Jane Caroline, b. Feb. 12, 1846.
2257. Lucy Amy, b. Feb. 5, 1848.
2258. Mary Wheeler, b. Sept. 17, 1850; d. Nov. 3, 1852.
2259. Albert David, b. Oct. 17, 1852; m. Oct. 8, 1874, Rebecca C. Strong.

M 1439

George Washington Reed, son of Simeon and Miranda (Morton) Reed.

b. Feb. 23, 1825, in Whately.

m. Nov. 3, 1847, Helen M. Pease, daughter of Jabez Pease of Whately; b. Nov. 23, 1827; resided in Whately on the Ferguson place.

CHILDREN

2260. George Le Forrest, b. Sept. 17, 1848; d. young.
2261. Merrill Pease, b. Sept. 4, 1854; m. Nov. 29, 1879, Lillian E. Miner; m. 2nd. July 11, 1890, Margaret R. McCormick.
2262. Helen Marion, b. Aug. 15, 1857; m. Frank J. Waite.
2263. Curtis Babcock, b. Oct., 1865; d. young.

M 1442

Rev. Edwin Dwight Reed, son of Levi and Nancy (Pratt) Reed.

b. March 22, 1812, at Leverett, Mass.; d. April 28, 1888, at Georgetown, N. Y.

m. in 1838 Sophia Redfield, who was a descendant of John Alden.

He graduated from Hamilton Theological Seminary in 1838. Was a Baptist preacher, and over forty years a pastor, not a day out of a pastorate; was much beloved, and very successful in his ministry.

CHILDREN

2264. Frances Amelia, b. July 19, 1839; m. May 18, 1864, William A. Briggs, a Baptist preacher, and nephew of Gov. Briggs, of Mass. No children.
2265. Charlotte Maria, b. Dec. 28, 1840; m. March 14, 1872, Calvin Beach, of Blue Rapids, Kansas.
2266. Mary Elizabeth, b. Nov. 4, 1842; d. Aug. 24, 1864, at Cassville, N. Y.
2267. Franklin Kendrick, b. April 20, 1846, at Truxton, N. Y.; d. May 20, 1851, at same place.
2268. Harriet Emily, b. Sept. 10, 1849; d. Sept. 15, 1850.

M 1443

Franklin Levi Reed, son of Levi and Nancy (Pratt) Reed.

b. Nov. 7, 1814; d. Feb. 9, 1880.

m. Harriet A. Bennett; b. Jan. 14, 1825; d. Oct. 31, 1882.

CHILD

2269. Sanford Bennett, b. May 28, 1847; d. Oct. 26, 1877.

EIGHTH GENERATION

A 1452

Silas Richmond Reed, son of Silas and Mahala (Harris) Reed.

b. Oct. 9, 1818.

m. 1st. July 14, 1839, Josephine Bailey, of Duxbury.

m. 2nd. Aug. 22, 1841, Louisa Raymond, of Middleborough; m. by Rev. Wales Lewis.

Of Abington, Mass.

CHILD OF SILAS AND JOSEPHINE

2270. Mahala Harris, b. April 8, 1840; m. April 29, 1860, John J. Lewis; after the death of her mother she changed her name to Josephine.

CHILDREN OF SILAS AND LOUISA

2271. Horace L., b. in 1843; d. in 1844.
2272. Levi R., b. March 27, 1851; unmarried.
2273. Eldridge, b. July 7, 1853; unmarried.

A 1453

Edwin Harris Reed, son of Silas and Mahala (Harris) Reed.

b. Aug. 30, 1822; d. July 30, 1899.

m. ———, Mary Porter Reed, daughter of Adam Reed; she died Sept. 27, 1899.

Lived at Whitman, Washington street, near Abington Line.

Of Whitman.

CHILDREN

2274. Mary Mahala, b. July 24, 1848; m. David S. Smith.
2275. William F. S. A., b. March 30, 1851; unmarried.
2276. Emily P., b. June 24, 1853; unmarried.

A 1454

Salmon Reed, son of Silas and Mahala (Harris) Reed.

b. March 31, 1824.

m. 1st. July 7, 1849, Maria Sanford; d. April 7, 1857, at West Bridgewater.

m. 2nd. ———, Lucia Kidder (no children).

Of Abington, Mass.

CHILD OF SALMON AND MARIA

2277. Ella, b. in 1850; m. ———.

A 1455

Evander Reed, son of Silas and Mahala (Harris) Reed.
b. May 27, 1827.
m. 1st. June 3, 1849, Lucy C. Humble.
m. 2nd. Oct., 1851, Mary E. Jenkins.

Of Abington, Mass.

CHILD OF EVANDER AND LUCY

2278. Lucy, b. March 9, 1850; m. May 9, 1875, Phillip P. Trufant.

CHILDREN OF EVANDER AND MARY

2279. Aza Evander, b. Jan. 6, 1854; d. 1869.
2280. John Jenkins, b. Oct. 8, 1855; m. Dec. 3, 1875, Lizzie Wade.
2281. Lucia Wilkes, b. Oct. 12, 1862; m. Frank Wade; had one child, which died.

A 1456

Obadiah Reed, son of Obadiah and Deborah (Reed) Reed.
b. Jan. 30, 1832; d. Nov. 12, 1866.
m. Dec. 25, 1856, Sarah E. C. Noyes, of Ipswich, Mass.; she was born in Newburyport, Mass., Oct. 3, 1832, and died Nov. 10, 1887.

Of Ipswich, Mass.

CHILDREN

2282. Earnest Howard, b. April 25, 1858; m. June 29, 1881, Mary E. Sherburn.
2283. Lizzie Bell, b. Jan. 12, 1865; m. Jan. 11, 1887, Arthur Franklin Tilton.

A 1460

Edward Richmond Reed, son of Israel and Louisa (Humble) Reed.
b. Aug. 19, 1839.
m. June 6, 1869, Ella L. Wales.

CHILDREN

2284. Edward Everett, b. July 2, 1874.
2285. Mary Louisa, b. May 17, 1877.

A 1461

Salmon Willson Reed, son of Israel and Louisa (Humble) Reed.

b. Feb. 24, 1847.

m. Aug. 11, 1873, Clara Ella Keene.

CHILD

2286. Bradford Willson, b. Oct. 11, 1878.

A 1466

Harvey Williams Reed, son of Matthew and Thirza (Harris) Reed.

b. Feb. 14, 1831; d. April 26, 1861.

m. Feb. 16, 1860, Helen M. Tirrell.

CHILD

2287. Harry Irving, b. June 20, 1860; d. Nov. 29, 1883; m. Jan. 1883, Harriet Louisa Seymore.

A 1467

Hiram Farwell Reed, son of Matthew and Thirza (Harris) Reed.

b. April 29, 1833.

m. 1st. Emily J. Loud Reed, April 25, 1857.

m. 2nd. June 11, 1874, Selina Huntington Nash.

Of Abington, Mass.

CHILDREN OF HIRAM AND EMILY

2288. William Durant, b. June 8, 1859, in Philadelphia, Pa.; m. Jan. 22, 1885, Alice Brown, of Pembroke, Mass.
2289. Charles Edward, b. 1861, in S. Weymouth; d. in infancy.
2290. Mary Wallace, b. March 20, 1865, in Abington; m. Sept. 6, 1881, James Fobert, of Italy.

A 1469

Matthew Gordon Reed, son of Matthew and Thirza (Harris) Reed.

b. Feb. 11, 1837; d. April 17, 1896.

m. May 1, 1861, Harriet Maria Bicknell, of East Weymouth.

CHILDREN

2291. Lillian Franklin, b. May 15, 1862; d. Oct., 1878.
2292. Emma Gordon, b. ———.
2293. Frank Gordon, b. Aug. 29, 1869; m. Sept. 23, 1893, Sarah Lillian Belcher, of E. Weymouth.
2294. Jennie Beatrice, b. Jan. 15, 1876.
2295. Annie Ardell, b. May 6, 1878; m. June 19, 1895, William Henry Pierce.

A 1472

Henry Lendall Reed, son of Matthew and Thirza (Harris) Reed.

b. March 28, 1842.

m. Sept. 17, 1864, Susan Adelaide Pratt.

CHILDREN

2296. Henry Morton, b. July 3, 1866; m. Jan. 10, 1889, Nettie Nash, of Abington.
2297. Warren Lendall, b. March 21, 1870; d. April 4, 1888.
2298. Alton Maltiah, b. Nov. 13, 1872; d. Aug. 19, 1873.
2299. Arthur Watson, b. July 1, 1877.
2300. Susie Adelaide, b. April 15, 1882.
2301. Alice Minnie, b. Sept. 26, 1887.

A 1473

Nahum Augustus Reed, son of Matthew and Thirza (Harris) Reed.

b. Feb. 4, 1844.

m. 1st. June 7, 1868, Isabella Frances Bicknell, of East Weymouth.

m. 2nd. April 1, 1888, Sarah Whitman Spilsted, of East Weymouth.

CHILDREN OF NAHUM AND ISABELLA

2302. Henry Bicknell, b. July 14, 1869; m. Oct. 5, 1892, Florence Talbot.
2303. Edith Harris, b. Oct. 19, 1870.
2304. George Augustus, b. Nov. 26, 1872; m. Jan. 10, 1891, Clara Howard Bates, of S. Weymouth.

CHILDREN OF NAHUM AND SARAH

2305. Harold Whitman, b. April 8, 1889.
2306. Harris Spilsted, b. Feb. 5, 1892.

A 1477

Alonzo H. Reed, son of Albert and Polly (Reynolds) Reed.

b. ———.

m. June 28, 1866, Olive Amelia Jacobs, daughter of Hosea Stodder and Lucy A. (Waterman) Jacobs; she was born Aug. 10, 1841; died June 7, 1877.

CHILD

2307. Charles Albert, b. ———; m. ———; lives N. Main street, Brockton, Mass.

A 1483

Francis Baylies Reed, son of Harvey and Mary Thaxter (Nash) Reed.

b. Dec. 30, 1844.

m. May 28, 1879, Clara Raymond, daughter of George F. and Susan W. (Burrell) Raymond.

He is a jeweler and resides in East Weymouth, Mass.

CHILD

2308. Mary Thaxter, b. Dec. 17, 1882.

A 1492

Lucius Alston Reed, son of Lucius and Lydia (Shaw) Reed.

b. Feb. 6, 1847.

m. June 7, 1877, Emma Lincoln Reynolds.

CHILDREN

2309. Carl Burton, b. Aug. 12, 1878; d. July 24, 1897.
2310. Mabel Lincoln, b. Oct. 20, 1880.

A 1501

John Porter Reed, son of John P. and Polly (Ramsdale) Reed.

b. July 29, 1819.

m. ———, Adaline Brown.

Lived in East Bridgewater, Mass.

CHILDREN

2311. Amelia, b. ———.
2312. Albion B., b. ———.

A 1502

Lloyd Watson Reed, son of John P. and Polly (Ramsdale) Reed.

b. Jan. 7, 1822.

m. ———, Lucy Bryant, daughter of Cephas and Lucy (Lincoln) Bryant, of Hingham.

Lived at South Abington, Mass.

A 1504

Thomas Baldwin Reed, son of John P. and Polly (Ramsdale) Reed.

b. July 29, 1827.

m. ———, Olive B. Perkins.

Lived at East Boston, Mass.

CHILDREN

2313. Herbert W., b. Feb. 14, 1852.
2314. Nathan Franklin, b. Sept. 4, 1856.
2315. A son, b. April 6, 1858.

A 1506

Homan Thaxter Reed, son of Thaxter and Mehetable (Brown) Reed.

b. Aug. 5, 1833, at South Abington, Mass.

m. 1st. Nov., 1854, Caroline Jenkins; b. June —, 1832, in East Bridgewater; d. Dec., 1855; daughter of Marion and Betsy Gannett (Reed) Jenkins.

m. 2nd. Dec. 25, 1857, Maria L. Soule; b. in South Abington, daughter of James and Leah (Bennett) Soule.

Newton Center and Newton Highlands, of Newton, Mass.

CHILDREN OF HOMAN AND MARIA

2316. Homan Erfurth, b. Sept. 11, 1860, in S. Abington; m. July, 1880, Frances A. Leach.
2317. Amelia Soule, b. Jan. 18, 1868, in Havilah, Cal.; d. Oct. 31, 1870, at Taunton, Mass.
2318. Alice Thaxter, b. March 3, 1872, in Boston, Mass.
2319. Ethel Gardner, b. Dec. 16, 1877, at Boston, Mass.

A 1508

George Augustus Reed, son of Ebenezer and Patience (Penniman) Reed.

b. Oct. 3, 1831.

m. ———, Susan Maria Gurney, daughter of Chandler and Sally (Vining) Gurney; b. Aug. 20, 1833.

Of East Bridgewater, Mass.

Removed later to Whitman, where he has a dry goods store.

CHILD

2320. Anna Josephine, b. Feb. 6, 1855; m. Feb. 9, 1875, Elmer W. Noyes.

A 1509

William Henry Reed, son of Ebenezer and Patience (Penniman) Reed.

b. April 12, 1833.

m. Feb. 2, 1859, Lucy Ann Dyer, daughter of James B. and Lucy White (Hersey) Dyer.

Of Whitman, Mass.

CHILDREN

2321. Charles Franklin, b. in Abington, Nov. 19, 1860; m. Feb. 5, 1891, Alice M. Gurney.

2322. William Ashton, b. in Abington, April 26, 1862; d. in Whitman, April 5, 1863.

2323. Edward Augustus, b. in Abington, Sept. 7, 1863.

A 1516

Newton Briggs Reed, son of James A. and Lydia M. (Stockton) Reed.

b. Aug. 22, 1861.

m. May 28, 1885, Rachel Blessing.

Resides in Albany, N. Y., is assistant treasurer of the Hudson River Telephone Company; is a solo tenor singer and sang in the Clinton Square Presbyterian Church choir.

Of Albany, N. Y.

CHILD

2324. Lydia Stockton, b. June 20, 1886.

BORN - 1788
SUSANNA (NOYES) WIFE OF JOSHUA
E. (NORTON)
SAMUEL W.
IDA M.
CHARLES K.
CARRIE (BOSWORTH)
EVA (HIMES)
CHESTER A.
BERTHA M.
REED
MONA A.
6th - 7th
8th - 9th
GENERATIONS

A 1523

Charles Keller Reed, son of Samuel W. and Adaline (Norton) Reed.

b. April 20, 1851, at Huntington, Mass.

m. July 6, 1873, Carrie S. Bosworth; b. May 21, 1852, at Barrington, R. I., only daughter of Leonard Smith Bosworth (Lumber and Coal Merchant) and Laura Ann (Dunn) Bosworth, b. at Andover, Mass.

Taxidermist and dealer in naturalists' supplies; also inventor of a patent oval convex glass for covering birds. His place of business is at 75 Thomas street, Worcester, Mass.

Of Worcester, Mass.

CHILDREN

2325. Bertha May, b. March 16, 1874.
2326. Chester Albert, b. Jan. 10, 1873; m. June 6, 1900, Eva M. Himes.
2327. Ralph Warner, b. Feb. 26, 1878; d. April 7, 1878.
2328. Mona Alma, b. July 16, 1892.

A 1530

Seth Dean Reed, son of Seth and Sally (Blanchard) Reed.

b. June 19, 1840.

m. 1st. Sarah Isabelle McConihe, daughter of James and Sylvia (Raymond) McConihe.

m. 2nd. July 10, 1886, Annie V. Grant Bigelow, daughter of John C. and Annie (Mortemore) Grant; b. in England.

Sarah Isabelle McConihe was born in Middleborough, Mass., Dec. 19, 1838, and died Sept. 19, 1900.

Of Abington, Mass.

CHILDREN

2329. Alice Weston, b. Abington, Feb. 4, 1859; d. Jan. 1, 1888; m. Nathaniel E. Arnold.
2330. An infant son, b. Abington, Aug. 26, 1860; d. there Sept. 19, 1879.
2331. Emma Estelle, b. Sept. 20, 1864; d. Nov. 7, 1885.
2332. Marie Antoinette, b. Jan. 28, 1868; m. Benjamin E. Stanley.
2333. Agnes Isabelle, b. March 19, 1873; d. Dec. 26, 1889.

A 1573

Henry Lyman Reed, son of William and Elizabeth Kent (Sayre) Reed.

b. Sept. 15, 1851.

m. Oct. 14, 1875, Lizzie S. McLean.

Of Greenfield, Mass.

CHILD

2334. Jennie, b. 1896.

A 1578

Charles Andrew Reed, son of Samuel and Caroline (Nash) Reed.

b. June 16, 1836.

m. 1st. June 27, 1870, Welthea (Noean) Dean, of Taunton; she died June 30, 1884.

m. 2nd. June —, 1889, Myra L. Dean, sister of his first wife.

He graduated at Amherst College in 1856; taught school and was principal of Hanover Academy in 1858. Studied law in Taunton and practiced his profession there after he graduated. He was representative from Taunton in the General Court in 1881-2. He was a member of the State Senate in 1886-7, was a member of the committee to revise statutes in 1882.

Of Taunton, Mass.

CHILDREN OF CHARLES AND WELTHEA

2335. Silas Dean, b. June 25, 1872.

2336. Frances A., b. 1875; m. Dec., 1898, Walter B. Clark, of Pawtucket, R. I. They have one child, Edwin Reed Clark.

A 1580

George Milton Reed, son of Samuel and Caroline (Nash) Reed.

b. Jan. 8, 1840.

Graduated at Amherst College in 1862; studied law and practiced in Boston, became Associate Justice of Municipal Court for Dorchester, District of Boston.

Of Boston, Mass.

A 1582

Samuel Willard Reed, son of Samuel and Caroline (Nash) Reed.

b. Dec. 31, 1849.

He studied law at Taunton with his brother, Charles A. Reed; was secretary of Weymouth Historical Society, the object of which is to gather material relative to the history of the town and of Weymouth families.

Of Weymouth, Mass.

A 1584

John Reed, son of John and Emma (Dill) Reed.

b. Dec. 7, 1822; d. Dec. 18, 1899.

m. Dec. 25, 1853, Mary Elizabeth Pope, daughter of William and Mary (Dill) Pope.

Resides in Hull, Mass. He was one of the most prominent men of that section. He was a selectman for many years, besides filling many other prominent offices. He was a well-known Prohibitionist. He leaves a widow and four daughters.

CHILDREN

2337. John Wesley, b. Dec. 2, 1854; d. Jan. 18, 1855.
2338. Harriet Swain, b. May 13, 1856.
2339. Annie Clark, b. May 7, 1857; d. Dec. 14, 1857.
2340. Horace Edgar, b. Oct. 6, 1859; d. Nov. 25, 1859.
2341. Fannie Sturges Tudor, b. May 5, 1865; m. Oct. 19, 1887, Francis S. James.
2342. Jane Binney Tower, b. July 17, 1866; m. Oct. 30, 1889, Charles H. B. Waterhouse.
2343. Mary Cora, b. Oct. 22, 1867; m. Oct. 15, 1890, G. Frank Austin.
2344. Ira Daniel, b. Feb. 21, 1870; d. March 10, 1870.
2345. Bertie, b. Nov. 14, 1872; d. Nov. 16, 1872.

A 1585

Daniel Dill Reed, son of John and Emma (Dill) Reed.

b. Jan. 13, 1827.

m. July 14, 1852, Esther B. L. Rachford, daughter of Thomas and Anna Rachford, of Halifax.

Of Scituate, Mass.

CHILDREN

2346. Esther Sophia, b. June 12, 1854.
2347. Emma Jane Binney, b. March 3, 1856.

A 1593

George Williams **Reed**, son of Phillip and Saphira (Howland) Reed.

b. Sept. 29, 1826.

m. June 18, 1846, Lucy Ann Cook, daughter of Asa and Pamelia (Hersey) Cook; b. June 17, 1827.

Of South Abington, Mass.

George W. Reed enlisted in Company K, 7th Mass. Vol. Infantry, April 27, 1861. Was commissioned as 1st Lieut., was ordered into camp June 13, 1861, mustered in June 15, 1861. Left camp for Washington July 12, 1861. Was stationed in Washington until March, 1862. Served through the Peninsula Campaign. In battles of Williamsburg, Fair Oaks, Glendale Farm, Malvern Hill, and during the Seven Days before Richmond, Va. After the battle of Williamsburg, Genl. Devens in command of the brigade, mentioned him very flatteringly in his report August 27, 1862. He was struck down with malaria, sent to Davids Island, N. Y. harbor, was discharged from the hospital at his own request, and sent to Washington with a detachment of convalescents. He was detailed for duty at the convalescent camp, then transferred to paroled prisoners camp, was in command the first fortnight. In November, 1862, he sent in his resignation on account of continued ill health, and on Dec. 17, 1862, he received an honorable discharge, dated Dec. 6, 1862. He was promoted captain August 1, 1861. Mr. Reed also represented the town of Abington at the General Court.

CHILDREN

2348. George Bancroft, b. April 13, 1847; m. Margaret Kennedy.
2349. Florence Augusta, b. Sept. 9, 1849; m. Thomas Wineborn.

2350. Franklin W., b. May 30, 1852; went to California, 1874; was not heard from after 1876.
2351. Lucy Ann, b. July 5, 1854; m. Edgar Benson.
2352. Oliver Henley, b. March 4, 1856; d. 1890, was drowned.
2353. Ella M., b. April, 1858; m. Frank Caswell.
2354. Henry W., b. 1860; moved to Georgia, and has a family.

A 1596

George A. Reed, son of Isaac and his first wife, ———, Reed.
b. 1832.
m. Dec., 1858, Nancy Watson Brown.
Reside in Whitman, Mass.

CHILD

2355. Jennie P., b. Aug. 21, 1869; m. Albert M. Harding.

A 1600

Clinton W. Reed, son of Nahum and Maria (Wetherell) Reed.
b. Sept. 4, 1842.
m. Jan. 1, 1868, Mehetable Nash ~~Gurney~~.

He resided in Whitman, Mass. Was a corporal in 20th Co., unattached from Aug. 11, 1864. (See His. of Abington, p. 311.)

CHILDREN

2356. Harry S., b. March 29, 1869; m. May 15, 1887, Elva Etta Totman.
2357. Nahum, b. May 27, 1873; m. April 27, 1898, Marion Leslie Soule.
2358. Carl A., b. June 4, 1882.

A 1601

Nahum S. Reed, son of Nahum and Maria (Witherell) Reed.
b. May 6, 1845.
m. Nov. 4, 1869, Mary E. Ferris. No children.

They reside in Waterville, N. Y.

Of Waterville, N. Y.

A 1603

Frank Austin Reed, son of Nahum and Maria (Witherell) Reed.

b. July, 1852.

m. Oct. 27, 1878, Alberta Thompson.

They reside in Brockton, Mass.

CHILD

2359. Dwight Bickford, b. July 14, 1886.

A 1610

Clarence Derwood Reed, son of James Thaxter and Elizabeth Ann (Keith) Reed.

b. March 29, 1857.

m. Dec. 25, 1889, Harriet Davis, of North Easton, Mass. Reside at Whitman, Mass.

CHILDREN

2360. Ruth Severance, b. Nov. 30, 1890.
2361. Clarence Searles, b. May 25, 1894.
2362. Rachel, b. July 13, 1899.

A 1619

Marshall Reed, son of Nathaniel and Betsy M. (Bartlett) Reed.

b. Sept. 13, 1841.

m. Sept. 28, 1863, Helen M. Penniman, daughter of George and Nancy (Dyer) Penniman; b. Feb. 15, 1841.

CHILDREN

2363. Lizzie M., b. S. Abington, Oct. 29, 1866; m. Jan. 22, 1896. Amasa Tucker.
2364. George E., b. S. Abington, May 20, 1868; d. June 26, 1868.
2365. Everett B., b. at Abington, Nov. 10, 1870; unmarried.
2366. William D., b. S. Abington, Oct. 1, 1872; d. Aug. 2, 1873.

A 1631

Andrew Hobart Reed, son of Oakes and Lettice Barker (Hobart) Reed.

b. May 15, 1833; d. May 15, 1869, at East Bridgewater.

m. —, 1856, Elizabeth E. Keene, daughter of Nahum Keene.

Of East Bridgewater, Mass.

CHILDREN

All born at E. Bridgewater, Mass.

2367. Catharine Parris, b. April, 1857; d. young.
2368. Edith Hobart, b. April, 1859; m. Wyman Clapp.
2369. Everett Elsworth, b. June, 1861; d. April 19, 1877.
2370. Anna Keene, b. July 6, 1863; m. John Lawrence.
2371. Eliza W., b. June 19, 1865; m. James Ryder.

A 1635

Calvin Payson Reed, son of Oakes and Lettice Barker (Hobart) Reed.

b. Nov. 2, 1844, at East Bridgewater, Mass.

m. June 25, 1877, Cora Maria Beal, daughter of Bradford Wentworth and Catharine O'Neal Beal. She was born at Abington, Sept. 14, 1857.

Of Whitman, Mass.

He is an engineer, and has run a stationary engine for over forty years, and is now running the engine at the power station in Whitman, for Brockton Street Railway Company.

CHILDREN

All born at S. Abington, Mass.

2372. Everett Hobart, b. Dec. 23, 1879.
2373. Ethel Wentworth, b. Nov. 20, 1882.
2374. Aileen Payson, b. July 14, 1885.

A 1638

Henry Dyer Reed, son of Lucius and Celina (Dyer) Reed.

b. Feb. 4, 1842.

m. Jan 21, 1875, Louisa Parker, of Whitman, Mass.

Of Whitman, Mass.

CHILDREN

2375. Charlotte Stetson, b. Jan. 23, 1876.
2376. Lucy Dyer, b. Dec. 19, 1879.
2377. Celina Dyer, b. Nov. 19, 1885.

A 1639

Aaron Alden Reed, son of Aaron and Hannah (Fullerton) Reed.

b. April 25, 1839.

m. July 23, 1876, Eunice Maria Slack.

Of Whitman, Mass.

Was a private in Company "E" 4th Mass. Volunteer Inf. Was wounded and lost a leg in the service.

CHILDREN

2378. Florence Marin, b. Feb. 2, 1878.
2379. Alden Roy, b. Dec. 5, 1879.

A 1641

Daniel Lyman Reed, son of Daniel and Mary Ann (Smith) Reed.

b. April 7, 1847.

m. 1st. ———, Lucia Whitman.

m. 2nd. ———, Marcia Edson.

Of Whitman, Mass.

No children.

A 1642

Forrest Samuel Reed, son of Daniel and Mary Ann (Smith) Reed.

b. Oct. 9, 1852.

m. ———, Louie Holbrook.

Of Whitman, Mass.

No children.

A 1652

Horatio G. H. Reed, son of Horatio G. and Wealthy (———) Reed.

b. April 12, 1828, in Mansfield.

m. April 2, 1850, Esther M. Cole.

Of Marshfield, Mass.

A 1661

Judge Warren Augustus Reed, son of Augustus and Laura Ann (Leach) Reed.

b. July 1, 1851, in Boston.

m. Dec. 3, 1878, Nellie A. Crocker, daughter of Bradford Lincoln and Mary (Perkins) Crocker.

Full sketch of him in History of Brockton, Mass.

Judge Warren Augustus Reed filled many important positions in Brockton, Mass., taking a great interest in education and the progress of the town and is at present its police justice.

CHILDREN

2380. Nellie, b. in Boston, March 30, 1880; d. April 5, 1880.
2381. Lawrence Bradford, b. in Boston, Feb. 22, 1881.
2382. Robert, } b. in Brockton, March 2, 1886; d. March 4, 1886.
2383. Malcolm, }
2384. Warren Augustus, b. Aug. 20, 1887; d. April 21, 1890.
2385. Clarence Crocker, b. in Brockton, Aug. 30, 1889.
2386. Mildred, b. Sept. 2, 1890; d. Oct. 1, 1890.

A 1669

William A. Reed, son of William Q. and Harriet (Leach) Reed.

b. Oct. 21, 1841, in Borne county, Ind.

m. March 11, 1869, Katie Hoyt, of Jefferson county, Pa. They were married in Rock county, Wis.

He served in Company "H" 42nd Wisconsin Infantry.

CHILDREN

2387. Frank D., b. Dec. 8, 1869, in Rock Co., Wis.
2388. Cora E., b. March 17, 1872, in Merrick Co., Neb.; d. Dec. 12, 1874.
2389. George, b. Jan. 15, 1876, in Chequest Co., Iowa.
2390. Arthur, b. Sept. 7, 1877, in Rock Co., Wis.
2391. Lottie, b. Jan. 8, 1880, in Rock Co., Wis.

A 1672

Cyrus Joy Reed, son of Prentice J. and Jedidah (Kingsbury) Reed.

b. June 20, 1836.

m. ———, 1864, Annette Smith, of Newbury, N. Y.; were married in Independence, Iowa.

Was a private in Company "E" 5th Iowa Infantry Regt., during the War of the Rebellion.

CHILDREN

2392. Grace Irene, b. April 2, 1869, in Dubuque, Iowa.
2393. Samuel, b. 1873, in Dubuque, Iowa.

A 1673

Samuel A. Reed, son of Prentice J. and Jedidah (Kingsbury) Reed.

b. Dec. 2, 1838; d. July 1, 1890.

m. ———.

Was Capt. of Co. "A" 5th Iowa Regt. in the War of the Rebellion. The "National Tribune" of Washington says: "He is in the Insane Hospital at Independence, Iowa, from the effects of a rebel bullet, at Champion Hill. As he raised his head to fire, he lost consciousness. He came to the next morning, when a comrade told him that he had been picked up on the field for dead and put into a trench with others and was about to be covered up, when a twitching of the limbs was noticed, and he was taken out; a rather close call he thinks. He was promoted to a captaincy, and held his position throughout the rest of the war, but while he lives he will suffer from the rebel lead."

For a while after Samuel returned home from the war he studied law, but owing to improper treatment of the wound in his head, his brain became affected and his reason tottered and he was sent to the hospital as before stated, where he died July 1, 1890.

A 1675

Benjamin K. Reed, son of Prentice J. and Jedidah (Kingsbury) Reed.

b. June 19, 1843, in Euclid, Ohio.

m. June 2, 1881, Philomena Digman, in Joliet, Ill.

CHILDREN

2394. Annie Caroline, b. Oct. 1, 1881, in Denver, Colo.; d. Jan. 17, 1883.
2395. Gertrude, b. Jan. 17, 1884, in Denver, Colo.

A 1680

Samuel Clark Reed, son of Hiram Joseph and Eliza (Keyes) Reed.

b. Jan. 21, 1852.

m. Oct. 17, 1884, Julia Baker; b. April 6, 1861.

CHILDREN

2396. Nellie Jane, b. April 7, 1886.
2397. Hiram Clark, b. Oct. 5, 1888.

A 1685

Fordyce Daniel Reed, son of Daniel W. and Electa (Hubbard) Reed.

b. Dec. 21, 1850, in Orleans county, N. Y.

m. Feb. 8, 1875, Mina Zilpha Andrus; b. July 17, 1853, in Watson, Mich.

Of Allegan, Mich.

CHILDREN

2398. Sarah Millie, b. July 5, 1879, in Watson, Mich.
2399. Daniel Williams, b. Nov. 2, 1881, in Watson, Mich.
2400. May Electa, b. Sept. 12, 1883, in Watson, Mich.
2401. Martin John, b. Jan. 28, 1886, in Watson, Mich.

A 1686

Elijah Reed, son of Horace and Mahalah (Hitchcock) Reed.

b. ———, 1842.

m. ———.

He went to Kansas, married and died leaving two children, of whom there is no trace. I shall have to record them as a "lost tribe."

A 1688

Lyman A. Reed, son of Napoleon B. and Czarina Hall (Glazier) Reed.

b. Jan. 2, 1840, in Orleans county, New York.

m. 1st. Jan. 28, 1858, Elizabeth M. Tutner; b. Aug. 12, 1836, in Montgomery county, N. Y.; d. June 30, 1861.

m. 2nd. April 15, 1865, Rachel Hoare, of Dorchestershire, Eng.; b. March 4, 1842.

He enlisted as a private in Co. "C" 105th N. Y. Infantry; was taken prisoner at the Weldon R. R. Aug. 18, 1864, confined at Petersburg, Richmond, Belle Isle, and Salisbury, N. C. Resided in 1888 at Cooper, Mich.

CHILDREN

2402. Eva Rosalie, b. June 10, 1866, in Orleans Co., N. Y.; d. Dec. 2, 1866.
2403. Elsie C., b. Oct. 5, 1867, in Orleans Co., N. Y.
2404. Charles Fred., b. Aug. 6, 1870, in Kalamazoo, Mich.

A 1691

Napoleon B. Reed, Jr., son of Napoleon and Czarina Hall (Glazier) Reed.

b. Feb. 13, 1846.

m. 1st. March 19, 1868, Marian Phillips, of Monroe county, N. Y.; b. May 6, 1847; d. Feb. 6, 1883.

m. 2nd. Sept. 13, 1885, Mrs. Nettie Sutherland; b. June 3,1848.

CHILDREN

2405. George N., b. June 29, 1869; d. Jan. 1, 1876.
2406. Hattie H., b. Feb. 17, 1871.
2407. Czarina R., b. Oct. 13, 1872.
2408. Marion B., b. Feb. 9, 1875, in Michigan.
2409. Georgiana P., b. July 4, 1877.

A 1692

Daniel E. Reed, son of Napoleon B. and Czarina Hall (Glazier) Reed.

b. Feb. 8, 1851, in Orleans county, N. Y.

m. April 2, 1871, Emeline Hayes, of Kalamazoo county, Mich. Married in Mich.

CHILDREN

All born in Kalamazoo Co., Mich.

2410. Alva N., b. April 1, 1873; d. April 29, 1873.
2411. Minnie, b. April 18, 1874.
2412. John W., b. Feb. 28, 1878.
2413. Emeline M., b. Feb. 20, 1880.

A 1699

Rev. Amer Alanson Reed, son of Samuel and Sarah M. (Partridge) Reed.

b. Dec. 22, 1851, in Orleans county, N. Y.

m. Sept. 16, 1875, Libbie Jessie Simmons; b. Feb. 9, 1856. Married in Orleans county, N. Y.

CHILDREN

2414. Leonard Amer, b. July 24, 1877, in Farnham, Va.; d. Sept. 18, 1878.
2415. Jesse Samuel, b. March 10, 1879, in Alleghany Co., N. Y.
2416. Carrie Belle, b. Sept. 15, 1880, in Alleghany Co., N. Y.
2417. Etta Malina, b. Feb. 13, 1882, in Alleghany Co., N. Y.
2418. Grace Myrta, b. Feb. 12, 1884, in Alleghany Co., N. Y.
2419. William Haynes, b. 1890, in Wyoming Co., N. Y.

A 1700

Orra Partridge Reed, son of Samuel and Sarah M. (Partridge) Reed.

b. Dec. 22, 1853, in Orleans county, N. Y.

m. Dec. 31, 1878, Ida B. Hall; b. July 27, 1857.

CHILDREN

2420. Helen M., b. Nov. 17, 1879, in Orleans Co., N. Y.
2421. Mina M., b. Nov. 6, 1883, in Orleans Co., N. Y.

A 1711

Waldo Simeon Reed, son of Hiram S. and Amanda (Noyes) Reed.

b. Feb. 2, 1847.

m. May 1, 1878, Luella Annette Miller; b. Sept. 23, 1857, in Hamburg, N. Y.

Married in Conneaut, Ohio.

CHILDREN

2422. Fred. Hiram, b. April 14, 1879, in Erie Co., Pa.
2423. Ralph Waldo, b. Oct. 8, 1882, in Erie Co., Pa.
2424. Grace Margaret, b. July 12, 1888, in Erie Co., Pa.

A 1713

Hiram Elwin Reed, son of Hiram S. and Amanda (Noyes) Reed.

b. Feb. 14, 1855, in Erie county, Pa.

m. ———, Hattie E. Allen; b. Aug. 12, 1860, in Conneaut, Ohio.

CHILDREN

2425. Bessie Amanda, b. April 14, 1881, in Cheyenne Co., Neb.
2426. Hiram Karl, b. July 9, 1883, in Cheyenne Co., Neb.
2427. Josie, b. Oct. 12, 1886, in Rock Creek, W. T.; d. Aug. 3, 1887.
2428. Sophia May, b. Jan. 16, 1887, in Cheyenne Co., Neb.

A 1714

Noyes Willard Reed, son of Hiram S. and Amanda (Noyes) Reed.

b. Sept. 25, 1857, in Erie county, Pa.

m. Dec. 28, 1887, Addie Florence McHenry; b. April 3, 1863, in Seneca county, Ohio.

Married at Chippewa Lake, Mich.

CHILDREN

2429. Hazel M., b. Sept. 30, 1888, in Erie Co., Pa.

A 1722

George H. Reed, son of Simeon S. and Adaline (Olds) Reed.

b. May 19, 1845, in Geauga county, Ohio.

m. June 16, 1869, Ella S. Colton; b. May 27, 1854, in St. Albans, Vermont.

Married in Dodge county, Wis.

CHILDREN

2430. Nellie May, b. Dec. 14, 1870, in Rock Co., Wis.
2431. Charles Dwight, b. Dec. 16, 1873, in Monroe Co., Wis.
2432. Bert Jay, b. July 18, 1877, in Martin Co., Minn.; d. July 5, 1889.

A 1724

Franklin Dwight Reed, son of Simeon S. and Adaline (Olds) Reed.

b. Sept. 24, 1851, in Rock county, Wis.

m. Feb. 18, 1873, Mary E. Speelman; b. Nov. 7, 1851, in Montgomery county, Ohio.

Married in Douglas county, Ill.

CHILDREN

2433. Florence, b. Aug. 29, 1874, in Rock Co., Wis.
2434. Jennie, b. Feb. 1, 1877, in Rock Co., Wis.
2435. Charles Joseph, b. Feb. 24, 1880, in Rock Co., Wis.
2436. Carrie, b. Aug. 18, 1884, in Rock Co., Wis.

A 1734

Elon Joseph Reed, son of Freeman Williams and R. Lucina (Cole) Reed.

b. Oct. 6, 1852, in Rock county, Wis.

m. Jan. 19, 1879, Isabella S. La Plant; b. May 7, 1863. in Olmstead county, Minn.

Married in Minnesota.

CHILDREN

2437. Joseph Freeman, b. Jan. 6, 1880, in Douglas Co., Minn.
2438. Bessie Isabel, b. Aug. 7, 1882, in Todd Co., Minn.
2439. Levina Blanche, b. Feb. 13, 1887, in Freeborn Co., Minn.
2440. Paul Marion, b. April 16, 1889.
2441. Mildred Joy, b. Sept. 26, 1896.
2442. Esther Fay, b. Aug. 1, 1899.

A 1740

Joseph Frank Reed, son of Rev. Joseph Wiram and Martha J. (Howard) Reed.

b. Feb. 9, 1866, in Richland county, Wis.

m. Jan 28, 1893, Sarepta E. Bundy; b. ———, 1866, in Vernon county, Wis.

A 1741

Joseph E. Reed, son of Daniel and Huldah E. (Damm) Reed.

b. Aug. 18, 1874, in Le Sueur county, Maine.

m. Oct. 23, 1895, Augusta Marzinske.

CHILDREN

2443. Charles P., b. May 25, 1896.
2444. Esther, b. June 4, 1898.
2445. Roy Otto, b. March 10, 1900.

A 1748

Frank De White Reed, son of Elisha Rice and Isabelle Owen (Brown) Reed.

b. July 15, 1869, in Washington, D. C.

m. June 28, 1894, Sarah Storm.

CHILD

2446. Sarah Isabelle, b. Aug. 13, 1895; d. Feb. 2, 1899.

A 1763

William Nelson Reed, Jr., son of William and Lucy Maria (Stevens) Reed.

b. Jan. 31, 1848.

m. April 27, 1871, Charlotte Louisa Daniels, of Roxbury, Mass., who was born Dec. 21, 1849.

Their children were all born in Roxbury, Mass.

CHILDREN

2447. Alice Gertrude, b. June 27, 1875.
2448. Henrietta Lillian, b. Aug. 26, 1878.
2449. Lucinda Daniels, b. May 3, 1880.
2450. Florence Elizabeth, b. Jan. 18, 1888.

A 1770

George Fernald Reed, son of David Keyes and Caroline A. (Fernald) Reed.

b. Sept. 20, 1862, at Roxbury, Mass.

m. Sept. 22, 1891, Rebecca Frances Hovey, daughter of Col. Charles H. Hovey.

Of Roxbury, Mass.

In business with his father under the firm name of D. K. Reed & Son. The family now reside at Wellsley Hills.

CHILDREN

2451. Paul Spencer, b. in Roxbury, July 13, 1892.
2452. Helen Sampson, b. in Roxbury, Jan. 29, 1894.

A 1777

Horace Luther Reed, son of Charles Franklin and Sarah (James) Reed.

b. April 24, 1862.

m. April 3, 1892, Annie L. Hamilton, of W. Va.

He resided at Beach Hill, W. Va. The rest of Charles and Sarah's children reside in Florida.

CHILD

2453. Horace Leslie, b. Feb., 1893.

A 1790

Capt. William Elisha Reed, son of William Gurney and Sophia (Witherell) Reed.

b. June 17, 1837; d. Oct. 31, 1863.

m. ———, Annie Hyde, of Chestertown, Mass.

No children. Served in the Civil War three years and was promoted to Captain of Co. H, 32nd Mass. Vol. Militia. He was severely wounded and received an honorable discharge.

Of Easton, Mass.

A 1795

Charles Davis Reed, son of Charles H. and Mary (Davis) Reed.

b. May 6, 1842, at Boston.

m. Aug. 19, 1867, Mary Clark, b. March 29, 1842, in Philadelphia; daughter of James and Eleanor (Wunder) Clark.

Of Newark, Ill.

CHILD

2454. Mary Eleanor, b. Sept. 14, 1868, in Newark, Ills.

A 1796

Henry Lyman Reed, son of Charles H. and Mary (Davis) Reed.

b. Dec. 3, 1843, at Boston; d. Dec. 26, 1878, at Easton, Mass.

m. April 28, 1868, Ellen Farley Stearns; b. Sept. 29, 1841, at Sterling, Mass.; daughter of Thomas and Charlotte (Blood) Stearns.

Henry Lyman Reed was a graduate of Bridgewater Normal School. He and his wife were both school teachers. Taught in Maryland and further South after the war. They were Unitarians. He served in the 6th Regt., Co. F, and afterwards in the 62nd Mass. Regt., but in that regiment never went into service, as the war was then closed.

Of Easton, Mass.

CHILD

2455. Jennie McLean, b. Sept. 5, 1876; m. Oct. 23, 1895, Lewis Claud Evans.

A **1797**

George William Reed, son of Charles H. and Mary (Davis) Reed.

b. Sept. 12, 1852, at Boston; d. May 23, 1887, at Easton, Mass.

m. May 25, 1881, Fannie C. Wilber; b. Feb. 20, 1860, at Little Compton, R. I.; daughter of Stephen B. and Martha Ann (Pease) Wilber.

He was a graduate of Bristol county, Mass., Academy, and lived at Easton, Mass., and attended the Unitarian Church. He was a bank clerk; shoe manufacturer, of the firm of Reed and Lincoln; served four seasons as baggage master on steamer "Old Colony."

Of Easton, Mass.

CHILDREN

2456. Walter Gurney, b. Sept. 25, 1882, at Fall River; d. Jan. 24, 1883, at Easton.

2457. Roy Brightman, b. Jan. 2, 1885, at Easton.

A **1804**

Samuel Payson Reed, Jr., son of Samuel Payson and Rachel Ann (Brown) Reed.

b. May 20, 1856.

m. ———, Matilda Lydard.

Of Howard county, Md.

CHILDREN

2458. Ann Laura, b. March 9, 1884.
2459. William Edgar, b. June 21, 1887.

W 1836

Daniel Edward Reed, son of Daniel and Hannah (Gurney) Reed.

b. Feb. 9, 1813; d. Dec. 13, 1884.
m. Dec. 28, 1843, Sophia L. Whittier.

He was a farmer; communicant of the Congregational Church; Republican. Lived in East Madison, Me.

Of East Madison, Me.

CHILDREN

2460. Sophia Whittier, b. Feb. 23, 1845; m. March 9, 1864, Albert Kettridge Perkins.
2461. William E., b. Oct. 8, 1848; d. Dec. 26, 1863.
2462. Newell D., b. Oct. 9, 1851; d. May 7, 1865.
2463. Ella R., b. Oct. 28, 1854; d. Nov. 2, 1863.
2464. Clara B., b. Nov. 5, 1859; d. Feb. 3, 1883.
2465. Flora D., b. Nov. 22, 1864.
2466. Infant son, b. May 7, 1866.
2467. Ruel E., b. April 12, 1871.

W 1837

John Gurney Reed, son of Daniel and Hannah (Gurney) Reed.

b. July 11, 1817.
m. Jan. 16, 1851, Hannah French.

He was a farmer; Republican; church attendant. Lived in East Madison, Me.

Of East Madison, Me.

CHILDREN

2468. Hannah Jane, b. Oct. 29, 1851; m. Jan. 12, 1872, Marcus L. McKenney.
2469. Anna C., b. Aug. 4, 1855; d. June 10, 1875.
2470. John Minot, b. Feb. 14, 1860; d. June 9, 1860.

W 1838

Turner Reed, son of Daniel and Hannah (Gurney) Reed.

b. Sept. 19, 1825.
m. ———, Anna C. Flower.

Farmer; communicant of Congregational Church. East Madison, Me., is his residence.

Of East Madison, Me.

CHILDREN

2471. Sumner T., b. June 17, 1857; d. Nov. 16, 1863.
2472. Elmer E., b. Feb. 16, 1862; m. May 13, 1882, Ida W. Woodman.
2473. Henry, b. Sept. 11, 1864.
2474. Viola S., b. Sept. 12, 1873; d. Feb. 26, 1882.

W 1839

Deane Elbridge Reed, son of Deane and Elizabeth (Norton) Reed.

b. Sept. 14, 1813.

m. 1st. Oct. 25, 1841, Electa Burns; b. April 1, 1823; d. Oct. 9, 1847.

m. 2nd. Oct. 24, 1848, Hannah Spaulding; b. Nov. 11, 1822; d. ———.

Farmer; church communicant; active in church work; strong Republican; lives in East Madison, Me.

Of East Madison, Me.

CHILDREN OF ELBRIDGE AND ELECTA

2475. Thaxter, b. Sept. 21, 1842.
2476. Ann Elizabeth, b. Aug. 1, 1844; d. July 24, 1872.

CHILDREN OF ELBRIDGE AND HANNAH

2477. Lucilla, b. Oct. 30, 1850.
2478. Luellyn, b. Oct. 23, 1856; d. Oct. 10, 1883.
2479. Susan, b. Sept. 15, 1858.
2480. Florence M., b. Aug. 9, 1860.

W 1840

Samuel Norton Reed, son of Deane and Elizabeth (Norton) Reed.

b. Oct. 1, 1817; d. Nov. 1, 1845.

m. (pub.) Aug. 18, 1833, Serusha Bailey, of Scituate.

Of East Madison, Me.

CHILDREN

2481. Serusha, b. June 27, 1834.
2482. Rowland, b. Oct. 13, 1836.

2483. Martha, b. Nov. 13, 1838.
2484. Sophia, b. Oct. 3, 1840.
2485. Anna, b. Nov. 30, 1844.

W 1841

Sheldon Reed, son of Deane and Elizabeth (Norton) Reed.
b. Nov. 17, 1820.
m. 1st. 1849, Betsy D. Reed; b. March 24, 1825; d. Aug. 24, 1860.
m. 2nd. Jan. 1, 1867, Martha R. Blanchard (of Madison).

Farmer, Aroostook Region.

Of Madison, Me.

CHILDREN OF SHELDON AND BETSY

2486. Orilla, b. Nov. 30, 1850; m. Oct. 1, 1873, Samuel N. Blanchard.
2487. Frank S., b. June 19, 1853; m. Dec. 25, 1885, Margaret H. Everett.
2488. Willis, b. Dec. 23, 1855; m. Aug. 17, 1888, Elvira G. Sweatt.
2489. Mary E., b. Aug. 24, 1857.

CHILDREN OF SHELDON AND MARTHA

2490. Eunice Maria, b. Oct. 20, 1867, in Madison, Me.; m. June 16, 1888, Ernest M. Ames.
2491. Winnefred, b. Aug. 3, 1869, in Madison, Me.
2492. Lotta Blanche, b. July 22, 1871, in Madison, Me.
2493. Daniel, b. April 20, 1877, in Madison, Me.

W 1842

Webster Reed, son of Deane and Elizabeth (Norton) Reed.
b. June 10, 1822.
m. 1st. 1844, Sophia Cook; d. Feb. 23, 1855; aged 27 years.
m. 2nd. Sept. 13, 1855, Electa S. Howes; d. June 27, 1866.
m. 3rd. Nov., 1866, Louisa L. Reed; d. May —, 1873.
m. 4th. July 3, 1874, Annie E. Pratt.

Lived in Madison, Aroostook Region; church communicant; farmer.

Of Madison, Me.

CHILDREN OF WEBSTER AND SOPHIA

2494. Samuel N., b. March 4, 1845; d. June 28, 1871.
2495. Webster, b. Aug. 23, 1846; drowned Dec. 3, 1869.
2496. Clara N., b. April 30, 1848; m. Nov. 27, 1874, Wm. B. Longley.
2497. Emma F., b. Oct. 1, 1849.
2498. Hattie, b. June 23, 1852; d. Aug. 23, 1854.

CHILDREN OF WEBSTER AND ELECTA

2499. Philo, b. Jan. 11, 1860.

W 1844

Woodbridge Brown Reed, son of David and Elizabeth (Brown) Reed.

b. Nov. 19, 1810, at Abington, Mass.

m. Jan. 19, 1842, Orinda Neal; b. Feb. 14, 1818, in Madison, Me.

Residence, Skowhegan, Me.; occupation, farmer; Republican; church attendant.

Of Skowhegan, Me.

CHILDREN

2500. Lyman, b. Feb. 28, 1843, at Skowhegan, Me.; d. Aug. 31, 1888.
2501. George Watson, b. July 26, 1845; d. Nov. 2, 1848.
2502. Henry Watson, b. Sept. 21, 1848; d. June 19, 1852.
2503. Ann Maria, b. Sept. 10, 1850; m. Jan. 1, 1885, Charles Henry Magoon; b. May 17, 1844, in Cornville, Me.

W 1855

Charles W. Reed, son of David and Delia (Smith) Reed.

b. May 26, 1849.

m. Dec. 25, 1871, Abbie A. Plummer; b. Sept. 3, 1846.

Residence, East Madison, Me. Farmer; Republican.

Of East Madison, Me.

CHILDREN

2504. Cordelia, b. Jan. 30, 1876.
2505. Lena M., b. July 28, 1878.
2506. William G., b. March 25, 1881.

W 1856

Anson Reed, son of David and Delia (Smith) Reed.

b. Aug. 20, 1853.

m. Oct. 20, 1875, Augusta H. Plummer; b. Feb. 16, 1852.

Lewiston, Me.; hotel keeper; Republican.

Of Lewiston, Me.

CHILD

2507. Leon Lewis, b. May 6, 1876.

W 1857

Jesse Reed, son of Jesse and Lucy (Reed) Reed.

b. June 27, 1819, at Abington.

m. Oct. 23, 1842, Eliza Emeline Curtiss; b. Oct. 26, 1823; d. Oct. 26, 1876, at Abington; daughter of John and and Eliza (Holbrook) Curtiss.

Jesse Reed and his wife lived in East Abington; they were educated there in the public schools. Were members of the Orthodox Church; were both tall and large. He was a shoemaker and farmer.

Of East Abington, Mass.

CHILDREN

2508. Sarah Emeline, b. March 5, 1844; m. May 5, 1866, John H. Harper, of E. Abington.

2509. Eliza Johnson, b. Nov. 1, 1846; m. Jan. 17, 1870, Benjamin Wormelle.

2510. Albert Curtiss, b. April 4, 1850; m. Nov. 19, 1873, Lillian Sherman Fletcher.

2511. Jesse Edwards, b. Sept. 1, 1860; m. Jan. 16, 1884, Melissa Jane Swett.

W 1859

Turner Reed, son of Jesse and Lucy (Reed) Reed.

b. April 8, 1826, at Abington.

m. Oct. 3, 1848, Sarah H. Curtiss; b. June 1, 1826, at Abington; daughter of John and Eliza (Holbrook) Curtiss.

m. 2nd. April 23, 1862, Sarah Moulton; b. Jan. 5, 1829, at Attleboro; daughter of Royal and Cynthia (Wiltnarth) Moulton.

Of Abington, Mass.

CHILDREN OF TURNER AND SARAH

2512. Clifford Wayland, b. Dec. 3, 1849; m. Helen L. (Reed) Norris.
2513. Frederick Eliot, b. Aug. 4, 1853; m. Flora Weston Chamberlain.

CHILDREN OF TURNER AND SARAH MOULTON

2514. Mabel Sarah, b. April 29, 1864; d. Sept. 25, 1865.
2515. Henry Turner, b. May 17, 1865.
2516. Wilmot Dean, b. Nov. 1, 1866; d. Feb. 25, 1876.
2517. Frank Alfred, b. Nov. 29, 1868.

W 1867

George Fearing Reed, son of Ezekiel and Cephisa (Studley) Reed.

b. May 31, 1834, at Abington, Mass.

m. May 31, 1855, Maria Antoinette Faxon; b. March 4, 1833, at Abington; daughter of Calvin and Althea (Curtis) Faxon.

Of Abington, Mass.

CHILD

2518. Althea Cephisa, b. Oct. 1, 1866; m. Ernest Florian Lamson.

W 1870

Charles Reed, son of Ezekiel and Cephisa (Studley) Reed.

b. July 19, 1847, at Abington, Mass.

m. Nov. 28, 1878, Ellen M. H. Foote; b. Aug. 4, 1853, at Northfield, Conn.; daughter of Frederick and Celestia (Tuttle) Foote.

Charles was educated at Williston Seminary, Easthampton, Mass. and at Yale University, class of 1871. He received the degree of B. A. in 1871, M. A. in 1874, LL. B. in 1874. He lived at Ansonia, Conn. from 1878 to 1885, since at Abington, Mass. He is an Attorney-at-Law, was Judge of Probate for District of Derby, Conn. in 1881-2.

Of Abington, Mass.

CHILD

2519. Celestia Foote, b. Jan. 9, 1882.

W 1872

Thomas Reed, son of Thomas and Lydia (Jenkins) Reed.

b. April 25, 1812; d. Nov. 30, 1844.

m. 1st. Nancy Hunt.

m. 2nd. June 12, 1840, Achseh Wesson (she married the 2nd time July, 1851, Brackley Shaw, Jr., whose 1st wife was Adaline, daughter of Thomas and Joanna (Shaw) Reed of Rockland).

Of Abington, Mass.

CHILD

2520. Ferdinand, b. June 12, 1842; d. May 19, 1854.

W 1874

Henry Watson Reed, son of Thomas and Lydia (Jenkins) Reed.

b. Dec. 29, 1819; d. Sept. —, 1843.

m. ———, Emily Howard.

Emily Howard remarried July 20, 1845, Lysander Cushing, the husband of Lydia Jenkins Reed, her deceased sister-in-law.

Of Rockland.

No children.

W 1878

Washington Reed, son of Goddard and Marcia (Reed) Reed.

b. July 6, 1820.

m. June 2, 1839, Harriet R. Corthell, ——— Pearl street, Boston.

He was an extensive boot and shoe manufacturer (see His. of Abington, p. 295). Lived in a handsome residence (see His. of Abington, p. 432). His son Henry Harrison Reed was a private in the Civil War from East Abington (see His. of Abington, p. 299).

Of Rockland, Mass.

CHILDREN

2521. Henry Harrison, b. Aug. 12, 1840.
2522. Joanna, b. May 7, 1846.
2523. Charles Goddard, b. April 28, 1852.
2524. Marcia, b. Nov. 26, 1853.

W 1882

Lorenzo Reed, son of Ebenezer and Lucy (Jenkins) Reed.

b. May 26, 1818, in East Abington, Mass.; d. Jan. 28, 1845.

m. in 1841, Sarah P. Brockway; b. ———, 1815, at Salioduck, N. Y.; daughter of Jeremiah and Sarah (Swift) Brockway, she afterwards married Henry Weiderwax of North Chatham, N. Y.

Lorenzo was a drover and lived in East Abington until his death. He attended the Congregational Church. After his death his widow and family moved to North Chatham, N. Y.

Of East Abington, Mass.

CHILDREN

2525. Cordelia, b. Nov. 6, 1842, in Nassau; m. Peter B. Walter.
2526. Lorenzo, b. July 29, 1845; m. Jan. 19, 1868, Vesta A. Hunt.

W 1887

Simeon Gannett Reed, son of Simeon G. and Rachel (Burgess) Reed.

b. April 23, 1830, at East Abington (now called Rockland) Mass.; d. Nov. 7, 1895.

m. Oct. 17, 1850, Amanda Wood, who was born at Quincy, Aug. 26' 1832. Her father's name was Henry Wood, he was born at Hollis, N. H. Her mother's maiden name was Sarah Hollis, who was born at Quincy, Mass.

Of Portland, Oregon.

From data furnished by himself, we have the following interesting sketch of the life of Simeon Gannett Reed:

He received a good New England education, and after leaving school at about the age of 15, he spent a year as a boy in a wholesale dry goods store in Boston. His wages were $75 the first year, and he had to board and clothe himself with a prospect of an increase of salary of $25 each year for the next two years.

The outlook did not seem very encouraging and boy-like he

SIMEON GANNETT REED.

felt like making a change, so he gave up the dry goods business and went back to East Abington and learned the shoe cutter's trade at Jenkins Lane's. He soon got the hang of this and as the work was piece work he was more or less master of his own time, and yet he felt like getting into some business for himself. An opportunity finally presented itself, and he embarked in the grain and flour business at Quincy, Mass., when about 18 years of age, and while there married his wife.

He left Quincy for California in the spring of 1852, remained in San Francisco until after the big Sacramento fire of that year, when he came to Oregon with the expectation of buying lumber, but as he could not buy lumber he bought a lot of flour and shipped it by steamer to San Francisco where he sold it to good advantage.

Not succeeding in establishing himself in any permanent business in California, and having thought all the time that Oregon was a good country for a young man to start in and grow up with, he returned to Oregon in the spring of 1853, where he resided until his death.

He first started a small lumber business at Rainier on the Columbia river, opposite the mouth of the Corrlitz, and finally sold out his business there and took a position with W. S. Ladd & Co. of Portland and remained there until Mr. Ladd went into the banking business, when in connection with his two brothers they bought Ladd Brothers out, and went into business under the firm name of Ladd, Reed & Co., they were in business for a number of years and were very successful.

He was one of the original incorporators of the Oregon Steam Navigation Co. in 1860, was elected vice-president of the company in 1864, and retained that position until July, 1879, when the company sold out to Henry Villard and merged into the Oregon Railway and Navigation Co., of which latter company he was vice-president and manager until he resigned in 1880.

He was also more or less identified with the mining inter-

ests of the northwest. First in building a water ditch for placer mining some thirty miles long in Baker county, Oregon, and afterward in the purchase and development of a free-gold bearing quartz mine on Conner creek, a tributary of Snake river, located about twenty miles below Huntington station, on the Oregon Short Line Railroad in Baker county. That mine has a thirty-five stamp mill run by water power and has been in successful operation for a number of years.

He was also interested with A. Onderdonk and D. O. Mills in the contract for building the Canadian Pacific Railway in British Columbia. The contract was from Port Moody (on Burrard's inlet) to Kamloop's lake, the work was heavy and amounted to several million dollars.

He also organized "The Oregon Iron and Steel Co.," of which he was president and the largest stockholder. The location of the company's works was on the Willamette river, seven miles south of Portland. They had a fine vein of brown hematite ore, from seven to fourteen feet wide, and extensive water power, and unlimited fir timber for charcoal. They had two and a half miles of narrow gauge railroad, connecting the mine with their works, which consisted of a first-class blast furnace with fire-brick stoves and all modern improvements, with a capacity of fifty tons of pig iron a day; also a twenty-five-ton cast-iron pipe plant (the only one on the Pacific coast). He went somewhat into detail regarding his connection with the iron business, because he thought it would cut quite a figure in the future development of the coast.

In 1887 he purchased the celebrated "Bunker Hill and Sullivan Mines," located near the town of Wardner in the Coeur D'Alene district, Idaho Territory. They were silver and lead mines, and were the largest producers in the district, having produced in twenty-three months and twenty-six days from the time the concentrator started up, 15,255.96 tons of concentrates of the gross value of $1,353,008.21; the average assay being thirty ounces of silver and sixty-eight per cent lead per ton.

He was quite extensively interested in farming and fine stock. Had one farm of over 3000 acres in the Willamette valley in high cultivation with over fifteen miles of Osage Orange hedge, and well stocked with imported Clydesdale stallions and mares, Clydesdale bays, short-horn cattle, Cotswold and Leicester sheep and Berkshire pigs.

He was somewhat interested in Portland, Oregon, real estate, having erected a five-story office building 100 by 100 with elevator and all modern improvements, heated throughout with steam, which he named the "Abington Building" after his native town.

W 1888

Samuel Colburn Reed, son of Albert and Maria (Colburn) Reed.

b. June 2, 1832, at East Abington, Mass.

m. April 22, 1893, Marguerite Bulkley, daughter of Joseph Bulkley of New York City.

He was educated at Columbia College Law School; admitted to the bar in 1859, went to war at its opening on the staff of Col. Vosburgh of the 71st Regiment, represented the 13th district in the New York Legislature in the year 1864-5, being the only Republican member from New York City, save one other in 1864, and two in 1865, was chairman on the committee of Federal Affairs, also joint chairman with Senator Andrew B. White. Present Ambassador to Germany of the Committee of Literature. Mr. Reed is a member since 1868 of the Union League Club, and for three years on its executive committee, for several years was treasurer of a Traveller's Club, also member of the Athenaeum Club, and life member of the New England Society. For two years was counsel to the department of buildings of New York City, and candidate for Judge of the Superior Court in New York in 1867; and for many years was referee in many important Supreme Court cases.

Of New York City.

W 1890

Amos Newton Reed, son of Amos Shaw and Hulda B. (Loud) Reed.

b. May 21, 1829, at East Abington, Mass.

m. Sept. 10, 1851, Sarah Elizabeth Boynton; b. May 12, 1832, at Boston. Her father's name was William Boynton, and her mother's maiden name, Sarah Curtis Butler.

Married by Rev. J. N. Parker. Resided in East Abington. Engaged in the grain, flour and coal business, under the firm name of A. N. Reed & Co. His son Harry Duncan Reed being his partner.

Of East Abington, Mass.

CHILDREN

2527. Harry Duncan, b. May 21, 1854.
2528. Grace Lillian, b. June 18, 1861; m. John A. Cross, of Providence, R. I.

W 1892

Edward Payson Reed, son of Amos S. and Rachel B. (Reed) Reed.

b. Sept. 21, 1836, in East Abington; d. at Boston May 29, 1894.

m. Sept. 6, 1864, Georgiana Spencer Loud; b. Feb. 13, 1842, at East Abington; daughter of Reuben and Betsy (Whiting) Loud.

He was educated in the public schools and Union Academy of East Abington. He was a lumber dealer. Has been Justice of the Peace since 1864, was State Senator in 1874.

He was 1st Lieut. of 12th Mass. Vol. June 26, 1861, Capt. June 25, 1862, Major May 6, 1864. Mustered out as Capt. July 8, 1864. (See History of Abington, p. 314.)

Of East Abington, Mass.

CHILDREN

2529. Minnie, b. March 14, 1866; m. Nov. 23, 1887, Perry Hare, of Braintree, Mass.
2530. Arthur Burgess, b. Sept. 8, 1867.
2531. Edward Loud, b. July 29, 1874; d. Feb. 22, 1878.
2532. George Gordon, b. June 16, 1880.

W 1902

Samuel Reed, son of Samuel and Polly (Corthell) Reed.
b. May 26, 1811.
m. ———, Elizabeth Wilkes.

Lived in East Abington. Was selectman for one year.
Of East Abington, Mass.

No children.

W 1904

Levi Reed, son of Samuel and Polly (Corthell) Reed.
b. Dec. 31, 1814; d. Oct. 18, 1869.
m. April 20, 1837, Louisa C. Drake.

Lived in East Abington, was a Justice of the Peace, also a member of the Senate.

Son Samuel Bryant was a private in the 56th Regt. Mass. Vol. Infantry.

Of East Abington, Mass.

CHILDREN

2533. Louisa Maria, b. Jan. 10, 1838; m. James Edward Nash.
2534. Henrietta Bryant, b. March 17, 1840; d. Jan. 13, 1842.
2535. Samuel Bryant, b. Sept. 10, 1841.
2536. Henrietta Manly, b. Aug. 15, 1846; d. June 21, 1849.
2537. Mary Emily, b. July 27, 1850; m. J. D. Page; lives in Brookline, Mass.
2538. A son, b. March 1, 1852; d. March 23, 1852.
2539. George Baxter Hyde, b. July 24, 1853; d. Feb. 2, 1857.
2540. Alfred Levi, b. Oct. 9, 1855.

W 1905

Dexter Reed, son of Samuel and Polly (Corthell) Reed.
b. Nov. 10, 1816; d. April 4, 1894.
m. ———, Catherine Stetson.

He always lived in East Abington, except a few years, which he spent in California.

Son Lewis was a Capt. in 54th Regt. Mass. Vol. Infantry, Frederick in 2nd Regt. Heavy Artillery.

Of East Abington, Mass.

CHILDREN

2541. Frederick, b. Feb. 11, 1841; m. 1st. Jan., 1866, Mary A. Holmes; m. 2d. Clara A. Jacobs.
2542. Lewis, b. Oct. 26, 1842; m. Nov. 12, 1865, Selina James Weston.
2543. Edith Catherine, b. Sept. 3, 1845; m. Nov. 23, 1861, Charles Merritt, of Scituate, Mass.
2544. Mary Alice, b. Dec. 21, 1846; m. Oct. 9, 1870, Walter Scott Lovell, of Rockland, Mass.
2545. Ruthena, b. Jan. 5, 1850; d. April 20, 1853.
2546. Eveline, b. Dec. 1, 1851; d. March 31, 1853.
2547. Abraham Lincoln, b. March 4, 1861; m. Nov. 30, 1893, Jane L. Donoghue.

W **1916**

Walter Reed, son of Abiah and Jane (Gurney) Reed.
b. July 24, 1821.
m. 1st. ———, Sophronia Josselyn.
m. 2nd. April 1, 1849, Cordone Keen.

Son Edward Stanley in 2nd Regt. Heavy Artillery, Mass. Vol.

Of East Abington, Mass.

CHILD OF WALTER AND SOPHRONIA

2548. Edward Stanley, b. Feb. 25, 1847; m. Clara A. Josselyn.

CHILDREN OF WALTER AND CORDONE

2549. Sarah Jane, b. May 8, 1850; m. Edward Curtis.
2550. Henry Walter, b. Nov. 27, 1851; m. Nov. 22, 1874, Susan Ellen Sullivan.

W **1924**

Isaac Thaxter Reed, son of Isaac and Eliza F. (Shaw) Reed.
b. March 15, 1834, in Roxbury.
m. ———, Susanna Jones of Whitman, Mass.

Of Whitman, Mass.

CHILDREN

2551. Bradford Thaxter (Whitman, Mass.); m. Minnie Gurney, daughter of Elbridge Gurney.
2552. Eve, b. ———; m. ——— Elbridge.

W 1928

Henry Wallace Reed, son of Isaac and Eliza F. (Shaw) Reed.
b. Jan. 15, 1843.
m. ———.

Of South Abington, Mass.

CHILD

2553. Frank, b. ———.

W 1934

Horace Richmond Reed, son of Horace and Lurana (Bates) Reed.
b. Aug. 12, 1852; d. Dec. 4, 1881.
m. Jan. 16, 1879, Susan Hersey, daughter of Jason Hersey.

After the death of her husband the widow of Horace Richmond Reed lived with her son, Henry Richmond Reed, at her father's, Jason Hersey, in Whitman, Mass.

Of Whitman, Mass.

CHILD

2554. Henry Richmond, b. July 24, 1880; lives in Whitman.

W 1935

Arthur Elsworth Reed, son of Horace and Lurana (Bates) Reed.
b. April 3, 1861, at Abington.
m. Oct. 6, 1887, Nellie F. M. Bunting; b. July 24, 1861, in Swampscott, Mass.; daughter of David C. and Lucy (Cole) Bunting.

He was a clerk in the employ of Messrs. Cobb, Bates and Yerxa.

Of South Abington, Mass.

CHILDREN

2555. Helen Lurana, b. March 11, 1891.
2556. William Richmond, b. May 18, 1892.
2557. Horace Bunting, b. May 13, 1894; d. Sept. 9, 1894.
2558. Olive Augusta, b. Aug. 23, 1896; d. June 9, 1897.

W 1940

Walter Lincoln Reed, son of William L. and Deborah (Chessman) Reed.

b. Nov. 5, 1859.

m. ———, Alice Rose.

Of South Abington, Mass.

W 1943

David Augustus Reed, son of David A. and Nancy (Loud) Reed.

b. Jan. 12, 1831; d. in spring of 1900; buried at Weymouth, Mass.

m. Nov. 3, 1850, Betsy D. Keith.

Was fond of music and had a fine base voice and sang in church choirs, both in Weymouth and Boston, where he resided at the close of his life.

Of Weymouth, Mass.

CHILD

2559. Herbert Augustus, b. June 28, 1851.

W 1944

Daniel Franklin Reed, son of David A. and Nancy (Loud) Reed.

b. May 10, 1834.

m. ———, Joanna Cushing.

Was a partner with Deacon Josiah Reed for many years in the manufacture of shoes, under the firm name of J. Reed & Co. Also represented the town of Weymouth at the General Court in 1859.

Of New Bedford, Mass.

CHILD

2560. Frank Edwin, b. Oct. 8, 1854; lives in New Bedford.

W 1947

George Reed, son of Thomas and Cynthia (Shaw) Reed.

b. April 19, 1824; d. Dec. 5, 1893.

m. ———, Maria H. Vinal, who died March 5, 1897.

Of Weymouth, Mass.

CHILDREN

2561. George Eaton, b. March 30, 1846; d. June 17, 1846.
2562. Thomas H., b. Oct. 5, 1847; d. Dec. 19, 1875.
2563. Adeline M., b. May 5, 1850; d. Sept. 5, 1865.
2564. George Everett, b. Aug. 2, 1852; m. Oct. 19, 1876, Clara A. Lowell, of Kennebunk, Me.
2565. Josiah Albree, b. Feb. 16, 1855; d. Sept. 25, 1861.
2566. Nathaniel B., b. July 21, 1857; d. April 5, 1876.
2567. Antoinette T., b. Oct. 14, 1859; d. unmarried.
2568. Josiah Burton, b. Oct. 21, 1862; m. Nov. 22, 1887, Clara Ford Martin, of Weymouth, Mass.
2569. Eaton Vinal, b. April 27, 1868; m. Nov. 11, 1891, Helen Merriel Tower, of Weymouth, daughter of Dr. Charles C. Tower, of Weymouth; no children.

W 1948

Josiah Reed, son of Thomas and Cynthia (Shaw) Reed.

b. April 18, 1826.

m. 1st. Sept. 3, 1845, Sarah C. Fogg.

m. 2nd. Oct. 25, 1864, M. Jennie Ainsworth; she died March —, 1871.

m. 3rd. July 22, 1874, Helen M. Flanders Matson.

He lived in South Weymouth, was known as Deacon Reed.

CHILDREN OF JOSIAH AND SARAH

2570. Amelia Caswell, b. March 15, 1846; m. John Worcester Field, of Dorchester (b. June 11, 1839, at Brighton).
2571. Cynthia, b. March 5, 1860; m. Dec. 16, 1885, James Halsey Elwell.
2572. Sarah Lora, b. Jan. 13, 1848; d. Feb. 17, 1865.
2573. Josiah Burton, b. June 7, 1852; d. Sept. 12, 1852.
2574. Henry Beecher, b. Oct. 1, 1853; m. Dec. 2, 1884, Mary Reid Clark.
2575. Fremont Sumner, b. July 22, 1856; d. July 4, 1879.

CHILDREN OF JOSIAH AND HELEN

2576. Ralph D., b. June 18, 1875; m. Aug. 29, 1901, Grace Holt.
2577. Stuart, b. May 23, 1877; d. Feb., 1880.
2578. Katharyne Isabelle, b. May 23, 1879; m. Nov. 22, 1900, Robert Low Pierpont, of Brooklyn, N. Y., by Bishop Chauncy Brewster, of Connecticut. He is a son of Henry E. Pierpont.

W 1957

Asa Reed, son of Thomas Jefferson and Clarissa (Belcher) Reed.

b. June 3, 1835.

m. Oct. 18, 1857, Elizabeth Bunker, of North Bridgewater, Mass.

CHILDREN

2579. Lizzie Jane, b. May 20, 1858; d. young.
2580. Fred., b. June 5, 1859; lives in Natick, Mass.
2581. Asa, Jr., b. Jan. 20, 1861; m. Louisa C. Jarvis, of Nova Scotia.
2582. Clara, b. Oct. 30, 1863; m. Herbert Bailey, of Brockton, Mass.
2583. George Franklin, b. May, 1865; lives in Brockton, Mass.
2584. Eva Frances, b. Oct., 1866; d. young.
2585. Charles Edward, b. July, 1868; d. young.
2586. Edward Ebenezer, b. Oct., 1869.
2587. Fannie Morne, b. 1871; m. Ernest Belcher, of East Randolph, Mass.
2588. Jennie, b. 1873; m. John Hanson, of Brockton, Mass.
2589. Eva Frances, b. Dec. 14, 1877; m. William Witherell.

W 1961

Edwin Reed, son of Thomas Jefferson and Clarissa (Belcher) Reed.

b. April 24, 1842.

m. ———, Alma Jennie Ford, of Hardwick, Vt.

CHILDREN

2590. Albert, b. ———.
2591. Edward Leroy, b. ———.

W 1962

George Minot Reed, son of Thomas Jefferson and Clarissa (Belcher) Reed.

b. Nov. 24, 1849.

m. June 16, 1874, Martha Belcher, of East Randolph, Mass., daughter of Thomas and Lucrecia C. (Dean) Belcher.

He has the old family bible with records.

CHILDREN

2592. Franklin Gilman, b. Dec. 27, 1874.
2593. Edith Lucrecia, b. April 3, 1881.
2594. Harvey Wilson, b. July 17, 1886.

W 1980

William Reed, son of William and Susan (French) Reed.

b. Oct. 30, 1832.

m. Jan. 12, 1859, Maria Louise Derby of South Weymouth, daughter of Capt. Martin and Mary (Burrell) Derby.

Of Braintree.

CHILDREN

2595. Susan Maria, b. April 23, 1860; m. Sept. 10, 1885, William Herbert Stevens; no children.
2596. William Park, b. Feb. 8, 1866; unmarried.

W 1983

Wellford Claiborne Reed, son of William and Lucy (Franklin) Reed.

b. Sept. 3, 1856.

m. Nov. 18, 1885, Hattie Relay McGee; b. Aug. 5, 1865; daughter of Thaddeus and Sally P. M. (Tucker) McGee of Raleigh, N. C.

Episcopalian. Dealer in leaf tobacco.

Of Richmond, Va.

W 1986

William Thomas Reed, son of William Block and Mary Ann (Larus) Reed.

b. Sept. 23, 1864.

m. Oct. 3, 1893, Alice Lewis Burwell, daughter of Lewis W. and Alice (Parker) Burwell.

In the tobacco business, manufacturer.

Of Richmond, Va.

CHILD

2597. Alice Burwell, b. July 19, 1895.

W 1989

Charles Clinton Reed, son of William Block and Mary Ann (Larus) Reed.

b. Jan. 13, 1873.

m. Dec. 15, 1898, Lyllian Marie Hancock, daughter of William T. Hancock.

Of Richmond, Va.

W 1994

Robert Hersey Reed, son of Charles Warren and Martha A. (Bullard) Reed.

b. Feb. 15, 1839.

m. 1st. March 1, 1861, Martha Louisa Fosgate of Boston, daughter of Mendal G. and Harriet (Parker) Fosgate of Northboro, Mass.

m. 2nd. June 21, 1882, Catherine Louisa Goodrich of New York, daughter of Alfred and Catherine (Carlisle) Goodrich of Newburgh, N. Y.

He has been in the employ of the Adams Express Co. for the past thirty years.

CHILDREN

2598. Charles Henry, b. Dec. 22, 1861, at Hingham; m. Nov. 9, 1893, Jennie Lucy Robinson, of Westboro, Mass.

2599. Frank Hersey, b. Nov. 26, 1863; m. June 4, 1899, Helen George, of Pittsfield, Mass.

W 1999

James Henry Reed, son of James Henry and Martha Ann (Wesson) Reed.

b. Dec. 15, 1872.

m. June 30, 1897, Mary Wade Page of Newton, daughter of Augustus and Mary Wade (Hallett) Page.

Of Newton, Mass.

CHILD

2600. James Henry, Jr., b. Jan. 28, 1901.

W 2003

John Kinsey Reed, son of John and Caroline (Kinsey) Reed.

b. April 18, 1846.

m. Nov. 25, 1875, Kate Vance.

Of Holden, Mo.

CHILDREN

2601. James Leighton, b. Oct. 19, 1876.
2602. Harlan, b. Dec. 21, 1878.
2603. Georgie Gray, b. May 15, 1881.

W 2004

James Leighton Reed, son of John and Caroline (Kinsey) Reed.

b. May 23, 1848.

m. Oct. 21, 1885, Emma Ellis of Brazil, Mo.

Of Brazil, Mo.

CHILDREN

2604. Mildred M., b. Sept. 14, 1886; d. Oct. 23, 1887.
2605. Clara Mary, b. Aug. 14, 1888.

W 2014

Charles Stedman Reed, son of Ezra and Jane A. (Wright) Reed.

b. Nov. 12, 1851, at South Weymouth.

m. Feb. 8, 1882, Ella Frances Colby of Vasselborough, Me., daughter of Rev. George Warren and Olive M. (Robinson) Colby.

He was an apothecary.

Of Holbrook, Mass.

CHILD

2606. Lenore, b. July 25, 1883.

W 2018

William F. Reed, son of Harvey H. and Ann (Ripley) Reed.

b. ———; d. Oct. 1, 1895.

m. ———, ——— Danforth.

CHILD

2606a. William F., b. ———; d. in 1899.

W 2032

Henry Horatio Reed, son of John Bradford and Emily Jane (Loud) Reed.

b. Oct. 16, 1853, at Weymouth, Norfolk county, Mass.

m. Nov. 12, 1885, Marion E. Crawford; b. Oct. 15, 1859, at Dunham Flats; daughter of William and Elizabeth (Townsend) Crawford.

They reside in Brockton, Mass. Of Brockton, Mass.

CHILDREN

2607. Elizabeth F., b. April 12, 1887.
2608. George Henry, b. June 30, 1891.

W 2035

Alvin Reed, son of Franklin and Pamilia (Thayer) Reed.
b. in Weymouth, Mass., May 19, 1860.
m. ———, Irene Hollis of Abington, Mass.

CHILD

2609. Ezra, b. at Whitman, May 23, 1884.

W 2039

Arthur Brown Reed, son of Frederick and Ellen Mehetable (Brown) Reed.
b. Feb. 24, 1874.
m. Oct. 7, 1896, Clara J. Warren of Abington, Mass.

CHILDREN

2610. Marion Burton, b. Feb. 27, 1897.
2611. Warren, b. Feb. 3, 1898.

W 2041

Harvey Dennett Reed, son of William Titterton and Ella J. (Harlow) Reed.
b. April 17, 1876.
m. June 21, 1899, Eva Stewart Arnold, daughter of Nathaniel W. and Alice (Mullaly) Arnold; b. Dec. 14, 1875.

T 2045

Luther W. Reed, son of Luther and Betsy (Hamilton) Reed.
b. Feb. 25, 1822.
m. ———, Lucy D. Cummins. Of Augusta, Me.

CHILD

2612. Ella Augusta, b. Oct. 2, 1855.

T 2048

Oliver Dean Reed, son of Oliver and Chloe (Briggs) Reed.
b. April 9, 1817.
m. ———, Sally Wilber.
Of Taunton, Mass.

CHILDREN

2613. Lucy Emma Jane, b. Nov. 12, 1850; d. Nov. 12, 1850.
2614. Mary A., b. April 19, 1855.
2615. Flora L., b. 1860; d. in 1860, aged two months.

T 2050

George Leonard Reed, son of Oliver and Chloe (Briggs) Reed.
b. Nov. 9, 1820.
m. May 23, 1851, Hannah K. Field.
Of Taunton, Mass.

CHILDREN

2616. Charles E., b. March, 1852.
2617. William W., b. June, 1854.
2618. Ardelia A., b. Aug., 1856.

T 2055

Lorenzo Revelo Reed, son of Oliver and Chloe (Briggs) Reed.
b. Sept. 11, 1832.
m. ———, Martha Hodges.
Of Taunton, Mass.

CHILDREN

2619. Martha M., b. March 18, 1853.
2620. Henry J., b. June 27, 1858.

T 2058

Jarvis Barney Reed, son of Barney and Rachel (Woodward) Reed.
b. March 14, 1821.
m. May 2, 1847, Elizabeth W. Eddy.
Merchant.
Of Taunton, Mass.

CHILD

2621. Arthur W., b. July, 1852.

T 2059

Salmon Leonard Reed, son of Barney and Rachel (Woodward) Reed.

b. Nov. 1, 1823; d. Jan. 20, 1851.

m. ———.

Of Taunton, Mass.

CHILD

2622. Leafy Ann, b. ———; d. Jan. 22, 1851, aged 4 years.

T 2060

John Quincy Adams Reed, son of Barney and Rachel (Woodward) Reed.

b. Sept. 20, 1825; d. Feb. 26, 1853.

m. Sept. 14, 1844, Arena C. Makepeace of Norton.

He was of Taunton; stable keeper.

Of Taunton, Mass.

CHILDREN

2623. Arvilla J., b. 1844.
2624. John F., b. 1846.

T 2076

Chester Allyne Reed, son of Chester I. and Elizabeth (Allyne) Reed.

b. April 26, 1860, in Taunton.

He was a lawyer and lived in North Attleboro.

Of North Attleboro, Mass.

T 2101

Charles Reed, son of Jonathan and Lydia Ann (Haskins) Reed.

b. Aug. 31, 1866.

m. Nov. 5, 1891, Sarah White.

CHILD

2625. Everett, b. Oct. 15, 1891.

T 2109

Curtis Henry Reed, son of Ira Madison and Adeline (Pratt) Reed.

b. Feb. 15, 1862; d. Sept. 29, 1894.

m. Nov. 20, 1884, Ellen Grace Tyndale of Taunton, Mass.

CHILDREN

2626. Helen Adeline, b. Oct. 26, 1885.
2627. Erma Taylor, b. July 18, 1889.
2628. Kennette Tyndal, b. Feb. 13, 1891.
2629. Marjorie Leach, b. Aug., 1893; d. Oct., 1893.

T 2111

Wallace Elmer Reed, son of Ira Madison and Adeline (Pratt) Reed.

b. Feb. 11, 1867.

m. June 5, 1895, Annie Louisa Fuller of Middlesborough, Mass.

CHILD

2630. Bernice Madison, b. May 17, 1896.

T 2115

George M. Reed, son of Freeman and Lamira W. (Jones) Reed.

b. June 3, 1835; d. March 24, 1869.

m. 1st. May 14, 1856, Elizabeth Howe; who was b. Nov. —, 1834; d. June 16, 1865.

m. 2nd. Dec. 7, 1869, Mary M. Adams.

T 2118

Ai M. Reed, son of Freeman and Lamira (Jones) Reed.

b. Oct. 31, 1845.

m. Dec. 1, 1868, Helen M. Henry.

CHILDREN

2631. Harry W., b. March 26, 1870; m. Nov. 23, 1897, Margaret M. Hayden; no children.
2632. Carl H., b. July 4, 1873; unmarried.
2633. Blanche, b. May 3, 1876; m. May 24, 1897, Ray A. Bullock. He was b. Aug. 26, 1873; no children.
2634. Bertha L., b. Nov. 10, 1879; unmarried.

T 2121

Charles E. Reed, son of Russell and Mary Ann (Edson) Reed.
b. April 24, 1847.
m. Feb. 25, 1872, Cora C. Andrews.
Of Northfield, Mass.

CHILD

2635. Alice F., b. Aug. 27, 1875.

T 2122

Guy M. Reed, son of Benjamin Porter and Harriet (Jones) Reed.
b. Jan. 9, 1847; d. Feb. 22, 1880.
m. Nov. —, 1870, Ellen Lea Rock.

No children.

T 2124

Henry C. Reed, son of Benjamin Porter and Harriet (Jones) Reed.
b. March 20, 1850; d. ———.
m. Feb. 8, 1876, Hattie M. Rowell.

T 2127

William P. Reed, son of Benjamin Porter and Harriet (Jones) Reed.
b. March 16, 1857.
m. Jan. 1, 1884, Sarah Rowell.

CHILDREN

2636. Guy, b. Jan. 21, 1885.
2637. Benjamin, b. Nov. 28, 1890.
2638. Fred., b. Feb. 22, 1892.
2639. Mildred, b. Sept. 6, 1896.

T 2131

George D. Reed, son of Benjamin Porter and Harriet (Jones) Reed.
b. Sept. 19, 1864.
m. Nov. 27, 1887, Kate Friend.

CHILD

2640. Ilda M., b. April 12, 1896.

T 2139

Richard Durfee Reed, son of John Richard and Julia P. (Breckenridge) Reed.

b. Feb. 4, 1862.

m. Sept. 16, 1891, Ethel W. Mallory of Westfield, Mass.

Of Westfield, Mass.

CHILD

2641. Julia Breckenridge, b. July 15, 1892.

T 2148

Romonzo Marvin Reed, son of David Wilson and Esther (Sanders) Reed.

b. June 23, 1830.

m. May 7, 1856, Cornelia White of Wayville, Dodge county, Wis.

Of Waukesha, Wis.

CHILD

2642. George Wilson, b. Nov. 17, 1858.

T 2154

Jason Lee Reed, son of Marvin and Eunice A. (Heath) Reed.

b. Sept. 15, 1839; d. Jan. 11, 1863.

m. Sept. 11, 1862, Mary Felicia Palmer; she was b. July 25, 1838.

He enlisted in the 10th N. Y. Cavalry, Sept. 7, 1862, and died in the service from the effects of disease. His widow married Francis H. Gillette.

Of Cortland, N. Y.

CHILD

2643. Jessie L., b. July 4, 1863; m. June 12, 1889, Chas. L. Munson.

T 2159

Howard John Reed, son of Marvin and Eunice A. (Heath) Reed.

b. Feb. 1, 1852.

m. June 7, 1881, Emma A. Sweetlove; b. Oct. 3, 1853.

Lightning Source UK Ltd.
Milton Keynes UK
UKHW040639050119
334856UK00004B/420/P

9 780484 878395